THE VIKING DIASPORA

The Viking Diaspora presents the early medieval migrations of people, language and culture from mainland Scandinavia to new homes in the British Isles, the North Atlantic, the Baltic and the east as a form of 'diaspora'. It discusses the ways in which migrants from Russia in the east to Greenland in the west were conscious of being connected not only to the people and traditions of their homelands, but also to other migrants of Scandinavian origin in many other locations.

Rather than the movements of armies, this book concentrates on the movements of people and the shared heritage and culture that connected them. This on-going contact throughout half a millennium can be traced in the laws, literatures, material culture and even environment of the various regions of the Viking diaspora. Judith Jesch considers all of these connections, and highlights in detail significant forms of cultural contact including gender, beliefs and identities.

Beginning with an overview of Vikings and the Viking Age, the nature of the evidence available, and a full exploration of the concept of 'diaspora', the book then provides a detailed demonstration of the appropriateness of the term to the world peopled by Scandinavians. This book is the first to explain Scandinavian expansion using this model, and presents the Viking Age in a new and exciting way for students of Vikings and medieval history.

Judith Jesch is Professor of Viking Studies at the University of Nottingham. Her previous publications include *Women in the Viking Age* (1991), *Ships and Men in the Late Viking Age: The Vocabulary of Runic Inscriptions and Skaldic Verse* (2001) and *The Scandinavians from the Vendel Period to the Tenth Century: An Ethnographic Perspective* (2002).

The Medieval World

Series editors: Warren C. Brown, Caltech, USA and
Piotr Górecki, University of California, Riverside, USA

Alfred the Great
Richard Abels

Christian-Jewish Relations, 1000–1300
Anna Sapir Abulafia

The Western Mediterranean Kingdoms
David Abulafia

The Fourth Crusade
Michael Angold

The Cathars
Malcolm Barber

The Godwins
Frank Barlow

Philip Augustus
Jim Bradbury

Disunited Kingdoms
Michael Brown

Violence in Medieval Europe
Warren C. Brown

Medieval Canon Law
J. A. Brundage

Crime in Medieval Europe
Trevor Dean

Charles I of Anjou
Jean Dunbabin

The Age of Charles Martel
Paul Fouracre

Margery Kempe
A. E. Goodman

Abbot Suger of St-Denis
Lindy Grant and David Bates

Edward the Black Prince
David Green

Church and People in the Medieval West, 900–1200
Sarah Hamilton

Bastard Feudalism
M. Hicks

The Crusader States and their Neighbours
P. M. Holt

The Formation of English Common Law
John Hudson

The Mongols and the West
Peter Jackson

Europe's Barbarians, AD 200–600
Edward James

The Cistercian Order in Medieval Europe
Emilia Jamroziak

The Viking Diaspora
Judith Jesch

Medieval Monasticism
C. H. Lawrence

Cnut
K. Lawson

The Age of Robert Guiscard
Graham Loud

The English Church, 940–1154
H. R. Loyn

Justinian
John Moorhead

Ambrose
John Moorhead

Charles the Bald
Janet L. Nelson

The Devil's World
Andrew Roach

The Reign of Richard Lionheart
Ralph Turner and Richard Heiser

The Welsh Princes
Roger Turvey

English Noblewomen in the Late Middle Ages
J. Ward

THE VIKING DIASPORA

Judith Jesch

LONDON AND NEW YORK

First published 2015
by Routledge
2 Park Square, Milton Park, Abingdon, Oxon OX14 4RN

and by Routledge
711 Third Avenue, New York, NY 10017

Routledge is an imprint of the Taylor & Francis Group, an informa business

British Library Cataloguing-in-Publication Data
A catalogue record for this book is available from the British Library

Jesch, Judith, 1954-
The Viking diaspora / Judith Jesch.
pages cm. — (The medieval world)
Includes bibliographical references and index.
1. Vikings—History. 2. Civilization, Viking. I. Title.
DL65.J468 2015
948'.022—dc23
2014047662

ISBN: 978-1-138-02076-4 (hbk)
ISBN: 978-1-138-02079-5 (pbk)
ISBN: 978-1-315-70833-1 (ebk)

Typeset in Bembo
by Swales & Willis Ltd, Exeter, Devon, UK

Printed and bound by CPI Group (UK) Ltd, Croydon, CR0 4YY

CONTENTS

TABLES

ACKNOWLEDGEMENTS

This book has its origins in the Viking Identities Network (2006–9), funded by the Arts and Humanities Research Council's strategic initiative for Diasporas, Migration and Identities.[1] The call for proposals under this initiative prompted the question of whether the concept of 'diaspora' could be useful and fruitful in understanding the migrations of the Viking Age and their aftermath. As far as I am aware, this was the first use of the term 'diaspora' in a Norse and Viking context, though it has become extremely common since.[2] I am most of all grateful to my colleagues Christopher Callow (University of Birmingham), Jayne Carroll (then University of Leicester, now University of Nottingham) and Christina Lee (University of Nottingham) for being my co-investigators on the project, for the discussions that led to the successful application to the AHRC, for the successes of the network itself, and for continuing discussions and collaborations since the end of the network. Although this book would never have happened without their collegial input, they should not in any way be held responsible for the ideas expressed here, nor for any errors or infelicities on my part. I am also grateful to the AHRC for further facilitating my work by awarding me a Research Fellowship in 2013. The bulk of this book was written during that time and the preceding semester of study leave generously granted by the School of English, University of Nottingham, though it builds on work done over many years.

I am also grateful to many colleagues in several countries who have, over the years, invited me to specialist conferences on different topics, often in fascinating places. These have acquainted me with the broad range of disciplines needed to understand the Viking Age and the Viking diaspora, stimulated my thinking on the subject, and given me the opportunity to try out some of the ideas presented here. In this era of Skype and video-conferencing, I still think there is huge added value in physically bringing scholars together, especially in those locations and landscapes where the Vikings themselves travelled and where their tracks can still be glimpsed.

Several sections of this book were in fact inspired by conference excursions to the places concerned and my enthusiasm for all things Viking and Scandinavian has only been fuelled by many years of travelling to these countries. I also thank the erstwhile Centre for Medieval Studies at the University of Bergen, the Centre for Advanced Study, Oslo, and the University of Uppsala for inviting me to join them for shorter or longer research visits within the last few years. All of these splendid institutions stimulated fruitful interactions with a variety of colleagues and in many cases these started off some of the ideas presented in this book, even when my visits were for some other purpose.

All interdisciplinary study is dependent on the generosity of colleagues in other disciplines sharing their knowledge. However invidious it may be to single out individuals, I would like to mention a few who provided specific help with and inspiration for some of the topics covered in this book:

- First and foremost (and not just alphabetically), Lesley Abrams for many years of fruitful and stimulating discussions, often on excursion buses or boats, for being an invaluable source of references and offprints, and for generally being on the same wavelength as me when it comes to all things Viking;
- Fedir Androshchuk for sharing his knowledge of, and unpublished work on, swords, and his published work on Vikings in the east;
- Michael Barnes for sharing his expertise on the Manx rune-stones, and much else besides;
- Kevin Edwards for advising me on palynology;
- Brean Hammond for alerting me to the work of Shlomo Sand;
- Jane Harrison for discussing settlement mounds;
- Elizaveta Matveeva for translating some Russian scholarship;
- Jan Erik Rekdal for introducing me to *Vágar*;
- Rebecca Reynolds for helping me to understand fishing.

Over the past thirty or so years, many other colleagues in many countries have, wittingly or unwittingly, contributed to my knowledge. I am only too aware that, both over my career and in this book, I have dabbled in many different disciplines in which I am not actually trained and which I may not fully understand. One reviewer of this project claimed that it would require a full interdisciplinary team of scholars to produce this book. Certainly such a book could be produced, with great trouble and at great expense, and it would be much larger than this one, no doubt more comprehensive and probably better. However, I believe that there is still value in trying to provide a personal vision, a rounded picture, coming out of a single scholar's engagement with as many aspects of the subject as possible. I am very aware that things can move quickly in some science-based disciplines, and that some of the interpretations presented here might already be out of date. I am also fully aware that I have not investigated every possible corner of the Viking diaspora, nor have I engaged with every possible discipline – to do so, even if I were capable of it, would make for far too voluminous a book. Rather, I have attempted to explore those aspects of the Viking Age and its aftermath that I believe are usefully illuminated by the concept of 'diaspora', and these aspects are no doubt influenced by my own interests and expertise which, as the reader will soon gather, focus on texts and the language(s) they are written in. I can only hope that any readers who find the concept of diaspora useful in this context will do their own research to test it further in areas and disciplines not well enough covered here, or to challenge my conclusions.

This book is in many ways the fruit of thoughts I have been developing for nearly three decades, ever since being in the unusual position of a language-and-literature person appointed (in 1985) to a lectureship in the then-unknown discipline of 'Viking Studies'. Many of my previous attempts to wrestle with both the required interdisciplinarity, and the challenges of making sure language and literature do not get lost among the shinier claims of archaeology, art history, history and science, are listed in the bibliography. Doubtless some readers will find that my thoughts have not developed that much over that time, but I hope nevertheless that most readers will be happy to read here about the things that have most excited me over a lifetime of studying the Vikings and what I have now learned to think of as the Viking diaspora.

My final debt is to my family, my parents Kati and Laci, and my partner Tom, all of whom have understood why I sometimes needed to work on this book rather than be with them.

Notes

1 www.diasporas.ac.uk, last accessed 18 November 2014.

2 For a summary of the activities of this network, see http://www.nottingham.ac.uk/research/groups/csva/research/funded-research-archive.aspx, last accessed 18 November 2014.

1

VIKINGS AND THEIR AGES

Definitions and evidence

Vikings and their Ages

The end of an era?

Around the year 1064, in the decade that is often seen as the end of the Viking Age, Þorfinnr Sigurðarson, the most powerful of all the Viking earls of Orkney, died and was buried at Christ Church in Birsay, the political and cultural seat of his earldom in northern Scotland.[1] His court poet Arnórr Þórðarson provided this fine poetical obituary of his patron, which presents his death as the end of an era:

> Bjǫrt verðr sól at svartri;
> søkkr fold í mar døkkvan;
> brestr erfiði Austra;
> allr glymr sær á fjǫllum,
> áðr at eyjum fríðri
> (inndróttar) Þórfinni
> (þeim hjalpi goð geymi)
> gœðingr myni fœðask.[2]

> The bright sun will become black, the earth will sink into the dark ocean, Austri's burden will break, all the sea will resound on the mountains, before a more glorious nobleman than Þorfinnr will be born for the Islands; God help that keeper of a hall-troop.

The poet's claim that the impossible would have to come about before the like of Þorfinnr was seen again in Orkney is couched in rich and complex language that not only evokes the landscapes of the north, but also alludes to both its shared ancestral culture and the shiny new possibilities of the future. In Norse mythology, Austri was one of the four dwarves who held up the earth, hence it is his 'burden'. Failure on the part of these dwarves would lead to the submergence of the known world by the dark ocean. The islands, mountains and seas of the stanza evoke not only Þorfinnr's homeland in the north of Scotland, but also the poet's own birthplace of Iceland, with its volcanic eruptions that darken the light of day. Arnórr's themes hark back to earlier Norse poetry, notably his fellow-Icelander Hallfreðr's memorial poem on the great Norwegian king Óláfr Tryggvason (d. *c.* 1000), and the anonymous Icelandic poem of creation, apocalypse and rebirth known as *Vǫluspá*.[3] Both of these literary models came about around the turn of the millennium in the crucible of the Christian transformation of the Scandinavian world. A little over half a century later, Arnórr prays for the Christian God's protection for his patron, even while still invoking old ideas of the cosmos and of Ragnarǫk, the end of the old world, as described in *Vǫluspá* and elsewhere.

In its linking of Þorfinnr to cosmic themes, the stanza does not do full justice to the extent of his power in this world. It is said in Chapter 32 of *Orkneyinga saga* that when Þorfinnr died he ruled nine earldoms in Scotland, as well as all of the Hebrides and a substantial realm in Ireland.[4] He amassed this power in the course of a long reign which was built on extensive raiding and military incursions in his youth, and on the extermination of his chief rival, his fraternal nephew Rǫgnvaldr Brúsason. But once Þorfinnr was established, his career changed tack. He set out on a long journey, first to pay homage to, and to receive the support of, the kings of both Norway and Denmark. Then he went on to Rome, where he sought out the Pope to be absolved of his sins. On returning to his earldom he gave up raiding and settled down to a life of governing, lawmaking and churchbuilding, in which peaceful state he died.

Þorfinnr's mixture of aggressive Viking and lawmaking Christian, of Scandinavian and insular, was built into his genes. On his father's side, he was a direct male descendant of *Torf*-'Turf'-Einarr, the first earl of Orkney and illegitimate son of a powerful Norwegian chieftain who, according to tradition, had been granted the islands by the Norwegian king Haraldr *hárfagri* 'Fine-Haired' in the ninth century. Einarr's son, Þorfinnr *hausakljúfr* 'Skull-Splitter', had a son Hlǫðvir who married Eðna, the daughter of an Irish king. Their son, Sigurðr *digri* 'The Stout', died in Ireland at the Battle of Clontarf in 1014, but not before he had married a daughter of a Scottish king who produced Þorfinnr. Thus Þorfinnr had more insular ancestors than Norse ones, including important men from both Scotland and Ireland. Yet he was given his great-grandfather's Norse name, married Ingibjǫrg, the daughter of a Norwegian nobleman, and presided over a powerful earldom that looked to Norway for its legitimacy in the eleventh century. We do not know what language Þorfinnr spoke when, as a child, he lived with his maternal grandfather in Scotland, but as an adult his rule in the Northern Isles encouraged culture in the Norse language, particularly skaldic verse, which required deep linguistic and cultural knowledge, as demonstrated in Arnórr's stanza quoted above.

Arnórr was Þorfinnr's chief propagandist, but he also worked for two kings of Norway, Magnús *inn góði* 'The Good' Óláfsson and Haraldr *harðráði* 'Hard-Ruler' Sigurðarson, as well as for Þorfinnr's rival Rǫgnvaldr Brúsason.[5] Þorfinnr's achievements are primarily remembered in *Orkneyinga saga*, written in Iceland, though with a strong basis in Orcadian traditions, a century and a half after his death, in the early thirteenth century.[6]

Even if Þorfinnr's death in 1064 was politically the end of an era, it was certainly not the end of Norse Orkney. The Northern Isles of Orkney and Shetland remained tributary lands of Norway (and, after 1397, of Denmark) until 1468–9, and Norse speech and culture persisted there long after the end of the Viking Age.[7] Such links between the Viking Age and its aftermath are characteristic not only of Orkney but of much of the Viking world. The linguistic, cultural and conceptual world in which people like Þorfinnr lived did not come to an end with the end of the Viking Age in the eleventh century. The various facets of this continuity are here summed up in the concept of 'diaspora' and are the subject of this book.

With his Norse ancestry, his family connections in Scotland and Ireland, his travels to, and political and personal connections with, Norway, Denmark and England, his pilgrimage to Rome, and his cultural connections with Icelanders, Þorfinnr epitomises the complex personal, political, religious, cultural and linguistic networks that developed as a result of what is usually termed the 'Viking expansion', or the 'Viking migrations', and that are here termed the 'Viking diaspora'. This terminology is based on the useful distinctions between 'migration' and 'diaspora' made by the social anthropologist Steven Vertovec, who defined:

> *migration* as physical movement, resettlement and re-establishment of key social institutions; *diaspora* as the consciousness of being connected to the people and traditions of a homeland and to migrants of the same origin in their countries; and *transnationalism* as the practices of exchange of resources, including people, across the borders of nation states. This implies that migration can occur without diaspora and transnationalism, but the two last-mentioned activities are always a result of migration.[8]

The implications of these distinctions will be explored more fully in Chapter 3. For the moment it should be noted that the term 'diaspora' is used throughout this book to highlight the fact that the Viking 'expansions' and 'migrations' were not the one-way movements suggested by those terms, but involved multi-directional contacts, networks and influences over a period of time, in a far-flung geographical world held together by the common language that we now term Old Norse, and by a distinctive culture rooted in this language.

Recently, an eminent Anglo-Saxonist declared that 'The "Vikings," as they were labeled, were a transnational imaginary constructed by the peoples with whom diverse groups from the countries that are now Denmark, Norway and Sweden came into contact.'[9] This book is an attempt to show how detailed knowledge of those groups from those countries, and their contacts, actually paints a very different picture. The Vikings were indeed transnational, but were not imaginary, and if they were constructed by anyone, it was by themselves, in the fruitful encounters of Scandinavians with new landscapes and new cultures.

The remainder of this chapter will consider definitions of Vikings and the Viking Age, the chronological parameters of the Viking Age, and the nature of the evidence for it, all prerequisites to understanding what is meant by 'Viking diaspora'. Chapter 2 will then outline the physical world within which the Viking diaspora developed. A more detailed exploration of the term 'diaspora', as used of the world that grew out of the Viking Age, will follow in Chapter 3. Chapters 4–6 will consider in detail the most salient themes of the Viking diaspora, those of gender, beliefs and identities.

Vikings and víkingar

'Of making of books about Vikings there is no end' is a common scholarly lament. The people labelled 'Vikings' and the period in which they lived, the 'Viking Age', have, since their rediscovery in the nineteenth century, been the subject of many books, learned or popular, good, bad or indifferent.[10] Vikings are widely taught about in primary schools around the world, and now increasingly in higher education. Vikings or pseudo-Vikings pervade popular culture of all kinds, and evidence of Viking ancestry is much sought after in those parts of the world where they settled, or are imagined to have settled. Clearly, modern concepts of 'Vikings' and the 'Viking Age' are familiar to many, and widely understood. Nevertheless, they need to be redefined on a regular basis, particularly when used in tandem with newer concepts such as 'diaspora'.

There are three possible approaches to understanding the word which in modern English is 'Viking' (sometimes 'viking', without a capital letter), which unfortunately are often confused in both scholarly and popular discussions. These are (a) etymology, or the original meaning and derivation of the word, (b) historical usage, or what the word meant to those who used its earlier forms in the Viking and medieval periods and in the language(s) of the time, and (c) current usage, or what the word has come to mean in our modern world, in both English and other languages. In particular, many popular (and even some academic) works about the Vikings commit the etymological fallacy, by assuming that giving an etymology of the word is equivalent to defining it. But words change or develop in meaning, while also often crossing into other languages, and all three approaches are needed for a full understanding of how to use the word now. Thus, etymology is useful in establishing how or where the word began, but cannot establish for certain what it actually meant in the Viking Age and later, since there is no guarantee that its original meaning was retained from when the word was first formed, nor can we say for certain when that was. Studies of how the word was used in the Viking Age itself provide insights which are useful for historical study but which sometimes bear little resemblance either to its etymology or to its later usage. Modern meanings of the word 'Viking' may have moved far beyond the earlier meanings, but they are inescapable.[11] Paradoxically, these are probably the most useful – 'Viking' seems to be a word, in English especially, that has expanded and developed to fill a gap, to give a name to a phenomenon which previously had no name but needed one.

It has to be remembered that there are actually two relevant words, those which appear in Old Norse as the nouns *víkingr* (m.), and *víking* (f.).[12] The former refers to a person, the latter to an activity, presumably the kind of activity typical of the person. It is possible that the abstract noun *víking* was primary, and that the common noun *víkingr*, denoting a person, is derived from it, but this is difficult to demonstrate.[13] Despite this, *víking* is less often considered by scholars, who tend instead to focus on *víkingr*. Cognates of *víkingr* are recorded in other Germanic languages from an early stage (for example Old English *wīcing*) and both the etymology of and the relationship between these cognates are a long-standing matter of dispute among scholars. It is not certain that the Old English word, for example, is from the same origin as the Old Norse word, or that it has the same meaning. In terms of etymology, it has variously been suggested that *víkingr* derives from Old Norse *vík* 'bay, inlet', or *Vík* 'the Oslofjord', or is somehow related to Old English *wīc* and Latin *vicus* 'dwelling place, camp'. These derivations thus posit that a *víkingr* is someone associated with one of these places or types of place, that is, a pirate who lurks in bays waiting to sail out and rob passing ships, or a coastal seafarer from the Oslofjord, or a traveller making temporary camps. Other suggestions relate the term to various verbs meaning 'withdraw, deviate, travel', more or less plausibly related to what Vikings are thought to have done. More specifically, it has been suggested that the word is related to the Old Norse verb *víkja* 'to turn aside' and is thus a reference to the practice of rowing in shifts, in particular the method of changing who is at the oars, back in the days before the adoption of the sail, and so before the Viking Age.[14] The overall argument is complex and far from resolved. But in any case, it has to be remembered that etymology aims primarily to reconstruct the original meaning of a word. While this can shed light on possible later meanings, there is no guarantee that the original meaning still applied in the time when we actually have records of the word in use. These later meanings can only be derived from actual usage.

The actual usage of *víking* and *víkingr* in the Viking Age and later shows that their meanings have moved on from whatever the original meanings were.[15] *Víkingr* appears in runic inscriptions from the Viking Age (as does *víking*), and also in skaldic poetry which is arguably from the Viking Age (see further on sources and evidence, below). Perhaps surprisingly, though, neither term is especially common, and their connotations in context are often ambiguous. More common than either term, in memorial inscriptions on Viking Age rune-stones at least, is *Víkingr* used as a personal name. This might suggest it had a positive connotation. But this positive connotation is not so well attested for the nouns, and particularly for *víkingr*. It can be used pejoratively, of enemies and opponents, suggesting it was not considered a positive concept. Again, etymology fails us, since it is impossible to say for certain whether the personal name has the same derivation as the noun; they might merely appear to be the same word. However, people in the Viking Age knew nothing of etymology, and are likely to have assumed that the personal name and the noun had some connection, so if people could be named *Víkingr*, it cannot have had entirely negative associations.

Although the terms are ambiguous, and seem to have been subject to regional and chronological variation, what their Viking Age uses do tell us is that none of the possible etymological meanings is at the forefront of the word as it was used then. Instead, usage suggests that *víkingr* (pl. *víkingar*) refers to people (always in groups) who were engaged in some sort of military activity, often but not always piratical or sea-borne. These groups of people could be either the comrades or (more often) the opponents of the person whose point of view is represented in the text. An interesting example is the eleventh-century rune-stone from Bro, in Uppland, Sweden (U 617), on which the person being commemorated is said to have been a *víkinga vǫrðr* – this could mean either a 'guardian of Vikings', and so imply the leader of a group of Vikings, or someone who guarded others against Vikings, a defender of his people against Viking raiders.[16] Scholarly consensus currently leans toward the former meaning, but both are possible.[17] Like this example, all the skaldic and runic instances of the word (with the exception of when it is a personal name) are in the plural, which may suggest something significant about Vikings, that they were typically a group of people doing whatever they did together. What they did seems to have been largely military in nature, and is often associated with the sea. But it is significant that there is no clear evidence for any ethnic or regional implication in the term.

After the Viking Age, our sources in Old Norse increase, especially but not only the sagas and other historical and literary texts produced in Iceland from the early twelfth century onwards (on which more below) and the meanings of the 'Viking' words are correspondingly broader.[18] Recent studies have focused on the use of this terminology in the historical sagas of the Norwegian kings and the legendary sagas, set in the pre-Viking Scandinavian past.[19] Here, we see the word *víkingr* used in an increasingly broad range of meanings and now used as a label for individuals as well as groups. In the kings' sagas, the pejorative connotations of *víkingr* used of opponents are strong, while the activities described as *víking* are shown in a more positive light, since they generally take place in faraway lands, carried out by those very kings. But both words are most commonly used of fellow Scandinavians. Again, there is no ethnic implication, and whether Vikings are viewed positively or negatively depends on context, both literary and geographical, rather than ethnicity. The range of the term is further extended in the sagas of ancient times, in which stories from the pre-Viking past of Scandinavia are retold in a style which shows the influence of the norms and conventions of European romance. Here, *víkingr* is the term used of native heroes who subscribe to a code which is closer to the chivalric ethos than to the codes of the heroes of the Viking Age. The ways in which the term is used in the sagas of Icelanders, the other main branch of saga literature relevant to this theme, mirrors the usage of the kings' sagas, with a generally pejorative reference to individuals, but a neutral or positive reference to 'Viking' activities.[20]

The modern meanings of 'Viking', in English at least, begin in the early nineteenth century, with the best-known example being in Sir Walter Scott's novel

The Pirate (first published in 1822), though the earliest recorded instance is somewhat earlier, from 1807.[21] This period is when the term acquires its basic modern meaning: 'One of those Scandinavian adventurers who practised piracy at sea, and committed depredations on land, in northern and western Europe from the eighth to the eleventh century . . . '[22] The use of the word really picks up in the nineteenth century, along with a growing interest in all things Viking in the Victorian period.[23] By the twentieth century, the range of usage of the word is very broad indeed. It is heavily used in advertising and marketing, to label everything from American football teams, to British suppliers of stationery or tyres. Sometimes these brand names are used to connote a Scandinavian heritage, as in the Minnesota Vikings (an American football team), at other times there is no obvious link between the company or product and anything Scandinavian, let alone 'Viking'. The tendency to use 'Viking' as a marketing brand is even stronger in Scandinavia than in the English-speaking world.

The most common usage of the term 'Viking' in modern academic contexts is already broader than the *OED* definition – it is most often used to characterise peoples of Scandinavian origin who were active in trading and settlement as well as piracy and raiding, both within and outwith Scandinavia in a particular historical period, variously defined, but generally within the broad range of 750–1100.[24] Some scholars prefer to restrict the term to those who indulged in the typical 'Viking' activities of raiding and pillaging outside Scandinavia, thus perpetuating the pejorative meaning of the word found already in the Viking Age. Other scholars find it convenient to use the term of all Scandinavians in Scandinavia and people of Scandinavian ancestry outside Scandinavia during the period in question, and most general books about 'the Vikings' use this more inclusive meaning. The inclusive meaning is useful because it acknowledges the complexities of the period and avoids reducing its history to one of just raiding and pillaging. Even piratical Vikings abroad had roots in Scandinavia, many of them began as or were subsequently transformed into peaceful farmers, either in their homeland, or in a new home across the sea, and once people of Scandinavian origin start going abroad, the term 'Scandinavian' is not always the most appropriate one for them. Iceland, for instance, is not geographically a part of Scandinavia, even though its language, culture, and political and economic affiliations place it firmly in the Scandinavian sphere. In modern scholarly usage, therefore, the term 'Viking' is useful for a broader range of meanings than the purely military because it connotes the expansive, complex and multicultural activities of peoples who were still in touch with their Scandinavian origins, language and culture, but who were also exposed to new landscapes, new neighbours, and new ways of living.

In both scholarly and popular usage the term 'Viking' has a tendency to seep into discussions of the subsequent, medieval period (it has to be remembered that, in Scandinavian scholarship, the terms 'medieval' and 'Middle Ages' are used to describe a period that begins only after the end of the Viking Age; see further on chronology below). Thus, a well-known collection of English translations of Icelandic sagas is known as the *Complete Sagas of Icelanders*, but has the subtitle

Viking Age Classics and a recent BBC programme on this literature had the even more blatant title *The Viking Sagas*. The distinction between the Viking Age and its aftermath is sometimes difficult for non-specialists to understand and no doubt the word 'Viking' is additionally thought to confer positive marketing benefits. But it may also be that the distinction is difficult to make precisely because of the multifarious connections between the Viking Age proper and its aftermath, between Vikings and their successors, up until the next major historical and cultural milestone of the Protestant Reformation in the sixteenth century. These connections are an important part of what this book is about.

Viking Ages

It is not always clear whether the 'Viking Age' is defined by 'Vikings', or the other way around, and there is some danger of a circular argument. If Vikings are Scandinavians operating outside Scandinavia, particularly in activities involving raiding and depredation, then the Viking Age must be defined on the basis of when such activities took place. But if Vikings include those who stayed at home in Scandinavia, or those who retired from the Viking life to become peaceful farmers, then defining their 'Age' becomes more difficult. Above, it was suggested that a generous definition would stretch from *c.* 750 to *c.* 1100, but it is worth looking a bit more closely at the milestones that scholars use to define the Viking Age within these parameters.

The beginning of the Viking Age is commonly assigned to the year 793, when our first reliable and dated record of a Viking raid comes in the *Anglo-Saxon Chronicle*'s report of an attack on Lindisfarne.[25] Using this date to define the beginning of the Viking Age prioritises the evidence of historical documents and the typical 'Viking' activity of raiding. Even so, the first recorded and dated raid is not necessarily the first raid, for example the *Anglo-Saxon Chronicle* also mentions a violent encounter, probably in Portsmouth, recorded under the year 789, but happening an undefined number of years previously, and there must have been others.[26] Moreover, the raids did not happen instantly, as there must have been a period of reconnaissance and preparation. Hence, the beginnings of the Viking Age can be pushed back to a notional 750. If we were to consider other evidence, and particularly other evidence from Scandinavia itself, we might be inclined to push the beginning date back to around 700. This is the date of the founding of the important trading centre of Ribe, while archaeological evidence has been taken to suggest contacts between Scandinavia and the British Isles in the eighth century.[27] Scandinavian handicrafts were being produced in Ladoga in Russia by the middle of the eighth century.[28] A number of categories of archaeological object considered characteristic of the Viking Age are now more securely dated to the middle of the eighth century.[29] Developments in runic writing in that century also suggest it was a time of major changes in Scandinavia.[30] Whether these contacts and developments were the cause of, or a result of, outward movements beginning in that century is a moot point, but either way they suggest the changes taking place at that time.

Another way of looking at the beginning of the Viking Age was suggested by Bjørn Myhre. Arguing, with particular reference to Norway, that there was no 'dramatic economic and cultural change' around 800, he nevertheless recognised that it was in the late eighth century that 'the Danish kingdom and the Norwegian petty kingdoms had reached such a level of political organization, and were so powerful, that chieftains felt strong enough to begin such attacks across the sea.'[31] It should also be remembered that there were contacts between Scandinavia and other parts of the world even before the beginning of the Viking Age, however we choose to define the latter. Whether the Viking Age represents an intensification or a change in the nature of these contacts, its beginning would remain relatively arbitrary, whatever date is assigned to it. In general, the picture seems to be one of steady developments in the seventh and eighth centuries leading inexorably to the explosion of outward-oriented activities in the late eighth.

While there is some consensus in finding its beginnings in the eighth century, scholars find the end of the Viking Age even more difficult to pin down. One option is to use the nice round year of 1000. This happens to be the year (though actually it was probably in 999) when Iceland adopted Christianity, according to historical accounts.[32] Certainly the adoption by Scandinavians of the organised, monotheistic religion of most of the rest of Europe is a major milestone in their history and the resultant changes can be seen as bringing about the end of the Viking Age. The problem is that the change is unlikely to have happened overnight, and there is great regional variation across Scandinavia and the Viking world in both when and how quickly this particular transformation took place. Christian missionaries were active in Scandinavia from the ninth century at least, and there is some rather obscure archaeological evidence which suggests the presence of Christians in Scandinavia (though not necessarily Christian Scandinavians) from an early period.[33] Scandinavians settled outside Scandinavia, particularly those in the British Isles, inevitably came into contact with Christianity and may have converted before their friends and relatives back home. Other evidence shows that the thorough Christianisation of the population, for example of Iceland, took several centuries.[34] At the same time, it is clear that the eleventh century was a key time in the religious, and therefore cultural and political, transformation of Scandinavia.[35] Most scholars would thus put the end of the Viking Age somewhere in the eleventh century, generally using such historical milestones as the death of *Hǫrða*-Knútr, or Hardicanute, the last Danish king of England, in 1042, or the death of Haraldr *harðráði* 'Hard-Ruler', attempting to become a Norwegian king of England, at the Battle of Stamford Bridge in Yorkshire in 1066.

Such dates are particularly favoured by historians, relying on specific events recorded in documentary sources, and with their own national bias, in these cases particularly towards the history of England. Beyond England, it is more difficult to pin down an exact date for the end of the Viking Age, especially if the conversion to Christianity is avoided as too imprecise or variable to be a marker. In Scandinavian Scotland, there is no major cultural or political break which could characterise the end of the Viking Age until the thirteenth century in the Hebrides or the fifteenth century in the Northern Isles. Military raids led by Scandinavian kings and chieftains continued well into the thirteenth century in Scotland, while such leaders also led crusades, not always so very different from earlier 'raids', to both the Mediterranean (particularly in the twelfth century) and the Baltic.[36] The disappearance of the Scandinavian colony of Greenland at some time in the fifteenth century, the Scottification of the Northern Isles around the same time, and the Protestant Reformation throughout Scandinavia and its surviving colonies in the sixteenth century combine to suggest that *c.* 1500 is as good a date as any for the end of the 'long Viking Age'.

Another approach to dating the Viking Age is source-based. It is a frequently repeated truism that our contemporary textual sources for the period are written from the outside, by the 'victims' of Vikings, or at least by foreign observers, in other languages such as Latin, Old English or Arabic. Our first manuscript sources in Old Norse begin to be written in the twelfth century (though surviving mainly in later copies). But the eleventh century is actually rich in two vernacular sources with deep roots in Old Norse culture: runic inscriptions and skaldic verse, the latter however an oral genre not recorded in writing until some time later than its period of composition.[37] These sources will be discussed in more detail below, but for the purposes of delimiting the Viking Age, it is worth noting that the eleventh century is a transitional period between orality and literacy in the Scandinavian-speaking world. Culturally, the end of the Viking Age is marked by the emergence of a fully literate manuscript culture in the twelfth century, a phenomenon that is also related to the Christianisation process, culminating in the glut of texts and manuscripts about the Viking Age from fourteenth-century Iceland.

If the eleventh century is a period of cultural transition, it is also a period of political transition. It is at this time that the three Scandinavian nations of Denmark, Norway and Sweden begin to emerge as nations in a modern sense, with established hereditary monarchies and administrative frameworks supported by the Church. Like Christianisation, the process of state formation is also a complex and long-drawn-out one, and many historians would not describe the Scandinavian nations as proper medieval states until the thirteenth century, when there is an increasing number of surviving administrative documents.[38] But there is no doubt that the process began in the eleventh.[39]

In this book, then, the Viking Age is a little arbitrarily defined as the period from 750 to 1100. At the same time, it is recognised that many aspects of the Viking Age can only be understood through a consideration of evidence emanating from the following centuries. (This is also true of the preceding centuries, though that is not a topic for this book.) This 'aftermath' of the Viking Age, which is here considered to extend to the sixteenth century (when there are several cultural and historical milestones, not least the Protestant Reformation) is integral to an understanding of the Viking diaspora. But before considering the aftermath, or the diaspora, a brief survey is needed of sources for the Viking Age, many of which extend into or derive from this aftermath.

Evidence

Sources for the Viking Age

The surviving evidence for this relatively distant period of the past is traditionally assigned to categories such as archaeological, art historical, documentary, epigraphical, historical, linguistic, literary, numismatic, onomastic and so on. The study of this evidence is thus often parcelled out among the academic disciplines with these names which specialise in dealing with these types of evidence. One result is that the different disciplines have differing views on which is the most useful kind of evidence for understanding the period. An apocryphal story has it that when certain Viking Age archaeologists got together, they would sing, to the tune of 'Land of Hope and Glory', and not entirely in jest, that 'only archaeology can reveal the truth'. The mix of available sources and the disciplines required to understand them is characteristic of all historical enquiry. Though the relative balance of different kinds of evidence will vary, most students of the past recognise the need for an interdisciplinary approach, and this has always been a characteristic of Viking Age studies. It is simply not possible to understand the Viking Age by only sticking to the linguistic evidence, or archaeological sites.

However, it is the particular balance of kinds of evidence that makes the Viking Age unique. Interdisciplinarity requires more than just a conglomeration of all possible sources for the period, and a team of specialists pooling their knowledge to achieve a grand synthesis. It also requires a more subtle understanding of the nature of the evidence and how the different sources relate or, often, do not relate to each other. While much of the available evidence is a product of the accidents of survival, there is nevertheless something about the particular mix of evidence for the period that is in itself revealing. For this reason, discussion of the available sources for the study of the Viking Age is not just a routine academic exercise but an important prerequisite to all further discussion. Rather than perpetuating the traditional academic divisions, it seems more appropriate to divide the evidence for the Viking Age into three broad categories which can be called the linguistic, the artefactual and the natural. Each category will be explained in more detail below, though it is useful to summarise them first.

Linguistic and artefactual evidence come about through human agency. The 'linguistic' consists of all evidence that is formed from verbal language. The survival of such evidence, for any period before the invention of sound recording, ultimately depends on its having been written down, so this category of evidence comprises written texts of various kinds, but also includes aspects of language (e.g. names) which have been recorded for their own sake and not necessarily in a narrative text, and many of which still survive. The 'artefactual' comprises all objects made by humans, from the smallest pin to the largest fortress. Such objects may be found by archaeological investigation, or they may turn up by chance, or they may still be visible in their original locations. The 'natural' is a term for all evidence that is formed by natural processes. Although the 'natural' cannot completely be divorced from that created by human agency, it is characterised by the fact that it is susceptible to investigation by the natural sciences, the methodologies of which have improved enormously in the last few decades. The remains of humans and animals, or of the rocks, soil and vegetation of the past, contain much useful information which is only just being revealed through the development of new scientific techniques. Although already very broad, these three categories of 'linguistic', 'artefactual' and 'natural' often overlap. Thus, a brooch with a runic inscription on it is both an artefact and a text. A comb is both an artefact and the organic remains of an animal which may be subjected to scientific investigation; it may even also bear a text, and be considered in all three categories. Such mixed evidence will require a variety of approaches, for what characterises the linguistic, the artefactual and the natural is that they require different frameworks of understanding.

Linguistic evidence

Since we have no direct access to the spoken languages of the past, we have to rely, by and large, on written interpretations of those languages, and to consider how well these written interpretations represent what was once spoken. It is true that modern-day spoken language can sometimes provide clues to the Viking Age. Thus, the language spoken in Iceland or the Faroes today is a direct descendant of the language taken to those places by migrants in the Viking Age and thus tells us something important, though rather general, about that migration process. Modern pronunciations of place-names, both in Scandinavia and elsewhere, may also provide important clues to their derivation. But apart from a few such instances, we can only investigate the spoken language of the past through the written word, in all its variability of survival. The written record includes inscriptions, documents, histories and chronicles, poetry and literary narratives. Many of these are important, not only for what they say, but for their record of linguistic artefacts such as names.

Place-names are an excellent example of language in use, since they generally have meaning as well as denotation when first given. When Scandinavians went to settle in new places, they had to name those places, and such names can tell us a lot about the language(s) they were using, as well as their first impressions of new landscapes, and what social and cultural features were important enough at the time to be recorded in names. Place-names in the Scandinavian homelands not only provide a basis for understanding names in the new settlements, but also give insights into social and religious structures before and during the Viking Age. Such facts are fossilised in place-names, from where they have to be dug out, as we very rarely have a written record of place-names from even roughly the time when the name was newly minted. When the first written record is from many centuries later, it takes specialist onomastic study to link a name to the time of its coining and to tease out its derivation and meanings at that time. Dating place-names is also very difficult, though it can be made easier by observing which place-name elements the Scandinavians took with them to their new settlements, and which were already too old-fashioned to be used then.

Another branch of onomastics is the study of personal names and nicknames. Personal names have to be used with care because they may depend more on fashion than on language, but it is possible to identify broad patterns in the ways in which they are used, which reveal much about population movements, and religious and cultural changes. Both personal names and nicknames can be recorded in place-names and can help to establish what names were particularly fashionable at the time, assuming that the place-names can be dated at least roughly. Other personal names (and place-names) are recorded on coins, a type of artefact which is extremely useful for chronological study, since they can normally be dated within quite a narrow time period. But personal names, and especially nicknames, are mostly recorded in written texts, and are thus subject to the same evidential constraints as those texts.

Inscriptions in the runic alphabet are the only texts which are both indubitably contemporaneous with the Viking Age and written in a Scandinavian language. In fact, the runic tradition in Northern Europe extends for a longer period than just the Viking Age, from around 150 to around 1500, and this corpus therefore also provides evidence for what went before, and what came after, the Viking Age.[40] The distribution of the runic evidence is uneven, both geographically and chronologically, and the texts are often not especially long or informative. Nevertheless, the approximately 3,700 separate inscriptions dated to the Viking Age are an important contemporary source for this period.[41] Like coins, runic inscriptions and the objects on which they are written are both artefacts and texts, and they provide a range of insights into language, naming practices, social structures, art, poetry and religion.

With the important but limited exception of runic inscriptions, the Scandinavians of the Viking Age did not have a literate culture. The bulk of the written sources therefore falls into one of two categories, those written by non-Scandinavians, and those written later than the Viking Age, though there are also some that are both. These sources were written in a variety of languages, either the native tongues of their authors, or in transnational languages like Latin or Arabic.

Given the extensive interactions that Scandinavians had with other cultures, the sources written by those with whom they came into contact cover a wide range and are in many languages. These include annals, chronicles and histories in Latin (mainly from the European continent, but also some from Britain and Ireland), in Old English (from England), in Middle Irish (from Ireland) or in Old Church Slavonic (from Kievan Rus). Many, though not all, of these are contemporary with the events they describe. Other contemporary sources include ethnographic accounts in Old English or Arabic. There is a range of contemporary poetry dealing with Vikings, in Old English, Old High German and Latin. Some of these international genres are also found in Scandinavia, after the establishment of a literate manuscript culture there by the twelfth century. So we have histories in Latin from both Norway and Denmark and histories and annals in the vernacular from Norway and, above all, Iceland.

The Icelandic histories are arguably as much the result of a native oral tradition as of the reception of international historiography.[42] And the bulk of the Scandinavian-language written evidence relevant to the study of the Viking Age and its aftermath comes in the poetry and prose deriving from this native tradition, most of it surviving in manuscripts written in medieval Iceland.[43] As already noted above, this literary tradition can be traced back to the twelfth century. One of the most difficult, but most interesting, questions in scholarship has been the relationship between the surviving texts and the oral tradition from which they are thought to have emerged. Scholarly opinion has veered, and continues to veer, between native oral tradition and European literary influence as the main mover behind the development of Old Norse literature. Nevertheless, most recognise not only the importance of both but also that this is a large body of literature and that there is unlikely to be one answer for all texts. The most relevant texts for the discussions in this book are those that are either concerned with, or seem to emanate from, the Viking Age past. This includes a range of different types of saga, especially the sagas of Icelanders (*Íslendingasögur*), the sagas of kings (*konungasögur*), and some of the sagas of ancient times (also known as 'legendary sagas', *fornaldarsögur*). Closely related to these are historiographical works such as *Íslendingabók* ('Book of the Icelanders') and *Landnámabók* ('Book of Settlements', literally 'Book of Land-Takings'). Embedded in many of these works, and especially in the kings' sagas, are extracts from skaldic poetry, generally considered an important and contemporary source for the Viking Age, even though mostly only recorded in manuscripts from around 1200 or later. Eddic poetry is the name given to a genre of mythological and legendary poetry which has also often been thought to originate in the Viking Age (or even earlier according to some). And handbooks of poetry and mythology, such as Snorri Sturluson's *Edda*, provide keys to both Eddic and skaldic poetry, as well as further examples of them.

These are the canonical works of medieval Icelandic literature, thought first to have achieved their written form in the twelfth to fourteenth centuries, but surviving mainly in manuscripts of the thirteenth century or usually later. An examination of their relationship to the Viking Age past will be one of the themes of this book, and it will be argued that the concept of diaspora is the most appropriate framework for understanding the nature of this relationship.

Artefactual evidence

Unlike the linguistic evidence, which is mediated through writing, artefactual evidence brings us into direct physical contact with the past, and with its material culture: the artefacts both large and small that were created, used and left behind by people who lived at that time. The range of artefacts from the Viking Age is vast, with the main categories being objects associated with or found in burials, settlement sites both rural and urban, monuments and buildings in the landscape, finds of small objects either discarded or lost, and underwater structures and vessels.

An advantage of artefactual evidence is that it continues to increase, as a result of both archaeological investigation and chance discovery, thus providing ever more data for interpretation, whereas, with the exception of runic inscriptions, it is very rare for a new text to be discovered. Like texts, artefacts need interpretation, and some archaeologists claim that objects, or sites, are 'texts' and therefore have both grammar and meaning. But this analogy is somewhat forced and the process of interpretation is different from that of interpreting texts.[44] As noted above, the term 'artefacts' is used here to denote everything made by the human hand, from the small, practical objects of everyday life to the largest constructions. Artefacts can be studied within categories of particular artefacts, or in their archaeological contexts. The various techniques for interpreting the artefacts of the past have largely been developed over the last century or so, as the discipline of archaeology has evolved.[45] These interpretations can focus on how, where, when and by whom the artefact was created, how, where, when and by whom it was used, and how and when it came to be in the place in which it was discovered in modern times. Depending on the type of artefact, archaeologists may want to classify it according to the ethnicity, gender or social status of the creator or user, or the style in which or techniques with which it is made. Another approach is to focus on relationships between different artefacts, either because they are associated with each other on the same site, or in order to establish a typology of similar artefacts across a range of sites. The materials from which artefacts are made can be studied using methods from the natural sciences, thus overlapping with the natural evidence, considered below. Larger-scale interpretations highlight questions of meaning, reading various types of meaning into the evidence, such as the physical, the traditional and the operational.[46]

The study of Viking Age artefacts has to engage with questions of both time and space. Chronology is an important key to the understanding of artefacts, and dating has played a very large part in studying them – dating which can be done on stylistic, typological or stratigraphical grounds, or using methods from the natural sciences. It is not only artefacts dated to the Viking Age which are of interest, though. Re-use of artefacts originally made in an earlier period is of interest, while some artefact types, especially of simple everyday objects, have a very long shelf-life and can be difficult to date. Spatial distribution is also an important factor in the study of artefacts, from the smallest to the largest scale. Distribution of objects within a building will provide insights into the uses of spaces within the building, while the movement of artefacts or artefact types far from their place of production has much to tell us about networks and connections in the Viking Age. While all artefacts travel with people, some provide evidence for migration and some do not. Coins, in particular, may pass through many hands to reach their far-flung destinations, while other artefacts are more closely associated with their owners and their movements may be taken to indicate movements of people.

Natural evidence

Natural evidence relates to the bodies of humans and animals and their natural environment, both organic and inorganic. Most dramatically, we may meet the remains of the people and animals of the past, in skeletal or other partial form, and usually because they have been deposited in a grave. These human and animal remains can be subjected to various forms of analysis by the natural sciences, such as DNA analysis, or oxygen or strontium isotope analysis of their teeth. Ancient DNA analysis is still developing, but can in theory establish the genetic links of the humans and animals concerned, both with other individuals from the same locations, and more generally with other populations. Stable isotope analysis, on the other hand, can establish the environmental influences on both humans and animals, by demonstrating what kind of geological environment they grew up in, or lived in subsequently, and whether these environments were the same as that in which their remains were found, or whether they came from somewhere completely different. Examination of the bones of both humans and animals can reveal not only many of the diseases from which they suffered, but also something about their physical activity in life, and the manner in which they died, especially if violent.

While actual remains of humans are rarely found other than in graves, both human waste and associated fauna can be found on other kinds of sites. Fossilised excrement from both humans and animals will reveal both what individuals ate and what intestinal diseases they may have suffered from. Fossilised insects and parasites found on domestic sites will show what kinds of human and animal activity took place on those sites. The bones of larger animals found on domestic sites will reveal what people ate, and how they interacted with and exploited both land and sea animals for food, for products made from them, and for agriculture and transport.

The natural sciences can also illuminate human interactions with their environment, and changes in the environment which may or may not be anthropogenic (caused by humans and their activities). Pollen remains reveal changes in the human use of both wild and cultivated plants. In places previously uninhabited, the introduction of crop plants such as barley indicate the arrival of human inhabitants. These pollen remains can then be subjected to advanced dating techniques, notably radiocarbon dating, which can then give an indication of the date when those humans arrived in that place. Other changes in the environment can also be used to date Viking settlements. Of particular importance in Iceland is the volcanic ash that periodically covers large parts of the landscape when there is an eruption. These layers can be identified on archaeological sites, and correlated with the same layers found in cores taken from the Greenland ice-cap, and thus dated, in the process known as tephrochronology. By this means, the arrival of permanent settlers in Iceland can be dated to just after the so-called *landnám* tephra, dated to 871±2, as discussed further in the next chapter.

As already indicated, analysis based on the natural sciences can also apply to artefacts as well as the remains of humans and animals, or the traces of their environment. Objects made of inorganic materials such as ceramics, metal, glass or stone can often be provenanced using various kinds of scientific analysis. Dendrochronology, or dating by tree-rings, can help to establish when wooden structures were built and, in the case of ships, where they were built if that is not where they were found.

Just as the Viking Age and its aftermath needs to be defined chronologically, and in terms of the evidence for it, so there are also geographical parameters to consider. Following this introduction to basic terms and concepts, the following chapter outlines the geographical extent of the Viking world, and considers some of the ways of understanding this environment and how it changed, before moving on to the themes of the Viking diaspora. Since these themes are impossible to cover in full detail, each of the following chapters will include a series of illustrative case studies.

Notes

1 Crawford 2005; *SPSMA* II, xcvii–xcviii. All dates in this book are AD, unless specifically stated to be BC.
2 *SPSMA* II, 258–9. Unless otherwise indicated, all translations from Old Norse texts in this book are by its author; the footnotes provide references to both source-texts in the original and published translations.
3 As noted by Whaley in *SPSMA* II, 258–9; for the texts see *SPSMA* I, 400–1; *Edda*, 1–16; *PE*, 3–12.
4 *ÍF* XXXIV, 81–2; *OS*, 189. The following account of Þorfinnr is largely derived from *Orkneyinga saga*. See also *SPSMA* II, xcvii–xcviii.
5 *SPSMA* II, 177–281.
6 Jesch 2005, 13–14.
7 Jesch 2005.
8 Mirdal and Ryynänen-Karjalainen 2004, 8.
9 Karkov 2012, 153.
10 On the rediscovery of the Vikings, see e.g. Roesdahl and Meulengracht Sørensen 1996; Wawn 2000; Kolodny 2012. For some good books about Vikings, see e.g. Roesdahl 1998, Holman 2007.
11 On Modern English 'Viking', see Fell 1987; on the concept in other European languages, see Böldl 2007, 705–7.
12 The most useful survey is by Andersson 2007, on which much of the following is based. See also Heide 2005.
13 Heide 2005, 44.
14 Heide 2005.
15 Jesch 2002a.
16 *UR* III, 28–39. All runic inscriptions discussed in this book can also be traced in *SR* using their identifier given in brackets.
17 Jesch 2002a, 112–13; Krüger 2008, 43–4.
18 Böldl 2007, 700–4.
19 Krüger 2008; Larrington 2008.
20 Böldl 2007, 703.
21 Fell 1987, 117–18.
22 *OED*, 'viking'.
23 Wawn 2000; Böldl 2007, 705–7; Kolodny 2012.
24 Böldl 2007; see below for more on this date range.
25 *ASC*, p. 36.
26 *ASC*, p. 35.
27 Myhre 1993; Feveile 2010, 98–9.
28 Duczko 2004, 68.
29 Steuer 1998, 145.
30 Barnes 2012a, 54–9.

31 Myhre 1998, 25, 27.
32 Jochens 1999.
33 Brink 2004; Søvsø 2010.
34 Vésteinsson 2000.
35 Callmer 2008, 450.
36 Jensen 2001; Lindkvist 2001; Jesch 2014a.
37 Jesch 2001a, 6–33.
38 Bagge 2010, 19.
39 Jesch 2004a.
40 Barnes 2012a.
41 This number is derived from *SR*.
42 Whaley 2000.
43 For further information on these and the texts mentioned below see chapters 5, 6, 16, 22, 25, 27 in McTurk 2005.
44 Hodder and Hutson 2003, 59–61, 168–9.
45 Hodder and Hutson 2003 is a useful survey.
46 Hodder and Hutson 2003, 236.

2

THE VIKING WORLD

Geography and environment

The northlands

Scandinavia

The distance from the northern tip of Norway to the southern border of Denmark is more than half the total length of Europe.[1] The modern countries of Denmark, Norway and Sweden are a vast and varied region, and one that has never been densely populated. It is usual to call this region 'Scandinavia', though strictly speaking that term applies only to the bifurcate peninsula of Norway and Sweden, while mainland Denmark is an extension of the European continent. But the peninsula and the continent are linked by Denmark's islands, which provide a geographical transition to Sweden in particular, and all three countries are linked by the seas which were especially important routeways in the Viking Age. Also, 'Scandinavia' is culturally and linguistically, if not always geographically, appropriate for the whole of the region.

This unity was already recognised in the 1070s when the German cleric Adam of Bremen, writing about the newly converted northlands in his *History of the Archbishops of Hamburg-Bremen*, called his fourth book *Descriptio Insularum Aquilonis* 'Description of the Islands of the North'.[2] While this heading disregards the fact that Norway, Sweden and the Jutlandic peninsula of Denmark are not islands, it enabled him to include other northern regions in his description, such as the islands of Iceland and Greenland, or *Vinland* (its location obscure to Adam, but somewhere in North America, as discussed further below). In his work, Adam places the Scandinavian homelands within a larger European context, specifically one of prelates and kings, but his ethnographic description of Book Four reaches beyond these homelands to the larger region that we now recognise as the Viking diaspora (this term will be discussed more fully in the next chapter). Adam's definition of the 'islands of the north' also includes areas in the east around the Baltic which would have been familiar to the Scandinavians, though not fully culturally integrated with them, as well as the Scottish isles and Ireland, which were very much a part of the Viking world in his day. For Adam, the coherence of this region lay not so much in any linguistic or cultural similarities, but in the fact that these were all regions newly converted to Christianity, and therefore a target of his aggressively expansive archdiocese. Yet, although his interest is religious rather than cultural, Adam's description unwittingly provides a snapshot of the Viking diaspora as it is still in the process of formation.

The geography of the Scandinavian homelands is, as one would expect of such a large region, very varied. In between the tundra and the frozen coasts of the far north, and the low green hills of Denmark in the south, are the mountains and fjords of Norway, the forests and lakes of Sweden, and the seas that bind them all together. The climate varies too, being maritime in the south and west, and continental in the north and east, as reflected in the vegetation, and with snow cover varying from a few weeks in the south to many months in the north. The large variations in altitude also affect temperature. Despite this variation, all the homelands share a harsh climate, especially in winter, and a rugged topography. However, temperatures are not as extreme as elsewhere on the globe at the same latitudes, due largely to the effects of the North Atlantic Current which brings warmth from the south. Many crops can be grown further north here than elsewhere in the world, due to the long hours of sunlight in summer as well as the warm air currents. In fact, the region is so vast, it comprises eight vegetation zones.

Access to timber, so vital for building ships and many other things, varies widely across Scandinavia. Mountain birch is the predominant species in the far north. Large parts of Norway are above the tree line, otherwise Norway and Sweden have predominantly coniferous forests (Norway spruce and Scots pine). Their southern regions and Denmark are in the temperate zone where there are deciduous species such as oak, beech, elm, maple, ash and linden. In general, the resource base of Scandinavia is much narrower than in the rest of Europe, though even in the Viking Age, certain goods such as furs and iron were sufficiently abundant to be exported.

By the beginning of the Viking Age, human colonisation had reached almost all of Scandinavia except for the very high grounds, although the area of settlement which subsisted from agriculture continued to expand into the sixteenth century. In the Viking Age and medieval times, settlements across much of the area were widely dispersed and often divided from each other by natural obstacles such as mountains or forests, while seas and lakes on the other hand made communication easier, also, or especially, when they were frozen in winter. Settlement in Denmark was largely village-based, in Norway farm-based, while Sweden had both villages and individual farms.

Norway

At its greatest extent, Norway is 1,750 kilometres long, with one-third of the present country lying north of the Arctic Circle. Agricultural land forms less than 3 per cent of the total area, but the very long coastline, with the so-called *skjærgård* 'skerry fence', an archipelago of small offshore islands, protecting the coastal sailing route, promotes both fishing and seaborne trade, and the majority of the population has been coastal since Palaeolithic times. While the perimeter of Norway measures 2,650 kilometres, the actual shoreline has been calculated at 83,281 kilometres, including 58,133 kilometres of offshore islands. There are extensive forests, both productive and unproductive, high plateaus, and dramatic mountains and fjords in the west and north. At its most extreme, for example in the Sognefjord, which was a point of origin for many Viking Age (and later) emigrants, the landscape has marked gradients of both climate and vegetation from the coast to the innermost district of Indre Sogn, and from sea level to mountains and glaciers. Norway has 84 per cent of Scandinavia's glaciers, and the largest ones in Europe. Much of Norway allows only small-scale agriculture, especially animal husbandry, though arable farming is also practised, especially in the south and east.

Sweden

Modern Sweden covers an even larger area than Norway, though in the Viking Age and Middle Ages it was considerably smaller, as parts of its modern territory belonged either to Denmark (see below) or to Norway. Even this smaller area took a long time to develop into a unified nation. In the 1070s, Adam of Bremen still recognised two separate entities, *Gothia* (modern Götaland) and *Sueonia* (modern Svealand), and these were not fully united until the thirteenth century.[3] The border to the 'Danish' territory in the south is marked by dense and extensive forests, especially in Småland, making a naturally impervious barrier for much of Sweden's history. The greater part of Sweden, like Finland, is located on a bedrock of granite and gneiss. The percentage of cultivable land is about 7–8 per cent, but with great regional variation, while something like 55 per cent of the present country is covered in forests, mainly coniferous (Scots pine and Norway spruce, as in Norway). Land uplift resulting from ancient deglaciation has caused the coastline to rise and it is still rising. In some parts of Sweden the coast is now up to 800 metres higher than a thousand years ago. As a result, the Mälar valley, for example, an important and wealthy region in the Viking Age, not least because it was connected to the sea, is now cut off from the Baltic and has become a large lake.

Important in the Viking Age were the large offshore Baltic islands, Öland and Gotland (now part of Sweden) and Bornholm (now part of Denmark). All of these were on well-trafficked trade and exchange routes to the south and east, and have distinctive geographies, and distinctive cultures which underline the diversity of Viking Age Scandinavia.

Denmark

Denmark, as it emerged in the Viking Age, consisted of several distinct regions. The Jutland peninsula, attached to, and physically an extension of, the European continent, had a more southerly political border than today. Danish territory also included some 500 large and small islands, and, until the seventeenth century, a substantial part, being the main arable areas, of what is now southern Sweden (Skåne [including Bornholm], Halland and Blekinge). These diverse areas were connected by seagoing traffic for most of Denmark's history, until the construction of major bridges in the late twentieth century. The Danish landscape is gently contoured, with the highest point in modern Denmark being only around 170 metres high, and a much larger proportion of its area can be cultivated than is the case with either Norway or Sweden. This, together with its long coastline, makes Denmark a land of both farmers and seafarers throughout its history. And it is this maritime connection that links Denmark culturally and linguistically to the areas to its north, rather than to the southern regions with which it is geologically and geographically connected.

It was from this vast region, so diverse geologically and geographically, yet intimately connected in its language and culture, that Scandinavian people set out in the Viking Age, on voyages of raiding, trading and settlement. While these three activities were undoubtedly connected, and often carried out by the same people, the focus here is on the lands in which they settled.[4] West, south and east of the northern homelands, these are the lands of the Viking diaspora.

The North Atlantic

Faroe

The Faroe Islands are an isolated group of 18 small, rugged islands, and many islets and reefs, with predominantly coastal habitation, inland pastures and dramatic bird cliffs along the western coasts.[5] The highest point is 882 metres above sea level. The underlying geology is an eroded basalt plateau and, as in Iceland, the islands lack trees and bushes, with the grass-, sedge- and heathlands providing grazing and the latter also peat and turf. Despite the warmth provided by the North Atlantic Current, the islands are at the climatic limit for growing grain, and less than 5 per cent of the land is cultivated today. Instead, sheep breeding has historically always played a dominant role in Faroese agriculture, as the name of the island group suggests (discussed further below). Marine resources are abundant, and fishing (both at sea and in streams and lakes) and the hunting of both whales and seabirds have always made an important contribution to Faroese subsistence. There is some evidence in the Faroes of human activity before the Viking Age settlements (discussed further below) but, as in Iceland, permanent human habitation seems to begin with those settlements and has been continuous since then. This apparently pristine character is what sets the Faroes and Iceland apart from the other regions of the Viking diaspora, where the incomers encountered indigenous inhabitants and an anthropogenic landscape, that is one that had been formed by human activities.

Iceland

Iceland lies just south of the Arctic Circle. Bestriding the Mid-Atlantic Ridge, it is geologically young, and still volcanically active (as the world discovered with the eruption of Eyjafjallajökull in April 2010). Like the Faroes, Iceland's climate is oceanic with relatively mild winters and cool summers. The Viking Age settlers who arrived in the late ninth century were the first permanent human population of this large island, somewhat larger than the island of Ireland. Two-thirds of Iceland consist of barren, uninhabitable highland, and there are four large glacier regions. The geology is basalt, though much younger than that of the Faroes, and all coasts except the south coast are indented by large fjords. Iceland also lacks trees and bushes, with the exception of some birch or willow woodland or scrub, and its agricultural activity is predominantly animal husbandry, though some grain can be grown. Before the arrival of people in the Viking Age, the flora and fauna of Iceland were very limited. There were for instance no land mammals at all except for the Arctic fox, and some polar bears which occasionally reached its shores by crossing winter sea-ice.[6] The first settlers encountered a landscape rather different from today's, 'a mid-Atlantic island with substantial arctic birch forest in the lower elevations, coastal sea mammal (including walrus) and sea bird colonies, migratory nesting birds, and the green grass that could feed their imported domestic livestock'.[7] The story of their impact on this environment is explained further below.

Greenland

The Faroes and Iceland still form a part of Scandinavia as broadly conceived today, and have belonged linguistically, culturally and politically to this region continuously since their settlement in the Viking Age. During that period, peoples of Scandinavian origin also reached further west, to Greenland. The descendants of these remained in Greenland well into the fifteenth century, and the country revived its associations with Denmark, and therefore with the Scandinavian world, in the eighteenth. Greenland is the world's largest island, but not obviously so as over 80 per cent of it is covered in ice and circumnavigation is impossible. The low-lying coasts of south-western Greenland are a sub-arctic landscape dominated by large fjords and their relatively southerly location (on roughly the same latitude as Orkney) makes animal husbandry a viable form of agriculture, as shown by the reintroduction of sheep-farming there in the twentieth century. The Viking Age and medieval population of Scandinavian origin began as farmers but also made extensive use of marine resources for both sustenance and trade. The Greenlanders ate seal and fish, and they benefited from the high medieval demand for luxury goods such as walrus ivory, narwhal tusk, polar bear skins and falcons. The exact reasons for which this population ceased to exist at some point in the fifteenth century are still not fully understood.[8]

Vínland

In the Viking Age, people of Scandinavian origin also reached various places in North America, though there is no evidence for any long-lasting settlement there. The exact location, and extent, of the *Vínland* mentioned in a variety of sources is disputed, and almost everywhere along the eastern seaboard of North America has been suggested. What is not disputed is the physical evidence of a short-lived Viking Age settlement excavated at L'Anse aux Meadows on the northern tip of Newfoundland, in Canada, which is most likely a particular point within a larger area that was called *Vínland*.[9] From this place, in existence for at most a quarter of a century around the year 1000, it is clear that people of Scandinavian origin made exploratory visits at least as far south as the St Lawrence River or north-eastern New Brunswick. The rather flat and barren area around L'Anse aux Meadows was not particularly attractive in itself. However, its nodal location at the entrance to the Gulf of St Lawrence made it a gateway to the regions further south which did have desirable resources in the form of hardwood, grapes and nuts. But the distance to these resources was great (*c.* 1,300 kilometres), so that the voyage proved not to be economical, and the gateway settlement at L'Anse aux Meadows was short-lived. There is however evidence that Greenlanders continued to access resources from areas to their north and west for some centuries afterwards.[10]

The west and south

Britain and Ireland

The North Atlantic settlements of the Viking Age included two (the Faroes and Iceland) that have survived to the present day as direct descendants of those first established in the Viking Age, while the Greenland settlement also persisted for half a millennium before its unexplained demise. Other settlements in the western Viking diaspora, particularly in the archipelago of Britain and Ireland, could be similarly long-lasting, as in the case of Orkney and Shetland, which remained politically Scandinavian for half a millennium (until 1468–9), but here the situation is more complicated. These regions were fully or partially inhabited when the Scandinavians arrived, and the impact of the incomers on the landscape and on human activity took place within existing local contexts, political, geographical, agricultural and cultural. The establishment of Scandinavian settlements could only be achieved through some sort of accommodation with indigenous populations, though some incomers may have been able to make use of underutilised or even deserted areas and thus avoided some of the problems of interaction. The extent to which the incomers displaced or replaced any existing populations, or whether they settled among them, either intimately together with, or separately from them, is still a matter of debate and undoubtedly varied from region to region.

In all the Scandinavian settlements of the British Isles, what happened after the Viking Age is also relevant to understanding this process. The places settled by Scandinavians continue to be inhabited, in some cases by people descended from those Scandinavians, but in all cases there have also been other incomers in later centuries. Together with general cultural and political developments, the end result has been the assimilation of the Scandinavian settlements into their local polities, with the gradual fading out of any recognisably Scandinavian language or culture.

There is great regional variation both in the Viking Age and subsequently, and the question of the 'Scandinavianness' of the different parts of Britain and Ireland must be decided for each locality on a fairly small-scale basis. This regional variation is in part determined by the great geographical variation of Britain, compared to its relatively small size. Mainland Britain and its surrounding islands encompass 'mountain, fen and bog, upland and lowland, wood and plain, field and pasture, river and stream' as well as a range of different types of coastline and many different types of waters around them.[11] Linked to these varied surface features are great differences of climate, vegetation and soil. This geographical variety of the British Isles must always be taken into account when studying historical and cultural conditions. But there is also marked cultural variety, with different parts of the islands inhabited by different cultural and linguistic groups, another important factor in understanding the Scandinavian settlements.

Most intensively settled and influenced by Scandinavian incomers are various regions of Scotland.[12] Scotland has been inhabited since the Mesolithic period (at least as early as *c.* 7000 BC), when hunter-gatherers lived in the forests that grew up quickly after the retreat of the ice. Some remarkable structures built by earlier inhabitants, ranging from Neolithic stone circles and chambered tombs to Iron Age brochs, are still visible in many areas today, and would have been even more prominent to the Scandinavians arriving sometime in the ninth century.[13] Although there is some evidence of Scandinavian settlement or at least linguistic influence in most parts of the modern country of Scotland, the main regions of Scandinavian settlement are north and west of the Great Glen, with particular concentrations in the archipelagos of the Northern and Western Isles (Orkney, Shetland and the Hebrides) and their adjacent littorals.

Scotland has a complex geology and varied geography, its post-glacial forest cover having largely disappeared before the Viking Age, with a concomitant expansion of heather moorland and blanket bog. The Scandinavian regions of Scotland are mainly composed of land suitable only for rough grazing, making animal husbandry the chief form of agriculture. However, some arable farming is possible, particularly in north-eastern parts (including Orkney), where the fertile lowlands and coastal inlets provided an environment not unlike that of western Norway. Elsewhere, subsistence cultivation was limited to the coastal fringes, most notably the Hebridean *machair*, windblown shellsand which provides fertile and easily tilled soil, also found in Orkney.[14] The archipelagic environment of the Scottish isles did however encourage both trade and the development of fishing in the late Viking Age and the Norse period.[15] At first this was largely inshore fishing for domestic consumption, but it soon expanded into deep-sea commercial fishing. Fowling also contributed to subsistence in many parts of Scandinavian Scotland.

Its situation along the coasts and beside the developing sea routes made Scandinavian Scotland central to the Viking diaspora and some of the main nodes in the social, cultural and economic networks of this diaspora are in this region. Thus Shetland is the nearest point to Norway, and was often the first port of call for travellers going west, especially to Faroe and Iceland. As a long north–south archipelago, it was easy to find by those sailing west. Orkney was also a key stop-over on these routes as well as on those heading further south, while the Hebrides lay along the important trading route to the Irish Sea region.

In the middle of the Irish Sea lies the Isle of Man, sometimes considered the southernmost island in the Hebridean chain, and certainly with many cultural links to Scandinavian Scotland, as well as the other Scandinavian settlements around the Irish Sea. The island, based on limestone and sandstone rocks, is fertile and was also extensively settled in the Viking Age. Due to its location at the intersection of several major sailing routes, the island's importance was political and commercial, as well as agricultural, and its ties were to England, Wales and Ireland as well as Scotland.

Ireland has also been inhabited since the Mesolithic (*c.* 7500 BC), with its early settlement patterns almost entirely rural, although in the early medieval period there was some nucleation in the form of monasteries. The first recorded Viking raid was in 795 and the ninth century saw intensification of this activity, with the establishment of small permanent settlements. The arrival of the Vikings is credited with introducing new forms of settlement into the Irish landscape, the much-discussed *longphuirt* (probably fortified land bases for Viking fleets) and the new urbanism, fuelled by trade, of Dublin, Waterford, Wexford and Limerick.[16] However, it is now recognised that Scandinavian influence extended beyond the trading centres into the rural and agricultural landscape of Ireland, although the evidence is still quite meagre and difficult to interpret.[17] A range of indicators, from rural settlements, agricultural tools and practices, crop remains, animal bones and linguistic evidence, suggests that there was two-way adoption of certain farming practices and equipment, leading to a merging of agricultural traditions which laid the foundations for the later socio-economic history of Ireland.

Wales is not extensively marked by Scandinavian influence in the Viking Age, though its location on the perimeter of the Irish Sea certainly brought it within range of the population movements occurring around those waters. Many of the prominent coastal features of Wales (and southwest England) have names of Scandinavian origin, indicating navigational routes, though such names do not always imply a settled community, but may derive rather from the international language of seafarers.[18] Place-names implying settled communities are rarer, but are supported by archaeological evidence for a limited degree of Scandinavian settlement, especially on the fertile island of Anglesey, more like the Isle of Man than the adjacent mountainous areas of Wales.[19]

At the time of the Viking settlements, the modern country of England did not exist as such, rather there were several small kingdoms, inhabited mostly by speakers of Old English (Anglo-Saxon). The Viking impact on these kingdoms and how it contributed to the creation of an English kingdom is well documented, particularly in historical sources such as the *Anglo-Saxon Chronicle*, and has been much written about.[20] From the geographical point of view, it is perhaps most important to recognise the variety of the English landscape and the resulting variety of Scandinavian influence. Thus it is probably no accident that the low rolling hills and flat expanses of Lincolnshire and East Anglia were settled by people from similarly contoured Denmark, while the mountainous regions of north-west England attracted people with their ultimate origins in Norway. As in Scotland, there is a marked regional concentration of Scandinavian influence, although some kinds of this influence, from different periods, can be found in many parts of the present country. In England, this concentration is in those parts which lie to the north and east of the old Roman road of Watling Street. A part of this territory was for some time under Scandinavian political control and is as a result known as the Danelaw.[21] Scandinavian influence outside the Danelaw is generally attributable to the eleventh century, when the Danish King Knútr (Cnut, Canute) sat on the English throne.[22]

In England, as in Ireland, Scandinavians contributed to the development of towns, and archaeological excavations in centres like York and Lincoln have revealed extensive Scandinavian involvement in manufacture and trade. Rural settlement in England is more difficult to pin down archaeologically, though it is clearly shown by the distribution of place-names of Scandinavian origin. Of all the parts of the British Isles settled by Scandinavians, Anglo-Saxon England was culturally and politically the most developed, and the debates about the extent, nature and effects of these settlements are still ongoing.[23] There is some evidence to suggest that the incomers favoured more marginal lands, or that they were able to populate regions that had been emptied by disease or other social factors, but more work is needed before these hypotheses can be confirmed. The question of how the Scandinavians mingled, if they did, with the indigenous population will be considered below, in Chapters 4 and 6.

The European continent

Although Scandinavian raids on the European continent are extensively documented, only a small part of this region can be included in the Viking diaspora. It has been pointed out that, despite the powerful but short-lived political effects of Scandinavian warbands and armies on the continent, 'the transfer of Scandinavian cultural elements . . . was virtually nil'.[24] This is even more true of distant regions in the Mediterranean and North Africa which we know experienced some Viking activity, but have no identifiable settlements.

However, just across the channel from England, in Brittany but especially in Normandy, the Scandinavians did establish, or attempt to establish, themselves in ways that may qualify for the designation 'diaspora'.[25] The very name of 'Normandy' originates from the 'Northmen' who, under their leader Rollo, established a Scandinavian polity in upper Normandy, around Rouen, in around 911, which was successively expanded westwards in 924 and then to the Cotentin in 933.[26] Place-names, some legal provisions and maritime organisation all attest to the existence of a Scandinavian community here, though it was short-lived and appears to have lost its Scandinavian flavour by the early eleventh century. Normandy's western neighbour, Brittany, has been described as 'the colony that failed'. The historical and archaeological evidence points to a Scandinavian military attempt to establish a colony that ended in a violent reconquest of their homeland by the Bretons.[27] Nevertheless, the Scandinavian activities in this north-western corner of the European continent should be seen as part of the larger movements in the region, across the Channel in the British Isles, and stretching back to the Norwegian homeland. In particular, the strong Scandinavian influence on the maritime culture of this region shows it to be closely involved in the networks of diaspora.[28]

The east

Finland

Together with Norway and Sweden, Finland forms the geographical region known as Fennoscandia. In modern parlance it is often considered to be a part of Scandinavia along with Denmark, Norway and Sweden, and indeed the North Atlantic territories, though it is culturally and, above all, linguistically distinct from them, as the Finns speak an unrelated language that is not even Indo-European. Nevertheless, Viking Age settlement from Sweden along the south-western coast of Finland and on the Baltic archipelago of Åland, now a semi-autonomous region of Sweden, places this region within the Viking diaspora. In fact, the Swedish settlement of Åland can be traced back to the sixth century.[29] Like Sweden, Finland has an archipelagic coastline in the Bothnian Gulf and Baltic Sea. It is low-lying and extensively (71%) forested, with thousands of lakes which, when frozen in winter, provide a superb communication network. Although there was a population increase during the Viking Age, only a small part of the country was permanently settled, with the rest a 'vast uninhabited wilderness'.[30]

The Baltic and Russia

The Baltic is the largest brackish sea in the world and links Scandinavia to regions in the east and south-east. Sweden was the point of departure for Viking Age trading voyages to the east, either via Åland to the southern Finnish coast, or across to Latvia, or the island of Saaremaa in present-day Estonia. In both cases the voyages would then continue south or east to Lake Ladoga, an important nodal point for voyages further south and east along the river systems of Russia, with the ultimate destination of Byzantium.[31] The region between Lakes Ladoga and Ilmen, and between the Upper Volga and its tributary the Oka, had the densest Scandinavian population in Eastern Europe.[32] Traders penetrated deep into Russia via great rivers such as the Vistula, the Dvina and the Niemen. Using light vessels and portages, they could access the Volga, Don and Dnieper rivers, flowing south and east, and reached both the Caspian and the Black Seas. The quantity of Viking Age Scandinavian artefacts (some of them dating to the seventh century) found in this large region (greater than the number of such artefacts found in Western Europe) is testimony to the liveliness of this traffic.[33]

While much of the Viking traffic in this region was associated with trade and was therefore transitory, there is evidence of permanent or semi-permanent Scandinavian settlements, or settlements where at least some of the population were Scandinavian or had contacts with Scandinavia, mainly in Russia. These were settlements of both rural and urban character, and which very clearly included Scandinavian women, and the evidence suggests a largish population of what has been called 'rural vikings'.[34] These rural vikings are also represented in some 141 place-names of Scandinavian origin, mainly from northern Russia, many of which contain Scandinavian personal names.[35] This rural picture is particularly true in the Lake Ladoga region, accessible by seagoing vessels from the Baltic, where there is evidence of Scandinavian settlement outside the towns, whereas in the areas further east and south, accessible only by portages, the evidence for Scandinavian women (and children) is primarily from burial grounds which served the population of the trading towns.[36]

The military and commercial elites of this region had close ties with the Scandinavian world up to the end of the twelfth century.[37] Many Scandinavians served in the Varangian Guard of the Byzantine Emperor and one of them, King Haraldr *harðráði* 'Hard-Ruler' of Norway, married the Russian princess Ellisif. She was already half-Scandinavian, as her father Jaroslav had in his time married a daughter of the King of Sweden.[38] There were other dynastic marriages between Russian or half-Russian princesses and Scandinavian royal houses.[39] But these exchanges were more an expression of elite politics at an international level than of a broader diaspora.

It was mentioned above that, while Vikings extended their voyages to places as far away as the Mediterranean and North Africa, these regions (along with much of the European continent) do not form a part of the Viking diaspora, since there is little or no evidence of established settlements and long-term contacts. As shown above, Vikings did penetrate far into eastern regions and established settlements there, but here too they came into contact with regions and peoples among whom they did not settle. Most notably, there is a large number of Arabic sources which record encounters with Vikings, in a wide range of places, including Islamic Spain as well as further east, around the Caspian Sea.[40] These sources span six centuries, though the bulk of the evidence relates to the ninth and tenth centuries. Evidence in the other direction is in practice limited to the very large number of Arabic coins known as 'dirhems' found in Scandinavia and other Viking regions during the period.[41] Other than these coins, there is little evidence to show that the Arabs made the same impression on the Scandinavians as vice versa.

Wherever Scandinavians settled, their living conditions varied considerably, not only according to geography, but also according to whether or not the landscapes they encountered were previously inhabited.

People and environment – arrival

Arrival in a pristine landscape

The natural environment is not entirely natural – it has been subject to human impact and intervention since the earliest times. With modern scientific techniques, this impact can be measured and interpreted. An important source of evidence for the movement of Scandinavians into new regions comes from the analysis of their effect on the natural environment, particularly, though not only, on the environment of previously uninhabited areas such as Faroe and Iceland. Greenland, too, counts as a 'pristine' landscape in this sense as the indigenous inhabitants of Greenland at that time did not have settled agricultural systems nor did they live where the Scandinavian incomers settled.[42] It is also very rich in relatively undisturbed archaeological sites on which to examine the Viking Age human impact on the landscape. All three of these regions had little diversity of flora and fauna, and the arrival of new inhabitants can easily be traced in changes to this flora and fauna. New and improved scientific techniques in disciplines such as sedimentology, palynology and zooarchaeology provide suggestive results, in conjunction with the main environmental dating techniques of tephrochronology and radiocarbon. While most of the evidence comes from small samples at a restricted number of sites, it is constantly growing. We are not yet at the stage at which it is possible to generalise, but the cumulative evidence is already telling.

The immigrants who came to the Faroes in around 800 brought with them domestic animals such as sheep, goat, cattle, pig and horse, and also introduced cereal cultivation.[43] There has been some debate among scientists about possible evidence in the form of early field systems and radiocarbon-dated pollen which seem to suggest cereal cultivation, and therefore some sort of human habitation, before the Viking Age. Some of the results of recent research using high-resolution pollen sampling and small-sample radiocarbon dating are ambiguous, but suggest more than one stage of human impact on the environment. There is evidence of pollen from a barley-type of cereal (*Hordeum*) at *c.* 730, and similar grains were perhaps present at 540.[44] A more recent paper presents new radiocarbon dates from one archaeological site that place the earliest human settlement in the Faroes in the fourth to sixth centuries.[45] Underneath a ninth-century Viking Age longhouse (dated on the basis of carbonised barley grains) on the island of Sandoy, there appear to have been two periods of small-scale human settlement, during the fourth to sixth centuries, and sixth to eighth centuries, dated on the basis of burnt patches of peat ash of anthropogenic origin, including carbonised barley grains. Previously, the earliest radiocarbon dates from Faroese archaeological sites were estimated at 690–890 and 690–970. These ranges cannot be distinguished statistically and are both consistent with a date of arrival of Scandinavians, suggested on historical grounds, of about 800.[46]

The new dates are now declared by the scientists to be 'firm archaeological evidence for the human colonisation of the Faroes by people of unknown geographical and ethnic origin some 300–500 years before the large scale Viking colonisation of the 9th century', but the actual evidence remains rather small and the authors of the recent study resort to various explanations as to why there is not more of it.[47] While they keep looking for further evidence, and continue to refine the answers to the question of when the Faroes were first inhabited by humans, it remains clear for the moment that the major impact on the landscape came during the Viking Age. Other pollen data (and of course the archaeological, historical and linguistic evidence) support the likelihood of major human impact from about 800, on a scale different from any earlier impact. These data show a reduction in already scanty Faroese woodland species such as downy birch and juniper, as well as heather, various herbs and ferns, and also buttercup and common sorrel. The decline in these species can be ascribed to the introduction of grazing animals, while juniper might have been used for fuel and charcoal production.[48] Microscopic charcoal particles do not occur in pre-settlement sediments – since natural fires are unlikely in the damp Faroese climate, when they do occur they are a clear indication of human activity.[49]

In Iceland, the time of initial human impact has been precisely calculated by the dating of the so-called *landnám* tephra, a layer of volcanic deposits frequently found immediately below the earliest archaeological records at a large number of sites, and named after the 'land-taking', the first period of permanent settlement. The occurrence of trace elements of this tephra in the Greenland ice sheet has allowed the volcanic events which caused it to be dated fairly securely to 871±2.[50] Pollen samples associated with this tephra show a marked change in the environment. As in the Faroes, high-resolution pollen analyses show the introduction of barley-type (*Hordeum*) cereal at around 870, accompanied by a reduction in tall herbs, suggesting grazing, over the period 870–920.[51] After 920, the site of Stóra-Mörk shows the permanent decline of birch and the movement of native species into new habitats created by humans, both of which are clear evidence of settlement.[52] Although there is some evidence for human activity below the tephra layer, this evidence is sparse, sometimes ambiguous, and is generally very close to the tephra layer, leaving the rough date of the settlement of Iceland intact.[53]

In Greenland, too, evidence associated with the introduction of pastoral farming marks the arrival of peoples of Scandinavian origin. In both coastal and inland locations of the Eastern Settlement, dates derived from soil columns and excavated sites put the arrival of the Norse at or before 985, the same date as suggested by the historical sources. The Western Settlement has dates that are almost as early, again at both coastal and inland sites.[54] Unlike Faroe and Iceland, Greenland did have indigenous grazing land mammals such as the caribou and the musk ox, which helped to maintain the grasslands which would have attracted the Scandinavian pastoralists, as suggested by the name Greenland.[55] Nevertheless, an increase in pollen from grasses and a decrease in tree and shrub pollen are evidence for the expansion of hayfields and grazing land, at the expense of previous heathland and scrub, that is associated with this introduction of pastoralism. Associated charcoal particles suggest domestic fires, again demonstrating settlement.[56] The evidence for whether the Viking Age settlers were able to grow cereals or introduce other crops like flax is currently still ambiguous, but there is certainly evidence of the introduction of several new species of 'Old Norse' flora.[57]

As a result of Scandinavian settlement in the Viking Age, the formerly 'pristine' landscapes of Faroe, Iceland and Greenland became what has been described as 'ovigenic' landscapes, artificial landscapes reflecting human impact in the form of a large-scale introduction of herbivores, that is the domestic animals, cows, sheep and to some extent goats, of the Viking Age settlers, and also their horses.[58]

As well as the larger species introduced deliberately, scientists can trace the smaller species that inevitably followed in their wake, primarily parasites, beetles and flies.[59] The dung beetle, and beetles associated with hay storage, appear immediately above the *landnám* tephra on Icelandic sites. These are both associated with domestic animals and thus unimpeachable evidence for settlement by pastoralists. However, it is interesting that the dung beetle failed to establish itself in Norse Greenland, suggesting either that animals were more extensively stalled in winter, or that their dung was fully used up for fuel.[60] Some flies especially associated with sheep appear in the earliest deposits in Greenland and Iceland, confirming that the earliest settlers practised sheep farming.[61]

Humans also brought uninvited followers with them. Head lice, body lice and human fleas have been found in both the lowest- and highest-status settlements across the North Atlantic.[62] Sanitary, or rather insanitary, conditions in the North Atlantic are indicated by *Heleomyza serrata*, also known as the 'Viking housefly', which feeds on carrion and faeces, and has been found in the foulest residues, which in Greenland could include house floors.[63]

Arrival in an inhabited landscape

When the Scandinavians arrived in areas already settled by other humans, their impact on the environment is more difficult to measure, or even detect. However, there is pollen evidence from northern and western Scotland which may suggest the expansion of agriculture in the Viking Age, as evidenced by deforestation associated with larger amounts of cereal pollen, and expansion of grassland pasture.[64] Also suggestive of new arrivals are changes in diet and economy, visible archaeologically when the incomers introduce crops which do not seem to have been grown before, or make use of local resources that did not interest previous inhabitants.[65] Whether the incomers in inhabited regions brought their own domestic animals with them, or took over existing herds and flocks, can be hard to tell. At Pool, on Sanday in Orkney, for instance, the cattle and sheep were of the same type throughout the life of this settlement, but the goats seem to have been introduced by the Scandinavian incomers.[66] It is often the case that the incomers increased the pace of change, while still working from the same resource base. Thus at Pool, new crops were introduced, and dairying and fishing were intensified, but these were mainly a further (if quicker) development of changes already underway before the arrival of the Scandinavians.[67] Oats, found in a third of the samples from the Pictish phases at Old Scatness in the south of Shetland, go up to 80 per cent in the Viking period samples, and there is a similar picture at Belmont, Unst, Shetland.[68] Oats were a crop that could extend the amount of cultivable land, and they could be fed to both animals and humans, making for a much improved subsistence basis.[69] But the situation is complex, as shown by changes in the relative cultivation of oats and barley in different periods at Quoygrew, on Westray in Orkney.[70]

Flax, or *Linum usitatissimum*, is also a crop which has a variety of uses, as the seeds can be processed to make linseed oil, while the fibres can be used to make linen fabric, and both can be used for cattle fodder.[71] Flax can also be used for sails, nets and fishing lines.[72] Evidence for the introduction of flax as a crop seems to relate to the earliest phases of Norse occupation at sites such as Pool and Old Scatness, and it is also found at the Norse site of Quoygrew.[73] The growing of flax is labour-intensive and represents a major investment – the large amount of evidence for it at these sites suggests its cultural as well as economic importance, and a substantial and well-organised settlement dedicated to agriculture. Along with oats and barley, flax plays an important part in an arable agricultural tradition found across the North Atlantic, from the Northern Isles to Faroe and Iceland.[74]

Quantities of fish bones at Norse settlement sites, particularly in the Northern Isles, also indicate the presence of incomers making different use of the environment. The increased reliance on maritime resources by the Scandinavian incomers is demonstrated both by the wide range of species recovered from these sites, and also by isotopic analysis of human bones from a wide chronological range.[75] But this use of maritime resources also changed over time. At both Old Scatness and Quoygrew, there is a clear increase in the exploitation of shellfish in the late Norse period, either for food or for bait.[76] Fish bones at Norse settlement sites increasingly belong to the cod family, suggesting specialisation and offshore fishing, which in turn suggests the commercialisation of fishing during the eleventh to thirteenth/fourteenth centuries.[77]

A snapshot of a typical settlement of the Viking diaspora, a relatively uncomplicated one established in the tenth century near, but not directly on top of, pre-Viking settlements, is Quoygrew, on the island of Westray in Orkney. A survey of its landscape context illustrates the range of subsistence activities in such new settlements, many of which were in fact on islands large and small:

> Quoygrew was part of a landscape that included a landing place (for transportation and fishing), a rocky foreshore (for collecting shellfish and seaweed), cultivated fields (for barley, oats and flax . . .), wet meadows (for fodder), uncultivated hill land (for grazing, peat and turf), navigational landmarks (perhaps for locating fishing grounds in addition to safe passage).[78]

Such was the environmental setting for the development of the new cultures of the Viking diaspora, and it turns our focus to the people who inhabited these sites and made their living from them.

Human populations

Arriving in inhabited areas, incomers might be expected to have an impact on the population as well as on the environment. Genetics, a scientific discipline which has had a very high profile over the last few years, provides a promising approach for detecting Scandinavian input into the population of inhabited areas. Genetic studies can be of either present or historical populations, and can be applied to human beings, animals and even plants. Recovering usable genetic data (ancient

DNA or 'aDNA') from archaeological remains is still difficult and the results often unreliable, though techniques are improving fast. A further problem with historical studies is that sample sizes are small and it can be difficult to generalise from the limited evidence. Genetic studies of modern populations, on the other hand, can provide great quantities of reliable evidence, but the interpretation of their historical significance is difficult, and depends on complex models and theories of how modern populations relate to historical populations.

In modern populations, geneticists can identify different markers on the Y-chromosome, found only in males and passed down from father to son, and on mitochondrial DNA ('mtDNA'), found in everyone but passed on through the maternal line only. While by no means a watertight indication of origin, these markers have noticeably different geographical distributions so that it is possible to say that a preponderance of a particular marker is most likely associated with a particular part of the world. Thus, geneticists can distinguish the markers most characteristic of the present populations of Norway, of the Celtic parts of Britain and Ireland, and of those parts of Britain settled by the Anglo-Saxons (i.e. most of England). Modern populations are quite mixed, but when they include one or more of these types, there is a high probability that the mixture arose from immigration events in the past. Modern populations of 'Danish' type are much more like the 'Anglo-Saxons' than the 'Norwegians'. This means that genetic analysis cannot be used to determine the extent to which modern populations in the Danelaw, for instance, have Danish rather than Anglo-Saxon ancestry (of course historical interpretations already suggest that they are likely to have both). However, in some parts of England, such as the north-west, the clear distinction between the 'Norwegian' type and the 'Anglo-Saxon' type of genetic markers makes it possible to establish that a substantial proportion of the modern population has an ancestry similar to that of the Norwegians, and this accords with historical and linguistic evidence suggesting the immigration of people with an ultimate origin in Norway into that area.[79]

Similarly, both Y-chromosome and mtDNA studies have been used to establish the origins of the modern populations of the North Atlantic islands, and in particular to determine the extent to which these populations descend from Scandinavian immigrants, or whether some other populations were involved in the migrations. The results of these studies have been widely publicised within the last couple of decades, and appear to suggest that more than two-thirds of the male population of Iceland has Norwegian ancestry, while less than one-third can trace its origins to the 'Celtic' regions of the British Isles.[80] Interestingly, the genetics suggest that these proportions are reversed in the female ancestry of Iceland, raising all sorts of questions about how to explain this gender discrepancy (discussed further in ch. 4).[81] One widely cited study also compares the Icelandic results with evidence from several regions in Scandinavian Scotland.[82] In this study, the population of both the Northern and Western Isles of Scotland showed a significant Scandinavian element, though this was lower in the Western Isles (15%) than in the Northern Isles (30–44%). What was interesting was that, in both Orkney and Shetland, the 'Scandinavian' proportion of both male and female populations was roughly equal, which the authors of the study took to mean that the Scandinavian incomers arrived in family units. However, in both the Western Isles and Iceland, there was a much higher proportion of Scandinavian patrilineal ancestry than of matrilineal, roughly double in both cases, which was explained in part by their relative remoteness from Norway, and so their lesser attractiveness to family groups from there, compared to the Northern Isles. It was hypothesised that these were colonised by 'lone males' who acquired female partners in the British Isles. That there was a 'Celtic' element in the Icelandic population has long been known, and much discussed in the scholarly literature, based on some older studies of blood groups and other biological markers, some linguistic evidence and frequent references in Old Icelandic texts.[83] The results of the newer genetic studies suggest that this Celtic element was even more extensive than previously recognised and that it is important to pay attention to the gender dynamics of these migrations.

An intriguing element in the equation is the genetic profile of the Faroese population, which according to a recent study is very similar to that of Iceland, at least as far as the Y-chromosome distribution is concerned. In the absence of any evidence of emigration from Iceland to the Faroes, the authors of the study concluded that both the Faroes and Iceland were settled at roughly the same time and mainly by men from the same regions of Scandinavia (most likely Norway), with some coming from the British Isles.[84]

At the time of writing, the jury is still out on what all this genetic evidence actually means, and it is important to be aware of the uncertainties of such results. Close reading of some of the studies shows that they explicitly refer to the possibility of multiple interpretations of the evidence.[85] At population level, present populations are at best only an approximate model for past populations. Even if both the Icelandic and Faroese populations have been relatively stable in the sense that they have experienced little immigration between the Viking Age and the late twentieth century, emigration can also be a complicating factor, leading to the end of some genetic lines. Other genetic lines may have died out as a result of demographic bottlenecks, such as the early fifteenth-century outbreak of pneumonic plague that eliminated around half of Iceland's population, followed by another, almost equally deadly one at the end of the century.[86] Without a counterbalancing immigration, such factors have the effect of reducing genetic diversity and this reduction may not be entirely random. The original gene pool of a place like Faroe, with a very small population, is particularly prone to what is called 'genetic drift', in which the genetic pool becomes more homogeneous, as is Iceland.[87]

At the individual level, both Y-chromosome and mtDNA can each trace only a single ancestor among the much larger number of people (more or less doubled every generation over some 30 to 40 generations) who contributed to that individual's existence over the last thousand years. For the individual, this genetic evidence provides information on only a very small proportion of their ancestry. Individual analyses therefore have little or no validity, it is only when large samples are analysed that we can say something about the history of populations. Moreover, mtDNA is more weakly stratified among European populations than the Y-chromosome, which means it is more difficult to pinpoint precise originary locations.[88] There is an increasing acknowledgement of these problems in more recent publications by some of the same geneticists who published the original results.[89] The results of such historical genetic research can therefore only be described as provisional, but it has been useful in provoking further research into and interpretation of other, non-genetic, evidence for the founding populations of Iceland and Faroe. At the very least it has focused renewed attention on the fact that the population of Iceland was not a simple migration directly from Norway, a simplified version of history that still has widespread currency.

Animals

Genetic research into the animals that may have accompanied the North Atlantic settlers is still in its infancy. Undoubtedly such research, particularly into domestic animals, would be difficult, since it would be even less certain than with humans whether or not the present animal populations of the homelands are representative of their Viking Age predecessors and any study of the ancient DNA of archaeological specimens is subject to the same caveats as similar study of human remains (see below). The linguistic geography of terms for domestic animals in the North Atlantic has been thoroughly studied, and would provide a good basis for a global study of the genetic relationships between sheep, cattle and horses which might show up some interesting patterns.[90]

Involuntary animal emigrants may be more useful subjects in the present state of knowledge, such as a recent study of two subspecies of house mouse in Iceland, Greenland and Newfoundland, using both ancient and modern mtDNA.[91] Unlike the field mouse, the house mouse is heavily dependent on a human population and its introduction into the pristine landscapes of the North Atlantic is a strong indicator of human movements. The study concluded that the Icelandic house mouse (*Mus musculus domesticus*) originally came from either Norway or the northern part of the British Isles and has persisted there until the present day. These mice were then transported to Greenland, where they can be identified in the archaeological record, whereas the modern house mouse population in Greenland represents a more recent reintroduction (probably from Denmark) of a different subspecies (*Mus musculus musculus*) after the 'Viking' mice had become extinct. There is no evidence for the transportation of mice to Newfoundland in the Viking period. Further genetic research will enable scientists to distinguish more closely the place(s) of origin of the Icelandic and ancient Greenlandic mice, following on from an earlier study which suggested that the *domesticus* subspecies might as well have been transported from the British Isles to Norway as the other way around.[92] Although field and possibly house mice have been thought to have been introduced to northern Scotland by the Vikings, there seems to be earlier evidence for them at Old Scatness in Shetland, but the question is not yet fully resolved.[93]

Bones and food

If the DNA evidence is imperfect, attempts have also been made to measure the biological distance between human populations by bioarchaeological analysis of skeletal material, using nonmetric traits in human skulls that are thought to have genetic origins. Analysis of a range of skeletal samples from Norway, Iceland, Greenland and Ireland using this method suggested a rather different picture from that of the genetic studies, namely that 'the Norwegian contribution to the Icelandic population was somewhere between 60–90%', though this study could not distinguish for gender because of the poor state of preservation of the examined samples.[94] But such studies also have their caveats, namely that even though the observed variations have a genetic origin, they are not necessarily in a linear relationship with genetic distance. Nevertheless, the study has reminded us that, despite all of the DNA evidence for the Celtic connection, we must still reckon with a close biological relationship between Icelanders and Norwegians, a relationship that is also clearly indicated by the linguistic and artefactual evidence.

The study of ancient DNA (aDNA), that is the DNA of humans who lived in the past, as preserved in their remains, has not progressed as quickly as genetic studies of modern populations, primarily because of difficulties in recovering viable samples from skeletal material. However, techniques are improving all the time, and some studies have been published.[95] Such studies usefully suggest the limits of inference from modern populations. Thus, the aDNA of 95 individuals from pre-1000 Iceland showed that their mtDNA was in fact more similar to that of the present inhabitants of both Scandinavia, and Scotland and Ireland, than to the modern population of Iceland. What this again demonstrates is that the forces of genetic drift operated more quickly in the small population of Iceland than in the larger ones of the homelands. This is a timely warning against placing too much importance on the genetic structures of present-day populations as a proxy for past populations. The emerging study of aDNA in the Scandinavian homelands may also complicate our understanding of the genetics of the source populations with which we compare the emigrant populations. A study of 10 Viking Age skeletons from different cemeteries in Denmark, carried out under optimum conditions, showed interesting differences in the distributions of their haplogroups (i.e. their genetic types) compared to the modern population, but these cannot yet be considered significant given the smallness of the sample.[96]

Other information that can be extracted from ancient skeletons can indicate where people (and indeed animals) grew up and what they ate. In particular, the analysis of certain isotopes, namely radiogenic strontium, and stable oxygen, carbon and nitrogen, can help to track the movements of individuals.[97] Another study of early Icelandic skeletons applied strontium isotope analysis to 90 human individuals from both pagan and Christian burials in order to establish where they spent their childhood and, therefore, where they were likely to have been born, compared to the values of the place in which they were buried (and likely died).[98] The method depends on the difference between isotope values in tooth enamel (which do not change once the enamel is formed in early childhood) and in bones (the chemical composition of which changes every decade or so in response to diet and environment). The analysis showed that between 9 and 13 of the 90 individuals, all belonging to the earliest burials, were clearly migrants to Iceland, apparently from a variety of different places, though closer identification of their origins was not possible in that study. A much smaller study of 11 individuals from Viking Age and Hiberno-Norse Dublin found that all but one had spent their childhood in or near Dublin and all had spent their last years there.[99] The authors of this study argue that these results may support models of acculturation rather than a high number of first-generation immigrants, though this seems a bold conclusion to draw from some rather sparse evidence.

Importantly, isotope analyses can also be used to show movements within and into as well as out of Scandinavia. Thus, 48 skeletons from the Viking Age fortress at Trelleborg, in Denmark, were subjected to strontium isotope analysis.[100] These individuals appear to represent a military population in the fortress, with a preponderance of young adult males, though also some females and children. Thirty-two of these 48 individuals (including all three females) were determined to have been born outside southern Scandinavia, most likely in northern Scandinavia (Norway or central and northern Sweden), though Baltic origins are also possible.

The Icelandic study mentioned above also established that the individuals tested had different diets. Whether their food was primarily of marine or terrestrial origin depended only partly on whether or not they lived near the sea. Individuals with a high level of marine protein in their diet who were buried far from the sea may have moved there relatively late in life. Another study combined radiocarbon dates and stable isotope data from the collagen of 54 skeletons of the fourth to the sixteenth centuries found in cemeteries in Orkney.[101] The results show that the pre-Viking Age inhabitants of Orkney, despite living in island environments with good access to marine resources, preferred a largely terrestrial diet based on arable and pastoral farming. By contrast, individuals buried in the ninth or tenth centuries had far more marine protein (whether from fish or marine animals such as seals) in their diet than their predecessors, suggesting that the Scandinavian incomers had brought with them new foodways from their homeland. The marine content of the Orcadian diet increased even further between the eleventh and the thirteenth centuries, and then dropped off again. Analysis of a group of skeletons from a thirteenth- to fourteenth-century cemetery in Rendall, on the Mainland of Orkney, suggested a tightly clustered group of people, very local both in terms of their origins and their diet, although one of the individuals was from either the Hebrides or Shetland.[102]

People and environment – living in the landscape

Survival and adaptation

As the natural environment is constantly changing, and human beings are constantly adapting to these changes, or failing to adapt to them, any study of the migrations of the Viking Age also has to take account of subsequent developments in the overseas settlements to place the initial migrations in context.

Iceland and Greenland provide a useful pair of case studies in how humans adapted to a new and uninhabited environment, both immediately on arrival and also in the longer term, the longer term lasting half a millennium in Greenland, but being permanent in Iceland. We lack certain basic facts about the settlement of both Iceland and Greenland, such as the causes for it, how long it took, how exactly the distribution of land was managed, and how many settlers there were (though of course *Landnámabók* considered as a whole presents an interesting and relevant, though not always consistent, range of insights into all of these questions, as will be discussed in ch. 6, below). There is some scholarly consensus that Iceland was settled relatively quickly in the late ninth and early tenth centuries.[103] Estimates of the population once the settlement period was concluded range from 40,000 to 100,000.[104] It has also been argued that the settlement process was managed by a small group of high-status individuals, 'chieftains', who peopled the landscape with their clients and thereby increased their own wealth and influence.[105] There is a strong correlation between 'cattle, good grazing and chieftainship', replicating traditional sources of power from the homeland.[106] The reasons for some of these people then moving on to Greenland a century later have in the past been ascribed to a chronic shortage of land or the means of subsistence in Iceland, but are now rather seen as being the attractive economic opportunities which could further increase the power, wealth and influence of those who moved there.[107]

The initial settlers of both Iceland and Greenland undoubtedly brought with them a northern European farming economy that was familiar to them not only from the Scandinavian homeland, but also the British Isles. An ideal farm in settlement-period Iceland would have large numbers of cattle and pigs, with some sheep and goats. As time went on, and in a context of environmental change, North Atlantic farmers found that a different balance was more suitable, so that pigs and goats gradually disappear from the archaeological record, and while both cattle and sheep were maintained, the balance shifted more towards the latter.[108] Interestingly, some Greenlanders also imported the idea of an 'ideal' Norse farm, replicating the Norwegian model of a farm rich in cows and pigs, rather than the contemporary Icelandic model more intensively based on sheep.[109] Archaeologists interpret this as reflecting the status and ambitions of those Greenlanders, though it cannot be ruled out that it might be because they came directly from Norway rather than Iceland. Certainly, the landscapes of the new settlements were sufficiently similar in appearance to the homelands to lead the first settlers to conclude that their traditional practices could simply be transferred to their new home, and it was only experience that eventually told them otherwise.[110]

If the new settlers were somewhat conservative in retaining their traditional farming practices, they also showed a remarkable ability to adapt to new ways of ensuring survival and even creating wealth, with the earliest settlers of Iceland making use of various kinds of marine life. Iceland had resident walrus populations which the incomers were able to exploit for the ivory in their tusks, as shown by evidence from some of the earliest settlement sites (e.g. Aðalstræti, now in downtown Reykjavík).[111] Some of the earliest inland sites of the ninth and tenth centuries were being provisioned with saltwater fish that had been caught and processed elsewhere, while also being able to make use of freshwater fish from Mývatn.[112]

Seabird bones have, like marine fish bones, also been found far inland, suggesting a communal effort in hunting and distribution.[113]

Greenland presented rather different adaptive challenges to its new settlers, challenges which they appear to have had no difficulty in meeting. Unlike in Iceland, fish was not an important supplement to pastoral farming – here the main marine resource was seals, and these were important right from the start.[114] Although Scandinavians would have been familiar with seals from the homelands, the British Isles and even Iceland, these were mainly harbour and common seals. The most abundant resource in Greenland however were migratory harp seals and hooded seals, which could profitably be hunted in large numbers.[115] Seal bones from archaeological contexts show an increasing consumption of seal meat, supported by isotopic evidence for increased consumption of marine protein, which in Greenland was mainly seal.[116] Greenlanders also made use of local caribou, another animal which would not have been familiar to them from Iceland, though any with experience of Norway would have had knowledge of similar animals.[117] It is clear that hunting in Greenland was not only a means of assuring subsistence, but rather a means to increase wealth through trade, particularly the hunting of walrus (very abundant in the seas around Greenland) for their ivory, plus various fur-bearing animals, falcons and exotica such as narwhal tusks.[118] Indeed, it has been suggested that the opportunities offered by such items were the main motivation for establishing Norse settlements in Greenland.[119] The Icelanders seem to have killed off their local walrus population in the first few generations of settlement, making Greenland an attractive alternative.[120] Rather than being just an adjunct to subsistence farming, these hunting and trading activities were the basis of wealth creation in the Greenland economy, supported by subsistence farming.[121] That these activities extended across the community is indicated by the presence of seal and seabird bones at inland sites and caribou bones at coastal sites.[122]

Effects and ends

Those settlers who established themselves in 'pristine' landscapes undoubtedly had a more marked effect on the environment than those who settled in regions where human activity was already well established. Where the Scandinavian settlers arrived in a previously inhabited landscape, their arrival is generally more obvious in cultural features such as house-types or place-names, rather than in the zooarchaeological or archaeobotanical record, and their impact on the environment more difficult to measure.[123] Effects on the environment are much easier to measure in the 'pristine' landscapes, and raise the question of whether the new arrivals caused any harm to their unfamiliar environment.

The Scandinavian settlement in Greenland, as has already been mentioned, came to an end sometime in the fifteenth century. It is not clear whether this was a gradual dying out or whether there was at some point an emigration of a residual population. The causes of this failure (if that is what it was) are not fully understood, though the smallness (and hence unviability) of the population, climate change, epidemics, conflicts with neighbouring populations, and economic marginalisation have all been cited as contributory factors.[124] The Greenlanders have notoriously been blamed for failing to adapt fully to their environment and for unsustainable land-use practices in the face of a worsening climate and an environment not conducive to their desired lifestyle.[125] However, one of the problems in assessing the reasons for the end of the Greenland settlement is that we do not know the size of the population there at its height, with estimates ranging from 3,000 to 6,000.[126] The demographic effects of even a relatively small number of deaths or emigrants would have been proportionally greater the smaller the population, and it may be that the real cause was simply insufficient numbers to maintain the settlement, however well it had adapted to its environment.

Recent research suggests that maladaptation is unlikely to be the explanation for the end of Norse Greenland. Those who have studied its environment in detail have been able to show precisely that the population adapted very well to local conditions, increasing their consumption of marine protein and adapting their economy and household management to take account of the available resources.[127] The causes of the end of Greenland may therefore rather need to be sought in economic, cultural and demographic factors, and perhaps the breakdown of the social order that maintained the economy.[128] In particular, if, as suggested above, the main motivation for the settlement of Greenland was not to establish a pastoral society, but to benefit from the hunting opportunities, secondarily supported by a pastoral economy, then the end of Norse Greenland should rather be sought in the inability of a falling population to maintain the hunting way of life, and competition from new patterns of international trade, such as the stockfish export from Iceland.[129] Whatever the precise causes of the failure of Norse Greenland, it is likely that demography lay at the bottom of it. If the hunting of seals, seabirds, caribou and walrus was carried out as intensively as it seems to have been, and for export, then this implies a communal activity, carried out at a higher level than that of the household, as indicated by the large storage buildings at the bishop's seat in Garðar/Igaliku, for instance.[130] Such a complex system would have involved the communal allocation of labour to various kinds of hunting as well as farming and would have been particularly vulnerable to any dips in the population, even quite small ones, endangering the long-term viability of such activities.[131] The export of walrus ivory also seems to have suffered from the availability of the finer elephant ivory from the thirteenth century onwards.[132]

The survival of Iceland was also not a given. There was for instance a move to evacuate the whole of the island to Denmark, in the eighteenth century, after many years of epidemics, famine and volcanic catastrophe.[133] Adaptation seems to have been the key to the survival of the Icelandic population. In Iceland, changes in the environment were extensive, but not sufficient to put an end to human settlement there, even when the demographic profile was threatened. Around the time the Greenland settlement was coming to an end in the fifteenth century, the population of Iceland was drastically reduced by two separate plague episodes.[134] There were also several major volcanic events during that century. However, recent research suggests that such eruptions had only a small-scale and short-lived impact on settlements.[135] The frequent tephra layers enable close monitoring of how the population reacted to the major impact of the fifteenth-century plagues.[136] This evidence shows that the Icelanders were able to retrench and concentrate on the core functions of their economy, and that their adaptations promoted the resilience of the landscape and, ultimately, the long-term survival of the population.

Another aspect of environmental change with significance for the population is that of vegetation cover and soil erosion. It is famously claimed in *Íslendingabók* (ch. 1) that the first settlers found a landscape that was wooded from the shore to the mountains, implying that this was no longer the case already when that text was written in the 1120s.[137] It is clear from archaeology and palynology (the study of pollens) that what woodland there was in Iceland was quickly destroyed by the settlers in their need for building timber, fuel and charcoal, and grazing land. Hand-in-hand with these reductions in vegetation went soil erosion, which increased notably soon after the arrival of the settlers.[138] Overall, it has been estimated that 90 per cent of the forest and 40 per cent of the soil present at the settlement has since disappeared.[139]

However, more recent research tends to stress the complexity of the pattern of pre-settlement woodland patterns and woodland change in Iceland.[140] The disappearance of woodland may have been merely part of an ongoing process resulting from climate change, the worst effects of which were not felt until around 1500, exacerbated by a major volcanic event in 1477.[141] The effects of volcanic ash and tephra over the centuries led in some cases to animal mortality and related famine, or even to the abandonment of certain settlements.[142] Yet there is evidence that the inhabitants of Iceland attempted to preserve their environment. Thus it has been suggested that the abandonment of farms in Þórsmörk in the thirteenth century happened precisely to protect the surviving woodland from the soil erosion that had already affected the outfields.[143] And the undoubtedly extensive amount of wood needed for iron production in Mývatnssveit in northern Iceland seems to have encouraged a managed process of felling.[144] There is also regional variation in the speed with which woodland was cleared.[145]

Not all effects of the settlement on the environment were negative, and often there was a balancing out between positive and negative effects as the environment adapted to human activities. In terms of biodiversity, for example, the settlers increased the number of species of both fauna and flora in Iceland overall. However, their agricultural activities led to fewer floral species in any given area of land, as woodland was replaced by heaths, grassland or eroded areas, much of this the result of the introduced grazing animals, and the accidental introduction of insects and wild plants changed the nature of the flora.[146] In general, the Icelanders seem to have managed the consequences of their effect on the environment through legal means, regulating various aspects of land-use and livestock management, for the common good.[147] They also seem to have been able to manage wild resources in a sustainable fashion, as indicated by the millennium-old practice of waterfowl and egg collection around Mývatn in northern Iceland.[148] Thus, in the long term the

Icelanders were able to adapt to their environment in various ways that ensured the resilience and survival of their population even in the difficult times of the late medieval and early modern periods.

Naming the environment

The uses of place-names

The physical remains of the natural environment, as discussed above, are not the only evidence for the geography and environment of the Viking homelands and subsequent diaspora. Place-names are very revealing of human interactions with their environments, both familiar and new, and illustrate the processes of exploration, migration and adaptation very well.

Despite the very small number of written sources from before the twelfth and thirteenth centuries, the structures and chronologies of place-names in the Scandinavian homelands are quite well understood, having been the object of intensive philological study over the last century or more.[149] The giving of place-names is a continuous process in human history; some die out and are replaced, while new names are given to new places. Other place-names have a very long history and persist for centuries if not millennia, though often undergoing phonological or other changes. A place-name will capture the visual impression, or social or agricultural importance, of a place at a particular moment in time, the moment when that name was attached to that place, if only we can identify when that time was. Later on, the name becomes merely a label for the place, no longer meaningful in linguistic terms.

Going back to a seminal work by Magnus Olsen, scholars agree on a rough chronology of place-names in Scandinavia, and particularly in western Scandinavia.[150] Thus, it is possible to identify the earliest layer of names, which are mainly those of large landscape features such as lakes, islands and large rivers. Many of these names were first coined far back in prehistory. Names of human settlements within this landscape tend to be later, though the oldest layer of these is also closely related to the landscape, identifying the settlement in relation to features such as a nearby hill, or the peninsula on which it stands. These names often consist of only a single element, such as *Berg* 'Hill', or *Nes* 'Headland', or *Bœr* 'Settlement'. Later on, settlement names generally have two elements, the second of which (known as the 'generic') identifies the type of place and the first of which (the 'specific') in some way links the type of place to the actual place. The generic can be either 'habitative' (denoting some kind of inhabited site or dwelling, as in *Bœr*) or 'topographical' (denoting a landscape feature, which can also be transferred to a nearby inhabited site or dwelling, as in *Berg*). The specific can be descriptive, as in *Langanes* 'Long Headland', or it can link the generic to a person, creature or thing characteristic of the place, such as *Sauðanes* 'Headland of Sheep'. The generics of place-names change over time and Olsen established a relative chronology in which the following generic elements succeeded one another: *-vin* 'meadow', *-heimr* 'home(stead)', *-stað(i)r* 'place', *-land*

'land', *-setr* 'dwelling', *-ruð* 'clearing'. All of these elements are still recognisable in farm-names (many of them now the names of larger settlements) that have persisted into the twenty-first century in Norway. The situation is similar in Denmark and Sweden, though the details of the names are somewhat different. The discussion below will focus on the names of Norway, as these form the basis of the names of new settlements across the North Atlantic in the western Viking diaspora.

The established Norwegian chronology provides the basis for understanding the naming practices of the Viking diaspora, when Scandinavians migrated to other parts of the world, taking their naming practices with them. It is possible to date certain name-types to before, during and after these migrations, by whether or not they were used outside Scandinavia. To take some examples from Norway, scholars are generally agreed that place-names ending in *-vin* 'meadow' and *-heimr* 'home(stead)' mostly predate the Viking Age migrations, as they are rare or non-existent in the diaspora.[151] Other elements such as *-staðir* and *-bólstaðir* are common both in Norway and in the diaspora, showing that these were productive name-forming elements in the Viking Age (and sometimes later). Both refer to some kind of farm or settlement, though their exact implications are not clear.

Place-names ending in *-staðir* are by far the most common type recorded in the Icelandic Book of Settlements, *Landnámabók*: the 125 examples form 20 per cent of the farm-names in that work.[152] Hugh Marwick counted 23 examples in Orkney, using both medieval and later sources, and there are also a number of examples from Shetland and the Isle of Man.[153] Despite the fact that such names are also common in Norway, the evidence does not suggest a straightforward transfer of this naming element from the homeland to the new settlements. Rather, scholars are agreed that most *-staðir* names are not the highest-status farms, and seem to be secondary to the earliest settlements.[154] The element seems not to have been used for the earliest settlements and was productive well into the eleventh century (probably later in Iceland), in both Norway and the new settlements.[155] This may reflect parallel developments, but also fits well with the diaspora model with its continued contacts between the homeland and the settlements (as outlined in the next chapter). Similarly, it has been shown that *-bólstaðr* also applies mainly to secondary settlements, in the context of a 'prolonged' Scandinavian settlement in the west.[156] This explains why it is restricted to the Scottish isles and Iceland, where continued contact with Norway was most pronounced and longest lasting.

Naming practices

While providing evidence for the chronology of the Scandinavian migrations, place-names are also useful as a guide to both the natural and the built environments of the homelands and the new settlements. Names are a form of linguistic behaviour and the migrants of the Viking diaspora took these naming practices with them along with the language that they spoke. Most settlers will have come from a landscape context that was already fully named – in general names, especially of landscape features and major habitations, persist for many generations. Such settlers may not have had much experience of naming places until they arrived in a new place, and it is of interest to see what models they used in naming those new places – did they create new names on the pattern of the names they were used to from home, or did they simply transfer names from home to their new contexts? The latter is a common phenomenon well known from, for example, modern colonisations of North America or Australia (Boston, Perth). Some possible examples of this are found in the Viking diaspora. Thus, it has been suggested that both Uppsalir in Iceland and Upsall in North Yorkshire memorialise the Swedish place now known as Uppsala, and there are a few other possible examples.[157] But more commonly it seems that new names were created using the well-established patterns and the elements that were also being used in the homeland at the time.

Settlers arriving in an uninhabited landscape will first give names to landscape features, to help orientate themselves in their new surroundings. Many of these names describe a distinctive aspect of the feature, as in *Álptafjǫrðr* 'Fjord of Swans' or *Mývatn* 'Midge Lake'.[158] The buildings and farms in which the new inhabitants lived are then given names when there are enough of them that they need to be distinguished from others nearby. This name-giving process is quite complex and reflects many different aspects of these sites. They can be named after nearby natural features, which also helps to locate them in the landscape, as in *Gnúpr* 'Mountain With An Overhang', or *Hvammr* 'Small Valley'. Or they can be named after some characteristic or function of the site, as in the many sites named *Hof* or *Hofstaðir* which may indicate some kind of cult activity, or *Hjarðarholt* 'Stony Area (or Wood) of the Herd'. Or they can be named after a person, in which case we often assume that this reflects some kind of ownership of the site. Iceland is particularly rich in place-names with personal-name specifics, and the compilers of *Landnámabók* have often been suspected of inventing settlers from these specifics, as perhaps in Chapter 38 of the *Sturlubók* version:[159]

> Rauðr hét maðr, er nam land . . . upp frá Rauðsgili til Gilja ok bjó at Rauðsgili; hans synir váru þeir Úlfr á Úlfsstǫðum ok Auðr at Auðsstǫðum . . .
>
> There was a man called Rauðr, who claimed land . . . up from Rauðsgil to Giljar and lived at Rauðsgil; his sons were Úlfr at Úlfsstaðir and Auðr at Auðsstaðir . . .

Something like 32 per cent of Icelandic farm-names seem to have personal-name specifics, compared to parts of Norway and Faroe, where it can be as low as 4–5 per cent. Some of the Icelandic names may therefore in fact have other origins, or be later formations.[160] But the fact that many place-names of Scandinavian linguistic origin in both England and Scotland also contain personal-name specifics suggests that naming a place after a particular person, either its first occupier, or a later owner, was a common phenomenon in the Viking diaspora.[161]

Migrants arriving in an inhabited landscape face a different naming situation. The inhabited landscape will already have been fully named, both its natural features and its human habitations. Depending on the nature and extent of the new settlers' contacts with the indigenous inhabitants, a number of different kinds of name can result. Some names will simply be taken over by the new inhabitants. This is particularly common with natural features and especially with water features. Across Europe, and including Scandinavia, many water features still bear names that were originally given in long-lost languages. In these situations, it seems, the meaning of a name was not important. Existing place-names could also be taken over by the new settlers in a way that was meaningful, though possibly with some adaptation that ultimately obscures its meaning. The name of York is a good example here. Originally British *Eburācon* 'Place Abounding in Yew-Trees', and Latinised as *Eboracum*, it was reinterpreted by its Anglian inhabitants as *Eoforwīc* 'Wild Boar Farm' and its subsequent Norse inhabitants as *Jórvík* 'Coastal Creek of Pigs'.[162] Or new names could be formed, using a mixture of existing and new elements. In England, there is quite a number of hybrid place-names which contain a Scandinavian specific (often a personal name) and an English generic, as Aslockton or Toton in Nottinghamshire, in which the personal names *Áslákr* and *Tófi* are combined with the most common Old English place-name generic, *-tūn*.[163] It is not always clear whether the name is a completely new one, that is a genuine hybrid, or whether a new specific has replaced the first element of an already-existing compound name. And then there were completely new names. Again, it is not always clear whether this came about through the renaming of existing places which already had names (an example is Derby, renamed from English *Norðweorðig* 'Northern Enclosure'), or whether these new names reflect new places, carved out of previously uninhabited or deserted districts.[164]

Remembering that the naming of places is linguistic behaviour, another factor that is relevant to the naming of places by settlers in previously inhabited areas is that of language. Naming behaviour will vary depending on whether or not the incomers understand the language of the indigenous inhabitants and vice versa. Britain and Ireland provide a range of interesting examples showing the different ways in which these linguistic contacts took place. In England, the similarity of the two languages led to the extensive Scandinavianisation of Old English place-names in which existing place-names were adapted to the speech habits of the Scandinavian settlers, without losing their meaning, in addition to the creation of whole new names in the Old Norse language.[165] In the Hebrides, on the other hand, Gaelic names which were not transparent to the Norse incomers were also adapted to their speech, but usually without maintaining their meaning.[166] However, a very small number of names are translation loans, suggesting linguistic transfer based on bilingual speakers. Because the records are generally very late, we cannot however tell whether this happened in the Viking Age, or represents the translation of Norse names by Gaelic speakers long after the Viking Age, when the Gaelic language became dominant in the Hebrides.

First impressions

While the Icelandic sagas provide later accounts, by some centuries, of the Scandinavians' impressions of the new lands to which they sailed and in some of which they settled, we have no contemporary narratives to tell us what their first impressions were. However, place-names can provide a proxy, a set of mini-narratives which give expression to the geographical knowledge and observations of the travellers of the Viking Age.[167] Such names also suggest ways in which navigational information was transmitted, as many names have navigational import. Thus, names like *Straumsfjǫrðr* and *Straumsey* in the Vínland sagas parallel names of the same origin, from Old Norse *straumr* 'current', like Streymoy in the Faroes and Stromness in Orkney, and there are similar names in Iceland and Shetland. *Straumsfjǫrðr* is thus the fjord whose entrance is marked by strong sea-currents, and *Straumsey* the island in those currents. The Orkney town of Stromness takes its name from a peninsula engulfed by currents, on what is still the main sailing route into the heart of the island group. The island of Stroma lies in the Pentland Firth, in the midst of some of the fiercest tidal currents of the British Isles. These names not only help to identify the places, but also give important information to sailors who must navigate these currents.

Such names based on real geographical knowledge can usually be distinguished from the explanations given to certain names by authors unfamiliar with the regions they are describing. Most notorious is when Adam of Bremen explains the name of Greenland (Old Norse *Grœnland*) as deriving from the fact that '[t]he people there are greenish from the salt water'.[168] Less implausible is the explanation given by Ari Þorgilsson in Chapter 6 of *Íslendingabók*, in which he maintains that Eiríkr *enn rauði* 'The Red' gave the name to the country because 'it would encourage people to go there if the land had a good name'.[169] The name may have been given because parts of Greenland are noticeably greener (at least in summer) than parts of Iceland, and indeed the Norwegian author of the thirteenth-century manual *Konungs skuggsjá* knows that in Greenland 'the earth yields good and fragrant grass'.[170] But it may not just be about grass: the Old Norse adjective *grœnn* has quite general positive connotations, not just of pasture, and suggests the possibilities the migrants saw in this new land.

Iceland, on the other hand, was named several times before its name was established, at least according to the various accounts of *Landnámabók*, which probably represent a number of conflicting traditions (see further on this in ch. 6, below).[171] A 'Viking' called Naddoddr, swept off course to Iceland on his way from Norway to the Faroes, names the land *Snæland* 'Snow-Land' because snow was falling on the mountains as they set off back to the Faroes. A Swede called Garðarr set out to find *Snæland* and established that it was indeed an island by circumnavigating it – it was subsequently called *Garðarshólmr*, with *-hólmr* having the sense of a larger island, as in Bornholm, in the Baltic. Finally, the name *Ísland* 'Ice-Land' was given by a Norwegian called Flóki, who named it thus because he looked down from a mountain onto a fjord full of sea-ice. The name 'Iceland' might have suited Greenland better, with its extensive glacier cover, but clearly it was already taken by the time the latter was settled at the end of the tenth century.

The Icelandic environment as experienced by the first settlers is reflected in many of the names they gave to a variety of places, both natural features and human habitations. A study of the place-names recorded in *Landnámabók* shows that the majority of names, not only of landscape features but also of settlements, are topographical, reflecting the pattern established in Norway that the earliest settlements tend to be named after natural features.[172] The most common habitative elements deriving from landscape features give a useful summary of the location of those settlements in the landscape. In descending order of frequency (in *Landnámabók*) they are: *-fell* 'mountain', *-dalr* 'valley', *-holt* 'stony area or wood', *-nes* 'headland, promontory', *-vík* 'inlet, bay', *-hóll* '(isolated, rounded) hill, hillock', *-á* 'river', *-eyrr* 'gravel- or sand-bank'.[173] Most of these also occur as simplex farm-names as well as generics in Iceland. That these are very common elements is shown by the fact that they all also occur on the much smaller Isle of Man.[174]

The names also include some elements which particularly reflect the earliest environment. While the element *-mǫrk* normally refers to a forest, it can also mean 'unsettled, uncultivated land', so is less clear evidence for wooded areas than *-skógr* 'wood' or a few other words which do seem to indicate forestation of the pristine landscape.[175] The name *Rosmhvalanes* 'Walrus Headland' records the existence of these animals before they were eventually eradicated from Iceland, as discussed above.[176] The names also show the new settlers adapting their vocabulary to accommodate new landscape features. For example, in Iceland the element *hraun* refers to a ubiquitous feature of that country, a lava-field. In Norway (and in the Isle of Man), where there are no lava-fields, this element referred simply to rocky ground or rocky mounds.[177] Other elements adapted in this way include *reykr* (as in the capital Reykjavík 'Bay of Smoke'), a noun which normally means 'smoke' but in Icelandic place-names refers to the smoke-like steam arising from hot springs.[178]

Case study – the Sheep Isles

Sheep play an important part in the pastoral economies of most of the Viking world. The animals provide meat, dairy products and wool for a whole host of purposes, including clothing and sails for Viking ships. The Scandinavian migrants to uninhabited lands took sheep along with other livestock with them, to stock their new farms, as discussed above. Those who settled in inhabited areas may not have had to take their own livestock with them, but could have acquired them locally. Furthermore, it is possible that the immigrants found sheep in un- or thinly populated areas. Place-names provide some intriguing insights here.

The very name of the Faroe islands (Old Norse *Færeyjar*) means 'Sheep Islands', and it is of interest to ask whether the first Scandinavians to arrive there named them thus because they found wild or feral sheep throughout the otherwise uninhabited archipelago. Another explanation, suggested by the late twelfth-century Norwegian author of *Historia Norwegie*, is that the islands were so called 'for the peasants there have a rich abundant flock, and some of them own thousands of sheep'.[179] While this suggests that the name did not arise until after the Scandinavian settlers established themselves there, this would not fit well with the name itself. Linguistically the name is likely to be quite old, as it uses the word *fær* for 'sheep', which survives in East Scandinavian dialects, but seems to have been replaced in West Scandinavian dialects by *sauðr* at an early stage.[180] The variety of sheep words in the Scandinavian dialects is remarkable and reflects changes in agricultural practices. So in Iceland, the collective word for sheep is now most commonly *fé*, originally a word applied to all livestock, showing how this type of animal has become the most important in that country. In Norway, by contrast, generic livestock words mostly refer to cattle. However, *fær* was still in use at the time of the Viking migrations, as it gave its name to two islands in Orkney as well as at least one place in Shetland, and it survives in fossilised form in some compounds in Old Icelandic.[181]

There remains the question of whether the Scandinavian settlers named the Faroes after sheep that they already found there, or for some other reason. Kevin Edwards and Douglas Borthwick recently attempted to explain the palynological evidence which suggests a 'double *landnám*' or at least two phases of human impact in the Faroes of which only the second can be associated with archaeological evidence of Scandinavian settlement around 800.[182] They speculate (and challenge archaeologists to find evidence) that in the first phase, there was an:

> intention of leaving a stable population of sheep to reproduce sufficiently to sustain later immigrant colonizers before their crops and settlements became established. Assuming that untended sheep could survive successions of winters prior to the Medieval Warm Period proper . . . the palynological data suggest that subsequent human visits may not have occurred for perhaps two centuries.

This suggestion has some merit for explaining the name. Linguistically, the important point is that the name (given its plural form) characterises the whole archipelago of 18 islands. If the sheep had simply been left behind by Celtic hermits, this is unlikely to have been sufficient reason to name the whole group of islands after them, unless their number were uncommonly large. Given that names often have a defining as well as descriptive function, *Færeyjar* would make much more sense if the whole purpose of the islands' existence was precisely to be a place where sheep were kept, not just for later settlers as suggested by Edwards and Borthwick, but possibly also by Scandinavians stopping off there to reprovision on their way to and from points south.

More commonly, it is individual islands (usually quite small ones) that are named 'Sheep Island' and these generally reflect local use of such islands for grazing or keeping sheep. There are many such names throughout the Viking world, using both the *fær*-word (as in two Faras in Orkney) and the *sauðr*-word.[183] One interesting example of the latter is Soay, from Old Norse *Sauðaey*, 'Island of Sheep'.[184] This is one of the islands of the St Kilda group, off the Outer Hebrides, which has in its turn given its name to a rather special breed of sheep that have survived in the wild there, independently of any human management.[185] These sheep belong to a breed that had reached Orkney by about 4000 BC, and it is uncertain whether they reached Soay at the time of the first human population of the islands in the Bronze Age, or were introduced by Scandinavian settlers (possibly from Orkney or elsewhere in northern Scotland). The discontinuity between the Bronze Age and Viking Age populations of St Kilda, and the relatively late date of the latter, tend to suggest that the sheep were introduced by the Norse.[186]

Names and the changing Viking world

The extent to which Iceland was wooded when the Scandinavian settlers arrived has been discussed above. Unfortunately, place-names do not help much in this regard. There are some place-names formed of elements which seem to indicate wooded areas, but their exact import can be difficult to determine. For example *-holt*, a common place-name element in Iceland, does not necessarily mean a 'wood, thicket' as otherwise most commonly in the other Scandinavian and Germanic languages, but in Iceland develops the meaning of a 'stony, unproductive area, often slightly raised'.[187] The process of clearing the sparse original woodland of Iceland, as discussed above, may be represented in a number of place-names containing elements derived from the verb *brenna* 'to burn'.[188] Places called *Brenna* and *Brenningr* are recorded in *Landnámabók* and most likely reflect this early clearing of woodland by burning. However, already by the time *Landnámabók* came to be written, the former name was interpreted rather differently. Chapter 42 of the *Sturlubók* version tells of a feud arising from disputed ownership of an ox which, after several killings, ends with the burning of one of the protagonists in his house *þar sem nú heitir á Brennu* 'at the place which is now called *Brenna*'.[189]

But, as already discussed, the destruction but also management of woodland in Iceland has to be seen as a long-term process. Similarly, name-giving is not a one-off event that happens at the time of settlement, but is a dynamic process, and one of the difficulties of using names to study the past is to identify this chronological aspect of the evidence. Not only were names reinterpreted, as *Brenna* clearly was, but there is always the possibility that Scandinavian names in the new settlements were given, not at the time of first settlement, but at some point between that and the first recording of the name, as suggested for *-bólstaðr* names, and several of the other examples discussed above. This raises the question of whether the naming practices are simply a natural continuation of the use of the language the settlers brought with them, or whether these naming practices, or indeed this language use, was reinforced by continuing contacts with the language as spoken in the homeland(s). This question of continuing contact will be an important element in the discussion of the term 'diaspora' in the next chapter.

Notes

1 Roesdahl 1998, 25. The following account is heavily indebted to Fullerton and Williams 1972; Sporrong 2003; Seppälä 2005; and Jones and Olwig 2008.
2 *AB*, pp. 186–223.
3 *AB*, pp. 204–6; Lindkvist 2003, 221–8.
4 For accounts of trading and raiding in the Viking Age see, e.g. Sawyer 1997, 1–109, 134–81; Roesdahl 1998, 187–261, 277–92.

5 The following account is based on Fullerton and Williams 1972; and Arge *et al.* 2005.
6 Dugmore *et al.* 2005, 24.
7 McGovern *et al.* 2007, 29.
8 See e.g. Arneborg 2003.
9 Much has been written about this topic, but a useful summary with full bibliography is Wallace 2003, on which the following is based.
10 Arneborg 2003, 171; Schledermann and McCullough 2003, 202.
11 Roberts 1978, 3–4.
12 The following account is largely based on Crawford 1987, 11–38; and Edwards and Ralston 1997.
13 For a discussion of dating problems, see Barrett 2003b, 75–88.
14 Barrett *et al.* 2012, 31; Adams *et al.* 2012, 169.
15 Barrett 2003b, 88–90.
16 Ó Corráin 2008; Sheehan 2008; Wallace 2008.
17 Monk 2013.
18 Redknap 2000, 19–22.
19 Redknap 2000, 45–6, 65–74; Redknap 2004; Griffiths 2010, 92–3, 98, 109, 115–18.
20 E.g. Keynes 1997; Hadley 2006.
21 Holman 2001.
22 Lawson 2004.
23 Hadley 2006.
24 Callmer 2008, 450.
25 Abrams 2013.
26 Renaud 2008.
27 Price 2013.
28 Ridel 2009, 65–91.
29 Edgren 2008, 472.
30 Edgren 2008, 472–3.
31 Edgren 2008, 478; Valk 2008, 485–6; Shepard 2008, 506–7; and several chapters in Bauduin and Musin 2014.
32 Duczko 2004, 7, 60.
33 Androschchuk 2008, 517; see also many of the contributions in Bauduin and Musin 2014.
34 Jansson 1997; Duczko 2004, 9; Androschchuk 2008.
35 Svane 1989, 22–4.
36 Stalsberg 2001, 66, 70–1.
37 Blöndal and Benedikz 1978.
38 Blöndal and Benedikz 1978, 55; Franklin and Shepard 1996, 202.
39 Lind 2001, 133–4.
40 Summarised in Montgomery 2008, studied in Hraundal 2013.
41 Noonan 1994.
42 Perdikaris and McGovern 2008, 191.
43 Arge *et al.* 2005.
44 Edwards and Borthwick 2010.
45 Church *et al.* 2013.
46 Edwards and Borthwick 2010.
47 Church *et al.* 2013, 231–2.
48 Dugmore *et al.* 2005, 31.
49 Dugmore *et al.* 2005, 31.
50 Vésteinsson *et al.* 2002, 105.
51 Edwards *et al.* 2011.

52 Edwards *et al.* 2011, 73–4.
53 Vésteinsson *et al.* 2012, 207, 220, 225.
54 Vésteinsson *et al.* 2002, 106.
55 Dugmore *et al.* 2005, 27.
56 Edwards *et al.* 2011, 77.
57 Edwards *et al.* 2011, 78; Schofield *et al.* 2013.
58 Dugmore *et al.* 2005, 31.
59 Buckland *et al.* 1993, and Buckland and Panagiotakopulu 2005 are useful surveys.
60 Buckland and Panagiotakopulu 2005, 168; Vésteinsson *et al.* 2012, 225–6.
61 Buckland *et al.* 1993, 517.
62 Buckland *et al.* 1993, 516.
63 Dugmore *et al.* 2005, 32.
64 Owen and Lowe 1999, 66, 289; Barrett 2003b, 89–90; Hunter *et al.* 2007, 192–3; Adams *et al.* 2012, 184.
65 Dockrill *et al.* 2010, 94.
66 Hunter *et al.* 2007, 216, 520.
67 Hunter *et al.* 2007, 520.
68 Larsen 2013b, 209.
69 Dockrill *et al.* 2010, 193, 204.
70 Adams *et al.* 2012, 179–80, 185.
71 Bond and Hunter 1987.
72 Barrett 2003b, 88; Dockrill *et al.* 2010, 166.
73 Hunter *et al.* 2007, 143–4, 166, 186–8, 191–3; Dockrill *et al.* 2010, 12, 80, 88, 94, 193–5, 204, 362; Adams *et al.* 2012, 166, 181.
74 Larsen 2013b, 210.
75 Barrett and Richards 2004; Hunter *et al.* 2007, 144, 276–9.
76 Dockrill *et al.* 2010, 176–8; Milner and Barrett 2012, 112.
77 Hunter *et al.* 2007, 144; Dockrill *et al.* 2010, 166–7; Harland and Barrett 2012, 137–8.
78 Barrett *et al.* 2012, 46.
79 Bowden *et al.* 2008.
80 Helgason *et al.* 2000a, 2000b.
81 Helgason *et al.* 2001, 733.
82 Goodacre *et al.* 2005.
83 E.g. Sayers 1994 and further references therein. See also Mourant and Watkin 1952, 23; Sigurðsson 1988; Guðmundsson 1997; and Jacobsen 2005.
84 Jorgensen *et al.* 2004, 26–7.
85 E.g. Goodacre *et al.* 2005, 5.
86 Karlsson 1996.
87 Helgason *et al.* 2003, 295; Jorgensen *et al.* 2004, 26.
88 Helgason *et al.* 2001; Jorgensen *et al.* 2004, 20.
89 E.g. Helgason *et al.* 2003; 2009.
90 Bandle 1967.
91 Jones *et al.* 2012.
92 Searle *et al.* 2009.
93 Dockrill *et al.* 2010, 171–2.
94 Hallgrímsson *et al.* 2004, 266–8.
95 E.g. Helgason *et al.* 2009.
96 Melchior *et al.* 2008.
97 The method is explained in detail in Knudson *et al.* 2012, 309–12.
98 Price and Gestsdóttir 2006.

99 Knudson *et al.* 2012.
100 Price *et al.* 2011.
101 Barrett and Richards 2004.
102 Toolis *et al.* 2008.
103 Vésteinsson *et al.* 2002, 2012; McGovern *et al.* 2007.
104 Dugmore *et al.* 2005, 25.
105 McGovern *et al.* 2007, 35.
106 McGovern *et al.* 2007, 29.
107 Dugmore *et al.* 2007a, 15–16; Keller 2010, 1–3.
108 Dugmore *et al.* 2005, 27–8; McGovern *et al.* 2007, 40; Arneborg *et al.* 2012a, 128, 130–1.
109 Dugmore *et al.* 2005, 28.
110 Dugmore *et al.* 2005, 25; McGovern *et al.* 2007, 40.
111 Dugmore *et al.* 2005, 28; Perdikaris and McGovern 2008, 192; Pierce 2009.
112 Dugmore *et al.* 2005, 28–9.
113 Dugmore *et al.* 2009, 99.
114 Dugmore *et al.* 2005, 29; 2009, 97.
115 Perdikaris and McGovern 2008, 195–8; Dugmore *et al.* 2009, 97–8.
116 Dugmore *et al.* 2007b, 19; 2009, 103; Arneborg *et al.* 2012b.
117 Dugmore *et al.* 2005, 29; 2009, 100–1.
118 Dugmore *et al.* 2007b, 16.
119 Perdikaris and McGovern 2008, 193; Keller 2010, 3.
120 McGovern *et al.* 2007, 30; Perdikaris and McGovern 2008, 192.
121 Dugmore *et al.* 2007b, 17.
122 Dugmore *et al.* 2007b, 19; 2009, 104.
123 Perdikaris and McGovern 2008, 202.
124 Dugmore *et al.* 2007b, 13.
125 Diamond 2006, 178–276.
126 Dugmore *et al.* 2005, 26.
127 Dugmore *et al.* 2007b, 19; Perdikaris and McGovern 2008; Dugmore *et al.* 2009; Arneborg *et al.* 2012b.
128 Dugmore *et al.* 2007b, 13, 29.
129 Dugmore *et al.* 2007b, 17–18, 29; 2009, 96.
130 Dugmore *et al.* 2007b, 17; Perdikaris and McGovern 2008, 193, 197–200.
131 Dugmore *et al.* 2007b, 19–21; Perdikaris and McGovern 2008, 199; Dugmore *et al.* 2009, 101–4.
132 Roesdahl 2005.
133 Karlsson 2000, 177–82.
134 Streeter *et al.* 2012.
135 Dugmore *et al.* 2007a, 2.
136 Streeter *et al.* 2012.
137 *ÍF* I, 5; *BoI*, p. 4.
138 Dugmore *et al.* 2005, 30.
139 McGovern *et al.* 2007.
140 Lawson 2009, 36.
141 Dugmore *et al.* 2005, 30–1; McGovern *et al.* 2007, 39.
142 Dugmore *et al.* 2005, 23.
143 Dugmore *et al.* 2007a, 7–8; see also Dugmore *et al.* 2007b, 22–3.
144 McGovern *et al.* 2007, 38–9; Lawson 2009, 37.
145 McGovern *et al.* 2007, 45.

146 McGovern *et al.* 2007, 29–30; Dugmore *et al.* 2005, 30, 32.
147 McGovern *et al.* 2007, 40; Dugmore *et al.* 2009, 100. See e.g. *GrágásK*, II, 91–6, 106–22; *LEI* II, 111–18, 125–39.
148 McGovern *et al.* 2007, 41–2. See e.g. *GrágásK*, II, 122–35; *LEI* II, 139–50.
149 Brink 2008.
150 Olsen 1926.
151 A useful introduction to the place-names of Norway is Stemshaug 1985.
152 Bandle 1977, 60.
153 Jakobsen 1936, 100–1; Marwick 1952, 234–6; Broderick 2006, xiii, 218.
154 Bandle 1977, 61; Thomson 1995, 59; Sigmundsson 2009, 57–67, 269.
155 Stemshaug 1985, 105; Sigmundsson 2009, 399–410.
156 Gammeltoft 2001, 279–80.
157 Fellows Jensen 1972, 89; Sigmundsson 2009, 18.
158 All of the Icelandic names mentioned in this section are found in *Landnámabók*, see *ÍF* I and Bandle 1977.
159 *ÍF* I, 76; *BoS*, p. 30.
160 Sigmundsson 2009, 268–70.
161 Bandle 1977, 66; Parsons 2002; Abrams and Parsons 2004, 399.
162 Abrams and Parsons 2004, 393.
163 Fellows Jensen 1978, 177–98.
164 Fellows Jensen 1978, 43–4.
165 Townend 2002, 4–87; Abrams and Parsons 2004, 392–403.
166 Gammeltoft 2006, 58–60.
167 Jesch 2006; 2009a.
168 *AB*, p. 218.
169 *ÍF* I, 13; *BoI*, p. 7.
170 *KS*, p. 32; *KM*, p. 149.
171 *ÍF* I, 34–8; *BoS*, pp. 16–18.
172 Bandle 1977, 49, 62.
173 Bandle 1977, 62; Sigmundsson 2009, 192. For English definitions of some of these see also *EPNE*.
174 Broderick 2006, 197–220.
175 Bandle 1977, 58.
176 *ÍF* I, 66, 166–7, 391–3; *BoS*, pp. 63, 146.
177 Bandle 1977, 58; Broderick 2006, 155.
178 Bandle 1977, 67.
179 *HN*, pp. 68–9.
180 Bandle 1967, 365–8.
181 Jakobsen 1936, 146–8; Marwick 1952, 52; Bandle 1967, 367.
182 Edwards and Borthwick 2010, 75.
183 There is also a Fårö off Gotland, but it is uncertain whether the first element is the sheep-word (*GS*, p. 23).
184 Coates 1990, 59–60. The name type is frequent both in Norway (Stemshaug 1985, 76) and the overseas settlements (Sigmundsson 2009, 229).
185 Clutton-Brock and Pemberton 2004.
186 Coates 1990, 5–6; Emery and Morrison 1995, 41.
187 Bandle 1977, 57–8; *EPNE*, 'holt'.
188 Lárusson 1939, 64.
189 *ÍF* I, 82; *BoS*, p. 32.

3

THE VIKING DIASPORA

Introducing the Viking diaspora

The long, broad Viking Age – continuities in time and space

Archaeologists recognise that Scandinavia is characterised by 'remarkable patterns of continuity which link the distant past to the present'.[1] These patterns can be seen, not just in archaeological evidence, but in many cultural practices particularly associated with the Viking Age. The continuities suggest that some evidence for the Viking Age is best considered in a chronological context broader than even the generous framework of 750–1100. This broader chronological context was outlined in Chapter 1, where it was argued that it should be extended to *c.* 1500. Because the Viking Age is the period when many Scandinavians left Scandinavia, often permanently, it is also important to widen the geographical range, and consider evidence from all the areas touched by Scandinavian settlement in that period. Just as much of the evidence stretches the chronological boundaries of the Viking Age, so there is also much evidence, whether natural, artefactual or linguistic, that stretches those geographical boundaries, and which can only be considered in the context of the larger Viking world. This geographical framework was outlined in Chapter 2, above.

The purpose of this chapter is to show by means of a small number of examples how this long, broad Viking Age works in practice, in connection with various kinds of natural, artefactual and linguistic evidence for the Viking Age. This does not mean that there is no space for the local, the regional and the otherwise particular. There have been some recent studies which have emphasised local variations in cultural practices even within Scandinavia, let alone outside it, and which have therefore argued against any pan-Scandinavian, unifying concept of the Viking Age, indeed against any overarching concept including the word 'Viking'.[2]

It would of course be surprising if there was not variation of many kinds across a long period of time and a very broad and varied geographical range. Yet certain continuities, both chronological and geographical, must also be present if the Viking Age and its aftermath are justifiably to be termed a diaspora. Some such continuities are outlined here to demonstrate that, even allowing for local regional variation, some aspects of the Viking Age have a greater reach in both space and time.

The term 'diaspora' will also be explored more closely, particularly in relation to this question of continuity vs. variation. It will be suggested that 'diaspora' is precisely the term that can resolve this paradox. The processes of diaspora counteract the tendency to variety and difference by selecting and emphasising certain cultural features and thereby creating continuity across time and space, and by discovering or even manufacturing other aspects of continuity. This can be seen across the range of natural, artefactual and linguistic evidence, and across both the chronological and geographical range.

Natural evidence

What has been defined as 'natural evidence' (see ch. 1) is in many ways the most difficult to incorporate into a diasporic understanding of the Viking Age, which is predominantly concerned with cultural processes best represented by the artefactual and linguistic evidence. However, natural evidence is still extremely useful in understanding the migrations that were the prerequisite of diaspora, as outlined in Chapter 2. The natural environment is always changing, and those changes which mark significant events in the Viking Age have to be considered in the context of the environmental and climate change that are a constant in human history, and which are sometimes caused by humans and sometimes not. The previous chapter has shown some of the impacts of Scandinavian settlers on their new environments, both the pristine and the already inhabited. Some of this research has placed the Scandinavian environmental impact in a longer historical context, such as the destruction of Iceland's original woodland, a process that seems to have spanned many centuries from the settlement era to the early modern period. Other research is still in the development phase, for example the strontium stable isotope analysis of sheep's wool which shows promise for the future provenancing of textiles and therefore a better understanding of patterns of both trade and migration.[3] But the most obvious example of natural evidence from a much later period that has been used to illuminate Scandinavian activities in the Viking Age is that of population genetics.

Case study – genetics

Most genetic studies purporting to give insights into Viking Age migrations are in fact based on inferences from the genetic patterns of current populations, on the basis that a large enough, well-chosen sample will reflect the history of that population in some measure. A classic example is Iceland which had some important advantages for DNA studies as the technology for these burgeoned in the 1990s. Its population is small, enabling the recording of DNA information for the whole population, primarily for the purposes of medical research, but with side benefits for historical research. And the history of that population is well known, at least in outline, with no significant immigration since its settlement in the Viking Age, so justifying the assumption that the late twentieth-century population was a good proxy for the founding population over a thousand years ago.[4] These studies produced the much-touted results which identified the origins of the Icelanders as being both in Norway, and in Britain and Ireland. As already noted in the previous chapter, this result was not unexpected, but the scientists claimed to be able to establish the nature of these origins in more detail. In particular, they claimed to have demonstrated that there was a considerable difference between the ancestry of the founding male population, over two-thirds of which had DNA similar to the present population of Norway, and the ancestry of the founding female population, two-thirds of which conversely seem to have had their origins in the Celtic parts of the British Isles.[5]

Since those pioneering studies, there is a greater recognition of the problematic nature of such historical DNA studies based on modern populations. Comparisons of founding populations with the current populations of their supposed homelands depend on the genetic evidence for those homeland populations, which may have its own problems of quantity and quality (and nowhere is as thoroughly mapped as Iceland). Also, such comparisons do not take into account any changes there might have been in the homeland populations since the Viking Age, not a topic which has been much studied in, for example, Norway. Furthermore, small populations like Iceland (and even more so the Faroes) are particularly susceptible to genetic drift, in which various factors eliminate some genetic lines from the population creating bottlenecks between past and present population structures. These factors include disease, in particular epidemics, and famine, both of which are known to have made a substantial reduction in the Icelandic population, and emigration, which was considerable in the nineteenth century.[6] Geneticists are of course aware of all of these issues, and they use mathematical modelling to get round some of the problems, but more popular presentations often ignore these problems with the evidence and simplify the results.[7] The scientific studies are also subject to reinterpretation in what has been called 'applied genetic history'. The reduction of an individual's complex genetic history to a matter of 'Viking descent' plays into the creation of individual and familial narratives of origin and belonging, which in turn affect the self-selection of those who submit themselves to testing.[8] Any discussion of the value of the genetic evidence must take these factors into account.

In larger populations, particularly in England, where surnames have been established since the Middle Ages, the obvious connection between the Y-chromosome and surnames, both being passed down from father to son, has enabled the better-targeted selection of samples.[9] In areas with high immigration in modern times, descendants of these more recent immigrants can be excluded through the selection of subjects with surnames attested in the area in late medieval times, giving a population sample chronologically closer to, and therefore more likely to be representative of, the historical population. A study of just such a population sample in the north-west of England demonstrated a substantial proportion of members (in the region of 50%) whose direct male ancestor had a Y-chromosome type most commonly found in Norway, a fact which was then explained by the Viking Age settlement of the area already suggested by place-names, archaeology and some documentary sources.[10]

Thus, studies from both Iceland and the north-west of England have shown that modern population genetics can make a contribution to understanding Viking Age migrations, though the limitations of and constraints on such evidence must always be borne in mind. Also, like all natural evidence, but unlike, on the whole, the artefactual and the linguistic evidence, genetics provides insights which depend on the deployment of modern scientific methods, insights which could not possibly have been available to people in the Viking Age itself. For this reason, the natural evidence is a useful check on the artefactual and linguistic evidence, which was actually produced by people in the past, and vice versa. For example, the genetic study of the north-west of England can only tell us that some males of Norwegian descent, perhaps in considerable numbers, must have passed through the area and left their sperm behind. But a study of the artefactual and linguistic evidence from the same region is needed to understand the broader context for this and, in particular, whether this injection of sperm took place in a context of Norse speech and cultural practices, which included women of Norwegian origin or descent as well as men, as will be discussed further in Chapter 4.

Artefactual evidence

One of the more spectacular indications of archaeological continuity over a long period of time are the farm mounds, or rather settlement mounds, since the inhabitants might also have carried out other types of activity such as fishing. These are found in various places, most notably in northern Norway, but also in Orkney, Faroe and Iceland.[11] They are accumulations of settlement debris which build up as the inhabitants of the settlement discard both household and agricultural rubbish, and renew their living accommodation and farm buildings. They indicate stability and a favoured location. Some of these, with modern farm buildings still on top, have a continuous history of habitation going back around 2,000 years, although the majority seem to have started to accumulate around the turn of the last millennium. In places like Sanday, Orkney, it is possible to see modern farms still operating on top of mounds which have their origins in the Viking Age migrations to the islands. Even without a farm mound, the Viking Age and late Norse site of Belmont on Unst, Shetland, lasted in essentially the same form for a minimum of 400 years, while Quoygrew, on Westray in Orkney, provides a millennium-long sequence of continuous archaeology from the tenth to the twentieth centuries.[12]

Apart from actual sites, there are other kinds of continuity which relate to form and type rather than specific instances. Buildings can provide interesting evidence across both time and space. The Viking Age rural dwelling, for instance, was based on a fairly standard model which gradually developed over time into a more complex structure and domestic space. But this standard model also had to be adapted to local conditions, particularly in regard to the available building materials, which would vary enormously from the wood-rich regions of the homelands to the generally treeless settlements of the North Atlantic where the buildings were made of stone or turf. Whether built in wood, stone or turf, the basic shape and dimensions of the three-aisled rectilinear houses with curving walls and about 20 metres long are found in the Northern Isles and across the North Atlantic, suggesting the community of ideas informing their construction, and deriving from models in the Scandinavian homelands.[13] Sometimes cultural imperatives would override the constrictions of local building materials, as when wooden buildings were imported wholesale into Iceland from Norway, such as the building known as Auðunarstofa, built for the Norwegian bishop of Hólar in northern Iceland in 1317.[14] Building types also reveal cultural connections. Thus, Greenland has the standard Scandinavian-type longhouses, as described above, and found across the North Atlantic, reflecting perhaps the origins of its settlers in Iceland. But it also has a house-type which reflects Scandinavian urban architecture from the eleventh century onwards, and which appears to be evidence for direct contacts between Greenland and Norway after the initial settlement, contact not necessarily mediated through Iceland.[15]

Not all artefactual evidence shows continuities with the homeland, or across a long period of time. Some artefacts seem to have been developed as a consequence of the Scandinavian migrations, without any obvious link to any homeland, but with links across several of the overseas settlements, and thus have a wide geographical range. For example, small metal bells that have been termed 'Norse bells' are found in a range of contexts and in substantial numbers in England, but also in Scotland, the Isle of Man, north Wales, Ireland and Iceland. A recent study has described these as 'a Scandinavian colonial artefact' on the grounds that, while there are no parallels for them from the Scandinavian homelands, their distribution is clearly related to a Scandinavian presence in those places where they are found.[16] They appear to date mainly to the tenth century and their function is uncertain, though the most likely explanation seems to be that they were used as necklace pendants by high-status women, for the purpose of ostentation, possibly with an amuletic function as well.[17] Their distribution suggests a fashion which arose through contact between a range of different Scandinavian communities, including the Danelaw and the Irish Sea region, reflecting the tendency of diaspora to create new cultural forms, as will be discussed further below. Both the gender associations of these little bells and their geographical distribution provide interesting insights into the nature of and links between various Scandinavian-origin communities in the west, but during a relatively restricted period of time.

Case study – steatite

A material that is particularly characteristic of the Viking Age in some regions, and enables the tracking of migrations throughout the Viking world, but also illustrates connections across the long Viking Age and around the Viking world, is that of steatite, also know as soapstone or kleber.[18] Steatite is a useful mineral, found extensively in Norway, but also in Shetland and Greenland. When newly exposed, it is soft and easily carved with either metal or stone tools. It then hardens with use, or on heating, making it suitable for domestic vessels of all kinds, for both cooking and storing food. Other uses are for textile tools such as spindle whorls and loom weights, lamps, fishing weights or even beads and gaming counters, often recycled from larger vessels.

The Norwegians were very used to this handy material: instead of pottery they generally made their domestic vessels from steatite, and the quarrying and working of steatite were major industries in Viking Age Norway.[19] With the arrival of Scandinavians in Shetland, there is a noticeable decrease in ceramic pottery in the archaeological record and an increase in the use of steatite, which characterises the earliest Norse phases at Old Scatness in Shetland and also Pool in Orkney.[20] The increase in the quantity of finds in the Viking Age, and the archaeological assessment of the earliest finds as coming from Norway, suggest that these items were brought with the incomers.[21] At sites like Belmont, in Unst, the steatite finds include not only fragments of imported Norwegian vessels but also a large amount of both worked and unworked steatite and manufacturing waste.[22] There are eight steatite outcrops close to the site and it is likely that the quarrying of steatite and manufacture of objects from it played an important part at Belmont, as elsewhere in Shetland.[23] The new Shetlanders built up a profitable trade in the material, to the neighbouring islands of Orkney in particular, but also to the Faroes and the Hebrides.[24]

Steatite goods found at markets such as Kaupang in Norway and Hedeby in Denmark indicate that they were traded widely. Kaupang had intensive manufacture and distribution of steatite vessels, and seems to have been a centre for their export to southern Scandinavia from around 800, while the steatite found at Hedeby is probably of Norwegian origin.[25] A fair number of steatite objects of probably Norwegian origin have also been found at ninth- and tenth-century sites in Russia, where the artefacts are predominantly of a Scandinavian type, raising the question of whether the steatite was traded or brought there by immigrants.[26]

Later on, Shetlanders made more use of their local resource, but also continued to import Norwegian vessels. Petrological analysis of steatite is still developing, but it is now possible to distinguish examples deriving from Shetland from those manufactured in Norway.[27] The extensive outcrops of steatite in Shetland provided a useful source for topping up supplies, a development dated to the second half of the tenth or the eleventh century at Pool, and in Orkney, steatite could be imported from Shetland as well as Norway.[28] A new type of vessel commonly made of steatite, known as a bakeplate or a bakestone, was manufactured earlier in Shetland than Norway, and then reimported to Shetland from Norway.[29] Bakeplates were used in Norway from the middle of the eleventh up to the seventeenth century. At the Shetland sites of Jarlshof, Da Biggins and Sandwick, they are found in late Norse levels, especially from the thirteenth and fourteenth centuries.[30] At Da Biggins, in particular, the large numbers of these vessels, used for making flatbread and imported from Norway, are part of a larger body of evidence which reveals the close contacts at least some of the inhabitants had with Norway from the twelfth century onwards.[31] Steatite fragments from St Kilda also come from a late Norse bakeplate, associated with a pottery fragment dated to 1135 ± 170.[32] They are also used in Iceland between *c.* 1100 and 1500.[33]

Steatite continued to be valued by Norwegians even after the Viking Age and after the introduction of other materials to make domestic vessels, indeed the use of steatite in that country has been called 'a cultural trait'.[34] The cathedral in Trondheim, the construction of which began in the twelfth century, is built from a number of different kinds of stone, but from 1200 onwards the main material for both its construction and its decoration is steatite. The reason for this has been linked to local traditions of using steatite for everyday vessels and other objects (since there was no tradition of building in stone in Norway before the arrival of Christianity), and certainly some of the same quarries were used for both vessels and architecture. However, it is more likely to represent the development of local expertise in building with stone.[35] The earliest phases of the cathedral would have been built by foreign masons, who used the kinds of stone with which they were familiar. By around 1200, local expertise had developed sufficiently to cast off imported ideas of the most appropriate building stone and use that which was abundantly locally available and most suitable for the purpose. This architectural use of steatite is a good example of the Norwegian, and indeed Scandinavian, ability to take up new ideas and adapt them to their own traditions. It is particularly appropriate that the cathedral containing the relics of Norway's national saint should be made of Norway's national stone.

It is always important to consider negative evidence, too, for example where and when steatite is not used despite cultural propensities. In the Hebrides, the Scandinavian immigrants continued the local practice of using ceramic vessels rather than importing steatite as they easily could have done. Whether this was because the immigrants were fewer, or took a different attitude to local customs, is not clear. Yet even here the Scandinavians put their own stamp on the cultural practices they borrowed. Finds from excavations in the Outer Hebrides show both continuity and change in the production and use of pottery in early Viking contexts. Thus, simple handmade pottery continued to be manufactured using local materials as in the pre-Viking period, but the arrival of the new inhabitants is shown in new manufacturing techniques and the size and shape of vessels made, though the dating of these new forms is still uncertain.[36]

This continuity in the use of pottery suggests some kind of continuity of population, or at least contact between the old and the new populations, in a way less clearly evidenced in the Northern Isles, although there is some evidence for the production and use of coarse pottery in Unst, despite the proximity of a steatite outcrop.[37] This differential pattern between the Western and Northern Isles is also evident in other forms of evidence, such as genetic studies of the modern populations of the different island groups. These suggest that the Hebrides were, like Orkney and Shetland, settled by family groups from Norway, but that the proportion of these in the population was smaller than in Orkney and Shetland, leading to the possibility of greater contact with indigenous inhabitants, as evidenced by the pottery.[38] While the use of steatite in places like Shetland is undoubtedly bound up with its local availability as well as connections with Norway, in a place like Orkney it seems to have been a cultural choice. The Viking Age settlers of Orkney chose to import (from Norway or Shetland) the material familiar to their culture, rather than learn or adapt more local traditions of pottery, as happened in the Hebrides. The islands of St Kilda, with very few Viking and Norse finds, nevertheless have some associated finds of both pottery and steatite, which are dated to 1135 ± 170, reflecting their intermediate cultural position between the Hebrides and the Northern Isles.[39]

Linguistic evidence

The long and broad Viking Age is most easily demonstrated in various forms of linguistic evidence. The runic inscriptions of the Viking Age have their origins in the development of this form of writing in Scandinavia before 150.[40] The runic alphabet then continued to be used for some centuries after the Viking Age and even after the introduction of the roman alphabet, not only in all three of the homelands but also in regions settled in the Viking Age, especially Scotland, Iceland and Greenland. Less long-lived in time, but even more distant in both physical and cultural space, are the Scandinavian runic inscriptions found in Russia, and as far east and south as the Black Sea, Istanbul and Athens.[41]

Poetry also shows a remarkable continuity between around 300 and 1500, as evidenced by some early runic inscriptions as well as later manuscripts.[42] The basic structures of Scandinavian poetry, especially its metres and diction, are maintained right through the major change from orality to literacy that happened between the late Viking Age and the twelfth century, accompanied by further changes in the cultural and social functions of poetry through this period.[43] Although best attested in medieval Iceland and Norway, the geographical range of Scandinavian poetry is also wide, including Sweden and Denmark, and the diasporic lands of England, Scotland and Greenland, as will be discussed further in Chapter 6.

As already noted (ch. 1), many of the written sources for the Viking Age were composed or put down on vellum, or both, in a later period and it is not possible to study the Viking Age without taking those sources into account. It is not, however, simply a matter of distinguishing between 'contemporary' and 'later' sources and assuming that the former are preferable. Traditionally, sources such as the *Anglo-Saxon Chronicle* or the Frankish annals have been highly valued for their contemporary insights into some aspects of the Viking Age. But such texts usually represent particular political or cultural agendas, and the doings of Vikings form only a part of what they choose to record, which is then usually also presented in a way that accords with those agendas.[44] Moreover, some such annals which are considered to be contemporary are nevertheless preserved only or mainly in later manuscripts, including most Irish annals.[45] Other annalistic texts were clearly written at a later date but seem nevertheless to incorporate some contemporary information, such as the *Russian Primary Chronicle*.[46] The process of historiography is generally an ongoing one, and Viking Age history is indebted to many sources from the twelfth century and later, such as the Irish *Cocad Gaedel re Gallaib*.[47] Similarly, and as already noted (ch. 1), some texts in the Scandinavian vernacular, notably skaldic poetry, are arguably contemporary (oral) sources from the Viking Age, even though not committed to writing until the twelfth century or later. These poems are often incorporated into sagas, which have their own complex relationship with the Viking Age.

Although the number of surviving texts in a Scandinavian language that can confidently be assigned to the Viking Age is relatively small, language is still an important form of continuity in the Viking diaspora, indeed language, though often ignored in these discussions, is acknowledged by some scholars to be one of the main 'shared cultural elements' of the Viking diaspora.[48] Scandinavian settlers took their language with them to their new homes in the Viking Age, and this language (or its later forms) continued in use in those settlements until either the settlement died out (as in Greenland in the fifteenth century) or the language and its speakers were assimilated into the majority population and its language (as happened in England, probably around the eleventh or twelfth century).[49] In Faroe and Iceland, the language has survived (and developed) continuously since the settlement period. Even in Russia, there is evidence for Scandinavian influence on both language and naming practices.[50]

Various kinds of language use provide some of the best examples of continuity through the long Viking Age, an obvious example being the place-names of Faroe and Iceland that were given by the settlers and are still in use today. The maintenance of their ancestral language, in the face of other possibilities (e.g. the use of Celtic languages brought by the settlers), enabled the Icelanders to keep up close contacts with the Scandinavian homelands, and this continuing contact was an important factor in the development of Icelandic textual culture. There are a number of examples of post-Viking Age contacts across the Viking diaspora that depended on a common language and textual culture, such as the literature of twelfth- and thirteenth-century Orkney, or the runic inscriptions of medieval Greenland, but the richest body of evidence comes from the extensive literature of medieval Iceland.

Sagas and the past

Much of the prose narrative literature of high medieval Iceland has the Viking Age past as its theme. Apart from literature produced in the service of the Christian church (not discussed here) the earliest examples of this prose narrative literature are explicitly historiographical works such as *Íslendingabók* and *Landnámabók* (discussed further in ch. 6). These and some of the kings' sagas began to be written in the twelfth century, though many of the surviving versions are thought to have been revised or composed in their current form in the thirteenth.[51] Texts in this genre are rarely stable, continuing to change and develop into the late fourteenth century or even later.[52] The sagas of Icelanders (*Íslendingasögur*) are assumed to have been composed during the thirteenth and fourteenth centuries. While there is evidence for some of these sagas in the form of fragmentary manuscripts from the thirteenth century, many of them survive only in manuscripts of the fourteenth century or even later.[53] These texts, too, continue to develop, though the variation between the versions is not usually as extensive as in the case of the historiographical works. Similarly, the sagas of ancient times or legendary sagas (*fornaldarsögur*) are assumed to be a phenomenon that began in the thirteenth century, though the manuscript evidence is less clear here, and the genre was quite long-lived, with a concentration of manuscripts in the fourteenth century and even later.[54] It is not clear whether this fourteenth-century flourishing of different kinds of saga is merely an accident of survival, with later manuscripts more likely to survive, or whether the literary recreation of the Viking Age past was of particular interest to authors, scribes or audiences at that time, alongside the many other literary genres concerned with other themes that also flourished then.

Once upon a time, sagas of kings, Icelanders and ancient times alike were all taken to be accurate historical accounts of the Viking Age past, and this view led to several quite serious scholarly attempts to explain how the sagas of Icelanders in particular could represent the literate culmination of a reliable oral tradition about the past.[55] However the tendency of much saga scholarship in the later twentieth century and until today has been to view all three genres as, at best, literary reconstructions of that past, or using the past to mirror the present, or even outright fictions. It is acknowledged that much of the poetry in the kings' sagas and some of the poetry in the sagas of Icelanders and ancient times may be older than the sagas in which they are preserved, having been a source for them and providing some kind of a link with earlier periods. Otherwise, much literary scholarship of the last half century or more has avoided, or downright refused to engage with, the historicity of the sagas, preferring to study them purely as literary texts.[56] However, there are signs that some scholars, including archaeologists, have been interested in how they might reveal aspects of their contexts of composition (in the thirteenth or fourteenth centuries) or manuscript recording (in the fourteenth century or later).[57]

Yet one of the most interesting things about these three saga-genres in particular, along with the historiographical works, is precisely their across-the-board obsession with the Viking Age past as their main literary theme, and this relationship between the time in which the sagas were written and that past deserves further exploration. The position taken in this book is that this pervasive connection between a high medieval literary context and the Viking Age past is an inevitable product of the long Viking Age. This long Viking Age is, in its turn, a product of the Viking diaspora, which created lasting and wide-ranging cultural and linguistic networks and reciprocal connections between the Scandinavian homelands and the various regions settled by Scandinavians in the Viking Age. The Icelanders' interest in their Viking Age past was thus not simply a memory of that distant past, whether accurate or constructed, but a product of those ongoing relationships long after the Viking Age, which maintained and encouraged a sense of commonality and belonging in the present, based on a shared past.

Case study – Vágar

An example of how these literary links across the North Atlantic and through time worked in practice can be seen in the treatment by various texts of the northern Norwegian district of *Vágar* 'Bays' (modern Vågan), on the island of Austvågøy in Lofoten, roughly the indented coast between the modern-day towns of Svolvær and Henningsvær. Even today this district is the centre of a large-scale fishing industry, and there is evidence for such activity going back to the medieval and possibly even Viking periods.[58] This particular characteristic is quite evident in the sources, but the district also had other resonances, both political and religious.

To demonstrate this requires first a detour into early Norwegian history. Widely renowned in the sagas is a battle said to have taken place at *Hjǫrungavágr* (probably modern Liavågen in Møre og Romsdal, much further south in Norway) in which Norwegian forces led by Hákon Sigurðarson, earl of *Hlaðir* (Lade, in Trøndelag) defeated an invading Danish–Wendish coalition known as the *Jómsvíkingar*, in about 985. Hákon's origins and power base were in northern Norway, north of modern Trondheim, in the region known then as *Hálogaland*.[59] The jarls of *Hlaðir* ruled this region quite independently despite nominal allegiance to the rulers of southern Norway, who were at times Danish. Various accounts of the battle of *Hjǫrungavágr* mention that one of Hákon's supporters was a chieftain called Þórir *hjǫrtr* ('Hart') from *Vágar*.[60] Hákon was a noted pagan, and his followers were too.[61] When Hákon had been killed and Norway was ruled by the Christian missionary king Óláfr Tryggvason, Þórir reappeared as one of the northern chieftains who attempted to resist Óláfr's Christian mission and political ambitions, though they were ultimately unsuccessful and Þórir was killed by Óláfr.[62]

The religious history of the region is then obscure until over a century later when the Norwegian king Eysteinn Magnússon (d. 1122) is said to have built many churches in different parts of Norway, including one at *Vágar*, to which he also granted a prebend for its maintenance.[63] This seems to have marked the incorporation of the district into the medieval, Christian kingdom of Norway. The same king, Eysteinn Magnússon, along with his brothers Sigurðr and Ingi, is also said to have issued an amendment to the Frostathing law for the people of *Hálogaland*, regulating their economic activities, including fishing and the fur trade. This enactment specifically mentions that 'every man who catches fish in *Vágar*' must give five fishes to the king.[64] In revising the fish tribute required from the residents of *Hálogaland*, the enactment implies that fishing was already a thriving industry in that region and probably increasing in importance. This importance became so great that a further royal order of 1384 names *Vágar* as one of the three most important trading centres of western and northern Norway, alongside Bergen and Trondheim.[65]

What have these rather various references to *Vágar* in the far north of Norway to do with Icelanders and their sagas? Firstly, the battle of *Hjǫrungavágr* was a perennial favourite of the Icelandic authors of historical and pseudo-historical sagas. As well as the accounts of it in kings' sagas such as *Heimskringla*, the Icelanders produced no less than five versions of a saga known as *Jómsvíkinga saga*, in which an interest in the colourful exploits of the Baltic *Jómsvíkingar* are balanced by a West Norse perspective which is indicated by traditions recording the presence of several Icelandic poets at the battle, fighting on the side of Hákon. But Hákon's victory, though celebrated, was also the last of the old order, having been achieved in part by pagan supernatural means. In the Icelandic conception of history, paganism was destined to give way to Christianity, and in their own case this happened during the reign of Óláfr Tryggvason (d. *c.* 1000). In Norway, his reign was short and inconclusive, but he belonged to the Icelanders as the king who had brought them to Christianity, whereas in Norway that mission was not fulfilled until the reign of his successor and namesake Óláfr Haraldsson (later St Óláfr, d. 1030).[66] From an Icelandic point of view, Óláfr Tryggvason's killing of Þórir *hjǫrtr* both parallels and contrasts with his more peaceful persuasion of the Icelanders to adopt Christianity.

The recalcitrance of north Norwegian pagans was not the only association the Icelanders had with *Vágar*. The importance of this district as a fishing station and trading centre resonates through several sagas of Icelanders, where it is presented as having had that status already around the time of the settlement of Iceland, in the ninth and tenth centuries.[67] In Chapter 17 of *Egils saga*, the hero's uncle, Þórólfr Kveldúlfsson, who is based a little further south in *Hálogaland*, has his men fishing for stockfish in *Vágar*, though this is only one of his many sources of income.[68] *Hallfreðar saga* begins in the north of Norway and mentions in Chapter 1 a herring boat with men on it 'from *Vágar* in the north', on which two boys escape their pursuers.[69] *Vágar* appears in Chapters 20 and 22 of *Grettis saga* as a location the saga-hero Grettir visits twice while the market is on.[70] The late *Þorskfirðinga saga* also portrays (ch. 2) two visiting Icelanders sent north to *Hálogaland* to make money from stockfish in the time of King Haraldr *hárfagri* 'Fine-Haired'.[71]

These two different associations of *Vágar* in Icelandic sources, of paganism and fishing, raise the question of its significance for the Icelandic authors and audiences of these sagas. The pagan theme and the battle of *Hjǫrungavágr* (fought a century after the initial settlement of Iceland) make a straightforward link to Iceland's heroic past. As in so much medieval Icelandic literature, the literary presentation of this past allows for the recognition of Icelandic and other heroism in a pagan context that can still be celebrated even though it was destined to be superseded by Christianity. The presentation of *Vágar* as a fishing station and marketplace on the other hand suggests more prosaic memories of the past. In their internal saga chronologies, two of the references to it (in *Egils saga* and *Hallfreðar saga*) are set in ninth-century Norway, before the settlement of Iceland, though involving the ancestors of the Icelandic heroes of those sagas, while *Grettis saga* depicts an early eleventh-century setting in which the Icelandic saga hero visits a range of places in Norway. Could these be fictionalised representations of the past based on the undoubted later status of *Vágar* as a fishing and trading centre in the thirteenth and fourteenth centuries when these sagas were written?[72] Or do they represent the medieval Icelanders' memories of their pre-settlement history in Norway? The archaeological evidence suggests that the answer is probably both, the two reinforcing each other.

It has been thought that Iceland's own trade in exporting stockfish did not take off in a big way until the late thirteenth or even fourteenth century, though more recent zooarchaeological analyses suggest rather that it could have been underway by

1200.[73] The creation of wealth from the Lofoten fishing grounds, on the other hand, was not new in the thirteenth century, though how far back the lucrative large-scale export of fish actually went is more difficult to establish. In 1974, Thorleif Sjøvold could declare, based on the paucity of fishing gear found in the graves and stray finds of Arctic Norway, that 'fishing was of far less importance to the Late Iron Age population than would have been expected', but this impression now seems ill-founded.[74] The Norwegian king's interest in *Vágar* in the early twelfth century, as mentioned above, suggests that trade, quite probably in fish, was already important by then. Even earlier, the powerful Viking Age chieftain who had his seat at Borg, on the neighbouring island of Vestvågøy, is thought to have acquired his immense wealth through the exchange of local surplus or hunting products paid to him as tribute.[75] The archaeological evidence of boat-houses in the area, and more recently from the stable isotope analysis of fish-bones found in Hedeby, suggests that some of this local surplus was fish, and thus that fishing for long-distance export, particularly of stockfish, could have taken place in this region as early as the ninth century.[76] A recent isotope analysis of samples taken from 33 burials in the north of Norway shows an increase in the consumption of marine protein over time, and also that certain individuals changed their dietary habits later in life, suggesting a move to a coastal area.[77] Both phenomena are observed in the Viking Age (before 1030) and are consistent with households whose economy was based partly or primarily on the exploitation of marine resources, in connection with the expanding stockfish industry.

Landnámabók lists a number of Icelanders who came from *Hálogaland*, or even Lofoten, and it is likely that their descendants retained a memory of their home district and its source of wealth.[78] Several of the anecdotes told of these immigrants from northern Norway relate to their generosity and ability to provide food, such as Geirríðr who sat outside her house inviting passers-by in to eat, or Þuríðr *sundafyllir* who was called 'Sound-Filler' because of her magical ability to conjure fish into the waters of *Hálogaland* at times of famine.[79] Þengill *mjǫksiglandi* ('Frequently Sailing') may have been named thus because of his fishing exploits.[80] These anecdotes seem to preserve truthful memories of the fish-basket that was *Hálogaland*. Any such memories of the settlement period would have been strengthened by continuing contacts with the Norwegian homeland at the time the sagas were being written and in the context of the continuing flourishing of the fishing industry there. The strong paganism of *Hálogaland* is also reflected in these anecdotes. As well as Þuríðr with her magical ability to conjure up fish, a certain Eyvindr is said to have made sacrifices, and Óláfr *tvennumbrúni* 'Double-Eyebrowed' is said to have been *hamrammr mjǫk* 'a great shape-changer' and to have been buried, pagan fashion, in a mound.[81] Unlike the memories of the fishing industry, such anecdotes are less likely to have been strengthened by continuing contacts with the Norwegian homeland, which was by then no longer pagan. Rather, they plug into the literary fascination with the north of Norway that is evident in the *fornaldarsögur*.

By way of contrast to the Icelandic perspective, we have a glimpse of *Vágar* from that of a thirteenth-century Norwegian, the anonymous author of *Konungs skuggsjá*, an instructional text for an ambitious young man who aspires to be a merchant. For this author, *Vágar*, and its northern neighbour *Andarnes* (modern Andenes), are characterised by neither paganism nor fishing but by their latitude. To this up-to-date and scientifically minded observer, instructing the future seafarer, *Vágar* is simply (and slightly inaccurately) the land of midday stars in winter and the midnight sun in summer.[82] The Icelanders' view of the same place, focused on its past paganism and its ongoing status as a major fishing port, is on the other hand an intermeshing of past and present, homeland and new land, which is characteristic of the literature of the Viking diaspora.

Understanding the Viking diaspora

Defining diaspora

The discussion so far has suggested some of the ways in which natural, artefactual and linguistic evidence demonstrate strong links between the Viking Age and what followed it. Several of the examples have also shown how these links depend on continuing cultural contacts between different parts of the Viking world, not always including the homeland. The question to be explored now is whether these connections across time and space justify the concept of a Viking diaspora, emanating from Scandinavia, but extending both east and west, and developing into a series of complex, reciprocal networks between the homelands and the settlements that lasted for differing periods of time. In particular, an approach based on texts provides a diasporic interpretation that can then be tested against other types of evidence. This approach is outlined below and then exemplified in the following chapters.

Before going on to discuss the Viking diaspora, it is worth pausing to remember that the word 'diaspora' was originally applied to the dispersal of the Jews from their homeland in Palestine and it is sometimes argued that it is inappropriate to use it for other historical situations.[83] However, recent work by Shlomo Sand, although he does not use the word 'diaspora' very much, challenges the entrenched idea that the spread of Judaism was due to a traumatic dispersal of peoples, involving massive migration, and concludes rather that it came about through a dynamic process of conversion leading to the spread of the religion outside Palestine over a period of time.[84] However, whether or not the spread of Jews throughout the world is recognised as the prototypical diasporic experience, the term 'diaspora' is now used in a wide variety of contexts, both historical and contemporary, although usually still in contexts involving the movements of people.[85]

Steven Vertovec's distinction between 'diaspora' and 'migration' has already been cited in Chapter 1 but is repeated here for convenience. He sees:

> *migration* as physical movement, resettlement and re-establishment of key social institutions; *diaspora* as the consciousness of being connected to the people and traditions of a homeland and to migrants of the same origin in their countries; and *transnationalism* as the practices of exchange of resources, including people, across the borders of nation states. This implies that migration can occur without diaspora and transnationalism, but the two last-mentioned activities are always a result of migration.[86]

The third stage of transnationalism is less relevant in the present context, as it presupposes the existence of well-defined and recognised nations, although these did emerge during the period under consideration here, and some of the later diasporic connections identified below might just as well be seen as transnationalism.

The reciprocal relationship with the homeland which characterises diaspora in contrast to migration is further emphasised by Kalra *et al.* as follows:

> diaspora more often than not evokes two social spheres of interaction – the place of residence and the place from which migration has occurred. . . . It is the ongoing political, economic, social and cultural ties between multiple institutionalized spaces that characterize diaspora.[87]

This reciprocal aspect is often more than just binary (as recognised by Vertovec) and this complexity, which seems particularly relevant to the Viking Age and its aftermath, was formulated by the anthropologist James Clifford as the '[d]ecentered, lateral connections' of diaspora, which 'may be as important as those formed around a teleology of origin/return'.[88] Thus a full understanding of a diaspora has to move away from a focus just on the homelands and colonies, and recognise the importance of reciprocal, and ongoing, links between the different regions of the diaspora.

Diaspora theory was introduced to Viking Studies with the creation of the AHRC-funded Viking Identities Network in 2006.[89] Since then the term has been widely adopted in the field but with little justification or discussion. Steinunn Kristjánsdóttir, for example, gives a brief definition of diaspora ('a population sharing common ethnic identity, but that left freely or forced their settled territory and became residents in new areas') but without further exploration of the implications of this, nor any justification of her use of the term to discuss religion in early Iceland.[90]

There has been just one detailed discussion of the validity of the concept of diaspora for Viking Age studies, offered recently by Lesley Abrams.[91] Abrams cites Robin Cohen's proposed attributes of diaspora (see more on this below), but does not address them systematically or in detail, only noting that 'Some apply quite readily to the Viking Age, others are more problematic'.[92] Instead she proposes her own 'model of Viking-Age society that takes in the Scandinavian homelands and overseas settlements', which conceives the Viking diaspora to a great extent as a series of royal or elite courts in various kinds of contact with each other.[93] Abrams concludes that

> for a period the dispersed Scandinavian communities of the Viking Age acted like a diaspora, retaining, synthesizing, and expressing a sense of collective identity and constructing a common cultural discourse, while new circumstances generated innovations and developments which flowed back and forth between them.[94]

While this is not incompatible with the general argument presented here, it is a narrower vision, probably too cautious ('for a period', 'acted like a diaspora'), and the model is heavily dependent on evidence from the British Isles and continental Europe (not really considering the 'overseas settlements' where there were no 'host communities') and especially on material culture, as well as being restricted chronologically to the Viking Age proper and largely to elites. It is argued here rather that the concept of 'the Viking diaspora' is most useful when applied in the context of the full range of evidence and the extended chronology of the long and broad Viking Age as outlined above.

The most thorough, and seminal, account of diasporas is by the sociologist Robin Cohen. He proposed that, normally, 'diasporas exhibit several or most of the following features:

1. dispersal from an original homeland, often traumatically;
2. alternatively, the expansion from a homeland in search of work, in pursuit of trade or to further colonial ambitions;
3. a collective memory and myth about the homeland;
4. an idealization of the supposed ancestral home;
5. a return movement or at least a continuing conversation;
6. a strong ethnic group consciousness sustained over a long time;
7. a troubled relationship with host societies;
8. a sense of co-responsibility with co-ethnic members in other countries; and
9. the possibility of a distinctive creative, enriching life in tolerant host countries.'[95]

Cohen's analysis is based on recent history but many, in fact most, of these features can be demonstrated in the movements of the Viking Age and the societies and cultures that developed from these movements, sufficient to qualify them as a diaspora.

As noted above, Abrams did not address this paradigm point by point, and for her '[t]he most obvious practical difficulty in applying Cohen's diaspora paradigm . . . is inequality of information. It is very difficult to conceptualize society in the Viking Age, because our evidence is both slight and complicated'.[96] As a historian, Abrams is very concerned with the problem that our 'historical sources' are written by outsiders, or later than the Viking Age, and that material culture has its own problems of interpretation. Her model of the Viking Age diaspora is quite firmly based in contemporary evidence from the Viking Age itself, rather than in a more generous acceptance of evidence from a longer period and a broader geographical context. The latter is the method proposed here, which involves accepting the limitations of this evidence, but also recognising that it may still contain significant and revealing patterns, the 'remarkable patterns of continuity' mentioned at the beginning of this chapter. With such a broader perspective in both time and space, it is possible to address Cohen's points one by one in relation to a putative Viking diaspora, as seen in a range of selected examples from different places, periods, and based on different types of evidence. These examples are meant to be illustrative rather than exhaustive, and some themes arising from them will be considered in more detail in the following chapters.

'Dispersal from an original homeland, often traumatically'

This feature is instantly recognisable in the persistent Icelandic myth that its first settlers left Norway to escape the tyranny of King Haraldr *hárfagri* 'Fine-Haired'. Such a motif is widely found in those sagas of Icelanders that cover the settlement period, as expressed in the words of the Norwegian chieftain Ketill *flatnefr* 'Flat-Nose' in *Laxdœla saga* (ch. 2):[97]

> Sannspurðan hefi ek fjándskap Haralds konungs til vár; sýnisk mér svá, at vér munim eigi þaðan traustս bíða; lízk mér svá, sem oss sé tveir kostir gǫrvir, at flýja land eða vera drepnir hverr í sínu rúmi.
>
> I have heard true reports of King Haraldr's enmity towards us; it seems to me that we will not experience safety from that direction; it appears to me that there are two choices open to us, to flee the country or to be killed, each in his turn.

Ketill's sons want to go to Iceland, though the old man is less keen, preferring Scotland. It is characteristic that those who were dispersed from Norway in this way often ended up in a variety of places. Thus in *Eyrbyggja saga* (ch. 1) the noble men who left their ancestral estates are said variously to have gone across the Keel to Sweden, or west across the sea to the Hebrides or Orkney, before going on to Iceland (ch. 6).[98] Similarly, *Færeyinga saga* gives Haraldr's tyranny as the explanation for the settlement of the Faroe Islands 'and other uninhabited lands'.[99] Even those chieftains who were friendly with Haraldr, such as Ingimundr in *Vatnsdœla saga* (chs 8–12), are presented as having moved to Iceland at the time of and in the context of the unrest in Norway.[100] The traumatic dispersal westwards from Norway is also reflected in *Landnámabók*, which regularly notes that certain settlers left for political reasons.[101]

Similar traumatic dispersals can be found in other literary traditions of the Viking diaspora. The Middle English romance *Havelok the Dane* (from around 1300), written for a Lincolnshire audience still aware of its Danish heritage, tells the story of Havelok, the son of the Danish king Birkabeyn, who as a small child is imprisoned after his father's death along with his sisters.[102] Their supposed guardian kills the sisters, but Havelok escapes through the help of a kindly peasant, Grim, who eventually takes his whole family, including Havelok, to England, where he founds the settlement known as Grimsby. Havelok eventually marries an English princess and becomes king of England. Written from a later medieval perspective, the poem's primary purpose is to celebrate the harmoniously dual Anglo-Saxon and Viking heritage of the English nation, and to acknowledge the full assimilation of the Danish-origin inhabitants of Lincolnshire into this nation.[103] Havelok's trajectory from prince to pauper and back again is a common romance motif, but while it should not be taken too literally, the story does plug into local memories of the Danish migration to Lincolnshire. As an explanation for this migration, the tyranny of the Danish ruler presented in *Havelok* parallels the role of Haraldr *hárfagri* in Norway, and suggests that the story of traumatic emigration was useful elsewhere in the Viking diaspora than Iceland.

'Alternatively, the expansion from a homeland in search of work, in pursuit of trade or to further colonial ambitions'

Those settlers discussed above who are said to have gone to Iceland with the blessing of King Haraldr *hárfagri* might be said to have gone with 'colonial ambitions'. Similarly, *Orkneyinga saga* (ch. 4) has King Haraldr give Orkney and Shetland to his lieutenant Rǫgnvaldr, Earl of Møre, in compensation for the death of Rǫgnvaldr's son while serving Haraldr.[104] The first few chapters of the saga show some of the difficulties Haraldr had in establishing control over this colony. A colonial context is also implied in the account of the *Russian Primary Chronicle* telling how the 'Varangians from beyond the sea' first imposed tribute on a wide range of inhabitants in the east in 859, were at first resisted, and then were called back to reign over the unruly region.[105] England's 'Second Viking Age' culminated in the crowning of the Danish king Knútr as sole King of England in 1017. While there were many factors which brought this about, the Danelaw, a large region where many of the population were of Scandinavian origin, provided a useful launching-pad for the military activities that ensured Knútr's final success, making him into 'the most successful of all pre-Conquest rulers in Britain', but also one whose 'dominion and influence extended over much of the northern world'.[106]

Nevertheless, it is doubtful whether a culture that did not have a developed concept of the state could be said to have colonial ambitions. In any case, colonial ambitions could only be realised in particular circumstances and are perhaps rather a by-product than a cause of the Viking diaspora. In general, land-hunger or the opportunity to trade are more commonly adduced as important factors in the Scandinavian expansions to various parts of the world.[107] While trade need not lead to permanent settlements, in which case the applicability of the term 'diaspora' is questionable, land-hunger could and would bring about diasporic settlements.[108] The *Anglo-Saxon Chronicle* famously states that in 876, after a period of Viking raids in many parts of England, their leader 'Halfdan shared out the land of the Northumbrians, and they proceeded to plough and to support themselves' and similarly in 877 that they shared out some of Mercia.[109] Certainly the whole of *Landnámabók* conceptualises the settlement of Iceland as the creation of a farming society from scratch, with opportunities for all, and within six decades.[110] This variety of explanations for the Viking diaspora, both ancient and modern, undoubtedly reflects a multiplicity of causes for it.

'A collective memory and myth about the homeland'

The Norwegian origin of the Icelanders is stated very prominently in Chapter 1 of *Íslendingabók*, which also makes clear (ch. 2) that Iceland's first law code was brought from Norway, soon after the settlement.[111] This firmly establishes the

Icelandic polity as an offshoot of the Norwegian one. The *Russian Primary Chronicle* notes that '[t]he present inhabitants of Novgorod are descended from the Varangian [= Scandinavian] race, but aforetime they were Slavs'.[112] Both of these represent different collective memories about homeland origins. The collective nature of the Icelanders' memories about their homeland origins is illustrated on a larger scale in *Landnámabók*, which regularly specifies a precise place of origin for the first settlers, usually though not always in Norway, as well as in those sagas which begin with their protagonists' origins in Norway.[113]

In contrast, *Orkneyinga saga* (chs 1–4) presents a historicised myth about the Norwegian origins of the Orkney earldom, rather than a collective memory of individuals and their places of origin. In an elaborate story, Norway is envisaged as having been conquered in mythological times by two brothers, Nórr who rules the mainland and Górr who is king of the isles and skerries. The earls of Orkney are ultimately descended from Górr.[114] This myth establishes a link between the two countries but also emphasises their separateness. Norway is figured not so much as an ancestral home but more as a country of the same origin as Orkney which experienced parallel political developments. Preben Meulengracht Sørensen has argued that this Orcadian origin myth expresses 'a specific Nordic self-esteem and pride', indeed that it shows that the earls of Orkney are 'more Norwegian than the kings of Norway'.[115] However, the provenance of this myth is not clear, whether it is an Icelandic construction or an Orcadian interpretation of the past, nor is it clear whether it was part of the saga from its inception. Indeed the myth may have had more to do with political conditions in both places in the thirteenth or even fourteenth centuries than with any collective memories of the homeland. Even so it would show that origin-stories were still a matter of interest and possibly debate at that time.[116]

'An idealization of the supposed ancestral home'

It is debatable whether the Icelanders actually idealised their ancestral home in Norway, but they certainly took a great interest in it and its history. Theodoricus, a Norwegian monk who wrote a Latin history of Norway in the late twelfth century, explicitly notes that he has much of his information from the well-informed Icelanders.[117] Similar sentiments were expressed by the Danish historian Saxo Grammaticus, writing in Latin around 1200, and of course the Icelandic kings' sagas also included sagas of the kings of Denmark.[118] This suggests that the Icelanders' concept of their ancestral home, though focused on Norway, encompassed the larger cultural zone that we call Scandinavia. The heroic prehistory of Scandinavia is celebrated in many of the *fornaldarsögur*, which are mainly set in the northlands in a time before the settlement of Iceland, but often involving characters who are figured as the ancestors of certain Icelanders.[119]

Another aspect of this idealisation of the ancestral home can be glimpsed in naming habits. Place-names in the new settlements which seem to have been transferred from the homeland, rather than given afresh, suggest that the settlers had sufficiently good memories of their old homes to want to perpetuate their names in the new. Icelandic place-names such *Þelamörk*, *Finnmörk*, *Katanes* and *Sigtún* are most likely to have been named after Telemark and Finnmark in Norway, Caithness in Scotland and Sigtuna in Sweden respectively, rather than being coined because of any local considerations.[120] Since few of these names are recorded in very early documents, it is however possible that they were coined some time after the initial settlement, on the basis of continuing contact with or knowledge of these places.

'A return movement or at least a continuing conversation'

The reciprocal traffic between the diasporic lands and Scandinavia is well documented and certainly qualifies as a 'continuing conversation'. *Landnámabók*, in noting that Iceland was discovered and settled from Norway, gives a description of how to sail to Iceland, with a starting point at the prominent landmark of Stadlandet in western Norway, locating the two countries in an ongoing geographical relationship.[121] The description is expanded on the basis of personal knowledge in the version of *Landnámabók* written by Haukr Erlendsson, who spent much of his life in Norway in the early fourteenth century. The sagas of Icelanders show many a young man going to Norway for three or more years in order to establish himself, as well as some merchants who are active there even longer.[122] The kings' sagas (especially, but not only, *Morkinskinna*) regularly retail anecdotes about Icelanders (especially poets) at the courts of the eleventh-century kings of Norway.[123] Similarly, Norwegians are regularly to be found in Iceland, in a variety of sagas, and occasionally even represented as living there.[124] These Norwegians are presented as strangers, recognisably not Icelanders, and yet they are not as strange as any other non-Icelandic group would be, and there are a lot of them in the texts.

The place of Norway in the Icelandic consciousness can be deduced from the laws preserving various rights, particularly inheritance rights, of Icelanders in Norway. These legal rights come with reciprocal responsibilities to the king of Norway from Icelanders, and particular rights for the Norwegian king in Iceland.[125] The reciprocity of the provisions is clear, and is equally clearly derived from the Norwegian ancestry of the Icelanders, a fact used in the Icelanders' negotiations for these rights. The 'continuing conversation' was taken to its logical conclusion when the Icelanders submitted to the king of Norway in 1262–4. Patricia Boulhosa has argued that this was 'the result of a continuous development' in which Icelanders negotiated their way towards that relationship, a relationship which encompassed both positive attitudes towards the Norwegian king and the maintenance of certain aspects of the Icelandic way of life.[126]

The relationship with Norway was just as important in Orkney. The history of the earls of Orkney suggests that their power could only be maintained with the support of Norway, as noted in Chapter 1, above, in the case of Þorfinnr Sigurðarson in the eleventh century. Orkney's most notable twelfth-century earl, Rǫgnvaldr Kali Kolsson (d. 1158/9) was the offspring of an Orcadian mother and a Norwegian father, and grew up in Norway, and his near-contemporary and fellow-poet Bishop Bjarni Kolbeinsson had a similar background.[127] Marriage alliances with powerful families in Norway took place in Iceland just as in Orkney.[128]

In England, events leading up to its conquest by the Danish king Knútr in 1016 have been called England's 'Second Viking Age'. In fact, the archaeological evidence suggests three rather different stages to the contacts between England and Denmark in particular.[129] There was first an early stage of raids and attacks, followed by settlement in England. In neither of these stages is there much evidence of these interactions back in Denmark. However, the third stage, which starts under the reign of Sveinn *tjúguskegg* 'Forkbeard' in the late tenth century, brings in a whole new era of traffic and exchange back and forth across the North Sea, particularly in objects which draw on both traditions. Although doubtless facilitated by Knútr's joint rule of England and Denmark, this process continued well beyond his death in 1035, maintained by 'family ties and relations, the potential for trade, as well as the ecclesiastical organisation'.[130]

'A strong ethnic group consciousness sustained over a long time'

Much archaeological ink has been spilt in the last few decades on the question of whether and how material culture expresses or constructs ethnic or other group identities.[131] The nature of the association between material culture and any form of 'ethnic consciousness' is a complex matter not easily reduced to a simple equation. Easier access to 'consciousness' is provided by language and how it is used.

The group consciousness of the Viking diaspora is perhaps best expressed in a term used of its common language, the *dǫnsk tunga* 'Danish tongue'. This phrase encapsulates the linguistic unity of Scandinavia, perhaps because Danish territory would be where any Scandinavian returning home from the south would first feel linguistically at home. The phrase is recorded in the early eleventh century in a poem by the Icelander, Sigvatr Þórðarson, celebrating the return from the European continent of Óláfr Haraldsson to take up the kingship of Norway.[132] It is also used in one version of an early saga about King Óláfr Tryggvason, probably composed just before 1200, though describing that king's Christian mission two centuries earlier.[133] The context is the difficulty of this mission since the foreign missionaries were ignorant of or inexperienced in using the *dǫnsk tunga*. Since the text credits Óláfr with converting Shetland, Orkney, Faroe, Iceland and Greenland, it has to be assumed that the phrase refers to the forms of language spoken in all of those places, and shows an awareness of their close kinship with the languages of the Scandinavian homeland. The common Scandinavian nature of *dǫnsk tunga* is clearly expressed by Snorri Sturluson, thirteenth-century Icelandic poet, historian and mythographer. In his *Edda*, a work of mythology and poetry, he twice uses the phrase, once specifically equating it with all the northlands where a common language is spoken (as he also does in *Heimskringla*), and once contrasting it with the languages spoken in *Saxland* (roughly the northern part of modern Germany) and England.[134] In England itself, it seems that the word *denisc* 'Danish' was used of all Scandinavian peoples, before usage gradually became more specific.[135]

In Chapter 17 of *Knýtlinga saga*, King Knútr is said to have been 'the most powerful king and the one with the most land *á danska tungu*'.[136] While this might not be surprising in a king who was from Denmark itself, this comment comes immediately after an account of all the places in which he ruled, namely Denmark, England, Norway and even (probably incorrectly) Scotland. This is then followed by an account of Knútr's pilgrimage to Rome, and his establishing of hostels along the way for all of those who went there who were *af danskri tungu*. Even more generous was the Danish king Eiríkr Sveinsson (d. 1103) who, on his pilgrimage to Rome, left money for all pilgrims who spoke *danska tungu* to be given free wine and lodging at the hostel in Lucca (ch. 74).[137]

The most revealing use of *dǫnsk tunga* is however in the thirteenth-century Icelandic laws, where knowledge of this language is a prerequisite of full participation in the legal system. Thus, someone who has not learned to speak it in childhood cannot be nominated as a member of the court until he has spent at least three years in Iceland.[138] Special inheritance rights are given to heirs who speak 'our language', whereas those whose languages are less familiar, such as Englishmen, have to fulfil more stringent criteria.[139] There are several other provisions in the laws which show a clear sense of a common tongue with 'foreigners' who are Danish, Swedish or Norwegian.[140] This sense of a common tongue appears to have lasted in Iceland at least until the end of the fourteenth century.[141]

There are other words expressing a Scandinavian group consciousness. An adjective frequently used in the sagas of Icelanders is *norrœnn*, which normally means 'Norwegian', as opposed to 'Icelandic', as in Chapter 6 of *Valla-Ljóts saga*, in which a group of men newly arrived in the north of Iceland on a ship are identified as *suma . . . íslenzka, en suma norrœna* 'some . . . Icelandic and some Norwegian'.[142] In this sense, the adjective is equivalent to the noun *austmaðr* 'person from the east', which in an Icelandic context usually means a Norwegian.[143] However, these meanings are contextual and, in episodes set outside Iceland, *norrœnn* can just mean 'Scandinavian' (or more probably 'West Scandinavian'). Thus, in Chapter 53 of *Egils saga*, the unit of the English king Aðalsteinn's army at the battle of Vínheiðr is described as including *allir norrœnir menn* 'all the Norse men' who were at the battle, and they are equipped with 'Norse' shields and armour.[144] This unit is led by Egill's brother Þórólfr, both of them of course Icelanders. Similarly, the noun *norrœna* 'Norse' is occasionally used of the common language, rather than of the specifically Norwegian language. This, too, is used in contexts where the commonality of Scandinavian contrasts with other languages. The German character Tyrkir switches from speaking *á þýzku* 'in German' to speaking *á norrœnu* 'in Norse' in Chapter 4 of *Grœnlendinga saga*, and in Chapter 64 of *Eyrbyggja saga* an Icelandic merchant's ship is driven to a curious place southwest of Ireland where everyone seems to be speaking Irish, except for their leader who addresses the arrivals *á norrœnu* 'in Norse' (and who is thought to have been an Icelander, though the saga narrator is cautious on this point).[145]

There is plenty of evidence for a recognition of different nationalities within the larger ethnic group consciousness. The adjective *norrœnn* was also borrowed into English, where it is used to contrast 'Norwegian' with 'Danish', at least in northern dialects, where they may have been more aware of these differences.[146] A well-known episode in *Eyrbyggja saga* (ch. 50), shows the arrival in Iceland of a merchant ship from Dublin, on which are both Irish and Hebridean people, *en fáir norrœnir* 'but few Norwegians'.[147] Here, the Icelandic context suggests the 'Norwegian' meaning for *norrœnn*, but it is also of interest to note that one of the Hebrideans, Þórgunna, has a Norse name, suggesting that in this episode the Hebrideans and the Irish may actually have been Norse-speaking Scandinavians based in those places. Similar distinctions between ethnicity and place of residence may lie behind certain place-names in England, for example several places with names of the type Irby/Ireby in the north-west, which are usually assumed to be named after a Hiberno-Norse settler rather than an actual Irishman.[148]

Linguistic distinctions are not always the same as ethnic distinctions either. The mid-twelfth-century author of the *First Grammatical Treatise* identifies himself as belonging to the *Íslendingar* 'Icelanders'; while most commonly referring to their and his language as *várt mál* 'our language', he also once calls it *dǫnsk tunga*.[149] Snorri Sturluson, in his history of the kings of Norway, makes an interesting observation on the place-names of Northumbria, in England, noting that they are given *á norrœna tungu* 'in the Norse tongue', having just noted that the region was densely populated by *Norðmenn* (possibly 'Scandinavians' in this instance) and that *Danir ok Norðmenn* 'Danes and (?)Norwegians' had harried and ruled there.[150] The multiplicity of terms used here suggests a more general awareness of difference within the overarching linguistic unity of the Scandinavians.

'A troubled relationship with host societies'

The depredations of Viking raiders in Britain and Ireland, and on the European continent, are well documented from contemporary sources and have been covered extensively in previous scholarship.[151] That the violence was not all one way is demonstrated by two important recent archaeological discoveries from the south of England, the mass graves from Ridgeway Hill, Dorset, and St John's College, Oxford. These represent two separate massacres of young Scandinavian men (interpreted as raiding parties) in the tenth or early eleventh centuries.[152] In both cases the Scandinavian origins of the dead were established through stable isotope analysis. While the historical context for the Ridgeway massacre is uncertain, it was tempting to see the Oxford bodies in the context of a massacre of Scandinavians which, according to the *Anglo-Saxon Chronicle*, took place in Oxford on St Brice's Day, 13 November 1002. [153] In this case we know that the perpetrators were acting on the orders of the English king, and that the victims were said to have been *denisc* 'Danish', but their age and gender, or even number, is less clear. However, the dating evidence, though not conclusive, tends to rule out the Oxford burials as being the result of the St Brice's Day massacre, so that they represent a different event. These three events together provide extraordinary evidence for the extent of violence towards Scandinavians in the south of England within a period of 50 years at most.

It is not clear when the inevitable violence of raiding armies (or retaliations against them) turns into a 'troubled relationship', nor how much violence was needed for Scandinavian settlers to establish themselves in regions that were already inhabited. There has for instance been a long-standing discussion about the fate of the indigenous (Pictish) inhabitants of the Northern Isles, with some scholars arguing that they experienced what could only be described as genocide, while others maintain that the evidence rather suggests processes of transition and acculturation than conflict.[154] Even in Iceland, where there was no established indigenous population, there were memories of conflict with some Irish clerics who were *in situ* when the first Scandinavians arrived, according to *Íslendingabók* (ch. 1).[155] These clerics, however, simply left rather than resisting the incomers because, as Christians, they did not wish to co-exist with heathens.

'A sense of co-responsibility with co-ethnic members in other countries'

As well as recognising the special rights of those who speak 'our language', as outlined above, the Icelandic laws that were in force until the late thirteenth century (known collectively as *Grágás*) regularly legislate for the deeds and needs of 'co-ethnic members' from other countries. There are provisions for who should prosecute the death of a 'foreigner from Norway or the realms of the king of Norway' who is married in Iceland; if a Dane or Swede or Norwegian should be killed in Iceland, it is anticipated that they might have kin in the country who could prosecute the case; and provision is also made for how to prosecute a killing which took place in one of those countries.[156] There are complex inheritance provisions for the eventualities that a man might die abroad, or that his heir might be abroad, with several additions and alterations to the laws, suggesting that there was sufficient to-ing and fro-ing of various kinds to make such changes necessary.[157] In some cases it is clear that Norwegians (that is people from the whole realm of the King of Norway, including the 'colonies') were granted privileges not granted to other foreigners.[158] The Norwegian laws, however, only make rather sparse provision for people from the diaspora, and then only Icelanders, who are to have the same rights to atonement for personal injury as the Norwegian class of men known as *hauldar* when they are in Norway on trading voyages (though the law also envisages the possibility that they might stay for more than three years, when different provisions apply).[159] There is also a provision, presumably applying to both Norwegians and Icelanders, that, if someone dies in Iceland, or at any point more than halfway between Norway and Iceland, then Icelandic inheritance laws apply.[160]

After Iceland had lost its independence to Norway, new laws were introduced, based on Norwegian laws but revised for Icelandic conditions. The text known as *Jónsbók* was adopted in Iceland in 1281, with parts of it still valid today.[161] This law code makes quite clear distinctions between Norway and the Norwegians on the one hand, and Iceland and the Icelanders on the other. The Norwegians are often referred to as *útlenzkr* 'foreign', while Iceland is *hér* 'here' and one of its inhabitants *várr landi* 'our countryman'.[162] Nevertheless, the law still anticipates the possibility that a Norwegian dying in Iceland may have closely related kin in Iceland to take charge of the inheritance, but since the provision envisages the inheritance being taken back to Norway, we may assume any such kin would be travelling with the deceased, perhaps on a merchant ship.[163] The provision also extends to Swedes and Danes, but those 'of all languages other than Norse [*danskri tungu*]' can only inherit if they are father, son or brother.

The earlier Icelandic laws of *Grágás* on the other hand make provision for people from quite a wide range of countries, most of which can be considered to be a part of the Viking diaspora, though some other countries where the links might be more of just a trading kind are also mentioned. Greenland and sometimes Norway and the Scottish Isles are presented as places where the law is essentially the same as in Iceland, except that there are some matters that can only be dealt with in one place or the other and, in the case of Norway, some differences are emphasised.[164] The laws even make provision for getting rid of an unwanted illegitimate child fathered by someone from Norway and its wider realm, including Shetland, Orkney, Faroe and Caithness, in which case the child can be handed over to someone from the same region as the father.[165] The equivalent provision in *Jónsbók* implies a rather different social and economic context.[166] Firstly, it omits Caithness, more importantly, there is no provision for the child to be sent to its father. Rather, the law requires the father to leave money behind for it and, if he does not, then the law stipulates that a letter is to be written *í þann kaupstað er sá maðr sigldi af* 'to that market town where that man sailed from', requiring various local officials to send the money. It seems that the kinds of situation which could give rise to such problems were by this period most likely to be in a trading context.

The earlier laws also present a wide picture of the places Icelanders might have been expected to go in Britain and Europe. One particularly complex provision in *Grágás* envisages who can vouch for the circumstances of killings that took place either in 'western Europe north of Valland [i.e. north of Normandy and the lower Seine region]' or 'south of the realm of the Danes', the guarantors being men who had been 'in the realm of the king of the English or the king of the Welsh or of the king of the Scots or the king of the Irish or the king of the Hebrideans'.[167]

'The possibility of a distinctive creative, enriching life in tolerant host countries'

Some diaspora theorists have emphasised the cultural consequences of diaspora, its enhancement of creativity and cultural production.[168] The most obvious example here is the literature of medieval Iceland. This literary production is very considerable in both quantity and chronological extent and can by no means entirely be attributed to diasporic processes. However, it is noticeable that in the twelfth and thirteenth centuries in particular there is extensive literary interchange between Iceland, Norway and Orkney, much of this based on cultural and historical traditions common to all three areas, which seems to have acted as a spur to some of the later literary developments in Iceland.[169] For example, the poem *Háttalykill*, conceived both as a key to metres and a chronological history of Scandinavian rulers, was composed in mid-twelfth-century Orkney in a collaboration between an Icelandic poet Hallr Þórarinsson and the Orcadian earl Rǫgnvaldr Kali Kolsson.[170] It not only provided a model for Snorri Sturluson's key to metres, the *Háttatal* section of his *Edda*, but is also an early example of the impulse to compose native history, which seems to have started in poetical form before the flowering of historical narratives in prose from the end of the twelfth century. The geographical and historical scope of *Háttalykill* also prefigured the Norwegian and Icelandic writing of Scandinavian history from the mid-twelfth century onwards.

In an earlier, pre-literate period, rulers of both Scandinavian and native origin in England, Scotland and Ireland employed poets to sing their praises using the very distinctive metres and diction of skaldic poetry.[171] This poetry had its origins in early Viking Age Norway but most, though by no means all, of these praise poets were Icelanders. Skaldic verse can be found in the Scandinavian homelands in runic inscriptions from the late tenth century to the fourteenth and in both Norwegian and Icelandic manuscripts of a variety of genres. It was the Icelanders in particular who were able to exploit their expertise in this kind of poetry as a form of cultural capital throughout the diaspora, and this topic will be explored further in Chapter 6.

While the spread of poetry throughout the diaspora was largely a matter of extending certain cultural practices to new audiences and arenas, the Viking Age sculpture of the British Isles is an example of a whole new cultural product that came into being in the creative crucible of the Viking diaspora. With its origins in the ecclesiastical sculpture of early Anglo-Saxon England, combined with various artistic and cultural traditions from the Scandinavian homelands, the sculpture of northern England in particular is not just an amalgamation of its main sources, but 'a creative manifestation of religious and cultural integration' with 'a strong intellectual component'.[172] Many of these monuments are crosses or cross-slabs, and thus clearly derived from insular models. However, there is also one type of monument, the hogback, which has no obvious direct predecessors in either Britain or Scandinavia, and is clearly a new form which arose in an Anglo-Scandinavian context, though it also spread to Scotland, and possibly Wales, and has been described as a 'Viking colonial monument'.[173] The 'colonial' aspect of hogbacks may be disputed. Though it is common to view Anglo-Scandinavian sculpture as an assertion of local, secular lordship, this is only one possible explanation and is difficult to demonstrate from the surviving evidence.[174] What is clear is that these monuments represent a distinctive creativity that was capable of producing new artistic forms, and the Christian nature of these secular monuments also suggests a relatively easy accommodation of the incomers (presumably after their conversion) with their 'tolerant host communities'.

Themes of the Viking diaspora

All of the above demonstrate that the 'Viking diaspora' is not simply a new name for the Viking Age migrations, as is sometimes the case in recent usage.[175] Rather it is a phenomenon that has its origins in these migrations, but transcends them in time, through linguistic and cultural contacts assiduously maintained throughout the Viking world for some centuries after the migrations. As Kalra *et al.* put it:

> If there is any single theme that emerges from a study of diaspora, it is that of its multi-locational qualities, or the interaction between homes and abroads which cannot be reduced to one place or another.[176]

'Diaspora' thus relates to the processes and results of migration and to how migrants themselves think and feel about their situation. An understanding of these processes requires the following questions to be addressed, though not all of them are easily answered: Did they migrate in a group? Did they migrate to a place where there were other migrants from their home? Did they take their own social and cultural customs with them or did they adopt new ones? Did they give their children traditional names and encourage them to speak the old language as well as the new one? Did they assimilate into the culture of their new homes and if so how many generations did that take? (How indeed does one define 'assimilation'?) Did they still have any connection with their homeland? If not, did they nevertheless have a sense of where they had come from and a memory of how things were there? And were they in touch with other migrants from the same homeland who had migrated somewhere else entirely? In other words, diaspora is about the migrant's sense of connectedness:

- to the homeland;
- to other migrants from the homeland;
- to other regions with migrants from the same homeland;
- to their new home.

Once the actual migrations had taken place, there remained webs and networks of connections between all of these groups, and that is what 'diaspora' refers to, an ongoing connectedness that came out of a migrational event or events, though with time these webs and networks might become narrower or more specialised.

The remaining chapters of this book will look at the implications of a diasporic framework for understanding the following important themes characteristic of the long Viking Age:

- gender and family;
- cults, beliefs and myths;
- networks and identities.

Migration and diaspora are processes which involve individuals, families and communities. The next chapter sharpens this focus by considering the significance of the linguistic, artefactual and natural evidence for understanding gender roles in migration and diaspora.

Notes

1 Hodder and Hutson 2003, 140.
2 E.g. Svanberg 2003, I.
3 Frei *et al.* 2009.
4 Gillham 2011, 12–19.
5 Helgason *et al.* 2000a, 2000b, 2001.
6 Gillham 2011, 13; Karlsson 2000, 234–8.
7 Thomas 2013.
8 Scully *et al.* 2013.
9 King and Jobling 2009.
10 Bowden *et al.* 2008; King and Jobling 2009, 356.
11 Bertelsen and Lamb 1993, 545; Arge 2005, 26; Sveinbjarnardóttir 2011, 261; Harrison 2013.
12 Larsen 2013c, 215; Barrett 2012a.
13 Barrett 2012b, 13–15; Larsen 2013c, 214–15.
14 Gunnarsson 2004; *ÍF* XVII, 326–7; *LLBH*, p. 62.
15 Høegsberg 2009, 98, 103–4.
16 Schoenfelder and Richards 2011, 157.
17 Schoenfelder and Richards 2011, 160.
18 Much of the following is based on Forster and Turner 2009; Ritchie 1984 is a useful introduction.
19 Baug 2011, 311.
20 Hunter *et al.* 2007, 139, 412–33; Dockrill *et al.* 2010, 12, 80–1, 297–301.
21 Owen and Lowe 1999, 170–3, 293; Forster 2009, 65; Dockrill *et al.* 2010, 93–4, 266–72; Batey *et al.* 2012, 207.
22 Larsen and Dyhrfjeld-Johnsen 2013, 194–204.
23 Larsen 2013a, 205–6.
24 Larsen 2013a, 206.
25 Baug 2011, 318, 332, 335–6.
26 Khvoshchinskaya 2007.
27 Clelland *et al.* 2009.
28 Hunter *et al.* 2007, 432; Forster 2009, 68; Dockrill *et al.* 2010, 272–80; Batey *et al.* 2012, 212–17.
29 Forster 2009, 65–8; Dockrill *et al.* 2010, 280–3.
30 Owen and Lowe 1999, 293.
31 Weber 1999; Crawford 1999, 247.
32 Emery and Morrison 1995, 41.
33 Sveinbjarnardóttir 2011, 155–6.
34 Baug 2011, 332.
35 Storemyr 2003.
36 Lane 2010.
37 Brown 2013a, 2013b.
38 Goodacre *et al.* 2005.
39 Emery and Morrison 1995, 41.
40 Barnes 2012a, 9–14.
41 Jansson 1987, 61–2; Barnes 2012a, 89.
42 Jesch 2008a.
43 Gade 2000.
44 Dumville 2008; Jorgensen 2010, 1–28.

45 The table in Mac Niocaill 1975, 40, demonstrates that the majority of the manuscripts of the Irish annals are from the fifteenth century or later, and none is earlier than the eleventh century, even though they are assumed to have been compiled from the eighth century onwards, if not earlier (Mac Niocaill 1975, 19).
46 Shepard 2008; Hraundal 2013, 2–3.
47 Dumville 2008, 359, 361.
48 Abrams 2012, 23.
49 Townend 2002, 189, 204.
50 Svane 1989.
51 Jakobsson 2005.
52 See e.g. Jesch 2010 on *Orkneyinga saga*.
53 Sveinsson 1958.
54 Tulinius 2005.
55 E.g. Liestøl 1929.
56 E.g. Jakobsson 2013; see also Boulhosa 2005, 41.
57 E.g. Hjaltalín 2009.
58 Perdikaris 1999.
59 Today the name Hålogaland is used in legal and ecclesiastical contexts, but politically and administratively Lofoten lies in the county of Nordland. For more about Hákon, see *SPSMA* I, cxciii–cxcv.
60 E.g. *ÍF* XXVI, 279; *Hkr*, p. 180.
61 Abram 2011, 127–42.
62 *ÍF* XXVI, 308–9, 324–5; *Hkr*, pp. 199, 212–13.
63 *ÍF* XXVIII, 254–5; *Hkr*, p. 699.
64 *NGL* I, 257–8; *ENL*, pp. 404–5.
65 *NGL* III, 222–3; *NMD*, pp. 364–7.
66 On both kings, see *SPSMA* I, cxcviii–cciv.
67 Bertelsen 1992.
68 *ÍF* II, 41; *CSI* I, 50.
69 *ÍF* VIII, 136–7; *CSI* I, 226.
70 *ÍF* VII, 73, 78; *CSI* II, 82, 85. This market is also mentioned in an eleventh-century context in *ÍF* XXVII, 212, *Hkr*, p. 392, along with a fleet of ships known as *Vágafloti*.
71 *ÍF* XIII, 182; *Þorsk*, p. 134.
72 Perdikaris 1999, 395–6.
73 Karlsson 2000, 106–10; Amundsen *et al.* 2005; Keller 2010, 2.
74 Sjøvold 1974, 302–3, 352.
75 Näsman and Roesdahl 2003, 290.
76 Johansen 2003, 28–9; Barrett *et al.* 2008, 857–8. Perdikaris 1999, 398–9 argues that the North Norwegian stockfish trade in the Viking Age was for the purposes of 'chieftainly prestige' rather than for 'monetary profit' as later on. See also Bertelsen 1992.
77 Naumann *et al.* 2014.
78 *ÍF* I, 127, 186, 244, 257, 272–3, 282, 332, 348–9, 376; *BoS*, 46, 69–70, 95, 99, 103–4, 107, 126, 130–1, 140.
79 *ÍF* I, 127, 186; *BoS*, pp. 46, 69–70.
80 *ÍF* I, 272; *BoS*, p. 103.
81 *ÍF* I, 273; *BoS*, p. 140; *NIP*, col. 389.
82 *KS*, pp. 12, 131–2; *KM*, pp. 98–9.
83 *OED*, 'diaspora'; Safran 2005; Abrams 2012, 19 n.6.
84 Sand 2010, esp. 188–9.
85 E.g. Kalra *et al.* 2005, 8–10; Abrams 2012, 19.

86 Mirdal and Ryynänen-Karjalainen 2004, 8.
87 Kalra *et al.* 2005, 3.
88 Clifford 1994, 306; see also Kenny 2013, 39.
89 Jesch 2008b explains the rationale of the network and appears to have been the first published work to suggest the usefulness of the term 'diaspora' to the Viking Age and its aftermath; see also Abrams 2012, 17.
90 Kristjánsdóttir 2011, 431.
91 Abrams 2012.
92 Abrams 2012, 19–20.
93 Abrams 2012, 21.
94 Abrams 2012, 38.
95 Cohen 2008, 161–2; see also Abrams 2012, 19; and a similar list in Safran 2005, 37.
96 Abrams 2012, 20.
97 *ÍF* V, 4; *CSI* V, 2. See also *Egils saga* ch. 25 (*ÍF* II, 65; *CSI* I, 61), *Gísla saga* ch. 1 (AM 445c version, *ÍF* VI, 3), *Grettis saga* ch. 3 (*ÍF* VII, 6; *CSI* II, 51). In *Kormáks saga* ch. 2 (*ÍF* VIII, 204–5; *CSI* I, 180), the tyrannous king is Haraldr's son Eiríkr *blóðøx* 'Blood-Axe' and in *Þorsteins saga hvíta* ch. 1 (*ÍF* XI, 3; *CSI* IV, 303), Þorsteinn goes to Iceland after the death of his father who had to move within Norway because of the tyranny of Earl Hákon. See also Boulhosa 2005, 172–3, 176, 228–32.
98 *ÍF* IV, 3–4, 11; *CSI* V, 131.
99 *ÍF* XXV, 3; *ThoG*, p. 19.
100 *ÍF* VIII, 22–36; *CSI* IV, 11–17. As well as Ingimundr, the sons of Haraldr's closest follower Rǫgnvaldr Mœrajarl end up in either Iceland or Orkney. See also Boulhosa 2005, 179–82, on positive attitudes to Norway in *Finnboga saga*.
101 *ÍF I* and *BoS*: *Sturlubók* version chs 29, 84, 85, 112, 134, 135, 139, 144, 149, 154, 156, 159, 161, 166, 225, 241, 267, 341, 344, 356, 359, 371, 378, 392 and similarly in other versions. Some, though not all, of these examples reflect the influence of the sagas on this text. As in the sagas of Icelanders, there are some settlers (e.g. chs 284, 309–10) who went to Iceland in a state of friendship with the Norwegian king.
102 *Hav*.
103 Turville-Petre 2001, 348–54.
104 *ÍF* XXXIV, 8; *OS*, pp. 138–9.
105 *RPC*, p. 59; see Franklin and Shepard 1996, 38–9.
106 *ASC*, p. 97; Lawson 2004, 82, 196.
107 See e.g. Barrett 2010, 291–5, though he argues against a strict demographic or economic determinism as causes of the Viking Age; also Dugmore *et al.* 2007b, 15; Abrams 2012, 28.
108 Both Abrams (2012, 28) and Cohen (2008, 83–104) use the term 'trade diaspora', though this involves stretching the concept in a new direction which is not necessarily helpful.
109 *ASC*, p. 48.
110 *ÍF* I, esp. 396; *BoS*, p. 146.
111 *ÍF* I, 4–7; *BoI*, p. 4.
112 *RPC*, p. 60.
113 This will be discussed further in ch. 6.
114 *ÍF* XXXIV, 3–8; *OS*, pp. 135–9.
115 Meulengracht Sørensen 1993, 219, 221.
116 Rowe 2005, 316–36, discusses these chapters and related texts in detail.
117 *TM*, pp. 1, 5, 55.
118 *Saxo*, p. 5.

119 Quinn *et al.* 2006, esp. 278, 294.
120 Lárusson 1939, 64. For a more cautious view, see Sigmundsson 2009, 227–8.
121 *ÍF I*, 32–3; *BoS*, p. 16.
122 E.g. *Gunnlaugs saga* ch. 5 (*ÍF* III, 64), *Bjarnar saga hítdœlakappa* ch. 2 (*ÍF* III, 113), *Laxdœla saga* ch. 40 (*ÍF* V, 114–15), *Hallfreðar saga* ch. 4 (*ÍF* VIII, 150), *Kormáks saga* ch. 18 (*ÍF* VIII, 260), *Njáls saga* ch. 2 (*ÍF* XII, 11).
123 *Mork*, pp. 171–9, 187–94, 206–8, 211–15, 219–20, 222–3, 243–52, 255–61.
124 Callow 2004, esp. 330–1; Jakobsson 2007.
125 Boulhosa 2005, 85–6.
126 Boulhosa 2005, 209–13.
127 *SPSMA* II, 575, and I, 954.
128 Jakobsson 2007, 148.
129 Pedersen 2004.
130 Pedersen 2004, 67.
131 The classic study is Jones 1997; for the Viking Age, see Stig Sørensen 2009 and Gräslund 2009, 137–9, both with further references.
132 *SPSMA* I, 555–6.
133 *ÍF* XXV, 271; *SOTOS*, p. 102.
134 *SnESkskm*, pp. 52, 80; *SnE*, pp. 107, 129; *ÍF* XXVI, 3; *Hkr*, p. 3.
135 Pons-Sanz 2013, 221–2.
136 *ÍF* XXXV, 123; *KnS*, p. 40.
137 *ÍF* XXXV, 220; *KnS*, p. 110.
138 *GrágásK* I, 38; *LEI* I, 53; see also *LEI* II, 388.
139 *GrágásK* I, 229; *GrágásSt*, pp. 74–5, 95–6; LEI II, 11, 244–5, 247.
140 *GrágásK* I, 172, 244, II, 198; *GrágásSt*, pp. 74–5, 95–6; *LEI* I, 160; II, 24, 214, 244–5.
141 Jakobsson 2007, 151; see *Flat* I, 296 and *SPSMA* II, 454–5; VII, 27–8, 566.
142 *ÍF* IX, 250, *CSI* IV, 140.
143 E.g. ch. 1 of *Ljósvetninga saga*, *ÍF* X, 5; *CSI* IV, 194; *ONP*, 'austmaðr'.
144 *ÍF* II, 136–7; *CSI* I, 96 translates this word as 'viking'.
145 *ÍF* IV, 178, 180, 252; *CSI* I, 22 (ch. 3), V, 216. Compare ch. 21 of *Laxdœla saga* (*ÍF* V, 54; *CSI* V, 27).
146 Pons-Sanz 2013, 221–2.
147 *ÍF* IV, 137; *CSI* V, 195.
148 Fellows-Jensen 1985, 16–17.
149 *FGT*, pp. 208–9, 212–13.
150 *ÍF* XXVI, 153; *Hkr*, p. 98.
151 E.g. Keynes 1997; Nelson 1997; Holman 2007; Dumville 2008; Ó Corráin 2008;
152 Pollard *et al.* 2012; Loe *et al.* 2014.
153 *ASC*, p. 86.
154 See for instance the contrasting interpretations of Smith 2001 and Bäcklund 2001.
155 *ÍF* I, 5. For a more detailed narrative of conflict between Christians and heathens in the earliest stages of the settlement of Iceland, see *Landnámabók* (*Sturlubók* chs 23–4, *Hauksbók* ch. 21), *ÍF* I, 59–65; *BoS*, pp. 25-6; Jesch 1987.
156 *GrágásK* I, 170; 172–4; *GrágásSt*, 387; *LEI* I, 158, 160, 233.
157 *GrágásK* I, 226–7, 236–40, II, 195–8; *GrágásSt*, pp. 70–2, 74–5, 77–9, 88, 95–6, 98–9, 101; *LEI* II, 8–9, 17–20, 210–14, 244–7. For discussion see Boulhosa 2005, 75–9.
158 *GrágásK* I, 226; *LEI* II, 8; Boulhosa 2005, 79.
159 *NGL* I, 71; *ENL*, 145; Boulhosa 2005, 82–3. See also *LEI* II, 210, n. 96, and Boulhosa 2005, 61, on the 'Norwegian perspective' of some of the Icelandic provisions.
160 *NGL* I, 210; *ENL*, 332.

161 *Jb*, pp. xi–xiii.
162 E.g. *Jb*, pp. 30–1, 124–5.
163 *Jb*, pp. 124–5.
164 *GrágásK* I, 205, 239–40, 249, II, 195–7; *GrágásSt*, 389; LEI I, 184, 235; II, 19–20, 27, 210–13.
165 *GrágásK* II, 25; *LEI* II, 49.
166 *Jb*, pp. 140–1.
167 *GrágásSt*, pp. 388–9; *LEI* I, 234.
168 E.g. Kalra *et al.* 2005, 13, 37.
169 Jesch 2009b.
170 *ÍF* XXXIV, 185; *OS*, p. 269; *SPSMA* III, forthcoming.
171 *SPSMA* I, cxlix–cli; Abrams 2012, 25.
172 Kopár 2012, xxiv.
173 Lang 1972–4; Lang 1984; Abrams 2012, 36; Kopár 2012, 197–8.
174 Hadley 2006, 221–2; Kopár 2012, 200–2.
175 E.g. Barrett 2010, 289.
176 Kalra *et al.* 2005, 17–18.

4

GENDER AND FAMILY

Gender

The importance of gender

The social anthropologist Thomas Hylland Eriksen noted that there is 'a fundamental difference between gender systems and other systems of human differentiation, including ethnicity'.[1] If there is to be 'societal continuity', then women cannot be 'expelled, exterminated or ignored' as members of other categories could. Since the whole concept of diaspora implies various kinds of continuity, not only 'societal', but also linguistic and cultural, then the Viking diaspora can only be fully understood when gender is taken into account. Gender represents 'an important dynamic aspect of the interrelations between people, their bodies, and society's conception and interpretation'.[2] Gender relations, both between people and at the societal level, are also dynamic in the sense that they vary according to stages of the life cycle. In different contexts, gender is differently 'experienced, expressed, and made recognizable'.[3] All of these are interesting topics that deserve further discussion. But, for understanding the diaspora, fundamentally, gender boils down to the difference between female and male and how this difference can be detected in the available evidence, so as to understand their various roles.

Such a fully gendered approach contrasts with the traditional lopsided emphasis of much writing about the Vikings, with its primary focus on males, especially when 'Vikings' have been defined according to their mainly masculine roles as pirates, robbers, seafarers, warriors and merchants. With the broader view of the Vikings that was characteristic of the late twentieth century came a greater interest in the role of women in the period, and the evidence for it, to redress the balance, and that interest has continued up to the present.[4] More recently, there has also been a new interest in constructions of masculinity in the Viking Age, though such an approach has tended to focus on seafarers, warriors and lordship, where such constructions are easier to demonstrate, and where male roles are otherwise still taken for granted.[5] However, the interest in 'women' *per se* has not been matched by work on 'men' *per se*, nor have studies of 'masculinity' been matched by those of 'femininity'.[6] It is time to collapse this lopsided distinction and attempt a more inclusive account.

A broader view of the Viking Age, and of the subsequent diaspora, requires a broader view of gender roles, and in particular a view that concentrates on the interactions of these roles, rather than their separateness. Diaspora results in a range of forms of 'disruption to existing social arrangements' and these need to be investigated in relation to their effects on gender roles.[7] Basic questions such as who participated in the diaspora, whether as migrants or in the subsequent interactions, have still not been fully explored. Were the Scandinavian emigrants equally male and female? Were the immigrants to places like Iceland equally male and female, and were they all equally Scandinavian? If not, what part did gender play in any differences, along with other factors such as social status and age?

A prerequisite for the continuation of the societies established by the migrants who arrived in the pristine landscapes discussed in Chapter 2 was the presence of women of child-bearing age to ensure that these societies survived for more than one generation. In the case of migration to inhabited landscapes, the question is more complicated, since immigrant women were not necessarily required to ensure subsequent generations if indigenous women could fulfil this role. In both cases, the interesting question is who these women who ensured subsequent generations were, where they came from, and what their relationships were, both to the male migrants and to the homeland societies. Thus, while it is important to consider both genders in relation to each other, it is also important to remember that, without the participation of women, the Viking Age would have remained a military and economic phenomenon, whereas the key to understanding the Viking diaspora is precisely in the role of women and the family.

Before considering the role of both genders in migration and diaspora, some basic questions of how to study gender in the past must be addressed, in particular those of identifying men and women in the surviving evidence. Viking Age archaeologists have been much exercised by this question, partly because so much of their evidence comes from burials, where establishing the sex of the occupant is not always a straightforward matter, nor is there much evidence to enable complex analyses of the relationship between sex and gender.[8] It is also a problem for archaeologists that the sexes appear not to be equally represented in the burial record, and the meaning of this imbalance can be difficult to determine.[9] The imbalance is not always in favour of men. In a survey of the archaeological material from Scandinavian Russia, Anne Stalsberg found that there was numerically more evidence for objects attributed to women than men.[10] This has however probably resulted from an interplay of the factors of identification and survival. The women's metal brooches, as discussed further below, seem to be unequivocal 'ethnic symbols' of Scandinavian women, whereas Scandinavian men have no direct equivalent, at least not in any material that would survive in large numbers. If the imbalance is sometimes in favour of women because of such factors, then it follows that an apparent imbalance in favour of men in other forms of evidence may also be due to factors of survival and identification.

Burials are not the only form of evidence for gender roles and relations. It is clear, for example, that men and women dressed differently. While few textiles remain, many aspects of how people dressed must remain conjecture, but how they dressed also influenced their personal adornment, for which there is more evidence, as will be discussed further below. Much of the evidence for dress and personal ornaments comes from graves, but the increasing use of metal detectors has led in recent years to large numbers of loose finds of metal ornaments. Careful study of these can reveal the ways in which they formed part of male and female dress.[11]

Another important form of evidence is that of personal names and the sources in which they occur. Unlike some modern names, Viking Age personal names are rarely, if ever, ambiguous as to the gender of the person who bore that name, and these provide a rich, and largely untapped, material for studying gender roles both in society as a whole and within the narrower context of the family.[12] In fact, we know the names of thousands of Viking Age individuals, from inscriptions, place-names and from texts. The first two of these sources do not perhaps tell us much about those people as individuals, while the texts may tell us more but present problems of interpretation as outlined in Chapter 1, but the overall patterns are certainly instructive.

The discussion of gender in the Viking diaspora below will concentrate on evidence, whether archaeological or linguistic, which can reliably be associated either with female humans (girls and women) or male humans (boys and men), whether those female or male associations are determined biologically, as in the case of genetic or osteological evidence, or socially, as in the case of dress and ornament, or names. The fact that some of the gender-specific evidence can occasionally be associated with the opposite gender (such as the occasional female grave with weapons in it, or the odd male name that is grammatically feminine) does not invalidate the overall approach, since it is clear that nothing is ever entirely black and white.

Gender, genes and migration

What the genetic evidence of modern populations (together with a limited amount of ancient DNA) tells us about past populations and their migrations has already been outlined in Chapter 2. To summarise, the evidence indicates that the predominantly Scandinavian-origin male settlers of the North Atlantic islands reproduced in part with female settlers also of Scandinavian origin, but in Iceland in larger part with female settlers whose genetic origins were in Britain and Ireland. In Britain itself, however, there seem to be equal proportions of male and female Scandinavian ancestry in those places in Scandinavian Scotland where it has been possible to measure these, although the proportion of Scandinavian ancestry in the population overall varies between the different places. Elsewhere (in north-west England and Ireland), the contribution of females to the Scandinavian ancestry of the population cannot be or has not been measured, but in north-west England at any rate, there seems to be evidence for a fairly substantial male Scandinavian contribution to the historical population. Other parts of the Viking world have either not been studied in this way or have not yet yielded convincing results.

This partial and problematic evidence cannot be the final word on the subject, though doubtless further refinements of methodologies in genetics will allow more and more subtle explanations in future. But however problematic the evidence for historical purposes, it does raise many interesting questions about the Scandinavian migrations of the Viking Age which encourage the student of those to return to other types of evidence. In particular, some of the things that genetic evidence cannot tell us can in fact be discovered from a reconsideration of other types of evidence in the light of what genetics *can* tell us.

Case study – north-west England

The evidence of genetics for the input of Scandinavians into the population of north-west England has been extensively explored in both scientific and popular publications.[13] It is suggested that something like 50 per cent of the historical (i.e. pre-industrial) population of areas such as Cheshire and West Lancashire have their ultimate origins in Norway. Since such studies as have been done focus only on the Y-chromosome, this percentage applies only to the male population and, indeed, for any individual only to their direct paternal line. The power of explanation of these results is therefore much more limited than one might gather from some of the media reporting of the results. The most glaring question that remains unanswered by the Y-chromosome studies is that of the role of women. Did the Vikings simply pass through and leave a lot of babies behind, fathered on indigenous women, with or without their consent? Or was there a migration of families, including women and children? And if so, were those women also from Scandinavia or from somewhere else? The evidence of language sheds some light on these questions and the linguistic and cultural contexts within which any genetic interactions took place reveal a broader picture of what actually happened.

Language in the form of speech is a fundamental characteristic of human beings and their identities.[14] In normal circumstances, individuals acquire language at a very young age from the people around them, especially their immediate family. Most cultures have a concept of 'the mother tongue' since it is usually with its mother that the infant has the closest contact at the stage of its life when it is beginning to acquire language and, because of this close contact, the infant is most likely to learn its mother's language first. When people have acquired that language, they generally speak it for the rest of their lives, particularly if it is also the language of their father, and the rest of their family and community. However, some people can and do learn other languages, and can become equally fluent in two or more languages if they use them regularly, while others make a complete switch from one language to another, and yet other people end up in a situation where they speak two or more languages, but none of them quite fluently. A lot depends on the circumstances in which, and the age at which, the languages are learned, the situations in which individuals need to use one or the other language, and the extent to which individuals have contact with other speakers of the language(s) they use. These circumstances can be studied in modern speech communities, but it is difficult to identify the circumstances that pertained in the Viking Age. Nevertheless, the possibilities need to be kept in mind when considering the evidence.

The evidence, mainly from place-names (which will be discussed in more detail below), suggests that the Old Norse language was spoken in north-west England in the tenth century and for some unknowable time afterwards, on a substantial scale. This immediately puts into question any hypothesis of a purely genetic contribution by male Vikings and indicates the presence of women speaking the language. These women could have come from the Viking homelands such as Norway themselves, but other explanations are conceivable. For example, male Vikings who came to north-west England could have settled down there with women whom they taught to speak Old Norse and whom they persuaded to speak it with their children, creating these Norse-speaking communities. This could have happened, for example, if a male Viking had kidnapped and enslaved a girl in Ireland or the Hebrides and then taken her to north-west England, along with a group of other Vikings who had done the same thing. In such a situation it is likely that she would have had to learn Old Norse as well as her native Gaelic to function in this group. But a lot may have depended on whether or not she remained his slave, whether or not any Norse-speaking women were present at all, and also on whether or not the men in such a community spoke Gaelic as well as Norse.

That analogous situations did happen is suggested by a well-known story from *Laxdœla saga* (chs 12–13).[15] The thirteenth-century saga describes how, in the tenth century, the Icelandic chieftain Hǫskuldr buys a beautiful slave girl at a market in Scandinavia and takes her home to Iceland. She appears to be mute and refuses to speak to anyone. When Hǫskuldr brings his new slave home, his wife sarcastically points out that he must have spoken to her at some point, and indeed she gives birth to his child some months later. Hǫskuldr finds out that she can in fact speak a few years later when he overhears her speaking to her small son. It turns out that she is an Irish princess and the son, Óláfr, becomes a heroic figure in the saga. It is not specified at this point in what language Melkorka spoke to the child, or to Hǫskuldr, but later (ch. 20) she sends Óláfr off to visit his Irish kin, stating that she has prepared him for this journey by teaching him Irish.[16] And, as there is no indication in the saga that Hǫskuldr had been to Ireland nor spoke any Irish, we assume from the reported conversations that Melkorka had also learned Old Norse, in spite of her long initial silence.

A similar situation in north-west England could have resulted in a Norse-speaking community, though if it happened on a large scale we would rather expect a bilingual community with the resources to maintain the Gaelic language as well as functioning in Old Norse. There is some evidence for this in a few place-names which show just this linguistic interaction between Norse and Gaelic speakers, although the evidence does not indicate widespread speaking of Gaelic. There are no names which are entirely Gaelic (in the way that there are names which are entirely Norse), that is, in which both elements of the name (not including personal name specifics) are Gaelic words. The most common Gaelic word in the place-names of this region is *ǽrgi*, a word whose meaning is not entirely certain but which probably refers to a hut or building used in summer pasturing arrangements, or a 'shieling', as it is often translated.[17] However, this word had by then been borrowed into Old Norse and is therefore not in itself evidence for the speaking of Gaelic. The Viking settlers learned it somewhere in the Irish Sea region and found it useful even though they already had their own word for summer pasturing arrangements (*setr*), found in names like Arnside or Hawkshead, both in Cumbria.[18] So when the element *ǽrgi* is compounded with an Old Norse personal name, as in Anglezark (*Óláfr*) or Grimsargh (*Grímr*), both in Lancashire, such place-names are in fact more likely to be evidence for Old Norse speech.[19] Further evidence for the naturalisation of this word in Old Norse is that it appears with Old Norse grammar (i.e. the dative plural form) in Arkholme in Lancashire.[20]

Occasionally the *ǽrgi*-word is compounded with a Gaelic personal name, as in Goosnargh (the personal name in question is *Gussān*) in Lancashire, which might in theory be taken as evidence for Gaelic speech since then both elements are of Gaelic origin.[21] By comparison, the name Becconsall in Lancashire, which consists of the Gaelic personal name *Beccān* and the Old Norse element *haugr* 'mound' is evidence of Norse linguistic usage, not Gaelic, since the language of the place-name is determined by the second, generic, element.[22] The mound may have belonged to, or commemorated, a person with an Irish name, who may or may not have spoken Norse, Gaelic or both. But the people who gave the mound its name used the Norse language in identifying it. In this way, even a name like Goosnargh, made up of two Gaelic elements, could be given in a Norse-speaking community, as the generic is an Old Norse word, albeit of Gaelic origin. Therefore, rather than suggesting a large Gaelic-speaking population accompanying the Viking settlers to north-west England, these examples are more likely to reveal traces of such contact before they got there.

When the migrants (speaking Norse or Gaelic or both) arrived in north-west England, they found there an indigenous population speaking Old English. This too suggests interesting questions. What would the linguistic situation be if a lot of Scandinavian-speaking males arrived and settled down with local, English-speaking women? Would they teach their wives to speak Old Norse and thus form a Norse-speaking community? This is surely less likely than in the case of any Gaelic-speaking wives, given that the English women would be on their home territory and still plugged into their family networks and local cultures. Even if Viking settlement was in areas that were sparsely or not at all inhabited by the locals, any such communities would not be too far away from English-speaking ones. It is therefore difficult to believe in completely Norse-speaking communities in this context unless the women were predominantly native speakers of that language, although bilingual communities do seem possible. Whereas the place-name evidence for communities speaking both Gaelic and Norse is not strong, the situation is rather different for Old English and Old Norse. One reason is that Old English and Old Norse were closely related languages, perhaps even mutually intelligible, facilitating everyday interactions without the need for interpreters or extensive bilingualism.[23] Indeed it has been argued that 'Late Anglo-Saxon England was . . . a bilingual society in which both Old English and Old Norse were spoken', by individuals who were not necessarily bilingual themselves.[24]

In summary, for there to have been any extensive use of the Old Norse language in the communities of north-west England, there must have been a fair number of women whose first, and most natural, language was Old Norse. Any establishment of Norse-speaking communities, who would give their localities names in Old Norse, would require a substantial migration of Norse speakers, including women and children.[25] Although women are not especially visible in either the historical records or the archaeological evidence, they are in fact the key to understanding what really happened in north-west England in the Viking Age, and elsewhere. The genetic evidence reveals only that there was a lot of Viking sperm about. The evidence of language, especially in the form of place-names, provides a fuller picture of the community. It indirectly shows the crucial role of women in maintaining the language of the homeland.

Visible gender – clothing and accoutrements

The separate but complementary roles of men and women can also be deduced from the ways in which their gender was made visible. In most cases, a naked adult human is immediately identifiable as male or female. The distinctive body shapes and parts may also be visible through some types of clothing. As in many other cultures, Viking Age men and women were additionally distinguished from each other by the clothing they wore, the ways in which they adorned themselves and their clothing, and any tools or other accoutrements they might carry about, as well as the ways in which they wore their hair and, in the case of men, whether or not they let their facial hair grow. These gender distinctions appear to have been quite strictly policed in Scandinavian societies. Thus, the medieval Icelandic laws in *Grágás* prescribe a penalty of lesser outlawry not only for women wearing 'men's clothing, or whatever male fashion they adopt in order to be different' but also for men who 'adopt women's fashion, whatever form it takes'.[26] Another version of the same law penalises women who cut their hair short or carry weapons.[27] The provision that anyone can bring such a case if they wish suggests that this policing of gender-appropriate clothing is done by the community as a whole.

Unfortunately, the laws do not specify, even in outline, what the essential difference between men's and women's clothing was, and we may wonder to what extent such a law was open to different interpretations, manipulations and possible malicious prosecutions. There are some hints, however, in a well-known episode in *Laxdœla saga* (chs 34–5), in which the heroine Guðrún divorces her husband in order to marry a new one, both of them using their respective partners' gender-inappropriate clothing as pretexts for their divorces.[28] Guðrún makes her husband a shirt with a low-cut neckline. What shape and depth is required to make this garment feminine is not entirely clear, though it appears that baring the nipples is one criterion. Guðrún's lover Þórðr in his turn divorces his wife Auðr for wearing men's clothing which is described in somewhat more detail. She wore breeches, with the added details that these had some kind of triangular insert (perhaps a codpiece) and that their lower legs were wound around with bands down to her shoes. After the divorce, Auðr puts on some breeches and rides to take revenge on her ex-husband by stabbing him in both nipples with a knife, thus breaking the other legal taboo of women bearing arms. The emphasis on male nipples in both parts of this story is remarkable, suggesting that breasts and nipples were a strong marker of femininity and thus an embarrassment to men. This might imply that women could or did wear garments that showed off their breasts, either by baring them, or at least by showing them through a thin garment, but there is little other concrete evidence for this. And in a famous episode in *Vínland* from Chapter 11 of *Eiríks saga rauða*, the heavily pregnant Freydís pulls one of her breasts out from her clothing, in order to terrify the indigenous people by slapping it with a sword, suggesting that it was in fact covered up, though easily accessible.[29]

The reconstruction of Viking Age clothing is difficult, since the textiles from which it is mostly made do not survive well archaeologically, and any contemporary depictions are usually too stylised to be useful. Reconstructions are thus based on either earlier or later evidence, as well as careful interpretation of some key texts.[30] However, in the absence of much information about clothing, quite a lot can be discovered about gender identities through the jewellery and other accoutrements worn by or associated with women and men. Based primarily on burial finds, the two genders have been most closely associated with their jewellery (women), or their weapons (men), though these may not have been everyday items in either case. While jewellery in general and oval brooches in particular are more closely associated with women, men also made use of certain types of brooch both as fasteners and for display, and other metalwork dress items, such as belt-slides and strap-ends, as well as beads and bone pins, can be counted as male jewellery, found both in burials and as stray finds.[31] As already suggested, weapons could also be considered as bodily adornment. Both jewellery and weapons provide some further insights into gender roles in the Viking Age.

Case study – oval brooches

When *Women in the Viking Age* was published in 1991, the illustration for the front cover, an oval brooch from Ågerup (Sjælland, Denmark) more or less chose itself.[32] The oval brooch, sometimes misleadingly known as a 'tortoise' (or, even worse, 'tortoiseshell') brooch from its perceived shape, though tortoises are generally less oval, is the one object most closely associated with women in the Viking Age. The Ågerup brooch had the additional merit of being decorated with four small female heads, so the gendered associations of the object were practical, symbolic and illustrative. Oval brooches were normally worn in pairs (usually, though not always, matching) as part of the distinctive costume worn only by Scandinavian women at that period, and are thus considered a marker of Scandinavianness as well as of femaleness. In fact, the ways in which they do (or do not) mark gender, status and ethnicity are much more complicated than the simplistic view which sees them as *the* badge of a Viking woman. Moreover, their widespread, if selective, use throughout time and space is very revealing about many aspects of the Viking diaspora.

Women in the Viking Age wore a variety of brooches of different types and functions. Although there was undoubtedly much variation, the typical Scandinavian woman's outfit in the ninth and tenth centuries consisted of several layers of clothing in different materials and fastened by different types of brooch.[33] Innermost was a thin shift, usually of linen, fastened at the neck by a small disc or ring brooch. Over this was a woollen strap-dress which reached the armpits, and which was suspended from two shoulder straps fastened on the woman's front with a pair of oval brooches, usually made of gilded copper alloy.[34] Other brooches, especially those of trefoil, lozenge and equal-armed shape, were mainly used for fastening outer garments such as a shawl or cloak, and there were doubtless other layers to the costume which did not require decorative metal fastenings.[35]

Although by no means the only possible attire for women in the Viking Age, the strap-dress held up by oval brooches was nevertheless widespread in both time and space, judging from the distribution of those oval brooches. Because of their construction, oval brooches could only be worn in one way and had only one possible function, which was to hold up this type of dress. Their distribution is thus a strong indicator, not only of this fashion, but of its Scandinavianness.[36] In 1985, Ingmar Jansson attempted to summarise the numbers of oval brooches known then, which came to at least 3,600.[37] Of these, the two largest groupings were from Sweden and Norway, with around 1,500 each. Denmark was far behind, with only about 120 examples, compared for example to Russia, from where some 160 examples were known. Jansson also counted around 75 from Britain and Ireland, and 35 from Iceland. All of these numbers now need revision upwards, as oval brooches continue to be found, not least through the activities of metal-detectorists. Danish examples now (counted slightly differently) number close to 400, though they remain low compared to Norway and Sweden, undoubtedly because this type of dress went out of fashion earlier in Denmark than elsewhere.[38] The relatively small number of oval brooches found in England may be due to its strong links with and hence emulation of Denmark, although recent finds may change this picture. There are now oval brooches from a single burial at Adwick-le-Street (Yorkshire), found in 2001, a Viking Age cemetery at Cumwhitton (Cumbria), found in 2004, and several fragmentary stray finds from Norfolk and Yorkshire, so that the most recent total amounted to 15.[39] In Iceland, Michèle Hayeur Smith recently counted 44 oval brooches (including 14 pairs), though some of these are now lost.[40]

The question of where such large numbers of items were produced, and acquired by their wearers, still needs further investigation, though some preliminary studies have produced suggestive results. Their long period of use, varying quality and wide geographical distribution indicate that oval brooches could be produced on both small and large scales, in both local and urban workshops. Søren Sindbæk's study of some early types produced in Ribe and Birka reveals a paradox that, despite the wide distribution of these types even then, they have distinct styles which reflect strong civic identities of the craftspeople who produced them in those towns.[41] Yet such origin-specific types were accepted by consumers across Scandinavia, showing that wide-ranging distribution networks were already in place. The overall pattern seems to have changed in the ninth century, when the site-specific traditions were abandoned in favour of common types that were produced equally in a wide range of urban centres, marking a move towards 'international production patterns'.[42] As a result of this international production, certain types, in particular the most common ones known as P37 and P51, are 'highly standardized and serially produced', with the latter, for example, providing 10 out of the 15 brooches found in England.[43] They are also characteristic of the Norse graves in an ethnically mixed cemetery in Shestovitsa, in Russia.[44] Apart from Denmark, where oval brooches were already going out of fashion, P51 brooches, dated to the late ninth and tenth centuries, predominate as the Viking diaspora extended out of the Scandinavian homelands. Thus, P51 brooches comprise 40 per cent of all oval brooches known from Norway, 65 per cent of those from Iceland and 60 per cent of those from Scandinavian Russia.[45] Such patterns show the processes by which a cultural phenomenon that was well-established in the homeland (in Norway oval brooches are attested from before the Viking Age) extends across the diaspora. The diaspora not only created an opportunity for the spread of this phenomenon, but also a need to establish a more standardised common identity across it. The question then is, what aspect of identity do the brooches represent, apart from their clear association with female gender?

Apart from their practical function as dress fasteners, it is clear that oval brooches meant or symbolised something, both to the wearer and to those with whom she interacted. It is thus relevant to ask in what contexts the strap-dress and oval brooches were worn. Since most of the finds of oval brooches are from burials, it is possible that they represent some kind of 'best dress' in which women were buried, perhaps even a specific burial outfit. If so, the meaning of the oval brooches was something understood primarily by those who prepared and attended the funeral. The significance of the brooches would then be restricted to within the family, perhaps as an heirloom, a marker of relationships with earlier generations. This seems to be supported by the fact that some oval brooches appear to be quite antique when put in the grave.[46] But even so, such a brooch must have had some kind of use before it was buried, that is, that it was worn rather than just kept for several generations, and then it might have had a different meaning.

If the brooches were regularly worn, as they seem to have been, then the question is what they meant when worn, whether on a daily basis or for special occasions. In the diaspora, it is assumed that they signify the Scandinavianness, or at least a

Scandinavian affiliation, of the wearer, particularly in those contexts, such as England or Russia, where there were also indigenous inhabitants from whom the wearer might have wished to distinguish herself. In the homelands, however, or those parts of the diaspora with no competing indigenous inhabitants, such as Iceland, the brooches must have had some other meaning. Certainly, the craftsmanship and metals involved in making an oval brooch show that the wearer had sufficient wealth to acquire such jewellery, and they could therefore indicate her social rank or status. However, this rank is not of the highest. Oval brooches are most often made of copper alloy, gilded, and thus of a metal which resembles gold but is much cheaper to produce, suggesting an aspirant status.[47] The oval brooches are also often seen by modern scholars as the symbol of a free woman, the female equivalent, and wife, of the 'free farmer' beloved of Scandinavian historians. Another suggestion is that they are the mark of a married woman.[48] These categories do overlap, as there is plenty of evidence for a layer of society consisting of free and prosperous male householders, who would normally each have a wife who herself had a position of standing both in the household and the wider community.[49] Even in the diaspora, it is likely that use of oval brooches indicates a similar position in the local community, rather than, or perhaps as well as, being a badge of ethnicity. In places like England, Ireland and Russia, oval brooches could at the same time have an inward meaning (social position) to the Norse-speaking community, and an outward meaning (Scandinavianness) to neighbouring indigenous communities. In diasporic contexts such as Iceland, where there were no neighbouring indigenes, but the immigrants came from different parts of the homeland, or even elsewhere, the oval brooch could rather signify the woman's kin-group or ancestral community.[50] We cannot be certain what, probably multiple, meanings the oval brooches had, but there is no doubt that they served to establish a common female identity across a large part of the Viking diaspora.

Study of other types of mainly female jewellery found in England provides evidence for its being used to indicate a Scandinavian identity, as shown by the work of Jane Kershaw on metal-detectorist and other finds recorded by the Portable Antiquities Scheme. In a detailed analysis of these, Kershaw was able to show that the different kinds of metal brooch in this material could be classified either as 'Scandinavian' or 'Anglo-Scandinavian'. The former indicate 'the presence of significant numbers of Scandinavian women, dressed in a traditional Scandinavian manner', while the latter 'are best understood as a response on behalf of indigenous women and probably also women of Scandinavian descent to the influx of new Scandinavian dress styles'.[51] However, unlike the oval brooches, which do seem to have some symbolic meaning regarding the woman's social or economic status, the other brooches, which form the majority of Kershaw's material, signal a more amorphous 'Scandinavian cultural affiliation' which is quite difficult to pin down in detail.[52]

Case study – swords

The male equivalent to the woman buried with jewellery, especially oval brooches, is the man buried with one or more weapons, especially a sword. There are many parallels in the distribution and dating of oval brooches and swords around the Viking world.[53] Just as women were buried with other jewellery as well as oval brooches, so the weapons found in male graves could include spears, axes, shields and arrows as well as swords, and it was quite usual for the grave to contain more than one of these. Swords and axes were the most common (and often occur together), as shown by an older study of North-Norwegian graves which found that, out of 230 finds, 123 included swords and 144 included axes.[54]

Although large numbers of Viking Age swords have been found in both the Scandinavian homelands and elsewhere, there is also significant local variation. A survey by Fedir Androshchuk counted at least 1040 finds from Norway, 644 from Sweden and 70 from Denmark.[55] Outside Scandinavia, he counted 61 from England, 90 from Ireland, 108 from present-day Russia and Ukraine but only 20 from Iceland.[56] Androshchuk's numbers are in many cases based on older sources and the present-day number is undoubtedly higher, as finds continue to be made.[57] For example, while finds of complete swords are rare, Viking Age pommels are regularly recorded by the Portable Antiquities Scheme in England.[58] These large numbers and the wide distribution of swords support Androshchuk's conclusions that sword-finds do not indicate a warrior aristocracy, as is sometimes suggested, but rather that 'Viking Age swords were used by all the socially active male inhabitants'.[59] This suggests a flat social structure, rather than a hierarchical one, though the key lies in the precise meaning of the term 'socially active', and just who these men were is difficult to define. In a forthcoming study of mainly Swedish evidence, Androshchuk concludes that the distribution pattern of Viking Age swords and rune-stones is often strikingly similar.[60] Although the dates of the swords and rune-stones are somewhat different, there is other evidence of social continuity in those regions of central Sweden he studies. This social continuity is represented by the class of free farmers, or *búendr*, a class wider than one that could accurately be described as 'elite', and the same class as postulated for the wearers of oval brooches – Androshchuk also notes similarities in the distribution of oval brooches and swords.

A sword was an expensive weapon and a valuable gift, as shown in skaldic poetry, and could hardly have been borne by just anyone.[61] Certainly, some swords were richly decorated – these would most likely have been the weapons of a small elite.[62] Yet the large numbers of mostly less richly decorated swords hardly suggest a narrow elite for the ownership of swords in general. The existence in some graves of swords which were hardly usable suggests they had symbolic as well as practical value.[63] In this as in other things there does seem to be a clear parallel between these two badges of masculinity and femininity, the sword and the oval brooch, and it is likely that they represented the male and female members of the same social group.[64] This group is probably not quite as small as the 'sub-group' of a 'small section of the population' envisaged by some archaeologists.[65] But neither is it representative of all Vikings, but rather a group of some wealth, standing and aspiration.

However, unlike oval brooches, which seem to be a fairly standardised pan-diaspora phenomenon, a detailed study of swords reveals rather variation and inter-regional contacts.[66] Icelandic swords are generally of Norwegian type, as are most of the swords from England and Ireland and even Denmark, whereas swords from the

East are most closely paralleled in Sweden. This discrepancy no doubt arises from the fact that swords could not be mass-produced in the same way as oval brooches. There are also regional differences between weapon burials and brooch burials which suggest that their symbolism could be different in different places. Dawn Hadley has argued that the difference between the relatively small number of female graves of Scandinavian type and the much larger number of better-equipped male graves of Scandinavian type in England arises from a particular political context. Rather than 'the simple transference to England of normal Scandinavian funerary practices' this preponderance of particular types of male graves suggests that 'burial strategies were deliberately modified in response to the circumstances of conquest and the processes of making claims to land and status in newly-occupied territories'.[67] According to Hadley, these male graves both constructed ancestral memories and mediated the processes of conquest, while female graves played no part in these. Hadley finds a similar masculine bias in the tenth-century funerary sculpture with its range of warrior-images which also 'conveyed messages about the status and attributes of the person for whom they were commissioned', though presumably to a wider audience than the graves.[68] However, as already noted, there is variation in the numerical discrepancies between male and female graves in different parts of the Viking world, and these discrepancies are not always easy to explain.

A better explanation might be that, unlike oval brooches, swords *per se* (or indeed weapons of any kind) are not a uniquely Scandinavian artefact – obviously, since Scandinavians were not the only perpetrators of violence. Viking Age warriors could acquire weapons and armour of foreign manufacture when victorious on the battlefield, and presumably also by trade. Most swords were composite artefacts, as different parts could be replaced or repaired as needed. Indeed, many 'Viking' swords had blades manufactured in the Frankish Empire, though Scandinavian smiths were able to copy them, and in both cases the hilts were most commonly of Scandinavian manufacture.[69] Aidan Walsh identified 10 of the 90 'Viking' swords from Ireland as 'of Anglo-Saxon type', even though they were found in Viking contexts and were likely to have been used by Vikings.[70] Thus, although parallel to oval brooches in many ways, swords could not carry the same meaning of Scandinavian ethnicity as oval brooches did, though, like oval brooches, they did indicate social standing.

However, the significance of a sword to indicate an individual's gender (and therefore potential warrior status) remains. This is clearly demonstrated by an Icelandic weapon burial from Öndverðarnes, of an individual aged 18–20.[71] Osteological analysis has revealed that this individual was male but suffered from reduced or absent testosterone, meaning that he may have had characteristics which would suggest either a woman or an immature male, such as a delicate bone structure, lack of facial hair and breast development. Despite these characteristics, he was buried as a fully adult male, with a warrior kit of sword, spearhead, shield, knife and bone pin.

Gender, individuals and names

Presumably the individual from Öndverðarnes also had a male name to go with his gender identity. Scandinavians had a rich and varied system of naming people, based on the same principles as those that governed name-giving in the other Germanic languages, and attested from before and during the Viking Age in runic inscriptions.[72] Names were created from originally meaningful semantic elements and could be either monothematic (made up of only one element) or dithematic (made up of two elements).[73] Given that Old Norse, like the other Germanic languages, had grammatical gender, the general rule was that names were formed from nouns with either masculine or feminine grammatical gender, and that these should match the gender of the person to whom the name was applied. In the case of the dithematic names, the second element (or deuterotheme) gives the gender of the whole name, and the grammatical gender of the first element (the prototheme) is irrelevant. As a result, the personal names that we find in large numbers in Old Norse sources can readily be identified with the gender of the persons that bore them, and therefore provide a basis for the discussion of gender roles. While it is difficult to generalise about personal names, since they are subject to changing fashion and both regional and chronological variation, the extensive corpora of names raise interesting questions about gender and gender relations in the Viking diaspora in a number of ways.

Occasionally, the names are ambiguous, not because they were intended to be so, but because we lack full information about them. It has already been mentioned that there is a small class of male names which have feminine grammatical gender. A classic example is the name *Sturla*, borne by several members of the powerful Sturlung family in twelfth- and thirteenth-century Iceland (including the father of Snorri Sturluson). This name was originally a byname, possibly derived from the verb *sturla* 'to confuse, disturb', and inflected according to the rules governing weak feminine nouns.[74] There appears to be a similarly constructed name on the well-known eleventh-century rune-stone (E 2) found in St Paul's churchyard, London.[75] The incomplete inscription records that **: k-na : let : legia : stin : þensi : auk : tuki :** 'Ginna had this stone laid, and Tóki'. The ending on *Ginna* is grammatically feminine, and the question is whether it is here a woman's name, which is known but quite rare, or a man's name, unknown, but created on the same principles as *Sturla*. In Scandinavian runic inscriptions, it is rare, though not unheard of, for a female name to precede a male name in the commemorative formula, which might suggest the male name. On the other hand, women can be named first, particularly in cases where the commissioners are a woman and her son(s) commemorating her husband and his/their father, especially if we suspect that the sons were underage at the time. This possibility, allied with the recorded existence of *Ginna* as a female name, combine to suggest that the female interpretation is the most likely for this inscription.

We should not draw too hasty conclusions from the numerical imbalance of names in the surviving sources. The Viking Age rune-stones of Scandinavia record the names of several thousands of people, both those who were being commemorated by these monuments and their family members (or occasionally others) who commissioned the monuments in their memory. There is no doubt that there is a gender imbalance in the people mentioned in this way. Taking the whole

Scandinavian corpus of Viking Age (mainly tenth- and eleventh-century) commemorative stones together, only a small number of women are mentioned. Birgit Sawyer, in a wide-ranging study of the complete inscriptions of the rune-stone corpus, established that approximately 4 per cent commemorate women, while 3.5 per cent commemorate both men and women. In nearly 12 per cent of inscriptions, women act as commissioners of the monument on their own, and a further 15 per cent involve women acting with men.[76] But these are figures for the commissioners and commemorated of the monuments only, yet other people are also mentioned, usually other family members. While no one has counted the numbers of women mentioned in the overall corpus, a study of the largest sub-corpus, memorials from Uppland in Sweden, has shown that while just under half of these inscriptions include mention of women as either commemorated or commissioners, only about 15 per cent of the total number of people mentioned in these inscriptions are women.[77] Thus, even when women are included in the inscriptions, this is frequently in the context of just one woman and several men who are named. There are various explanations for this imbalance. Birgit Sawyer's suggestion that these percentages reflect inheritance patterns has some merit, assuming that the inscriptions are inheritance documents as she maintains, though this is likely to be only part of the story.[78] An alternative suggestion, put forward by Anne-Sofie Gräslund, is that this dearth of females is evidence for female infanticide, leading to fewer daughters.[79] This hypothesis depends however on the inscriptions providing a random sample of the population, which is clearly not the case, particularly since Uppland, with around 15 per cent mention of females, actually has a higher percentage than other rune-stone areas.[80]

A similar situation pertains in *Landnámabók*, that extensive catalogue of the settlement of Iceland, in which far fewer women are mentioned than men, although, interestingly, 13 of its over 400 land-claimants are said to have been female. Like the runic inscriptions, this is a corpus of a large number of personal names, often with little information about these people beyond their names. Of the approximately 3,500 people named in the text, only about 13 per cent are women, not dissimilar to the proportion of females mentioned in the Upplandic runic inscriptions, as discussed above. This relative paucity of female names in *Landnámabók* has similarly led to suggestions of female infanticide as one cause of this numerical imbalance.[81]

While the overall demographic patterns of the Viking Age and subsequent centuries are still obscure, and may well have included a high sex ratio (as discussed further below), it is more difficult to accept such conclusions when based merely on the imbalance of numbers in imperfect sources. As Chris Callow wrote recently of *Landnámabók*, 'neither the total number of women identified as female primary colonists nor the ratio of men to women can be taken to represent any kind of historical reality for the first generations of Norse settlers in Iceland'.[82] Both *Landnámabók* and the runic inscriptions are about memory, and in particular a collective memory of individuals. The choice of individuals to be remembered in these ways clearly favoured men. Women were underenumerated in life (e.g. as commissioners of the runic monuments) and undercommemorated in death (e.g. as the commemorated of the runic monuments, or in the genealogies of *Landnámabók*), and there are a number of reasons for this including patriarchal attitudes, inheritance laws or lack of information. However, there is no simple correlation between numbers of women named in these biased sources and numbers of women on the ground at the time.

This underrepresentation of women can also be found in burials across the Viking world, as already discussed, in the personal names used in the coining of place-names, in skaldic poetry and in the sagas. This consistent pattern across a range of evidence cannot easily be linked to demography but is more likely to indicate a society in which women were substantially (but not entirely) absent from public forms of expression, be those place-names or poems, monuments or memorial documents. The more private roles of women make little or no appearance in these kinds of evidence and are probably best deduced from the archaeology of domestic space, though there it is generally not possible to link the evidence to specific individuals.

More promising for understanding the social and cultural role of women is the study of name-giving practices and how they change over time. As noted above, the names given to Scandinavian children were governed by the same principles as used in the other Germanic languages, but each linguistic region had its own name-giving fashions, and the Scandinavians also innovated in their name-giving practices, in ways that suggest that girls were often given more unusual or innovative names, while the naming of boys was more likely to be quite traditional.[83] The reasons for this may be related to the importance of males to inheritance, where clear lines needed to be drawn to the past. Again, this reinforces the impression gained from the runic memorials, for instance, that men maintained their links with and loyalty to their family of birth throughout their lives, while women's kin loyalties were not so closely tied to their family of birth, as they were expected to marry and join a new family.[84]

Gender in poetry and myth

Kennings, while also known in other poetic traditions, are a highly developed and characteristic feature of skaldic poetry. While not strictly speaking names, kennings behave quite like names in that they denote men and women, and in the ways that they represent them. Structurally, they are formed on the same principles and there is overlap in the elements from which kennings for men and women are created, just as there is overlap in the elements used for men's and women's names. But alongside these structural similarities, there is also a keen sense of differentiation, based on both grammatical gender and personal roles and accoutrements.

Kennings have been defined as 'a noun phrase combining two nouns in a genitival relationship (or a compound noun with an implicit genitival relationship between two distinct elements) . . . used by a poet as a substitute for a noun referent'.[85] Whether a phrase or a compound, a kenning consists of a base-word and a determinant – the base-word may have no relationship with the referent, and it is the determinant which creates that relationship. A classic example is when a camel is called a 'ship of the desert'. A camel is quite unlike a ship (the base-word), but the determinant 'desert' helps to make the connection, in that a camel is, like a ship, a mode of transport, but one appropriate to the desert. Kennings cover a wide range of referents both animate and inanimate, including men and women, and the system is too complex to explain here in detail. However, kennings for people are relatively simple to understand, and those which are compound nouns are particularly similar in structure to personal names. The determinant of any person-kenning behaves just like the deuterotheme in a personal name, in that its grammatical gender must match the sex of the person being referred to.

People-kennings are summarised in Snorri Sturluson's *Edda*, although the actual practice of poets is much wider-ranging than that suggested there.[86] In Snorri's rather simplified account, men and women are compared to trees, which then form the base-words of the kennings for them. Given that some Old Norse tree-words are grammatically masculine, and some are grammatically feminine, these words can then be used in the appropriate kennings. Thus, in man-kennings, the base-word can be *askr* 'ash' or *hlynr* 'maple' or *reynir* 'rowan', or a more general word associated with trees such as *viðr* 'wood' or *lundr* 'grove'. Woman-kennings, on the other hand, will use a grammatically feminine tree-name like *selja* 'willow'.[87] In this way, male and female are defined as belonging to the same category, both are trees, but nevertheless distinguished by the grammatical gender which mirrors their sex. This differentiation is then further established by the determinants linked to these base-words. According to Snorri, men are referred to by their actions and their possessions, which include *farar* 'journeys', *athafnar* 'undertakings', *vígar* 'killings', *sæfarar* 'sea-journeys', *veiðar* 'huntings', *vápn* 'weapons', *skip* 'ships', and *fé* 'wealth'. Women are also referred to by both their actions and their possessions, though these are rather different. Firstly, they are distinguished by *kvenbúnaðr* 'women's accoutrements', which are *gull* 'gold', *gimsteinar* 'gems' and *glersteinar* 'beads'. But woman is also associated with *ǫl* 'ale', *vín* 'wine' and other drinks 'which she serves or gives', as well as *ǫlgagn* 'ale-containers' and other equipment she needs in order to serve these drinks. There are many other types of kennings for both men and women, but these present the clearest picture of Viking Age attitudes to gender.

The skaldic poetry in which we find these kennings is highly stylised, esoteric and quite far removed from daily life, and the actual use of kennings is often much more complex than the simple account above. But it is clear that kennings are one rather particular realisation of the parameters for what it meant to be male and female in the Viking Age. These parameters extended well beyond the world of poetry and are also realised in other evidence, notably the burials discussed above, in which there is the same strong association between women and jewellery and men and weapons. While kennings present an idealised world, the oval brooches, swords and names discussed above belonged to real people, those who inhabited the Scandinavian homelands and the regions of the diaspora.

No discussion of gender can ignore the fact that any culture's perception of gender is mediated through stories, myths and beliefs, which may or may not reflect 'real' life closely. While the kennings just discussed present a fairly narrow view of the associations and roles of men and women, a broader look at mythology shows a wider range of attitudes to gender divisions, though still with many of the same concerns.

The story of how the god Þórr retrieved his hammer from the giants, as told in the Eddic poem *Þrymskviða*, reinforces the rigidity of gender boundaries precisely by allowing the gods to cross and thus stretch them.[88] In this well-known myth, the giant Þrymr, who has stolen Þórr's all-important hammer, with which he protects both gods and humans, promises to give it back if he can have the goddess Freyja as his wife. When Freyja understandably refuses to marry a giant, the ambiguous figure Loki suggests that Þórr dress up as Freyja, while Loki will accompany him dressed as a serving-maid. Despite Þórr's resistance, as he is worried he will be thought effeminate, they do so, and successfully deceive the giant. An important point in the story is that Þrymr is too stupid to recognise that 'Freyja' is not what she seems. The giant sees only the feminine accoutrements of a bridal headdress, a necklace, keys, a long dress and jewellery, and does not recognise the significance of a 'bride' who puts away a whole ox, eight salmon and three casks of mead in addition to the delicacies meant for the women. In the end, Þórr's masculinity (which was never really in doubt, except to the giant) is restored along with his hammer, and the giants destroyed.

Case study – valkyries

Although there are many aspects of Old Norse mythology which seem designed to perpetuate and reinforce gender divisions, some aspects are more ambiguous. A persistent question about the Viking Age, particularly emanating from the multifarious amateur scholars who populate the internet, is whether the culture had women warriors. The questioners rarely specify what exactly they mean by 'woman warrior' though if they mean a fully armed and trained warrior who regularly participated in combat alongside and on an equal footing with similarly equipped men, then the answer is almost certainly 'no'. Nevertheless, there are some archaeological examples of women buried with weapons, and there are also literary examples of women bearing and using arms in different contexts, some quite realistic, others more fantastical.[89] What these examples show is that people in the Viking Age and its aftermath were perfectly capable of imagining women as warriors, or at least as imagining them carrying and using weapons, whether this occurred in real life or not. Doubtless it did occur in real life, since human beings are capable of most things, whether or not it is considered 'normal' for them to do so, but the strong emphasis on gender distinctions in Viking Age society already outlined suggests that it did not happen very often.

However, it is precisely these strong gender divisions which make imagining those who do cross them so interesting to a culture that otherwise polices the distinctions tightly. One example of the way in which gender roles can be collapsed in the Viking imagination is the valkyrie (Old Norse *valkyrja* lit. 'chooser of the slain'), a mythological being with widespread currency in the Viking diaspora, since she appears in art, archaeology and a wide range of literary texts. Valkyries were defined by Snorri Sturluson as figures

> whose job is to serve in Valhall, bringing drink and looking after the table-ware and the drinking vessels . . . These are called valkyries. Óðinn sends them to every battle, they choose who is to die and allot victory.[90]

Snorri does not specify that they bear arms, though this might be deduced from the second aspect of their role. The figure is further developed in Old Norse literature, often with a strong romantic angle involving love between a valkyrie and a male warrior, and Snorri himself testifies to the enduring popularity of this figure in the thirteenth century.[91] But the two functions of valkyries identified by Snorri have their origins in the Viking Age, where they can be traced in the material culture, as well as in both Eddic and skaldic poetry.

The first of the functions identified by Snorri can be seen in pictorial representations. Some of the earliest examples are scenes on several Viking Age (eighth- to eleventh-century) picture stones from the Baltic island of Gotland, which show female figures proferring drinking horns to warriors about to enter a building that can be interpreted as Valhǫll, the mythological hall of the slain.[92] This image is repeated in art, particularly metalwork, but also sculpture, from across the Viking world.[93] Even the scene of Mary Magdalene at the Crucifixion on the tenth-century Gosforth cross in Cumbria has been seen by most scholars as owing something to this visual tradition.[94]

Images of armed female figures are less common. However, an exciting metal detectorist discovery from Hårby on the island of Fyn in Denmark in 2012 appears to represent just such a figure.[95] The small (3.5 cm) silver figurine has long hair, knotted into a pony-tail, and is wearing a long dress with what looks like an apron, while carrying a shield in her left hand and holding a drawn sword in her right. This is a very rare, perhaps unique, visual representation of a female figure with a sword. When valkyries are represented in literary texts as being armed, their weapons of choice tend to be a spear and protective armour, but not swords, as in Stanza 15 of the Eddic poem *Helgakviða Hundingsbana I.*[96] There, the valkyrie Sigrún arrives with some of her mates in the middle of Helgi's battle with Hundingr, and they are said to have helmets, blood-spattered mailcoats, and shiny spears. The figurine from Hårby has none of these attributes.

However, a closer study of skaldic poetry does show an occasional association of valkyries with swords, though mostly indirectly, in kennings. In a large number of kennings, battle is figured as a storm, or tumult, or din, or meeting, which is further determined by a term for weapons, or for a valkyrie, either her name, or a further kenning for her.[97] Thus, simple kennings call battle *þing hrings* 'assembly of the sword' or *gný Gunnar* 'din of Gunnr', with Gunnr a valkyrie-name.[98] A more complex battle-kenning such as *snerra geirvífa* 'onslaught of the spear-women' incorporates a valkyrie-kenning with her traditional attribute of the spear.[99] Occasionally, such valkyrie-kennings do associate them with swords, though most often embedded in more complex kennings where the direct association of valkyries and swords is less clear. Thus, a kenning for ravens or eagles figures them as the *gjóðir dísar dolgeisu* 'ospreys of the woman of battle-fire', in which 'battle-fire' is an embedded kenning for sword.[100] But in the same way, valkyries can be associated with other weapons such as bows, or just with weapon-points in general.[101] Thus, the skaldic evidence suggests the possibility that any female figure associated with weapons of any kind can be interpreted as a valkyrie.

Clearly, many people in the Viking Age were interested in valkyries, and such an interest can be quite clearly demonstrated in late Viking Age England.[102] Indeed they seem to have been one aspect of a widespread ideology that actually got warriors out and fighting. In themselves, though, these figures from art and literature do not yet prove the case for warrior women, or for any association between women and the weapons of war other than as an aspect of myth and ideology. It would be difficult in any case to pin down any such association in real life, though burials, despite their heavily symbolic nature, might give a clue. We know that warriors were men, and we know that many men were buried with weapons. This does not make every man buried with weapons into a warrior, as discussed above, but the association is widespread and consistent. Thus, if there were a burial or two which appeared to be female but which included weapons, we might be justified in concluding that women could also be warriors. A recent study of a small and problematic sample of Scandinavian-type burials in England by Shane McLeod has noted the presence of weapons (strictly speaking, weapon parts) in some burials that have been osteologically sexed as female, though these consist only of one woman buried with an axe and 'sword pieces' and another buried with a sword hilt grip. [103] McLeod is more concerned to demonstrate a higher female participation in the early Viking Age settlement of eastern England than to speculate on the reasons why such women might have been buried with ostensibly 'male' grave-goods, so it is difficult to know what conclusions he would draw from this limited evidence. There are a few other examples of women buried with weapons, though their number is not great, and some of the 'weapons' could be interpreted just as readily as practical tools for everyday life.[104] At the same time, a male burial with oval brooches from Claughton Hall, near Garstang in Lancashire, is explained as a husband buried with a memento of his wife.[105] Most of these burials are problematic in some way, many of them antiquarian finds with inadequate contexts. Nevertheless, it seems likely that occasionally people could be buried with items more commonly associated with the opposite gender (and of course there are many grave-goods that are gender-neutral). The reasons for these very occasional deviations from the norm are difficult to discern from this distance, and could be various, including the items belonging to someone else in a double or mass burial, or the finds from two adjacent burials becoming mixed, or even people being buried with items belonging to their (deceased?) partner. But that the very few women buried with weapons were warrior women in life seems the least likely explanation of all.

Family in the Viking diaspora

The sex ratio in early Scandinavia

As already discussed, the paucity of women in a variety of sources has led to suggestions of the widespread practice of preferential female infanticide and a high sex ratio (in favour of males), based on a hypothesis that the underrepresentation of women in the sources reflects their underrepresentation in life. Carol Clover even developed this argument to explain the whole phenomenon of the Viking Age, arguing that the very success of Viking raiders and traders led to a preference for sons over daughters.[106]

While Clover's argument was based largely on written sources and cross-cultural comparisons, Nancy Wicker attempted to marshal the archaeological evidence more thoroughly.[107] In particular, she went beyond the purely numerical assessment of male vs. female graves (with all their problems of identification) to look for 'direct archaeological evidence of infanticide' and found only 'scattered archaeological traces of infants who were not buried with an adult-type burial rite', the interpretation of which is 'problematic'. Nevertheless, she concluded that 'the testimony of hundreds of graves seen within the context of the literary and historical evidence is a potent source of information'.[108] But in the end, Wicker is more cautious than Clover in attributing the causes of the Viking Age to this practice, arguing only that female infanticide contributes to explaining 'the scarcity of archaeological remains of women in some Scandinavian regions from the late Iron Age, c. AD 600, through the end of the saga period, c. AD 1300', rather than using it to explain what happened in the Viking Age.

Clover's was not the only attempt to explain the causes of the Viking Age through gender relations: a recent study by James Barrett similarly calls on demographic reasons for Viking Age expansion. Having dismissed various other possible causes of the Viking Age, he accepts Clover's and Wicker's arguments for female infanticide, and then develops the argument in terms of what he calls 'the marriage imperative'. His argument is similar to Clover's except that he sees the preference for sons over daughters in Scandinavia as resulting from the 'increasingly militaristic competition associated with Scandinavian state formation'.[109] Young men were driven abroad by the need to acquire a 'bride-price', the wherewithal to settle down. Barrett's argument does not, however, consider the question of what happened later, when these young men got their brides and finally settled down. Yet it is precisely when this process happened that the 'Viking expansion' can legitimately be called a 'diaspora', particularly since it is clear that not all the families established in this way were in the Scandinavian homelands, but many were rather overseas.

The extensive presence of insular treasure, from Britain and Ireland, in Norwegian Viking Age female graves suggests that many young men did take some of their plundered wealth back to Norwegian brides.[110] A possible example of this (though perhaps not from a grave, as its provenance is unknown other than that it came from Norway) is the insular copper reliquary with a runic inscription indicating female ownership: **ranuaik a kistu þąsa** 'Rannveig owns this casket' (N 541).[111] But of course we cannot rule out the possibility that Rannveig herself travelled west to acquire the casket, or that she bought it from someone who had been in the west. Of the large range of insular material in Norwegian graves in general, two kinds of such potential 'bride-wealth' stand out. Horse harness mounts reused as jewellery are characteristic of the graves of a few rich women in particular, while items of insular metalwork from ecclesiastical contexts remodelled as female jewellery are more widespread, with over a hundred and fifty finds, containing over three hundred items, known in 1998, a number that has certainly increased since then.[112] Overall, the distribution of insular items in general suggests a gendered aspect to these imports: around 85 per cent of graves with insular imports are female graves, and the implication is that they were brought back to Norway as loot from raids in the Irish Sea region in particular.[113] Egon Wamers' study of this material ruled out extensive trading of these items as an explanation, so it must be assumed that the looters took them home to their brides as gifts, though of course we cannot exclude the possibility that mothers, sisters or daughters benefited in this way too.

Language in the diasporic family

But many other Vikings either never returned home, establishing their families elsewhere in the Viking world, or if they did return, then they may later have chosen to take their families to one of the new settlements of the diaspora. The genetic and linguistic evidence for family migrations, particularly to the west, has already been discussed, along with the evidence for the fact that families established elsewhere may then have migrated even further west, for example from somewhere in Britain or Ireland to Iceland, as discussed in Chapter 2, above. The genetics appear to confirm a model in which a substantial proportion of the female founding population of Iceland had its origins in Britain and Ireland. This model receives support from a detailed statistical analysis of *Landnámabók* by Grethe Jacobsen.[114] This study examined the proportions of reported males and females, correlated with their social and marital status, and ethnicity, within each of the first five generations of Icelanders, making use of *Landnámabók*'s extensive descending genealogies as well as its records of founding settlers. The sex ratio of males to females is indeed high in the first generation, but improves significantly after that. There are also notable differences between those settlers said to have come from Norway, whose wives are more frequently reported, and those who were of Norwegian origin but came from the British Isles, whose wives are less frequently reported. The author concludes that 'men of lower social status and/or who came from the British Isles are more likely to have unreported wives or mistresses who mothered their reported children'.[115] According to Jacobsen, these unreported mothers in the first generation were of Celtic origin and possibly of slave status, and this under-reporting is therefore a conscious omission of such women from Icelandic genealogies. Whether this reflects a bias on the part of the compilers of *Landnámabók*, or in Icelandic society more generally, is not clear from the evidence, nor whether the bias is ethnic or social, though if most Celtic women were slaves it could be both. The uneven sex ratio reported by *Landnámabók* is thus not necessarily an effect of bias against women *per se*, as argued by other scholars (as discussed above), but only against certain kinds of women.[116]

This model would explain why the bias (as reflected in the sex ratio) diminishes after the generation of the founding settlers. Presumably the children born to these women were accepted into their paternal family and future generations would be recorded as full members of these families, as in the example from *Laxdœla saga* discussed above. Jacobsen's argument does depend on a fairly quick and extensive settlement of Iceland, a model that is supported by some archaeologists, while others argue for a more complex and drawn-out process.[117] Another aspect of the argument that needs further discussion are the linguistic and cultural consequences. A relatively quick assimilation of the children born to Celtic/slave mothers into their paternal families of Norwegian origin raises once again the question of language. Did the Celtic mothers continue to speak their own language with their children, or with other women in the same situation? Did their children become bilingual, and if so, then how? To what extent were Celtic languages spoken in Iceland and by whom? *Landnámabók* also mentions male slaves with Celtic names – were there therefore communities of Celtic-speakers? The evidence is remarkably sparse and difficult to interpret.

An obvious, if complex, indicator is that of personal names. While these are not in any way a necessary indication of ethnicity, there is no doubt that personal names of other linguistic origin generally enter a language because of some kind of contact and are therefore evidence of that contact. While both *Landnámabók* and the sagas mention a number of slaves and settlers with Celtic names, of more relevance is the prevalence or otherwise of names of Celtic origin given to people born in Iceland after the initial settlement. The hero of probably the greatest of Icelandic sagas, Njáll of *Njáls saga*, has a Celtic name though no obvious Celtic family connections, as does Kormákr of *Kormáks saga*. Another well-known saga-hero, Kjartan in *Laxdœla saga*, also has an Irish name, though this is less unexpected, since he is the son of Óláfr *pái* 'Peacock' and grandson of the Irish princess Melkorka, whose story has already been discussed above. Óláfr grew up bilingual and was clearly proud of his Irish heritage, and indeed the saga (ch. 28) explicitly states that he named his son after his own grandfather Mýrkjartan.[118] However, Óláfr's other six children all have Norse names.

The number of Icelanders later than the settler generation who have Celtic names and are mentioned in *Landnámabók* is not particularly large. One example appears to bear out Jacobsen's thesis.[119] A man called Vilbaldr is said to have come to Iceland from Ireland, no wife is mentioned, and he has three children, a son and daughter with the Irish names Bjólan and Bjollok, and a further son with the

Norse name Ǫlvir. But elsewhere in the text, both Vilbaldr and his brother are said to be the sons of a man with an Irish name, and Vilbaldr itself may be an English name.[120] Vilbaldr's brother, meanwhile, had the Norse name of Áskell (though with a Celtic byname, *hnokkan*). There is no mention of Áskell's wife, but his only named son has the Norse name of Ásmundr. The ethnicity of this family is obviously complex and it is not clear where the Norse element comes in, though a likely explanation is that it was from the unnamed mother of Vilbaldr and Áskell, potentially a Norse-speaking woman married to an Irishman in Ireland, grandson of a king. At this point it is worth recollecting the genetic evidence, which shows that a proportion of the male ancestry (albeit smaller than the female ancestry) of Icelanders is also from Britain or Ireland. Not all of this Celtic DNA need have come from slaves, and it may not always have been just the Celtic female ancestors that went unrecorded in the genealogies.

Similarly, Erpr, a slave freed by the great female settler Auðr, was the son of a Scottish chieftain and the grandson (on his mother's side) of an Irish king. In Iceland, he was given land by Auðr, and had a family of five sons and one daughter, of whom only one son had the Celtic name of Dufnall.[121] Again, no wife is mentioned, and we are left to wonder whether she was also a freed slave and what language she spoke. Erpr and his mother had in fact served Auðr's family for some time before he arrived in Iceland, so it is quite likely that he was already a Norse-speaker by then, and he may even have forgotten his mother tongue. It is sometimes suggested that his name is Pictish, but its occurrence in the early Eddic poem *Hamðismál* (sts 8, 14, 28) suggests it could have been Norse and, if so, it may have been given to him by his Norse owners.[122]

A few names of Celtic origin became relatively popular in later generations in Iceland, such as Kjallakr, Kjartan, Koðrán, Konáll, all masculine names, as feminine personal names of Celtic origin are vanishingly rare.[123] The diasporic origins of these names are suggested by the fact that they do not appear to have been borne by any Norwegians.[124] What little evidence we have suggests that it was the father who chose the child's name, and these names might be further evidence that some male Icelanders had both Celtic origins and the desire to celebrate those origins in naming their children. Once the names were established in the anthroponymicon, then they were of course available to anyone. A complicating factor in the other direction is that not everyone with a Norse name necessarily had Norwegian origins – both slaves and others living in Iceland might have been given, or chosen to take, Norse names in order to function better in a Norse-speaking society, as many immigrants do today.

If the genetic evidence for the proportion of people of Celtic origin in the Icelandic founding population is anywhere near correct, then one might reasonably expect the Icelandic language to show evidence of this contact. As well as the relatively small number of personal names, there are a number of loan-words suggestive of such contact. A study by Helgi Guðmundsson analysed 46 proposed words borrowed into the various forms of Old West Norse (Norwegian, Faroese, Icelandic and insular Norse) from Gaelic.[125] This number is not large, and becomes even smaller if examined closely. Fourteen of the words do not occur in Icelandic, but only in one or more of the other languages, while ten occur in Icelandic and only one other language (six in Faroese, two in Norwegian and two in insular Norse). Of the 32 words recorded in Icelandic, some are found only in the post-medieval language, which leaves open the possibility that they were later borrowings. Others are recorded in rather special contexts which suggest that they were learned or nonce-borrowings, and not established in the language. Snorri Sturluson, for example, seems fond of showing off his knowledge of words like *bjannak* 'blessing' and *díar* 'gods', and several other words are recorded only in the word-lists of his *Edda*.[126] Other words relate specifically to episodes involving people of Celtic origin, such as *minnþak*, a concoction of flour and butter prepared by some Irish slaves, referred to in *Landnámabók* to explain the origin of the place-name Minþakseyri.[127]

After close consideration, there seems to be only a handful of words that were firmly established in the Icelandic language in the medieval period and these are rather a mixed bunch. The three most frequently recorded words are *bagall*, *gjalt* and *kapall*.[128] The most commonly recorded is *bagall* 'crozier, bishop's staff', a word ultimately derived from Latin *baculum*.[129] This word appears in the well-known passage from *Íslendingabók* which relates the items (Irish books, bells and croziers) that the *papar*, defined by the text as Irish Christians, left behind to be discovered by the first Scandinavians when they arrived in Iceland.[130] The next most frequent word is *gjalt* which in prose occurs only in the phrase *verða at gjalti* 'to go mad, insane', cp. Middle Irish *geilt* 'a panic-stricken fugitive from battle'.[131] An early borrowing of this might be suggested by its occurrence in Stanza 129 of *Hávamál*, which explains that warriors who look upwards in battle become *gialti glíkir* 'like a *geilt*'.[132] The third most common word is *kapall* 'pack-horse', an interesting borrowing into a language which did not lack words for horses.[133] But apart from three relatively early examples of the compound *kapalhestr* '*kapall*-horse' (the redundancy of which suggests the first element was not fully understood), most of the records of *kapall* are from the fifteenth century or later.

Despite this interesting range of loan-words, the evidence does not suggest a thoroughgoing influence of Gaelic on the Old Norse language of Iceland. None of the words discussed above suggest the linguistic influence of a slave class speaking Gaelic, let alone a gendered subgroup of that. Some of the less common words discussed by Helgi Guðmundsson do relate more closely to daily life and may reflect such influence, though it is hard to pin them down to the settlement period. The evidence for Gaelic influence on Faroese is slightly stronger, particularly when we take into account the almost total absence of medieval texts from the Faroes, with the suggested loan-words recorded either in place-names or the modern dialect. Their relatively substantial survival in this way suggests a more extensive influence in the settlement period. This stronger Gaelic connection is what we would expect from the geographical proximity of the Faroes to Britain and Ireland, and also from other evidence of Celtic cultural contacts.[134] Other than names and loan-words, very little research has been undertaken on the possible influence of the Gaelic language on Old West Norse, and Icelandic in particular. It may be that such influence could be detected in aspects of morphology, syntax or pronunciation, but this must await further research.

Both the linguistic and onomastic evidence suggest rather that the bulk of Norse–Celtic linguistic and personal contact took place in Britain and Ireland, and perhaps the Faroes, rather than Iceland. The word *kross* 'cross', ultimately from Latin *crux*, seems to have found its way from Gaelic into both English and all forms of Norse, and it may have entered the former through the latter.[135] Most likely the influence travelled along multiple routes (see further discussion of its use on the Manx rune-stones, below). *Kapall* (also from Latin, this time *caballus*) is also found in Middle English, as for example when Chaucer uses it to characterise the speech of the northern students in the *Reeve's Tale*; it too is likely to have been borrowed along different routes in different languages.[136] A word like *ǽrgi*, a loan-word from Gaelic found in Norse contexts in England, and in the Faroes, is thoroughly assimilated into the Norse speech of those regions but did not make its way to Iceland.[137]

In general, the linguistic evidence is most easily explained by a situation in which people of Celtic origin went to Iceland already speaking Norse before they arrived there, having learned it through contact with Norse-speakers in the insular world, perhaps the same Norse-speakers who then took them to Iceland. If they still remembered their mother tongue by the time they got to Iceland, there is little evidence to show that they used it to any great extent there. This is not very different from the situation postulated for the north-west of England (above). But it should be stressed that the influence of Gaelic on Old Norse is an underresearched topic, and a more thorough study might well come up with different results.

Case study – the Isle of Man

While we surmise that most people lived in households that consisted of more than just the nuclear family, the importance of this particular unit is clear from a range of evidence, not least the memorial rune-stones of the late Viking Age which most frequently celebrate the commissioner's nearest and dearest. The inscriptions on the 30-odd rune-stones from the Isle of Man provide an illuminating example of this kind of family feeling in a diasporic context, while also further highlighting issues of language.[138]

These memorials are dated art-historically to the middle or end of the tenth century and are remarkable for their number in such a small island (at a time when the whole of Norway did not have twice that number), particularly if we include some 14 or so carved stone monuments in the same tradition, but without runic inscriptions. Both types of memorials make use of local elements in their style and form, combining crosses and cross-slabs in the artistic traditions of the Irish Sea region with Scandinavian decorative, iconographical and textual elements. Where there are inscriptions, these are written in Scandinavian runes and in the Old Norse language.[139] The monuments most frequently describe themselves as *kross* 'cross', a word borrowed into Old Norse from Gaelic, as compared to the majority of

Scandinavian runic memorials which almost without exception described themselves as *steinn* 'stone'. Like the monuments themselves, the society indicated by the personal names of those commissioning them and commemorated in them appears to have been quite mixed. This onomastic blending, combined with the imperfect grammar of some of the inscriptions, suggesting a bilingual community, and the relatively high proportion of inscriptions that mention women, all provide insights into the diasporic family in one small part of the Viking world.

In all, there are up to 48 persons named in 21 memorial inscriptions from the Isle of Man.[140] However, some of the names appear more than once, and if these multiples are removed we are left with 41 distinct names, representing somewhere between 41 and 48 individuals.[141] Of these 41 distinct names, 24 are masculine Norse names, 5 are feminine Norse names, 9 are masculine Gaelic names, and 3 are feminine Gaelic names.[142] While the number of feminine names is not large, it is remarkable that 7, or all but 1, of them are of the person being commemorated in the inscription: 4 wives (to which we can add an unnamed wife on Maughold V, IM MM175), 2 (foster-)mothers and 1 daughter. The eighth named one is a rune carver. In comparison with the rest of the Viking world, this is a high proportion of commemorated women, in fact it amounts to half of the inscriptions sufficiently well preserved to reveal who was being commemorated. Bearing in mind that a number of the inscriptions are fragmentary (with concomitant loss of names or relationship terms), only 8 commemorated men are mentioned: 2 fathers, 3 sons, 1 man commemorating himself, and 2 where the relationship is not explained or not known. Apart from Þúríðr the rune carver on the stone from Onchan (IM MM141; possibly a graffito and unrelated to the memorial inscription), the one aspect of runic memorialisation in which women in the Isle of Man did not apparently participate was in the commissioning of the monument and/or the inscription, whereas there are quite a number of examples of this in the memorial inscriptions of mainland Scandinavia.[143]

With a broad range of people being commemorated, the Manx memorials give some revealing insights into both the linguistic situation and family life on the island in the middle of the Viking Age. The monuments are all Christian and, as already noted, are crosses or cross-slabs with clear insular parallels, but no obvious Scandinavian ones. Nevertheless, some of the inscriptions are purely Scandinavian, such as Andreas II (IM MM131), on which it is said that 'Sandulfr the Black raised this cross in memory of Arinbjǫrg his wife', the only Gaelic element being the word for 'cross', which by this time had presumably been naturalised as a loanword in Norse. Others hint at a mixed family background, such as Braddan IV (IM MM135), 'Þorleifr *hnakki* raised this cross in memory of Fiak, his son, Hafr's brother's son'. Here, the father and the paternal uncle have Norse names, but the son has a Gaelic name, perhaps because he had a Gaelic-speaking mother. Meanwhile, an intriguing inscription on the stone from Bride (IM MM118) records that 'Druian, Dufgal's son, raised this cross in memory of Aþmiul, his wife'. As all 3 names in this inscription appear to be Gaelic, it is an unresolved question why the monument is written in Scandinavian runes and the Old Norse language, and whether that was the language of the people mentioned in the inscription. Even if these personal names reflect a local fashion rather than individual ethnicity, the fact that so many of the inscriptions record people with Gaelic names clearly suggests extensive personal contacts between the speakers of the two languages.

The inscriptions also suggest which aspects of family relationships were considered important. As in the case of Þorleifr, above, who noted his brother Hafr's name in the inscription, so Óleifr, commemorating his son Ulfr on the Ballaugh monument (IM MM106), also mentions that he himself is the son of Ljótulfr. Here we have three generations of men with Norse names, with the grandson's name consciously echoing that of his grandfather. Similarly, **iualfir** (the exact Norse form of the name is uncertain), who commemorated his mother Fríða on the Kirk Michael V stone (IM MM132), described himself as the 'son of Þórulfr the Red'. The commissioner of the German II monument (IM MM140; name unknown because the inscription is fragmentary) noted that his wife, Ástríðr, whom he was commemorating, was 'Oddr's daughter'. Gautr, who signed both the Andreas I (IM MM99) and Kirk Michael II (IM MM101) memorials, and claimed on the latter to have 'made all in Man', describes himself on the former as 'the son of Bjǫrn from Kollr'. This place has not been securely identified, but may be the island of Coll in the Hebrides.

These examples show the importance of recording paternal ancestry, whether it was Norse or Gaelic. Other inscriptions reveal genuine family feeling. Most intriguing is the Kirk Michael III inscription (IM MM130), which ends with the proverbial statement 'It is better to leave a good foster-son than a bad son.' From this we deduce that the inscription commemorates a foster-mother by her foster-son, though the exact names and relationships are difficult to clarify:

> **mal:lymkun : raisti : krus : þena : efter : mal:mury : fustra : si(n)e : tot(o)r : tufkals : kona : is : aþisl : ati + ¶ . . . etra : es : laifa : fustra : kuþan : þan : son : ilan +**
>
> <Mallymkun> raised this cross in memory of <Malmury>, his foster-mother, Dufgal's daughter, the wife to whom Aðísl was married. It is better to leave a good foster-son than a bad son.

The name of the commissioner cannot be identified with certainty with any recorded name, though it is fairly clear that it is Gaelic. The name of the commemorated appears to be equivalent to *Maelmuire*, a name which means 'devotee of Mary' and can be either male or female.[144] If it were a male name, then the following noun, **fustra**, would be grammatically correct and would represent the accusative form of *fóstri*, 'foster-father'. However, both the accompanying possessive **si(n)e** (presumably representing *sína*), and the following apposition **tot(o)r : tufkals** (*dóttur Dufgals* 'daughter of Dufgal') suggest that the carver meant to write **fostru sine** (*fóstru sína* 'his foster-mother'). There is further evidence of the carver's uncertainty in Old Norse grammar in the third apposition, **kona : is : aþisl : ati** (*konu es Aðísl átti* 'the wife to whom Aðísl was married'), in which we might have expected the accusative form **konu** instead of the nominative form **kona**. In fact, it is wrong to call such unexpected forms 'bad' grammar, as they may reflect how at least some people spoke on Man in the tenth century. This kind of interference in the inflectional system is just what might be expected in a bilingual society, and the names of the people in the inscription support this – of the four, only Aðísl has a Norse name.

While not exactly parallel to the Manx memorials, a rune-stone from Killaloe (IR 2; not a memorial), Co. Clare, Ireland, provides further evidence of Norse–Celtic linguistic and cultural contact within one monument.[145] This is a fragment of the shaft of a standing cross, of uncertain, though Viking Age, date. It is highly unusual, not just as a rare rune-stone from Ireland, but in having two inscriptions on it, one in runes and one in ogham, with related messages. The runic inscription states that 'Þorgrímr raised this cross', again using the Gaelic-derived word *kross* for the monument, as in the Manx inscriptions. The inscription in ogham (a form of writing associated with the Celtic languages) is in Gaelic and calls for 'A blessing on Þorgrímr' (spelled *Toroqrim*).

In their clear Christianity, the Manx memorials link individuals, family and religion. How far back the Christianity of these families went is difficult to tell, but it is certain that at some point in the past they had exchanged their old religion for the new one. The fascinating questions surrounding this transition are the subject of the next chapter.

Notes

1 Eriksen 2010, 212.
2 Stig Sørensen 2009, 255.
3 Stig Sørensen 2009, 256.
4 E.g. Jesch 1991; Gräslund 2001; Hayeur Smith 2004, 60–4, 71–8; Kershaw 2013; see also Stig Sørensen 2009, 258–61.
5 E.g. Jesch 2001a, 44–63, 180–265; Hadley 2008.
6 A recent handbook of Anglo-Saxon studies has one chapter on 'masculinity' and one on 'women' (Stodnick and Trilling 2012).
7 Stig Sørensen 2009, 264–5.
8 For a recent survey, see Moen 2011, 5–8; see also Bolin 2004; Stig Sørensen 2009, 254–6; Wicker 2012, 247–53.
9 Hadley 2008, 273; Moen 2011, 6.
10 Stalsberg 2001, 68–9; see also Bolin 2004, 176–7.
11 Kershaw 2013, 157–78.
12 Jesch 1994; Shaw 2011.
13 Bowden *et al.* 2008; Harding *et al.* 2010.
14 Joseph 2004.
15 *ÍF* V, 22–8; *CSI* V, 10–13.
16 *ÍF* V, 51; *CSI* V, 24.
17 *VEPN*, 'ærgi'.
18 Whaley 2006, 8, 157–8.
19 Fellows-Jensen 1985, 60, 64.

20 Fellows-Jensen 1985, 61.
21 Fellows-Jensen 1985, 64.
22 Fellows-Jensen 1985, 103.
23 Townend 2002, 181–5.
24 Townend 2002, 189, 202.
25 Abrams and Parsons (2004) make a strong case for the value of place-names as evidence for substantial communities of speakers of Old Norse. Though their work is mainly based on evidence from eastern England, the principle is more broadly applicable.
26 *GrágásK* II, 47; *LEI* II, 69–70.
27 *GrágásK* II, 203–4; *LEI* II, 219.
28 *ÍF* V, 93–8; *CSI* V, 46–9.
29 *ÍF* IV, 229; *CSI* I, 16.
30 Ewing 2006.
31 Hayeur Smith 2004, 59, 65–70; Kershaw 2013, 173–5.
32 Jesch 1991; Capelle 1968, plate 22. I am grateful to Else Roesdahl for suggesting it at the time.
33 Jansson 1985, 11; Ewing 2006, 24–45; Kershaw 2013, 21–2.
34 Kershaw 2013, 96.
35 Jansson 1985, 11; Ewing 2006, 50–2; Kershaw 2013, 159.
36 Kershaw 2013, 96.
37 Jansson 1985, 12.
38 Kershaw 2013, 96–7, 159, 227.
39 Kershaw 2013, 97, 99–100, 157–8, 225–6.
40 Hayeur Smith 2004, 27, 30–1.
41 Sindbæk 2011.
42 Sindbæk 2011, 417.
43 Capelle 1968, 66–70; Jansson 1985, 13; Kershaw 2013, 96–100.
44 Duczko 2004, 243–4.
45 Kershaw 2013, 98.
46 Hayeur Smith 2004, 78–9.
47 Hayeur Smith 2004, 93.
48 Hayeur Smith 2004, 71, 75–6; Ewing 2006, 39–40.
49 Gräslund 2001; Jesch 2011a, 38, 41–3.
50 Hayeur Smith 2004, 79.
51 Kershaw 2013, 216.
52 Kershaw 2013, 229.
53 Bolin 2004, 180–81; Androushchuk 2009, 96.
54 Sjøvold 1974, 263, 266.
55 Androushchuk 2009, 93.
56 Androushchuk 2009, 95; according to Eldjárn 2000, 323, there are 22 sword finds known from Iceland.
57 As acknowledged in a forthcoming study by Androshchuk, which recognises about 750 swords from Sweden, 91 from Denmark and 22 from Iceland. Martens 2004, 127–8, suggests 3,000 swords from Norway and 75 from Denmark.
58 A simple search of *PAS* using 'Viking sword' as the search term brings up nine Viking Age sword pommels recorded during the years 2009–12.
59 Androushchuk 2009, 102.
60 I am grateful to Fedir Androshchuk for allowing me to cite his forthcoming monograph on Viking swords. See also Jesch 2011a on the *búendr* in rune-stone inscriptions.
61 Jesch 2013b, 343–9.
62 Cf. the Dybäck sword discussed in Jesch 2013b and Androshchuk forthcoming.

63 Martens 1994.
64 Bolin 2004, 180–1.
65 Harrison 2010, 144.
66 Androschchuk 2003; Androushchuk 2009, 93, 95, 102.
67 Hadley 2008, 272–3.
68 Hadley 2008, 274–7.
69 Androschchuk 2003, 42–3; Martens 2004, 128.
70 Walsh 1998, 233–4.
71 Eldjárn 2000, 106–8; Hayeur Smith 2004, 62–3.
72 Peterson 2007.
73 Shaw 2011.
74 Janzén 1947b, 53–4.
75 *SRIB*, pp. 285–8.
76 Sawyer 2000, 69–70.
77 Jesch 1994, 151.
78 Sawyer 2000, 47–90.
79 Gräslund 1988–9, 235–7.
80 Sawyer 2000, 113, 123.
81 Clover 1988, 168.
82 Callow 2011, 12; see also Clover 1988, 173; Jacobsen (2005, 288–9) estimates that *Landnámabók* represents about 1–2 per cent of the total population in each generation.
83 Shaw 2011, 164, 167.
84 Jesch 1994, 160.
85 Clunies Ross 2005, 107.
86 *SnESkskm*, p. 40; *SnE*, p. 94.
87 This is the only example provided by Snorri, though other words appear in the surviving poetry, such as *bjǫrk* 'birch' or *eik* 'oak'.
88 *Edda*, pp. 111–15; *PE*, pp. 93–7.
89 Jesch 1991, 21–2, 138–9, 176–80, 191–4.
90 *SnEGylf*, p. 30; *SnE*, p. 31.
91 Jesch 1991, 169–75; see also Quinn 2007 and Kopár 2012, 128–33.
92 Ney 2012; Graham-Campbell 2013, 44–5, 161–3.
93 Price 2006, 180, 183; Jesch 2011b, 16, 22 n.30; Graham-Campbell 2013, 39.
94 *CASSS* II, 102; Kopár 2012, 98, 131–2.
95 Henriksen and Petersen 2013.
96 *Edda*, p. 132; *PE*, p. 112.
97 Cf. *SnESksksm*, pp. 66–7; *SnE*, pp. 117–18.
98 *SPSMA* I, 484.
99 *SPSMA* I, 168.
100 *SPSMA* I, 151; see also p. 256.
101 *SPSMS* I, 159, 291.
102 Jesch 2001b, 319; 2011b, 16.
103 McLeod 2011, 345.
104 Jesch 1991, 21–2.
105 Edwards 1998, 15.
106 Clover 1988, 171–2.
107 Wicker 1998.
108 Wicker 1988, 213–16.
109 Barrett 2008, 676–7, 680–1.
110 Wamers 1998, 38, 41–7.
111 *NIYR* V, 141–4.

112 Wamers 1998, 38, 41–7.
113 Wamers 1998, 42–4.
114 Jacobsen 2005.
115 Jacobsen 2005, 299.
116 See also the discussion in Wicker 2012, 254–6.
117 See the extensive debate in Vésteinsson *et al.* 2012.
118 *ÍF* V, 75; *CSI* V, 38.
119 *ÍF* I, 326; *BoS*, p. 124.
120 *ÍF* I, 326n., 327, 367; *BoS*, p. 137.
121 *ÍF* I, 138, 142; *BoS*, p. 53; see also *ÍF* V, 10; *CSI* V, 5.
122 *Edda*, pp. 270–1, 273; *PE*, pp. 231–2, 234.
123 *ÍF* I, 63, 78–9, 120–3, 148, 173, 180, 227, 243, 277–9; *BoS*, pp. 31, 44–5, 55–6, 67, 87, 94, 106; for later examples of these, see *A&N*, pp. 271–2, 274; see also p. 281 for later examples of *Njáll*. For a list of Celtic personal names recorded in Iceland, see Janzén 1947b, 139–40. The discussion in Guðmundsson 1997, 170–86, of 35 male and 8 female names, mixes together given names, bynames and names occurring only in place-names, and includes the names of both Icelanders and those born elsewhere, giving an impression of a greater spread of Celtic names in Iceland than is the case.
124 *NID*, cols 687–99, 713; *NIDS*, col. 557.
125 Guðmundsson 1997, 127–68.
126 *ÍF* XXVI, pp. 11, 13; *Hkr*, pp. 7–8.
127 *ÍF* I, 42–3; *BoS*, pp. 19–21.
128 These relative frequencies are derived from the online materials of *ONP*, which are an extensive but far from complete record of the language.
129 Guðmundsson 1997, 127.
130 *ÍF* I, 5; *BoI*, p. 4.
131 Guðmundsson 1997, 135.
132 *Edda*, p. 38; *PE*, pp. 30, 287.
133 Guðmundsson 1997, 137–8.
134 Hansen 2010.
135 *OED*, 'cross'.
136 *OED*, 'caple'.
137 *VEPN*, 'ǣrgi'; Guðmundsson 1997, 158–9.
138 Holman 1996, 86–172.
139 Barnes 2012b.
140 As of the most recent version of *SR* (2014), there are 34 stones with runic inscriptions from the Isle of Man. Two of these are not on Viking Age memorial stones and of the 32 memorial stones, 11 are too fragmentary to reveal any name.
141 The masculine Norse names *Gautr*, *Grímr*, *Oddr* and *Ófeigr*, and the masculine Gaelic name *Dufgal*, all appear twice, though both instances of *Gautr* almost certainly refer to the same person. *Þorbjǫrn* appears at least twice and possibly three times (though in the fragmentary form **þorb . . .** on Jurby (IM MM127) it could in theory rather be a feminine name such as *Þorbjǫrg*).
142 Assuming that the name **malmury** on Kirk Michael III (IM MM130) is feminine, as seems most likely from the context – see further on this inscription below. Some of the names are difficult to identify as to language and gender, particularly those described as 'Gaelic' above, though the Norse ones are on the whole clear.
143 Sawyer 2000, 70, 111–13.
144 O'Brien and Baumgarten 1973, 229–30.
145 *RIVAD*, 53–6, 78–9.

5

CULTS, BELIEFS AND MYTHS

Cults and beliefs

Myth and religion of the North

Half a century ago Gabriel Turville-Petre presented a full if rather monolithic picture of Scandinavian beliefs and traditions of the pre-Christian era entitled *Myth and Religion of the North.*[1] The general topic has long fascinated the modern mind, ever since the European rediscovery of northern culture from the sixteenth century onwards, but establishing what it might include is quite difficult. Turville-Petre, for instance, scarcely distinguished between 'myth' and 'religion', and presented a geographically and chronologically vast range of evidence. A more recent survey like Christopher Abram's *Myths of the Pagan North* puts more emphasis on 'myth', with 'religion' only becoming an issue with the coming of Christianity.[2] Like him, most scholars today are inclined to make more of a distinction between 'myth' and 'religion', and to emphasise regional variety and chronological difference in the matter of beliefs and traditions. But once it has been recognised that variation exists, it is still possible to see in both Old Norse myth and Old Norse religion 'a more or less uniform tradition with a relatively long temporal continuity'.[3] Andreas Nordberg draws an analogy between Old Norse religion and Old Norse language, which is of course subject to both synchronic and diachronic variation, but which is recognisably the same language over a long period of time, and where certain elements are common across a wide geographical range and persist over time.[4] And just as the Old Norse language spread during the Viking diaspora, so it needs to be considered whether the Old Norse religion did the same. While Nordberg's argument is focused on religion, the same questions apply to its close cousin, myth, which is even more closely entwined with language than religion is.

'Myth' and 'religion' are complex concepts which are impossible to reduce to simple definitions. Here, a working distinction nevertheless needs to be made because it was during the Viking Age that there was a change in Scandinavia, from a poorly understood set of practices that we call 'paganism' or 'heathendom', to the international and organised religion of Christianity. Despite this major change, many of the myths associated with the old practices persisted well into the time of the new religion, spanning the diasporic period being investigated, and this will be the focus of the second half of this chapter, after some consideration of evidence for religion and its practice.

'Myth', at the simplest level, can be understood as 'story' (the original Greek *mythos* means 'speech, narrative, fiction, myth, plot'), but is usually, as here, used to designate stories about supernatural or superhuman beings, or events of cosmic significance.[5] Such stories can reflect what people believed to be true, and may therefore be closely linked to religion. In other contexts they can be understood as having a more symbolic meaning, recognising their religious framework without any implication that they were believed literally to be true. Or they can simply be enjoyed as stories for entertainment or edification, without either belief or religion entering into the equation. 'Religion', on the other hand, is here understood as a set of practices based on belief in, or acknowledgement of, some supernatural power or powers. These practices might be individual, or they might be collective and involve special institutions, cult locations or cult professionals in rituals aimed at making contact with those powers. Religious beliefs may be alluded to in myths, or may require knowledge of certain myths, but myths do not necessarily represent belief *per se*. These concepts of 'myth' and 'religion' apply equally to Christianity as to what went before, though scholars rarely discuss them in these terms.

A large part of the evidence for both 'myth' and 'religion' in pre-Christian Scandinavia comes from just two works, both of which were products of thirteenth-century antiquarianism in Christian Iceland and both called *Edda*: the 'Prose Edda' of Snorri Sturluson, a treatise on poetry and mythology, and the 'Poetic Edda', a manuscript anthology of anonymous poems.[6] Both comprise material that is explicitly presented as older than the text itself, though how much older is not clear. A long-established scholarly view has been that the pre-Christian religion of Scandinavia was a fully developed system of beliefs and practices that was exported to Iceland during the Viking Age migrations. There, in this view, the conservative nature of that colony ensured the preservation of stories and myths in oral tradition relating to those beliefs and practices until the arrival of writing, when they could be recorded for posterity. In this view, the Eddas represent a codification of ancestral stories and myths. Furthermore, many scholars also viewed the Scandinavian evidence as an important relic of a wider religious system common to all the Germanic-speaking peoples, as found in the *Germania* of the Roman historian Tacitus in the first century.[7] In this broad view of the subject, a whole range of other kinds of evidence supplemented the basic outline provided in the Eddas, including a wide range of texts, often emanating from other cultures, archaeological sites and finds, artefacts with significant iconography, runic inscriptions, and personal and place-names.[8]

Although the traditional view of the 'myth' and 'religion' of the North as a rather static and monolithic system which hardly varied from Tacitus in the first century to the coming of Christianity a millennium later is no longer tenable, it cannot be denied that any approach to the question still has to grapple with this broad range of sources. For example, the medieval Icelandic sources give us the names and attributes of deities and supernatural figures which can then be identified in place-names or iconography. And even those who prefer to focus on the Eddas as literary constructs of the thirteenth century cannot maintain that everything in them was pure invention by medieval Christian authors, in the face of clear and close parallels in earlier material, such as sculpture. Nevertheless, it is important to make at least a conceptual distinction between evidence which directly illuminates people's beliefs, practices and traditions in the pre-Christian period, and that which is filtered through the minds of people who may or may not have been especially knowledgeable about beliefs, practices and traditions which were no longer current or directly relevant to them.

This chapter will thus start by attempting to assess the most useful evidence for understanding what people actually did and believed in the Viking Age. Since the Viking Age, as already noted (ch. 1), saw at least the beginnings of Christianity, both in Scandinavia and in the diaspora, the study of beliefs should encompass the Christian religion as well as whatever religion preceded it. Moreover, the subsequent adaptation and appropriation of older beliefs and traditions in the Christian period are such a characteristic aspect of the Viking diaspora that they cannot simply be ignored, in favour of a 'pure' concentration on the evidence for Viking Age paganism. These adaptations of Norse myths and legends will be considered in the second part of this chapter, once it has been possible to come to some understanding of the evidence for pre-Christian beliefs, practices and traditions. This will also involve some consideration of how and why the Viking diaspora had such a strong engagement with its pagan past well into the Christian era.

There is actually very little unambiguous evidence for religious beliefs and practices in pre-Christian Scandinavia. Nevertheless, two types of evidence are especially important, even if they need careful interpretation. Probably most important for a global understanding of the scope and nature of religious belief and practice is the evidence of names, mainly place-names, but to a limited extent also personal names, which provide a wealth of information on deities and cult locations across the whole geographical area of Scandinavia and the diaspora. Archaeological evidence is more diffuse and less evenly spread, but encompasses possible cult sites, as well as artefacts that may be associated with rituals, or that represent deities or other supernatural beings. However it has an advantage over place-names in that it can often be more closely dated.

Cult and beliefs in Scandinavia – place-names

It is a paradox that place-names are probably our most important contemporary evidence for cults and beliefs in the pre-Christian Viking Age. The paradox lies in the fact that the surviving evidence, namely the written forms of the names, is almost never older than the twelfth or thirteenth century in Scandinavia, very rarely older than that in the diaspora, and often later in both cases. Nevertheless, the special nature of place-names makes it possible to argue for the contemporaneity of some of them with pre-Christian beliefs. Firstly, it is a general rule that a name, once attached to a place, can and often will have a long life. The length of its life can vary, and places can change their names, but it is an axiom of name-studies that any place-name will have been given some time before its first record in writing, often long before. The philological method enables the reconstruction of the original form of the place-name from its earliest written forms. When done on a global scale, this also enables the establishment of a rough chronology of name-giving, as outlined in Chapter 2, above, and thus the identification of names given both before and after the coming of Christianity. Secondly, it is also axiomatic in name-studies that a place-name containing an element that clearly refers to a pre-Christian deity or cult site cannot have been given in the Christian period, since this would simply not be countenanced once the new religion was fully established.[9] The main difficulty in the interpretation of place-names is therefore not so much that of the date of the evidence as it is that of identifying those elements which unequivocally refer to religion.

There are basically two types of place-name elements which seem to provide evidence about pre-Christian beliefs, those which refer to deities and those which refer to cult sites.[10] Thus, there is a range of generic elements (the element which characterises the type of site, being either the second element in a compound place-name, or the only element in a simplex name) which may refer to cult locations, whether these are specific constructions, or landscape features. These elements (all to be discussed further below) include *hof*, *hǫrgr*, *vé* and *lundr*; these can also sometimes function as specifics (the first element of a compound name which defines the particular example of the type). Other specifics are either the names of deities, such as *Óðinn*, *Þórr*, *Freyr*, *Týr*, *Ullr*, or common nouns referring to deities in general, *áss* or *guð*, or nouns or adjectives referring to abstract concepts of sacrality, such as *heilagr*.

The challenges of interpreting names containing these elements have been clearly stated in an article by the Danish onomast Bente Holmberg.[11] Many place-name elements can have multiple meanings, and this applies particularly to those apparently designating cult sites. Thus, *hof* can refer to a cult building, but it could also mean 'mound' or 'farm'. Similarly, a *hǫrgr* can be a 'hill, stony ground' as well as some kind of cult location, and a *lundr* is a 'grove', which may or may not have had a sacral character. *Vé*, on the other hand, does seem to have just one meaning, again referring to some kind of cult site or sanctuary, and this is therefore the most secure onomastic indicator of sacrality. The problem with this element, however, is that in place-names recorded much later, it is easily confused with the common element *viðr* meaning simply 'wood'. But when it is compounded with a god's name, the religious meaning seems certain, as in Odense in Denmark (*Óðinsvé*).

The names of deities can also be difficult to identify. *Freyja* is hard to distinguish in place-names from an adjective meaning 'fertile, fecund', while the deity *Týr* is sometimes hard to distinguish from *týr*, a noun which does at least seem to mean 'god'. In these two cases, there is at least some relationship of meaning, but *áss*, also meaning 'god', is more problematic because it cannot always be distinguished from its homonym *áss* 'slope, hill'. In such cases, a knowledge of the local topography may help, but will not necessarily be decisive. Place-names containing the element *heilagr* 'holy' cannot always be distinguished from those containing the personal names *Helgi* (m.) or *Helga* (f.). Here, there is the added complication that *heilagr* has an additional, legal, meaning of 'inviolate'. Despite the apparently close connections between law and religion in the Viking Age, it is not certain that every legal site was also a cult site, or vice versa.

However, as with *vé*, the other element with which such ambiguous elements are compounded can reveal whether or not the name had a sacral character. Thus, names like Torshov in Oslo (*Þórshof*) clearly link the potentially ambiguous elements to the names of deities and therefore suggest their sacral character. A name like Helgum in eastern Norway (*Helgheim*) is unlikely to contain the personal name *Helgi* or *Helga* because elsewhere the element *-heim* is rarely if ever compounded with a personal name. But whether this place was 'holy' or 'inviolate' (in the legal sense) is more difficult to determine. Landscape features such as *akr* 'arable land', *vangr* 'field, meadow', or *lundr* 'grove' are often found compounded with gods' names (cf. Ullensaker, Ullensvang in Norway, and several Torslundas in Sweden). But even when this is the case, it is not always certain that such fields and groves were the actual location of cult sites, rather the relationship might have been something else, such as that the field or grove belonged to a cult site dedicated to that god.

Extra-linguistic factors can help to decide the meaning of an element, with topography and archaeology particularly important. A place-name containing the element *hǫrgr* which is in the close vicinity of rocky outcrops is more likely to have the topographical meaning than the sacral one. On the other hand, although it has been argued that *hof* may refer only to a large farm, the excavations at Hofstaðir in northern Iceland have revealed a large cultic feasting hall of exactly the type that many scholars imagine is represented in the sacral element *hof*.[12] Similarly, the excavations at Lunda, in Södermanland, Sweden, unearthed evidence of a sacred grove, a ritual space where votive offerings took place.[13]

The difficulties of interpretation can often be overcome by the methods described above so that the place-names of Scandinavia provide a very rich picture of the deities commonly venerated in the Viking Age, and their distribution, assuming that in general the place-names record the approximate locations of these particular deities' cults. The numbers of such 'theophoric' place-names, that is, those that contain gods' names, are large, particularly considering that some such place-names must have disappeared. It has been estimated, for example, that some 500 names in Norway alone refer to the pre-Christian religion in the ways outlined above.[14]

Further detailed work is still needed on the sacral names of Scandinavia, on the model of Per Vikstrand's micro-study of the Mälar valley in Sweden.[15] But some preliminary surveys give a good idea of the deities that were actively venerated in pre-Christian Scandinavia, and their geographical distribution.[16] Table 5.1 shows

TABLE 5.1 Theophoric place-names in the Scandinavian countries

	Denmark	*Norway*	*Sweden*
Freyr	1	22	38
Njǫrðr/*Niærþer[1]	3	13	17
Óðinn	11	11	49
Týr	33	1	0
Ullr	0	27[2]	48
Þórr	5	20[3]	57

Notes

1 In Old Icelandic tradition, *Njǫrðr* was a male god, and this is the name found in the Norwegian names. The Swedish names seem to point rather to a female deity whose name can be reconstructed as **Niærþer*, not recorded in the medieval sources. See discussion in Vikstrand 2001, 101–6.

2 This total rises to 35 if we include names that contain *Ullinn*, see below.

3 This total rises to 27 if we include names of the type *Totland*, which less certainly contain the name of *Þórr*.

the numbers of place-names in each of the modern Scandinavian countries which were judged by Stefan Brink as reasonably certain to contain the names of the deities in question.

This broad picture can be nuanced. Thus, the many *Freyr*-names in Sweden are geographically restricted, being concentrated in the Mälar valley. The Norwegian *Freyr*-names are also concentrated, this time around the Oslofjord, but many of these are less certain than the Swedish ones. *Óðinn*-names, on the other hand, are quite evenly distributed across Scandinavia, with the exception of western Norway. Similarly, *Þórr*-names are fairly well-distributed throughout Scandinavia, but lacking in the Trøndelag area of Norway. There may of course be reasons for these distributions other than variation in the veneration of particular deities. We cannot assume that all deities are equally likely to appear in place-names, and we must remember that 'absence of evidence is not evidence of absence'.[17] Nevertheless, some of these distributions ring true.

Freyr, Óðinn and Þórr are well-known deities from the pantheon as presented in later Icelandic sources in both poetry and prose. What is interesting about place-names is that they provide information about other gods that are much more fleetingly recorded in the later literary sources. Thus, Norwegian and Swedish place-names provide plenty of evidence for Ullr (and Ullinn, who may just be an alternative name for him), but he is entirely absent from Denmark. This is not surprising in light of the fact that the Icelandic mythological sources remember him as a god of skiing and hunting, the former activity not generally associated with Denmark.[18] That this god was actually venerated is indicated by the frequent occurrence of his name with the generic *vé*, as in the 23 instances of the name Ullevi in Sweden. If Ullinn was a separate deity, then the place-names suggest that his cult was restricted to central and western Norway. Týr, on the other hand, the god remembered chiefly for sacrificing his hand to the Fenrisulfr in an attempt to

TABLE 5.2 Viking Age personal names in Scandinavia containing sacral elements

Element	*No. of male names*	*No. of female names*	*Total no. of names*
Alf-	7	2	9
-alfR	1	0	1
-ælfR	0	10	10
Ās-	22	12	34
Dīs-	0	1	1
-đīs	0	8	8
Frøy-	4	4	8
Guð-	18	7	25
Helg-	1	1	2
Ōðin-	1	1	2
Þōr-	24	12	36
-þōrr	4	0	4
Vī-	18	6	24
-vēR	8	0	8
-vī	0	19	19

avert Ragnarök, was very popular in Denmark, but totally absent from Sweden, and with only one certain example in Norway.[19]

The picture provided by the place-names is supported by the evidence of personal names. Most early Scandinavian personal names consist of two elements (as explained in ch. 4), rather like place-names. The first element (the 'proto-theme') is often, and the second element ('deutero-theme') sometimes, identical with the name of a deity, or another word related to the religious sphere. Table 5.2, which is based on the contemporary evidence of dithematic names recorded in Viking Age runic inscriptions, shows the number of different names current in the Viking Age containing potentially sacral elements.[20]

Personal names present rather different problems as evidence for religion than place-names do. Even if the names, when first coined, had some connection with the deities or sacral concepts concerned, there is no necessary connection between the meaning of a personal name and its owner. Just as a person called *Steinn* is not a 'stone', so a person called *Þorsteinn* need have no connection with the god Þórr. Once a name has been introduced into the name-pool, it will have a life of its own and future users may not be concerned with, or even know the meaning of, the individual elements. Moreover, Scandinavian name-giving practice had a conservative effect on personal names, in that people were often named after a previous family member. This is clearly shown by the fact that many of the names containing pagan sacral elements persisted well into the Christian period and some even continuously into the present day.[21]

The runic corpus which is the basis of Table 5.2 is not representative of the Viking Age as a whole, since it is generally from the late Viking Age, and numerically biased towards Sweden. Moreover, the actual names in this corpus vary enormously in popularity – some are recorded only once, others had many bearers.[22] However, this corpus does provide a record contemporary with the Viking Age, and it shows fairly clearly that, with the exception of Þórr, people were not generally given names that contained god's names. Not reflected in Table 5.2 is the fact that simplex or uncompounded gods' names are even rarer than compounded ones (though there are a couple of possible examples of Þórr in Swedish inscriptions).[23] But although the gods tend to be avoided, the table shows a substantial sacral element in personal names, in the popularity of the elements meaning 'god' (*Ás-* and *Guð-*) and in the widespread use of the element *Vé-* (the West Norse form) or *Vī-* (the East Norse form) as proto-theme, or its variants *-vér* and *-ví* as deutero-theme. The use of this element in personal names is of course somewhat different from that in place-names. As a proto-theme in personal names it most likely has the same meaning as in place-names, that of 'sanctuary, cult site', but as a deutero-theme it is a derived form, probably referring to the male or female cult leader respectively.[24] However, it bears repeating that just because someone had a name containing this element did not mean that they had this function, once the name is established in the anthroponymicon. The role of cult leaders is discussed further below, after some consideration of the archaeological evidence.

Cult and beliefs in Scandinavia – archaeology

Like place-names, archaeological finds can also be ambiguous. Nevertheless, scholars have felt able to identify visual representations of the Norse gods and other supernatural beings in or on a range of different types of object. Since these deities were assumed to belong to a religion which predated the Viking Age, even objects from before that period have been interpreted in this way. Particularly often mentioned in this context are the small (often postage stamp-sized), thin gold foils generally known by the Danish term *guldgubber* 'little old men of gold' (or similar in Norwegian and Swedish), and dating to 500–800, so just reaching into the early Viking Age. They currently number around 3000 and have been found all over Scandinavia, but with a strong concentration on the Baltic island of Bornholm.[25] These mass-produced foils are predominantly decorated with anthropomorphic figures. Previously, scholars have thought they could identify some of the figures with Óðinn, Þórr and Freyr, and those with two figures on them, one male and one female, as representations of the story of Freyr and the giantess Gerðr, told in the Eddic poem *Skírnismál* and in Snorri's *Edda*.[26] Although the function of the *guldgubber* is still disputed, it is fair to say however that they are no longer widely regarded as images of deities.[27]

The *guldgubber* are mostly pre-Viking Age so even if they have a religious function, this will be an older one. From the Viking Age proper, there are some finds of small figurines, often in precious metals, both three-dimensional and two-dimensional, which have at one time or another been identified with the Norse gods or other supernatural beings.[28] A silver figurine from Rällinge, Södermanland, Sweden, which has a very obvious erection, is usually identified with Freyr 'or another fertility god'.[29] While the connection with fertility seems obvious, the specific interpretation as Freyr must remain speculative, in the absence of any name-tag attached to the object. A fascinating recent find is a seated figure found in Lejre, on the island of Sjælland, Denmark, in 2009. The figure is 1.75 × 1.98 × 1.25 cm, is made of silver with niello inlay, and weighs only 9 g.[30] It has been dated to the first half of the tenth century. Despite its minute size, it is very detailed and has excited differing interpretations. At first glance, the figure appears to be female, as it is wearing a long gown with an apron, a cloak and four strings of beads. Nevertheless, the proposed interpretation is that it actually represents Óðinn, because it appears to have only one eye, has two birds above its shoulders, and has certain masculine traits in spite of the apparently female dress. According to Snorri Sturluson, in Chapter 7 of *Ynglinga saga* (in *Heimskringla*), Óðinn was adept in the practice of *seiðr*, a form of magic which was otherwise considered to be unmanly and usually restricted to the *gyðjar* (a term discussed further below), and which had been taught to the gods by Freyja (ch. 4).[31] Others have argued that the figurine is Freyja, and draw attention to similarities between the Lejre figurine and another silver figure from Aska in Östergötland, Sweden, which is more clearly female.[32]

Scholars all seem to share the urge to identify these objects with particular figures from Norse mythology, especially deities. Yet, as the Lejre figurine shows, even those with very clear attributes can be ambiguous and interpreted in various ways, with the interpretations dependent on our later sources. And not all are necessarily deities, but could be other supernatural figures. Thus, the Lejre figure could represent a seeress, and many of the female figures are interpreted as valkyries, as discussed in Chapter 4, above. But as has been shown by Neil Price, such interpretations often read too much into these objects, which can often be understood in quite different ways.[33] He points out that many of the figures could represent supernatural beings of a different order from deities, such as trolls or dwarfs or spirits of various kinds. Or they could even represent human beings, whether aristocrats, legendary heroes, or even ancestors. The problem of interpretation is that each figurine has been studied in isolation, or in comparison with only its most obvious analogues, without considering this category of object as a whole. A wider-ranging study which took into account geographical distribution, context and dating would almost certainly reveal patterns which would aid in the understanding of these objects, the function (or range of possible functions) of which is in any case not yet understood. For the moment, the conclusion has to be that such figurines undoubtedly could provide insights into the thought-world of the Viking Age, but those insights still need to be pinned down, and whether they reveal much about religious practice in the Viking Age is still an open question.

The other main contribution of archaeology is in providing evidence for possible cult-sites. Adam of Bremen, who had never been to Scandinavia, nevertheless clearly imagined that the Scandinavians (or at least the Swedes in Uppsala) worshipped their gods in temples, much as the Christians did. Of the temple in Uppsala, he says:[34]

> In this temple, entirely decked out in gold, the people worship the statues of three gods in such wise that the mightiest of them, Thor, occupies a throne in the middle of the chamber; Wotan and Frikko have places on either side.

The hunt for archaeological evidence of temples has however produced only mixed results. A highly influential study by the Danish archaeologist Olaf Olsen in 1966 claimed that there were no separate cult buildings in pre-Christian Scandinavia, and that cult activities took place in the hall of the local chieftain.[35] He therefore also denied a previously popular theory that many Christian churches in Scandinavia were placed on former heathen cult-sites, most notably propounded by the Norwegian scholar Magnus Olsen.[36] Olaf Olsen's study was, however, heavily based on the Danish evidence with which he was most familiar, and conflates two arguments which need separate discussion, on the one hand the question of where pre-Christian cult activities took place, and on the other that of possible continuity between such locations and Christian cult buildings.

Within the last decade, a ritual building that has been described by some as a pre-Christian 'temple' has been unearthed in the archaeological excavations at Uppåkra in Skåne, southern Sweden.[37] The overall site is a very large one (40 hectares) with many interesting aspects, though still not fully understood in detail, and it covers a wide chronological range through much of the first millennium. The building in question is a small wooden one, 13.5 metres long and 6 metres wide, with three entrances and a central hearth, built and rebuilt in seven major stages, without significant changes to the layout. It was built with a stave-wall structure (a form of construction similar to a palisade), and the size of the posts supporting the roof suggests it was quite high. It was in use for some six hundred years, extending into the Viking Age. Although the building was in many ways similar to local domestic structures, the size of its roof-posts and the long sequence of use suggests rather a different sort of building, and this is supported by the finds from around the building. These finds included 111 *guldgubber*, the gold foils discussed above. The other finds, many from before the Viking Age, but some extending into it, included high-status vessels of both metal and glass, many objects of precious metals, and beads, crucibles and potsherds. Just west of the building, there were finds of fire-cracked stone and animal bones, possibly indicating sacrificial meals. To the north and south there were deposits of deliberately destroyed weapons and other items of warrior kit, along with some human bones. Although individually not especially significant, these items collectively suggest a cult site.

Like other examples of Scandinavian buildings which have been assigned some kind of cult function, the 'temple' at Uppåkra has its origins long before the Viking Age, and many of the finds appear to be related to this earlier period.[38] It can therefore be difficult to extrapolate Viking Age conditions from such sites. Larsson also makes the point that the proposed 'cult' buildings found across Scandinavia are quite various.[39] While they all seem to relate to cult activities of one sort or another, there is at present no evidence for a standardised cult building which could reasonably be described as the prototypical pagan temple, in the way that churches are built to a regular plan with fairly standard inventory. Nevertheless, it has already been pointed out (in ch. 3, above) that much of Scandinavian culture is characterised by long-lived continuities. Uppåkra does seem to be a site which illustrates how many aspects of pre-Viking Age cult activity continued into the Viking Age, though we still lack more detailed investigations of its finds which might indicate the kinds of changes that also took place there.

A site which does suggest continuity of cult practice from the pre-Christian to the Christian period is Mære, in Nord-Trøndelag, Norway. The present stone church was built in the late twelfth century, but excavations in the 1960s found beneath it at least one wooden church and churchyard, along with the remains of two even earlier buildings.[40] The older of these two was dated to around 500, while the later one appears to have been from the Viking Age and to have continued in use right up to the time of the building of the wooden church sometime in the eleventh century. In the post-holes of this Viking Age building were found 19 gold foils, as discussed above. These gold foils have been taken as evidence that there was a pagan cult building on the site, and it is of great interest that the later churches were built on such a site. A recent re-evaluation of the site has concluded that there was indeed cult continuity at Mære, in that there was little or no time gap between pagan and Christian rituals on the site and moreover that the Christian takeover happened in the middle or end of the eleventh century.[41]

This archaeological evidence finds an echo in saga-texts. Several episodes in the kings' sagas suggest that Mære was a stronghold of paganism at a time when Christianity was making inroads into Norway under the tenth- and eleventh-century kings Hákon *Aðalsteinsfóstri* 'Foster-Son of Athelstan', Óláfr Tryggvason and Óláfr Haraldsson.[42] In particular, the versions of *Óláfs saga Tryggvasonar* make clear that Mære was the chief temple for the region and a centre for *blót* 'sacrifice'. They describe the *hof* as a building containing images of Þórr, covered in gold and silver, and other gods, which are struck from their pedestals by King Óláfr.[43] These are fairly formulaic accounts of the king's slash-and-burn approach to conversion and, indeed, the people of Trøndelag are said to have turned to Christianity as a result, though several decades later Óláfr Haraldsson still found sacrifices taking place at Mære. Despite being filtered through later medieval perceptions of the pagan past, the anecdotes (and one from *Landnámabók* discussed below) do resonate in conjunction with the archaeological evidence in a way that suggests they preserve a kernel of truth about the status and functions of a *hof*, in this case an important one which later became a large stone church on a royal estate.[44]

Case study – cult leaders and cult buildings

Although actual pagan temples might be difficult to identify, a more interdisciplinary approach, also using some later sources, can provide tantalising evidence for the rituals, locations and leaders of the pre-Christian cults of Scandinavia. This is exemplified by the word *goði*, a term well known from medieval Iceland, where it referred to the 36, or later 39, chieftains (pl. *goðar*) who formed the country's oligarchical system of government.[45] Although in the Icelandic context the word referred primarily to secular leadership, there is evidence that people with this title may also have exercised religious leadership. This religious aspect to the role is suggested firstly by the etymology of the word, which is derived from *goð* 'god'. Secondly, it occurs in a number of runic inscriptions, at least one of which suggests religious leadership.[46] Two Danish stones, DR 190 Helnæs and DR 192 Flemløse 1, both from the island of Fyn, mention a man who is called *Hróðulfr* and who is said to have been a *goði*. While the inscriptions are obscure, they may refer to a group of people living in a particular district, over whom *Hróðulfr* exercised some authority.[47] The monuments give no clue as to whether this authority was secular or religious (or both), but the latter is certainly possible given their early date (before about 900).

The slightly later Glavendrup stone (DR 209), also from Fyn, does seem to indicate religious authority for the man being commemorated on it.[48] His name was Alli and he was also a *goði*. On that much scholars agree. The rest is however still not satisfactorily explained.[49] While the exact collocations of *goði* in the inscription are unclear, it may be related to a *vé*, or cult site, as discussed above. One possible interpretation is that Alli was the *goði* of the *vé* 'sanctuary'. Another is that he was the *goði* of some people known as the *Sølvar* in which case there is a parallel with the Helnæs and Flemløse inscriptions. As already discussed above, the word *vé* is our best example of a term associated with pre-Christian cult locations and its possible occurrence, and collocation with *goði*, in this inscription suggest at least an element of cult leadership for *goði*. That the Glavendrup stone emanates from a heathen context is in any case demonstrated by the undisputed imprecation *Þórr vígi þessar rúnar* 'Þórr hallow these runes'.

The word *vé* is more securely recorded in two runic inscriptions from Sweden which scholars have dated to the ninth century.[50] These give tantalising hints of what such a site might have involved, without revealing much detail. The Oklunda inscription (Ög N288) from Östergötland, carved in bedrock, records the fate of a certain Gunnarr who cut the runes, who fled to *vé þetta* 'this sanctuary' in a state of guilt (probably for homicide). The rest of the inscription is a bit more obscure, but what it indicates as a whole is the close connection between a cult site and legal asylum, which has parallels in medieval laws of church sanctuary. Indeed, there is very little to suggest what the religious role of the *vé* at Oklunda might have been, but it chimes with other evidence for the close connection between law and religion in Viking Age Scandinavia, both being communal activities that took place at designated places.

The iron ring from Forsa (Hs 7) in Hälsingland, in northern Sweden (until quite recently kept on the door of the church there), was once thought to be a medieval artefact, until it was reinterpreted as a Viking Age inscription in the 1970s by the runologist Aslak Liestøl. It has a long inscription which, in this re-interpretation, is a legal text regulating the maintenance of a *vé* by stipulating fines for when this duty is not carried out. Unlike Oklunda, there is no direct suggestion here that the *vé* itself was a legal site, but neither is there any other indication of what its function was, except that it was important enough to the community to be regulated in this way. Unlike the Oklunda inscription, which might well refer to an open-air site, the need for maintenance suggests that, at Forsa at least, a building was involved. Stefan Brink interprets both Oklunda and Forsa primarily as evidence for legal matters, the *vé* being an 'assembly place for legal, cultic and probably also other communal matters', and he concludes that sites named *hof* are similar, the difference between them being mainly one of geographical distribution.[51]

Landnámabók is also a fruitful source for the vocabulary relating to cult-sites and leaders. It mentions two men who were outlawed from Norway, each because he *vá víg í véum* 'committed a killing in the sanctuaries'.[52] One fled to the Hebrides and his descendants then to Iceland, the other one went straight to Iceland. These anecdotes confirm the inviolate nature of the *vé*, without telling us much about what that involved. Unlike the Glavendrup stone, when the word *goði* is used in a cult context in *Landnámabók*, it relates to a *hof* and not a *vé*; this may be because of regional differences between Norway and Iceland on the one hand and Denmark and Sweden on the other, as suggested above, or assumptions made by later Icelandic authors about the practices of their ancestors. Thus, a certain Þórhaddr *gamli* 'The Old' is said to have been the *hofgoði* at Mære in Trøndelag, the site discussed above:[53]

> Hann fýstisk til Íslands ok tók áðr ofan hofit ok hafði með sér hofsmoldina ok súlurnar; en hann kom í Stǫðvarfjǫrð ok lagði Mærina-helgi á allan fjǫrðinn ok lét øngu tortíma þar nema kvikfé heimilu.
>
> He felt the urge to go to Iceland and had dismantled his *hof* and took the soil of the *hof* and its pillars with him; and he arrived in Stǫðvarfjǫrðr and proclaimed the inviolability of Mære around the whole of the fjord and let nothing be killed there except the domestic livestock.

Again, the main idea here seems to be of the inviolability of a location, but in this case there is also mention of a building with pillars.

While Þórhaddr brought his sanctuary with him, another Icelandic settler originally from Sogn managed to keep up the family *hof* in Norway by returning there every three years:[54]

> Loptr fór útan et þriðja hvert sumar fyrir hǫnd þeira Flosa beggja, móðurbróður síns, at blóta at hofi því, er Þorbjǫrn móðurfaðir hans hafði varðveitt.
>
> Loptr went to Norway every third summer on behalf of himself and his maternal uncle Flosi, to sacrifice at the *hof* which his maternal grandfather Þorbjǫrn had had charge of.

Elsewhere it is explained that Flosi could not return to Norway because of some killings he had carried out there.[55] Although the word *goði* is not used in this connection, we get the same sense of someone in charge of a cult site, with an obligation to sacrifice there, and also that this role was hereditary.

In Iceland, quite a number of settlers are said to have raised a *hof* on their newly claimed lands, and the use of the verb *reisa* suggests that this was a building.[56] Several of these anecdotes also mention the obligation to maintain the *hof*, and these duties are further specified in a passage which is found only in the *Hauksbók* version:[57]

> Þá var landinu skipt í fjórðunga, ok skyldu vera þrjú þing í fjórðungi, en þrjú hǫfuðhof í þingsókn hverri; þar váru menn valðir til at geyma hofanna at viti ok réttlæti; þeir skyldu nefna dóma á þingum ok stýra sakferli; því váru þeir guðar kallaðir. Hverr maðr skyldi gefa toll til hofs, sem nú til kirkju tíund.
>
> Then the country was divided into quarters, and there were to be three assemblies (*þing*) in each quarter, and three chief *hofs* in each assembly-district; people were chosen [or 'elected'] to look after the *hofs* according to wisdom and justice; they were to pronounce judgements at assemblies and be in charge of the litigation; for that reason they were called *guðar*.[58] Each person was to give a payment to the *hof*, as now the tithe to the church.

This passage appears in the context of a longer passage outlining the heathen laws of Iceland, along with the legal duties of the *goði*, which have a clearly sacral character. Every chief *hof* was to possess an arm-ring weighing two ounces, and:[59]

> þann baug skyldi hverr goði hafa á hendi sér til lǫgþinga allra, þeira er hann skyldi sjálfr heyja, ok rjóða hann þar áðr í roðru nautsblóðs þess, er hann blótaði þar sjálfr.
>
> each *goði* should wear that ring on his arm to all those legal assemblies which it was his duty to call together himself, and he should previously redden it in the blood of those oxen which he himself sacrificed there.

The passage as a whole has a suspiciously antiquarian slant to it, as shown by the comparison with the church tithe of the writer's own day (the fourteenth century), and can hardly be relied on in detail as a description of pre-Christian practices in Iceland, let alone anywhere else. Nevertheless, there are some indications that the passage may contain genuine information about those practices, not least the parallels with the Forsa inscription discussed above. The connection between the law and religious cults is evident in a range of evidence, some of it from the Viking Age itself.[60] And the connection between the sacrifice of oxen and a place-name including the element *hof* has most recently clearly been demonstrated in the excavations at Hofstaðir.

Hofstaðir in Mývatnssveit in the north of Iceland first came to attention in the early twentieth century when rudimentary excavations were used to proclaim that it was indeed the site of a pagan temple, as the name suggested. This hypothesis was even accepted by Olaf Olsen to the extent that he saw it as a location for ritual feasts.[61] A comprehensive research programme in the 1990s revealed the site in much more detail, using the latest methods, and it is currently the largest known settlement from the Viking period in Iceland, its date range extending from the ninth to the eleventh century.[62] The settlement consisted of several buildings and was a self-sufficient farm, raising livestock, and producing textiles and iron.[63] Quite far inland, it participated in exchange networks to acquire various marine and freshwater resources. However, there were two unusual aspects to the site: its high consumption of meat and the unusually large size of the main building (termed an 'aisled hall' by the excavators), which at 38 metres is two to three times the size of the average Icelandic house of the period. These two factors have led the excavators to suggest that the function of Hofstaðir was 'to host seasonal gatherings of people . . . during which large scale feasting occurred'. Another interesting feature of the site are the 14 skulls of cattle which were probably hung on the outside of the building for display. These cattle were killed in a manner which, it has been suggested, was 'intended to dramatize death' and was therefore 'an act of sacrifice'. A religious interpretation of the feasts and sacrifices at Hofstaðir (as opposed to a socio-political one) is further suggested by the fact that the site was abandoned *c.* 1030, not only around the time Christianity was introduced in Iceland, but also around the time that a small church or chapel was built nearby. There are possible parallels to Hofstaðir at a couple of less-well understood sites in Norway, Hove in Nord-Trøndelag, and Løken in the parish of Hof, in Møre og Romsdal.[64] Like Uppåkra, discussed above, both of these stretch back into before the Viking Age, and they seem to come to an end around the turn of the millennium.

Current archaeological thinking leans to the view that we should distinguish between places that were sacred in themselves, such as sanctuaries, wells or groves, on the one hand, and religious rituals which could take place anywhere, but especially in 'halls', on the other.[65] The literary evidence points in the same direction, though with the added feature that the leaders of these religious rituals could also be women.

The feminine equivalent to the *goði* was the *gyðja*, a word that occurs only in Old Icelandic texts. An amusing anecdote from Chapter 2 of *Kristni saga* gives a medieval Christian view of what went on in pagan Iceland during the conversion period. The anecdote concerns a missionary Þorvaldr who is travelling around Iceland with a foreign bishop, preaching Christianity. They come to a place in the west called Hvammr, home of a *goði* Þórarinn *fylsenni* ('Foal's-Forehead'), who is away at the assembly carrying out his chieftainly duties. But his wife and son are at home, and the anecdote describes the wife, Friðgerðr, sacrificing in the *hof* at the same time as the missionaries are preaching the new faith, while the son, Skeggi, simply laughs at their efforts to drown out each other's words. Þorvaldr recites the following stanza, which contains a range of vocabulary signifying different aspects of the heathen religion:[66]

> Fór ek með dóm inn dýra,
> drengr hlýddi mér engi;
> gátum háð at hreyti
> hlautteins, goða sveini.
> En við enga svinnu

aldin rýgr við skaldi,
þá kreppi Guð gyðju,
gall um heiðnum stalla.

I brought the glorious *dómr* [i.e. *kristindómr* = Christianity], no one listened to me; I got mockery from the shaker of the sacrificial twig, the boy of the *goði*. And the aged dame crowed with no wisdom at the poet from the heathen platform. May God punish that *gyðja*.

All the elements of how we imagine pagan practices in Iceland are here: the twig for sprinkling sacrificial blood, some kind of platform for performing the rites on, and a female cult leader presiding. The prose places these rites within a *hof*, though in another version of the story, they simply take place *inni* 'inside' and could as well be happening in the main building of the farm, while the stanza gives no clues as to the location of the rites.[67]

We get a similar glimpse of female participation in such rites in some stanzas perhaps more convincingly contemporary than Þorvaldr's, but also deriving from the response of a Christian poet to strange pagan customs. They come from a sequence of verses (*Austrfararvísur* 'Verses on a Journey to the East') by Sigvatr Þórðarson, an Icelandic poet who was active in Norway during the first half of the eleventh century, describing a political mission he undertook to Sweden on behalf of King Óláfr Haraldsson, around 1019.[68] Stanza 4 describes the travellers' arrival at either a place called Hof (probably in Sweden, but possibly somewhere in Norway along their way), or a place which is a *hof*, where the door is barred to them by *heiðnir rekkar* 'heathen men' (or 'people'), presumably because they are Christians. In Stanza 5, Sigvatr cites the response of a woman (as in Þorvaldr's stanza, she is unflatteringly described as a *rýgr*, a term normally used for giantesses) who says she cannot let him in because she is in the process of holding an *alfablót í bœ sínum* 'sacrifice to the elves in her farmhouse'. Here, however, there is no indication of who is leading the rites, though it is of interest that they take place inside a dwelling. And although the woman makes reference to Óðinn, it is clearly not the deity to whom they are sacrificing, but to the elves. This resonates with the number of female personal names with the deuterotheme *-ælfr* in the predominantly Swedish runic corpus, as discussed above.

The Swedish and the Icelandic episodes which, if they really happened, were only about three decades apart, have clear similarities. Taken with other evidence presented above, the picture is consistent, even if it shows there was much variation. Religious rituals could be led by male or female cult leaders, they seem to have taken place indoors, most likely in dwellings, but we cannot completely exclude the possibility of dedicated buildings, they may have taken place on a special platform within the building, and they are described as *blót* 'sacrifice'. The connection with the name *Hof* or word *hof* is established in Stanza 4 of Sigvatr's *Austrfararvísur*. There is nothing here that is inconsistent with either the place-name or archaeological evidence, as described above, and these two literary images are probably the closest we can get to the rituals of the pre-Christian religion in both Scandinavia and Iceland. This is the basic outline from which other examples may be evaluated, the bottom line of what we think we know about that religion.

Deities in the diaspora

An interesting question, raised obliquely and in a rather different context by Neil Gaiman in his novel *American Gods* (2001), is what happens to deities when they cross the ocean. Names in particular, but also other forms of evidence, can be brought to bear on this question, though here again there are problems of chronology.

While the number of Viking Age runic inscriptions from Britain and Ireland is too small to draw many conclusions from (and heavily concentrated in the Isle of Man), we may still note that they record eight male names and one female name containing the element *Þór-*, and one male and one female name with *Ás-*.[69] The other name-elements discussed above are not represented. However, there are other sources for Scandinavian personal names in Britain, from documents, or extracted from place-names. While many of these documents are from later than the Viking Age, they do nevertheless testify to the vitality of personal naming practices in the Scandinavian parts of Britain. Thus, in a corpus of Scandinavian personal names from Lincolnshire and Yorkshire, including many recorded as late as the twelfth or thirteenth century, we find a number of names containing the cited elements (see Table 5.3).[70]

The overall pattern is very similar to that of the names in the runic corpus discussed above, though the number of elements recorded is fewer.

A similar exercise on the many thousands of names in *Landnámabók* produces the results shown in Table 5.4.[71]

TABLE 5.3 Personal names in Lincolnshire and Yorkshire containing sacral elements

Element	*No. of male names*	*No. of female names*	*Total no. of names*
Alf-	5	1	6
Ās-	12	1	13
Frøy-	1	0	1
Guð-	7	1	8
Ōðin-	1	0	1
Þōr-	20	4	24
-þōrr	3	0	3

TABLE 5.4 Personal names in *Landnámabók* containing sacral elements

Element	*No. of male names*	*No. of female names*	*Total no. of names*
Álf-	1	3	4
Ás-	11	9	20
Frey-	2	2	4
Guð-	6	6	12
Þór-	29	18	47
Vé	11	3	14

Both sets of names contain more or less the same elements in similar proportions, with the exception of *Vé-* which is common in Iceland but not found in England. But what these names represent is the export of the name-stock to the regions of the diaspora, rather than necessarily the export of particular religious beliefs.

While the popular personal names containing sacral elements continue to be popular, the transfer of theophoric place-names, a safer indicator of religious beliefs as discussed above, is much less common. Iceland does have a place named Njarðvík, presumably incorporating the name of the god Njǫrðr (though the sacral character of this has been disputed), and several places containing *Þór-*, including a river, a ?forest and a peninsula, though this element does not appear compounded with words for cult sites, as in mainland Scandinavia.[72] Much more common are the places named *Hof*, or *Hofstaðir*, or similar, mainly occupied sites but also some landscape features (one mountain and one bay). Thus, *Landnámabók* mentions nine places called *Hof*, four examples of *Hofstaðir* and four in which *hof-* is compounded with various words indicating a settlement or at least owned land. The element *hǫrg-* also appears a few times, though in the rocky landscape of Iceland it will be more difficult to determine a sacral meaning in these places, given the meaning of this element as discussed above.

Elsewhere in the diaspora, theophoric place-names are even thinner on the ground, with the notable exception of an unusual eminence in North Yorkshire now called Roseberry Topping, but most likely derived from an original *Óðinsberg*. This summit lies in the midst of an area with a substantial number of Scandinavian place-names and other evidence for Scandinavian settlement in the Viking Age. Some of the surrounding place-names, though not strictly speaking theophoric, suggest a landscape charged with Scandinavian cultural practices.[73] Within this context, it is perfectly possible to imagine cult rituals such as those described above taking place, though again it is important to remember the distinction between sacred places and cult sites. Names indicative of heathen cult sites in England are otherwise both very few and far from certain, though there is an outside chance that Hoff in Westmorland is a *hof*-name.[74] The picture is similarly thin in Scotland. Despite a variety of suggestions to the contrary, there is no certain example of a place-name containing the name of a Norse deity in Scotland, the most likely one being Thurso, in Caithness, perhaps from *Þórshaugr*.[75] In general, other explanations can be found for place-names which might appear to contain the names of Þórr or Óðinn, and of cult sites there is no direct evidence whatsoever.

However, the absence of theophoric names does not mean that the gods were not known, and possibly venerated. An important, though again limited, source of evidence for the Norse deities in the diaspora is that of the Viking Age sculpture that is abundant in many parts of Scandinavian England, some parts of Scandinavian Scotland, and richest of all in the Isle of Man. Although the sculpture is abundant, images of the deities are not. However, there are enough examples that are more or less certain to make this some of the most important evidence for the 'export' of the old gods to new homes. Thus, Þórr is certainly depicted only on the Gosforth Fishing Stone in Cumbria, though it has also been suggested that two

Manx monuments may depict his fishing expedition for the *Miðgarðsormr* 'World-Serpent'.[76] Óðinn is more alluded to than unambiguously depicted, but there is a reasonably certain depiction on one of the runic carved stones from Kirk Andreas, Isle of Man, which shows him being devoured by the wolf Fenrir at Ragnarǫk.[77] Along with other depictions of the events of Ragnarǫk, carvings showing warriors or figures with Odinic attributes and iconographic allusions to Yggdrasill (the tree on which Óðinn sacrificed himself) all suggest fairly extensive knowledge of myths about Óðinn in Anglo-Scandinavian England and the Isle of Man.[78]

Ragnarǫk imagery more broadly is quite common and this extends the range of gods depicted. Thus, Viðarr, the son of Óðinn, is shown avenging his father on the Gosforth cross in Cumbria.[79] Heimdallr, with his horn announcing Ragnarǫk, has been identified both on the Gosforth cross and on a carved stone from Jurby, Isle of Man.[80] The Gosforth cross also depicts the punishment of Loki for his role in the death of Baldr (and therefore Ragnarǫk), along with his wife Sigyn.[81] The Ragnarǫk imagery also includes two fairly certain iconographical references to the god Týr and his sacrifice of his hand to the wolf Fenrir on hogbacks from Sockburn in County Durham and Lythe in North Yorkshire.[82] In a rather different mode, a graffito now in Skipwith but possibly originally done in York, also seems to consist of Ragnarǫk imagery, possibly even depicting Óðinn.[83] Although the suggestion that it was done by a 'bored Viking warrior . . . [who] scratched his own vision of one end of the World onto a stone' is speculative, it is certainly a rather different form of picture than those on the monuments.[84]

Although the sculptural evidence for the god Þórr is not extensive, he seems to be ubiquitous in England (and is just present in Scotland) in the form of hammer amulets which have been identified as representing his weapon Mjǫllnir, along with other representations of hammers, for example on coins issued by the Norse kings of York.[85] The amulets in particular have grown in numbers in recent years due to metal-detecting, and there is now a risk that some of the finds are fakes. But these amulets are extensively paralleled throughout the Viking world, and it is interesting to observe that while the Christian mission latched on to Óðinn and the myth of Ragnarǫk, the everyday Viking was more likely to have been a devotee of Þórr, if the amulets are an indication of belief.

Paradoxically, and in a way that is typical of the diaspora, the contexts for the images on sculpture are almost always Christian, usually very clearly so. As was pointed out at the beginning of this chapter, myth does not necessarily equate to religion, and the use of the Norse myths in Christian contexts has occasioned much debate among scholars, who have come up with many theories about why and how images from Norse paganism could be used by or perhaps even for Christian audiences. The most common explanations are Christian mission and Scandinavian acculturation, which could be seen as two sides of the same coin. Thus, Lilla Kopár argues that the sculpture represents typology, or figurative thinking, a form of religious accommodation that facilitated the integration of the Scandinavian settlers through cultural convergence.[86] Similarly, though with a different emphasis, scholars such as Richard Bailey and John McKinnell have seen the sculptures as purely Christian products, merely using the heathen material to deliver a pre-determined Christian message, and the possibility of their having a teaching function in the context of mission has been raised by Lesley Abrams.[87] One scholar, David Stocker, sees in the sculpture of Northumbria the 'flowering of a hybrid religion which had characteristics of both paganism and Christianity'.[88] While few scholars would go this far, there is no doubt that the sculptural evidence for Norse paganism in England is inextricably linked with Christianity. In this context, it is worth remembering the point already made, that religious change does not happen overnight. Even in England, where there was undoubtedly strong pressure from the local situation for the pagan Norse to become Christian, it is not possible to pinpoint a particular moment when one religion ends and another begins.[89]

Also mediated through Christian, but importantly contemporary, eyes is the evidence of some texts from Anglo-Saxon England by the lay chronicler Æthelweard, writing in Latin, and the clerical authors Ælfric and Wulfstan, writing in Old English. These works have been discussed in detail by Matthew Townend, who has been able to demonstrate that these Christian authors knew of a whole range of Scandinavian gods.[90] Townend's linguistic analysis of their writings shows that Æthelweard knew of Viðarr and Baldr 'through Scandinavian contact'. While Ælfric and Wulfstan assimilate the Norse gods to their classical equivalents, Ælfric in particular seems to have known the Old Norse forms of the names of Þórr, Óðinn and Frigg. All in all, this evidence points to living traditions about Norse gods in tenth-century England, though the contexts in which these traditions were alive are difficult to reconstruct.

One particular context, however, is that of skaldic poetry composed in tenth- and eleventh-century England, which has a range of reference to Norse gods and myths that is even broader than those mentioned in connection with the evidence discussed above.[91] Although these poems represent a narrow cultural and social context, in that they are all composed by Scandinavian or Icelandic poets in praise of Scandinavian rulers in England, they have a fairly wide chronological range (from the mid-tenth to the late eleventh century) and can be placed geographically both in the heavily Norse regions of Northumbria, but also in the southern bastions of the eleventh-century Danish dynasty. The skaldic evidence also illustrates the way in which the processes of diaspora reinforce cultural knowledge and cultural practices from the homeland, in this case in the context of an elite diaspora, as discussed by Lesley Abrams.[92]

As discussed in Chapter 1, Viking Age burials are ambiguous in many ways. Do they reveal religious beliefs, or the fashion of the time, or do they express local or regional identities, or all three?[93] While burials may be social acts as much as, or even more than, religious acts, they may still provide evidence for the veneration of particular gods. For example, Guðrún Nordal has argued that the presence of horses and spears in the pagan graves of Iceland are veiled allusions to the worship of Óðinn.[94] Similarly, she argues that personal names of real people which are identical to those said to be alternative names for Óðinn (such as *Gizurr* and *Gautr*), or names containing elements referring to his familiars, the wolf and the raven, as well as names ending in *-geirr* 'spear', are similarly evidence of the followers of Óðinn, at least in earlier generations. As noted above, once adopted into the pool of given names, such names are not necessarily meaningful. Neither the 'Odinic' burials nor the names necessarily provide direct evidence of pre-Christian beliefs in Iceland, but taken together in an interdisciplinary way, they do suggest patterns which indicate that for the little over a century before Iceland became Christian, Óðinn was a respected and venerated deity.

The conversion to Christianity

The conversion of Scandinavians (whether at home or in the diaspora) to Christianity is probably the most thoroughly studied topic in this field. Over the last few decades, there have been several major international and interdisciplinary research projects, with many outputs, some also comparing the Scandinavian conversions with those of other northern European peoples. To summarise all the results of this massive scholarly effort is far beyond what is possible within the scope of this book.[95] Moreover, many of the published studies have focused on the introduction and gradual supremacy of Christianity, with much less emphasis on what went before, or even on the process of transition from one religion to another. In part, this is because, as outlined above, it is in fact very difficult to pin down the pre-Christian religion of Scandinavia as an organised and systematic religion, like Christianity, rather than as a miscellaneous set of beliefs and practices. Nevertheless, it is important to survey some of the frameworks within which scholars have approached the topic, in order to understand the role the diaspora played in this process.

Two aspects of the processes by which the Scandinavian homelands and the diaspora all became Christian have been particularly salient in the voluminous research into this subject. One is an important distinction between conversion and Christianisation, or between conversion moment and Christianisation process, and the other is that the latter could take a very long time, in a context of much geographical variation.[96] Conversion may be a personal thing, or it may apply to a whole country, such as when the Icelanders decided, collectively at their General Assembly, and literally overnight, to become Christians in the summer of 999.[97] Yet even that decision still allowed some pagan practices to continue for an unspecified time afterwards, namely the consumption of horseflesh and the exposure of unwanted children, and sacrifice if it was practised in secret, according to Chapter 7 of Ari Þorgilsson's *Íslendingabók*.[98] So even this classic account of a conversion moment recognises that religious transformation cannot happen overnight. Churches need to be built, priests educated, a bureaucracy established, and ordinary people taught the basics of both the new faith and what was now expected of them. In Iceland, it is estimated that the full Christianisation of the country, at least in terms of the establishment of the required infrastructure, took something like three hundred years.[99] This can be contrasted with the evidence from places like Hofstaðir, where what seem to be clearly pagan rituals can be shown to have come to an end just at the time when the earliest Christian rituals can be demonstrated nearby. This suggests that, even if the infrastructure took some time to evolve fully, either people were quick to make the changes themselves, or the Church was quick to stamp on those practices which it considered least acceptable.

In the homelands, the picture is more complex. On the basis of a number of studies which have compared in detail the archaeological evidence for different regions and localities in different parts of Scandinavia, it seems that there was considerable variation in burial practice, even in adjacent places. This applies both to the pre-Christian burial practices and the early Christian graves, suggesting that the process of Christianisation varied and had a different character in different regions.[100] This variety is undoubtedly a product of both geography and a variety of external influences, but probably also reflects the difficulty of changing the well-entrenched beliefs and practices of the Scandinavians, and suggests pockets of resistance in many places. This picture accords with the kings' sagas, which suggest multiple efforts at the Christianisation of Norway at least, by successive tenth- and eleventh-century kings. While the details of their efforts may not be strictly speaking historical, the overall picture of a lengthy and difficult process seems to be correct.

There is also evidence for a prehistory to the conversion of the homelands. The recorded evidence of Anskar's mission to Denmark and Sweden, in the mid-ninth century, and archaeological evidence in the form of Christian burials suggesting the presence of Christians in Scandinavia as early as the ninth century, all indicate at least two hundred years of Christian prehistory before the official conversions of the late tenth or eleventh centuries. In the early trading centre of Ribe in Denmark, archaeologists have recently found a cemetery of inhumation graves of clearly Christian character dating in some cases to the ninth century.[101] As these are Christian graves without grave-goods, the identity of the occupants cannot easily be established, and they are not necessarily Danish Christians. In an international emporium like Ribe, it would be no surprise to find foreign Christians in sufficient numbers for them to establish a Christian cemetery for those who died there.

There is a similarly early Christian cemetery on the island of Veøy in Møre og Romsdal, Norway. It is unclear whether the etymology of this name is from *vé* 'sanctuary, cult site' or *við* 'wood' (see discussion above), since both are supported by the spellings of the earliest documents, from the fourteenth to the sixteenth centuries.[102] The site consists of a number of inhumation graves of clearly Christian character, surrounding what might have been a wooden church (though nothing of this remains).[103] Based on radiocarbon dates, the earliest graves are dated to the ninth or tenth century. Although the excavator of the graves linked them to missionary activity by the Norwegian king Hákon *Aðalsteinsfóstri* in the tenth century, more recently Sæbjørg W. Nordeide has questioned this on the basis of recalibrated dates, and suggested that the site was 'an early, single Christian community, such as a monastery', which might have been there for missionary purposes.[104]

In Old Icelandic literature, the Swedes are notoriously presented as late and reluctant converts to Christianity. But even here, there is some archaeological evidence for early Christian burials from about the tenth century onwards.[105] Again, regional variation is important, as in some parts of Sweden pagan burials seem to have continued into the twelfth century. The several thousand rune-stones from Sweden, dated mainly to the eleventh century, are generally associated with a conversion period during that century. At Varnhem, in Västergötland, later an important monastery, the earliest wooden church seems to have been built in around the year 1000.[106] Christian burial, however, took place even earlier, with 10 graves from before that date, the earliest one from the late ninth century, and pagan burial practices seem to have died out in this region in the first decades of the tenth century.[107]

Scandinavians in those areas of the diaspora where they came into contact with indigenous Christian populations were presumably converted before the official conversions of the homelands, though here too there is much regional variation.[108] An under-explored question is the extent to which the conversion of the homelands was stimulated or facilitated by diasporic contacts with the newly Christian Scandinavians overseas. As already noted in the discussion of sculpture above, some aspects of the old religion seem to have persisted, not only beyond the conversion, but even under the aegis of the church, in Britain and Ireland. Here, the evidence of Christian burial, the normal practice of the indigenous inhabitants, will not reveal much about the conversion of Scandinavians (unless the new science of isotope analysis could identify the occupants of Christian graves who were born in Scandinavia). Pagan burials are relatively rare, so the process of the conversion of the Scandinavians has to be deduced from the fairly ambiguous evidence of historical documents and various kinds of stone monument.[109] Differences in the ways in which the Scandinavians in these regions became Christian are explained by differences in the socio-political circumstances.[110] In England, with a large immigrant population, the result was productive cultural fusion and positive partnerships between churches and the new Christians. In Ireland, powerful churches and rulers seem to have kept the two groups apart well into the tenth century. In the Scottish isles, lacking strong government in the conversion period, the process seems to have been natural and inevitable, and largely the result of interactions with nearby Christians.

Some of those interactions left their mark in Iceland where many of the early settlers came from the British Isles rather than directly from Norway. It has been suggested that the smoothness of the adoption of Christianity there in 999 derived in part from this previous acquaintance with Christianity on the part of some of the population, as well as the relatively short time in which ancestral pagan customs had to flourish in that country.[111] But, if burials are an index of paganism, then Iceland, with over 300 such burials, from 157 locations, in the archaeological record, certainly maintained some pagan customs.[112] In terms of the conversion process, it has been argued that two distinct types of church from the late tenth and eleventh centuries represent two different avenues for the introduction of Christianity into Iceland.[113] The turf churches are most closely linked to architectural traditions in some parts of western and northern Norway, Faroe, Ireland, Scotland and Greenland, and represent the influence of a Celtic style of Christianity which, in

Iceland, was brought by settlers from the British Isles. The timber churches on the other hand have their parallels in the Scandinavian homelands and seem to link to Anglo-Saxon missionary activity there, reaching Iceland through the Norwegian-instigated missionary activity of the late tenth century.

In Russia, the Scandinavian settlers encountered a very different situation. Here there was no organised Christian religion and the indigenous population were also pagans, though in a different way. The consequence of not needing to oppose Christianity directly was far fewer Thor's hammer amulets in precious metal, which are generally regarded as a response to Christianity, as opposed to the smaller and often multiple iron hammer pendants on iron rings, which are the traditional material culture of Scandinavian paganism, particularly in Sweden. The latter are quite commonly found in Russia, whereas no certain examples of the former are known from there.[114] Moreover, other than burials, there is little evidence for Scandinavian pagan cult activities in Russia, either in the form of cult buildings or the figurines discussed above. A recent survey has concluded that any pagan cult activities took place within the family home.[115] In Russia, Christianity was introduced in the tenth century hand in hand with the development of an interethnic society in which many of the ancestral traditions from Scandinavia had lost their meaning, and in which the population, both branches of pagan origin, though from different traditions, took on the new religion together. This merging of traditions is illustrated in the Russo-Byzantine treaties of 944–5 and 971, recorded in the *Russian Primary Chronicle*.[116] In these, the Rus have Scandinavian names and it is envisaged that some of them have been baptised, so they are variously to swear upon either the Christian God or the Slavic deities Perun or Volos.[117] There is no mention of the Norse gods, even though the Scandinavian names of the envoys include several people called Freysteinn and four people with names including the elements *Þórr-* or *-þórr*.

Myths

Recording myths and legends

Much of the evidence for the Norse deities in the Viking diaspora, as outlined above, also implies the existence of stories about the gods and other supernatural beings, which it is convenient to call 'myths'. Although a picture may be worth a thousand words, it cannot in itself tell a story, though it can allude to one. So, to the uninitiated, the Gosforth Fishing Stone simply shows two figures in a boat. But to those who know the story, significant details such as the serpentine figure and the ox-head beneath the boat, and the hammer-like object in the hand of one of the figures in the boat, show that the image alludes to the myth in which Þórr sets out with the giant Hymir to catch the Miðgarðsormr, the World Serpent. This story, which is also alluded to in art from Viking Age Scandinavia, is found in Eddic poetry (*Hymiskviða*), and in a variety of skaldic poetry recorded in Snorri's *Edda* (especially Bragi Boddason's *Ragnarsdrápa* and Ulfr Uggason's *Húsdrápa*).[118]

All the sculptures with imagery from Ragnarǫk presuppose stories about that event, or series of events, many different versions of which are recorded in the Eddas. They can also presuppose a narrative sequence, which is further evidence for a story. Thus, according to Snorri, Loki's punishment (for having arranged the killing of Baldr) will last until he breaks free of his bonds at Ragnarǫk.[119] So the presence of a scene clearly representing Loki's punishment on the Gosforth cross implies a chronology in relation to the images of Ragnarǫk elsewhere on the cross. While any material representation can only imply an actual narrative, the existence of which has to be presupposed or reconstructed, overall the sculpture suggests that a number of Old Norse myths and legends were known in some kind of oral story form in Viking Age England and the Isle of Man, available to be appropriated by the makers of Christian stone monuments. Such evidence raises the question of the form in which these underlying stories were known in England (and the Isle of Man), and one suggestion has been that oral poems similar to surviving Eddic poems were known in tenth-century England, though this is impossible to prove.[120]

It may well be that the situation in which these stories crystallised from earlier mythological motifs is precisely that of the encounter between paganism and Christianity, and a similar situation may have pertained in late Viking Age Norway. Christopher Abram has surveyed a range of skaldic and some Eddic verse which he argues was produced in Norway in the second half of the tenth century and which contains a lot of mythological material.[121] In particular, most of this poetry can be associated with the earls of Hlaðir, an aggressively pagan dynasty based in Trøndelag. There is, in this poetry, remarkable evidence for how paganism could be and was used in political contexts but, as Abram points out, these poems 'are still not quite what we could usually call "myths"', rather they are still very much making 'references to the Norse gods and other mythological figures'.[122] In this way, this poetry, and indeed most skaldic poetry with mythological content, is best compared to the iconographical references on sculpture, as both assume in their audience a familiarity with the figures and stories which can give meaning to their allusions. Both types of allusion, skaldic and sculptural, serve a dominant ideology, a pagan one in the case of the tenth-century Norwegian poetry, but a Christian one in the case of most of the insular sculpture, also largely from the tenth century.

Other than in nebulous and unreconstructable oral traditions, the recording of Norse myths as actual narratives rather than allusions to narratives, as recognisable 'myths' (remembering that this word basically means 'story'), can only take place in a written culture, when there is a will to record them as narratives. Thus, the references to Norse gods in Adam of Bremen, and in a variety of Anglo-Saxon texts, as discussed above, remain references, and do not tell stories about these figures. This narrativisation happens with the development of manuscript culture in Scandinavia and Iceland. Literacy in the roman alphabet, whether in the Old Norse or the Latin language, was introduced, as explained in Chapter 1, to Scandinavia with the conversion to Christianity. Although there is no direct evidence for a manuscript culture before 1100, soon after that the writing of texts in both Latin and the vernacular takes off. But the earliest authors did not rush to record their ancestral traditions – as the author of the *First Grammatical Treatise* pointed out, some time in the second half of the twelfth century, writing was first put to practical use by his predecessors for 'laws and genealogies, or interpretations of sacred writings, or also that sagacious (historical) lore that Ari Þorgilsson has recorded in books'.[123] But with this strong historical bent, it was inevitable that authors would soon turn to the stories of their culture that were even older than those of the earliest kings.

Two nearly contemporary authors stand out in this context, the Dane Saxo Grammaticus (*c.* 1150–1220), who wrote in Latin, and the Icelander Snorri Sturluson (1179–1241), who wrote in his native language. Even though their texts are different in many ways, both were pioneers in their attempts 'to turn traditional stories about the Scandinavian gods into a cohesive sequence of prose narratives'.[124] For Saxo, the context was a massive and florid account of the kings of Denmark from the earliest times, in which he avowedly turned to the Icelanders for material.[125] In this material, we can discern the outlines of some well-known Old Norse myths, but they are not presented as myth but rather as history. Like other medieval authors, Saxo's view of the old gods was through the lens of euhemerism, a doctrine which maintained that the gods were actually just people who were falsely believed to be gods.[126] Thus, the story of a feud between the Danish king Høtherus and a certain Balderus, son of Othinus, has echoes of the killing of Óðinn's son Baldr by Hǫðr that set off the events of Ragnarǫk, but it is far from the same story.[127] Saxo's picture of Othinus, however, is the same as in the medieval Icelandic sources: he is 'chief of the gods', he consorts with seers and soothsayers, he disguises himself with a large hat, and he gives victory to his followers.[128]

Snorri also wrote a compendious history, in his case of the kings of Norway, *Heimskringla*, which does have some important mythological material which he did not get from the same sources as those he used for the later parts of his history. His approach to the old gods is similarly euhemeristic in both *Heimskringla* and the preface to his main work in recording the old myths, his *Edda*. In the *Ynglinga saga* section of *Heimskringla*, Óðinn is a chieftain in Asia, but one who is in charge of a great *blótstaðr* 'sacrificial place' run by 12 *hofgoðar*.[129] Snorri's *Edda* is a complex work which is part handbook to poetry, and part guide to mythology. After the euhemeristic Preface, this viewpoint is largely lost in *Gylfaginning*, which presents the gods straightforwardly as gods, though within a narrative framework which is designed to emphasise their tricky and deceptive natures. *Gylfaginning* is the first attempt to present Old Norse mythology systematically, though Snorri did have precursors (and models) in some poems also known from the Poetic *Edda* (*Vǫluspá*, *Vafþrúðnismál* and *Grímnismál*, all three of which he cites extensively) which present either a coherent vision of the cosmos or an account of the world encompassing both its creation and its destruction.

The Poetic *Edda* is also a compilation, though of a rather different sort. It is a single manuscript, written in Iceland in the third quarter of the thirteenth century, which gathers 31 poems with mythological or legendary content, organised so that the 10 mythological ones come first.[130] The origins and dating of these poems have been the subject of much discussion over the years, without any real consensus.

Detailed studies of the manuscript suggest that its exemplar can probably be traced back to around 1200, though that still leaves a considerable gap back to a potential pre-Christian oral tradition.[131] However, most scholars would probably subscribe to the view of Preben Meulengracht Sørensen that many of the poems, particularly those which have mythological content, contain ancient material, even if the actual surviving texts are not necessarily a close representation of oral texts from the Viking Age.[132] A number of similar poems are found in other manuscripts, and are usually included in editions and translation of the Poetic *Edda*. All of these are important, but troublesome, evidence for the pre-Christian thought-world of the Scandinavians and the Viking diaspora.

Diasporic myths

The medieval texts discussed above which provide the main evidence for Old Norse myth emanate predominantly from Iceland. The traditional view which saw these Icelandic texts as written recordings of oral tales originally brought by the first settlers from their Norwegian homeland does not provide a model of whether, or how, stories of the old gods and heroes might have circulated elsewhere in the diaspora. If, as noted above, something like the Eddic poems were known in the British Isles, this would strengthen the argument that this kind of poetry did come to Iceland with the settlers from the Scandinavian homelands, though this would be quite a circular argument. But it cannot be denied that the sculpture of Viking Age England and the Isle of Man demonstrate, albeit indirectly, the existence of stories on mythological and legendary subjects that are earlier than any written record of those stories. There is a clear parallel between these stories which came to Britain from the Scandinavian homeland (most probably Norway) and those which were later recorded in Iceland, and the simplest solution is to assume that they reached Iceland by more or less the same processes that took them to the British Isles.

However, the exchange of stories did not stop there. It has already been noted that the Icelanders were the givers, to their diasporic cousins in medieval Denmark, of mythological tales euhemerised by the churchman Saxo into the history of his country, written around 1200. But it is unlikely that Saxo got all of his material from the Icelanders. In fact, he alludes to both oral poetry and runic inscriptions as a way of transmitting tradition in Denmark:[133]

> I should like it to be known that Danes of an older age, filled with a desire to echo the glory when noble braveries had been performed, alluded in the Roman manner to the splendour of their nobly-wrought achievements with choice compositions of a poetical nature; not only that, but they engraved the letters of their own language on rocks and stones to retell those feats of their ancestors which had been made popular in the songs of their mother tongue.

The reference to the Icelanders comes after this passage, suggesting that Saxo chose to use Icelandic sources because they resonated with what he already knew about the oral and runic traditions of his homeland.

Somewhat earlier than Saxo, the Earldom of Orkney was a centre for Norse cultural activity in the twelfth and early thirteenth centuries.[134] A closer focus on Norse myths and legends in this diasporic context can shed light on the ways in which such traditional material circulated in the diaspora at around the time that such myths were first being recorded.

Case study – Norse myth in Orkney

Two mythological narratives (though not directly stories about the gods) are located, at least in some versions, in Orkney. The Everlasting Battle, or *Hjaðningavíg*, is said in *Snorra Edda* to have taken place in *Háey* in the *Orkneyjar*, apparently the Orcadian island of Hoy.[135] The story tells of a princess, Hildr (whose name means 'battle') who is abducted by a king called Heðinn. They are pursued by her father Hǫgni to Hoy where the men refuse to be reconciled and begin a battle. In the night, Hildr wakes all the dead to life again, so that they can fight again the following day, and this fight and revivification happens every day and night until Ragnarǫk.

The other story involves a magic quern, or hand-mill, called Grótta or Grótti that grinds out whatever its owner wishes. While it belongs to a Danish king Fróði, he makes it grind out gold for him and works the slave-women, Fenja and Menja, who operate it hard. In revenge, they grind out an army that kills Fróði. The king Mýsingr who kills him and inherits the quern makes it grind out salt. So much salt is ground that Mýsingr's ship sinks, along with the quern which continues to grind, making the sea salt. In one version the quern is said to lie at the bottom of the Pentland Firth, at the spot where there is a *svelgr* 'whirlpool' (presumably that named as *Svelgr* in ch. 74 of *Orkneyinga saga*).[136]

These are both widespread and well-known tales, attested in a number of versions, not all of which have Orcadian associations. Thus, the *Hjaðningavíg* is not located in Orkney in its earliest version, Bragi's *Ragnarsdrápa*, where it is said simply to have taken place on an island.[137] Saxo's slightly different version of the story takes place mainly in Denmark, though there is a fight in the Orkneys.[138] In *Sörla þáttr* the narrative moves from Denmark to an island called *Há*, though the latter is not specifically said to be in Orkney.[139] The story of the salt mill/whirlpool is linked to the myth of the Danish king Fróði's magic quern Grótti and his slave-women Fenja and Menja, who grind out gold for him on it, by Snorri, as well as the version cited above. However, Snorri does not specify the location of the whirlpool, though he does call it a *svelgr*.[140] The Eddic-style poem *Grottasǫngr* that Snorri cites does not refer to either the salt mill or the whirlpool, and other versions of the story of Fróði do not mention slave-women or querns at all.[141]

This kind of variety is par for the course for traditional tales. It is impossible to pin down unitary 'origins' of such complex and multifaceted tales, but it is possible to explore in more detail the popularity of these tales in medieval Orkney. It so happens that both narratives are referred or alluded to in poetry attributed to the Norwegian-Orcadian Earl of Orkney, Rǫgnvaldr Kali Kolsson, active in the twelfth century, and both also appear in later folklore.[142] The narrative centring on the *Hjaðningavíg* is referred to in *Háttalykill*, a didactic poem composed jointly by Rǫgnvaldr and an Icelander Hallr Þórarinsson in Orkney in the twelfth century.[143] It devotes two stanzas to the story, told in question-and-answer form to illustrate a metre called *greppaminni*. These stanzas mention the main characters and the main elements of the story, but there is no reference to its location and the mythological dimension in which the warriors fight every day to be revivified by Hildr, while awaiting Ragnarǫk, is barely hinted at. *Háttalykill* thus seems to represent a rather different version of the story, which may have come to Orkney through the Icelander Hallr. Nevertheless, the poem is evidence that it was known there in the twelfth century if not before. The question-and-answer form of these stanzas (uniquely in this poem) may suggest that some instruction in the myth was needed. There is also a later Northern Isles connection in the form of a ballad recorded in eighteenth-century Shetland which clearly derives from this story and is set in Orkney.[144]

The salt mill story is more tenuously associated with Rǫgnvaldr. In one of his stanzas he uses the kenning *Fróða meldr* 'Fróði's meal' for 'gold'.[145] This kenning alludes to the first part of the myth, the magic mill that ground gold, rather than the salt mill/whirlpool story. However, there is a possibility that Rǫgnvaldr knew a version in which the two parts of the story were connected.[146] The argument is based on his use of the word *meldr*, which appears to be a non-Icelandic form in this meaning. Knowledge of the myth in Orkney may be further supported by evidence from later folklore about 'Grottie Finnie and Grotti Minnie and their Salt-Quern in the Pentland Firth' which were vaguely remembered by a couple of Orcadians around the turn of the twentieth century.[147] The names are significant here – if they derive from Fenja and Menja, as they seem to, then they link the two different parts of this myth (Fróði's slaves and the salt mill), as discussed above.

The *Hjaðningavíg* and the salt mill story are not the only mythological tales alluded to by Rǫgnvaldr. Poetry attributed to him and his twelfth-century associates contains a range of kennings based on the names of gods or mythological beings. It could be argued that such kennings are highly conventional and therefore not evidence of mythological knowledge. Snorri's *Edda* demonstrates that poetry containing such language could be remembered in the thirteenth century without the underlying mythology being fully known or understood, indeed the purpose of writing that text was to explain the myths. But there is a difference between kennings in which a mythological name merely stands for a category (e.g. 'goddess') and those which require an understanding of the underlying myth to make sense. Using this distinction, and disregarding the former, it is possible to identify the following allusions to well-known myths in twelfth-century poetry from Orkney:[148]

- gold as the bed of the serpent;
- gold as the speech of giants;
- gold as the brightness of water;
- poetry as Óðinn's drink;
- Óðinn hanged;
- Frigg's attempt to rescue Baldr from Hel.

There are also references to Norse myths and legends other than the *Hjaðningavíg* in *Háttalykill*. The content of this poem is essentially historical, listing the deeds of legendary heroes, starting with Sigurðr Fáfnisbani and going up through the legendary kings of Denmark to Hrólfr kraki.[149] Many of these legendary heroes are also mentioned in Snorri's *Edda* and may be assigned to a category of 'historical' myth which is too vast to take full account of here (though see further below on Sigurðr Fáfnisbani). It is of interest that *Háttalykill* mentions Ragnarr *loðbrók* ('Shaggy-Breeches') and that the name Loðbrók occurs in the runic graffiti of Maeshowe, contemporary with Rǫgnvaldr, though the reference is obscure.[150] *Háttalykill* then goes on to list kings of Sweden and Norway, many of them also legendary. The preservation of the poem is such that many of its kennings are obscure or difficult to decipher, nevertheless it is clear that there are few truly mythological kennings, in the narrow sense of those based on stories about the gods, rather than kennings which use mythological names to stand for a category. However, the following myths are alluded to:[151]

- poetry as the liquid of dwarves;
- gold as the bed or way of the serpent;
- the Rhinegold, gold as the fire of the sea;
- gold as the speech of giants.

These correspond to the myths alluded to in Rǫgnvaldr's other poetry, as listed above, and reflect the interest in myths about gold, in particular, that Guðrún Nordal has seen as characteristic of the twelfth and thirteenth centuries, and which she also sees as emanating from the diocese of Lund, in Skåne, present-day Sweden but part of Denmark at the time.[152]

The twelfth-century Orcadian interest in myths about gold and poetry continues into the thirteenth. There is evidence for poetic composition in thirteenth-century Orkney in the form of two poems attributed to the Norwegian-Orcadian Bishop Bjarni Kolbeinsson. Like *Háttalykill*, his *Jómsvíkingadrápa* is a poem about the heroic deeds of legendary heroes, though in narrative rather than catalogue form. It too has the occasional use of mythological names and the even more occasional allusion to a mythological narrative, namely poetry as Óðinn's drink, and Óðinn hanged. *Málsháttakvæði* on the other hand (more uncertainly attributed to Bjarni) is basically a collection of proverbs, many of which have parallels beyond the Norse world. But this poem, too, alludes to some legendary heroes, as *Háttalykill* does, and also to a number of myths:[153]

- gold as the tears of Freyja;
- gold as the speech of giants;
- Baldr in Hel, and Frigg;
- gold as the dwelling-place of the serpent;
- poetry as the mead of Óðinn.

In Stanza 8 the poet comments that the various allusions are *nú minni forn* 'old lore now', while in Stanza 9, the story of Baldr's death is said to be *heyrinkunn* 'very well known'. These comments would certainly fit the hypothesis that the poem was composed in an Orcadian milieu where Rǫgnvaldr and his associates had cultivated the poetic art and this kind of 'old lore' in the previous century. While neither *Jómsvíkingadrápa* nor *Málsháttakvæði* make much use of Norse myth, those myths that they do allude to, principally those embedded in kennings for gold and poetry, match those current in twelfth-century Orcadian poetry, as outlined above.

There is thus plenty of evidence for a learned and poetical interest in Norse myth in twelfth- and thirteenth-century Orkney, but such evidence is scarce in earlier poetry associated with Orkney. The poetry of the Icelander Arnórr *jarlaskáld*, who worked for two eleventh-century Earls of Orkney (see ch. 1, above, and ch. 6, below) contains few allusions to mythological narratives, as opposed to mythological names which may not refer to specific myths and which are thus, as suggested above, not necessarily evidence for mythological knowledge.[154] It is difficult to deduce how much such knowledge Arnórr expected from his Orcadian audiences. In his poem for Þorfinnr, Earl of Orkney, Arnórr alludes to Norse cosmological myth in the kenning *erfiði Austra* 'the toil of Austri' and to Óðinn's possession of the mead of poetry in the kenning *hrosta brim Alfǫður* 'mash-surf of the All-father [= Óðinn]'.[155] It is notable that Arnórr does not share the later obsession with gold-kennings, supporting Nordal's suggestion that these are a particularly twelfth- and thirteenth-century phenomenon.

In the twelfth century, Orkney was central to the study and practice of skaldic poetry, involving an academic knowledge of particular myths and legends that turned out to be influential for Icelandic practice in the thirteenth.[156] There is no way of determining whether this knowledge goes any further back than the twelfth century in Orkney. It may have had to be either imported or re-imported in the twelfth century, with the revival of interest in stories of the old gods and heroes that was characteristic of that period. As noted above, Guðrún Nordal has suggested a connection with the Archbishopric of Lund.[157] A Norwegian connection is also possible, through Rǫgnvaldr who spent his early years there – but it is just as difficult to reconstruct the kind of social and cultural milieu which taught him poetry and mythology there as it is to identify a similar milieu in Orkney. Or, the knowledge of poetry and mythology may have come to Orkney from Iceland, with Rǫgnvaldr's fellow-poets, trained in the old oral traditions that were only just beginning to be recorded there. The arrival of a lot of well-trained Icelandic poets in the upwardly mobile, wealthy and vibrant culture of twelfth-century Orkney, spiced by contact with Celtic peoples all around, may just have been the catalyst that sparked an explosion of interest in poetry and mythology which was then quickly transferred back to Iceland and continued to develop there, culminating in Snorri's *Edda*.

Whichever way the cultural transfer went, it is clear that, in the twelfth century, Orcadians had a strong diasporic consciousness that meant they took a detailed interest in stories that linked them both to the homeland and to the other colonies in the diaspora, and that harked back to a pagan past. Paradoxically, but not surprisingly, this happened at the very moment that the Norse society of those islands was opening up to a range of influences from further afield, in architecture, poetry and literacy. To what extent this twelfth-century interest in Norse mythology actually derived from traditions brought by the first settlers is impossible to say. On the available evidence it does not look very likely. Rather, it seems more likely that diasporic contexts ranging from Denmark to Iceland created an ideal environment for the transmission, discovery, invention or re-invention of stories with roots in the Viking Age homelands.

Reworking old legends

Not all the stories with their roots in the Viking Age homelands were necessarily mythological in the strict sense, that is, stories about the gods. In any case, in a world-view which incorporated many gods and other mythological beings, the borders of what is 'mythological' are fairly permeable. As the evidence from twelfth-century Orkney discussed above shows, the academic interest in the old myths characteristic of that period also encompassed an interest in stories about old legendary heroes and kings of the distant past, and many of the traditional stories reworked by Saxo are better described as 'legends' than 'myths'. The conceptually clear distinction between 'myth' and 'legend' is actually difficult to maintain in the face of the medieval evidence. Thus, both Snorri, in his *Edda* and *Heimskringla*, and the compiler of the Poetic *Edda* included stories of gods and heroes in the same work. The conceptual distinction can, it is true, be discerned, as the legendary material in Snorri's *Edda* is largely confined to *Skáldskaparmál* and in the Poetic *Edda* the mythological and legendary poems are grouped separately and may have come from originally separate collections. It may be that the distinction was irrelevant for the Christian authors and compilers of the thirteenth century, since they no longer believed in the gods of the mythological stories, indeed Snorri warns his readers against doing so.[158] They would therefore require no more suspension of disbelief than stories about human, if exceptional, heroes of the past, with neither a direct threat to Christian doctrine. Indeed, it seems that the mythological and the legendary were easily attracted to each other, as can be seen in the story of Sigurðr, the slayer of the serpent Fáfnir.

This is one of the most widely recorded stories of the Viking diaspora, and its various forms will be discussed in more detail below. Essentially, it is the story of how the human hero Sigurðr kills the serpent (or dragon) Fáfnir and acquires its treasure. Some versions have a prehistory, in which this treasure originates in a killing which takes place in the world of the gods. In many versions, the story then continues in a long cycle which relates the death of Sigurðr and the subsequent history of the treasure, along with the vicissitudes of the various characters associated with it, notably Sigurðr's wife Guðrún, her brother Gunnarr and his wife Brynhildr.[159] In the Codex Regius of the Poetic *Edda*, written in the late thirteenth century, this story-cycle occupies nearly half of the surviving manuscript and, given that some of that manuscript is now missing, is likely originally to have taken up fully half of it. The story is of course also known in other traditions, from the Middle High German *Nibelungenlied* to the operas of Wagner, and its origins are to be sought in shadowy semi-historical figures who lived on the European continent in the Migration Period (fourth to sixth centuries). But the Vikings made it their own, and its spread across the Viking world illuminates some aspects of that diaspora.

Although many studies of this story complex consider all the different versions together, it is useful to separate the evidence chronologically, as well as geographically, precisely in order to plot its variation during the Viking diaspora, and the possible meanings of that variation.[160] The Viking Age evidence (tenth and eleventh centuries) is primarily in the form of stone monuments, whereas from the twelfth century onwards there is a wealth of literary sources, as well as sculpture, primarily in wood.

Case study – Sigurðr Fáfnisbani in the Viking Age

As the Viking Age evidence for the story of Sigurðr is largely pictorial, it is important to establish which images actually depict the story, and this is not necessarily a simple matter. In essence the story involves a hero killing a serpent or dragon, and both warrior figures and serpentine forms abound in Viking Age art. In a seminal article, Sue Margeson established those diagnostic features which indicate that a particular image or set of images represents the Sigurðr story, rather than any other warrior and/or any other serpent. These features are:[161]

- association with a smith who forges a sword for the hero;
- the killing of the serpent from beneath;
- the roasting of the serpent's heart by a thumb-sucking hero;
- birds who warn the hero of the smith's treachery;
- a horse carrying the treasure.

This kind of detail has to be taken from the later literary sources, and here Margeson relied heavily on *Vǫlsunga saga*, one of the latest of these. But overall the argument is convincing and, even with the reductions which result from a strict application of this method, Margeson arrived at a substantial corpus of Viking Age pictorial representations that are fairly certainly those of the Sigurðr legend.[162]

Using this method, Margeson identified four tenth- or eleventh-century cross-slabs from the Isle of Man as having such representations, from Kirk Andreas, Malew, Jurby and Ramsey (the last of these, now at Maughold, is a little uncertain, as will be discussed below). From England, the tenth-century cross from Halton in Lancashire is a certain example, with one or two possible further candidates from Yorkshire in the same period.[163] The rest of the Viking Age corpus is to be found in Sweden, on four eleventh-century runic or pseudo-runic monuments, from Ramsund (Sö 101) and Gök (Sö 327) in Södermanland, and Drävle (U 1163) and Ramsjö (U 1175) in Uppland.[164] The contexts, distribution and dating of all of these monuments (most of them runic memorials to the dead) are all remarkable. As with other mythological sculpture discussed above, all of these depictions occur in contexts which are more or less explicitly Christian, and the same question arises as to what function this presumably pre-Christian (if not exactly pagan) story played in such a context. The Manx monuments (along with the Halton cross from Lancashire, which could be seen as emanating from the same tenth-century Irish Sea context) are not only the earliest certain references to the story but also perhaps an unexpected place to find evidence for a story that has its ultimate origins on the European continent and which we assume was brought to the Irish Sea region by migrants of Scandinavian, perhaps Norwegian, origin. The Swedish monuments are a little later, but again from a context in which Christianity was still quite new, and again show a remarkable concentration, as they are from a fairly restricted area of central Sweden.

The importance of identifying which sculptures allude to the Sigurðr legend, and to which parts of it, is demonstrated by two of the Manx stones and several of the Swedish ones. While most of the Manx images focus on the central part of the story identified by the features listed above, there may also be visual allusions to those parts of the story that happened before and after the serpent-killing on two of the stones. The cross-slab from Ramsey (now at Maughold) shows a splayed quadruped with a long tail and a fish in its mouth, which Margeson identifies with the otter and the salmon killed by Loki, the episode which in Snorri's account sets the whole story in motion.[165] This episode also links the story to the mythological world, since the treasure for which Sigurðr kills the serpent is taken by the gods from the dwarf Andvari to pay compensation for Loki's killing of the otter. Some scholars also see the otter alluded to in the mysterious quadruped which is an inexplicable element of the Ramsund carving in Sweden.[166]

A motif from much later in the story-cycle is that of the death of Sigurðr's brother-in-law Gunnarr in a snake-pit when his own brother-in-law Atli lured him to his court in order to try to get the treasure from him.[167] The cross-slab from Kirk Andreas, which has clear images of the serpent-killing, the heart-roasting, the bird and the horse on one side, also has an image of a figure surrounded by serpentine forms, with his hands tied, as Gunnarr's are said to have been, on the other side. The close relationship with the certain Sigurðr-images makes this plausibly a depiction of Gunnarr, though it lacks the harp that, in the later versions, he is said to have played with his toes. Similarly, some of the additional stones that Stern argues belong to this group seem to allude to aspects of the story that come after Sigurðr's slaying of the dragon and his death.[168] It has also been argued that some of the picture stones from the Baltic island of Gotland have images of both Sigurðr and Gunnarr in the snake-pit.[169] While these seem more debatable than the examples discussed above, if true this would show knowledge of the story-cycle both earlier and further east than the Swedish examples.

If the images discussed in the previous paragraphs do indeed refer to other parts of the story-cycle, then this has very interesting implications, in that it suggests that a variety of different stories, of possibly different origin, were already linked to each other in the tenth and eleventh centuries, some time before they were recorded in writing, though this argument is dangerously circular. But support for it is found in similar links suggested by skaldic poetry from the same period (first half of the eleventh century) which also allude to various parts of the Sigurðr cycle.[170] A poem in praise of the Norwegian king Haraldr *harðráði* 'Hard-Ruler' alludes to the following elements of the story:[171]

- Sigurðr killing the serpent with a sword;
- Sigurðr roasting the heart of the serpent;
- the wooing of Brynhildr;
- Atli's invitation to his brothers-in-law.

Another poem connected to Haraldr's older half-brother, King (later Saint) Óláfr Haraldsson, describes the killing of the serpent, and possibly the roasting of its heart in allusive terms.[172] The prose context of this stanza states that it was composed in response to a scene depicted on some wall-hangings. If correctly dated, then these poetical allusions importantly show that a longer version of the story-cycle was also known in Norway at roughly the same time as in the Isle of Man and Sweden. The second example may even provide evidence for a pictorial version, in a medium (textile) which is unlikely to survive, but which may have been a widespread method of disseminating such stories.

Case study – Sigurðr Fáfnisbani in the twelfth and thirteenth centuries

The earliest written evidence for the Sigurðr story comes in a text known as the *Leiðarvísir* of Nikulás of Þverá, a set of itineraries for Nordic pilgrims to Rome and the Holy Land, written by an Icelandic monk in the middle of the twelfth century. This is essentially a medieval road map, listing the names of all the towns and settlements along the way, and the time it takes to get from one to the other. Additional information is rather sparse and tends to focus on churches and bishops. But one of the ways to Rome passes through Mainz, in Germany, and on the way there from Paderborn, two minor places are mentioned, in the vicinity of which is to be found 'Gnitaheiðr, where Sigurðr attacked Fáfnir'.[173] The name *Gnitaheiðr* is recorded already in stanzas 5–6 of *Atlakviða*, generally considered to be one of the oldest poems in the Poetic *Edda*.[174] The implication seems to be that Nordic pilgrims would be sufficiently interested in the story of Sigurðr to stop off and visit this site on their way south. The *Leiðarvísir* also mention the 'snake-pit that Gunnar was put into', and somewhat bizarrely locate this somewhere in the region of La Lunigiana in Italy.[175] The two parts of the story-cycle are not closely linked, either in the text or in geography, but it may still be significant that these are the only references to legendary material in the text, apart from a mention of 'Þiðrekr's bath', located in Viterbo.[176] The other text in which Sigurðr, Gunnarr and Þiðrekr are linked is *Þiðreks saga*, discussed below.

At around the same time as *Leiðarvísir*, interest in the Sigurðr cycle can be seen in *Háttalykill*, the metrical tour-de-force composed in Orkney by Earl Rǫgnvaldr and an Icelandic associate, mentioned above.[177] The badly defective Stanzas 3–4 appear to have related the killing of the serpent by Sigurðr, a supposition heavily reliant on the fact that the following Stanzas 5–8 clearly tell the story of Gunnarr's decision to throw the treasure into the Rhine, after his brother-in-law Atli's attempts to discover its whereabouts by cutting out his brother Hǫgni's heart and putting Gunnarr into the snake-pit. While both *Leiðarvísir* and *Háttalykill* mention or allude to the killing of Fáfnir and the death of Gunnarr, neither of these makes any link to a mythological prehistory of the treasure which caused these deaths.

In the thirteenth century, as already noted, the story is extensively told in both the Poetic *Edda*, and in summary form in Snorri's *Edda*. The increasing tendency to the cyclical is apparent in the Poetic *Edda*, where the story of Sigurðr is preceded by that of his half-brother Helgi Hundingsbani, told in two poems. The cycle then proceeds through 16 further poems, interspersed with prose passages, telling the whole story from the birth of Sigurðr, 'the greatest of all men and the most redoubtable war-leader', through a range of tragic events to the deaths of Hamðir and Sǫrli, the sons of Sigurðr's widow Guðrún, in an attempt to avenge the death of their sister.[178] The poems are clearly pieces of various origins and dates, many of them overlapping in their subject-matter, collected by an anthologist using prose passages to bind them together into something more like a coherent narrative. Of particular note are *Grípisspá*, a poem designed to summarise the story of Sigurðr, rather than the whole cycle. This has nothing to say about the origins of the treasure, mythological or otherwise, concentrates on his relationships with Brynhildr and Guðrún, and concludes with a brief allusion to Sigurðr's death and to the fact that his wife Guðrún will have 'no joy . . . afterwards'. The mythological origins of the treasure are told in the mixed prose and verse of *Reginsmál*, which goes on to show Reginn adopting Sigurðr, making him a sword to avenge his father, and then egging him on to kill Fáfnir. *Fáfnismál*, also in mixed prose and verse, tells the central story of how Sigurðr killed Fáfnir (though not before having extensive dialogue with him), roasted his heart, heard the speech of the birds, killed Reginn, and took the treasure away on Grani's back. The rest of the poems tell of the subsequent events, often with overlapping content. Just as Sigurðr's story was introduced in summary form, so a prose passage entitled *Dráp Niflunga* 'Killing of the Niflungar' summarises the events leading to the death of Hǫgni, and of Gunnarr in the snake-pit, which are then told in the following poems.

As noted above, the Poetic *Edda* compilation can probably be traced back to around 1200 (even if some of the poems might be older), and Snorri must have known a similar anthology when he summarised the cycle in the *Skáldskaparmál* section of his *Edda*.[179] This summary comes in a section dealing with kennings for gold, and the whole story is motivated by the question 'What is the reason for gold being called otter-payment?', this being the mythological prehistory of the treasure. There are also scattered references to Sigurðr elsewhere in Snorri's *Edda* and there is a particularly interesting short anecdote in *Háttatal* about a shipwrecked poet who composed a poem *kveðit eptir Sigurðar sǫgu* 'based on the story of Sigurðr', although the poem itself is not cited and does not survive.[180] Anthony Faulkes has argued that this is not any 'written saga, but the story in the abstract as it appeared in Eddic poems known to Snorri'.[181]

But at around the same time or a little later, an anonymous Icelander did have the idea to write a saga based on the cycle. *Vǫlsunga saga*, surviving in a manuscript from around 1400, but probably written in the mid-thirteenth century, is closely based on an anthology of poems very like the Codex Regius of the Poetic *Edda*, since it can be shown to derive from 12 of the 18 relevant poems.[182] It also has additional material not found in either Snorri's or the Poetic *Edda*, particularly in the beginning, where it augments the mythological import of the story by giving Sigurðr an Odinic ancestry and Odinic assistance.

Also from the thirteenth century, a version of the story is incorporated into *Þiðreks saga*, a Norwegian retelling of the story of Theoderic of Bern, based on German sources.[183] This saga is believed to have been written in Bergen, in Norway, though whether by a Norwegian or an Icelander is disputed, at a time when there were plenty of Germans active there in connection with the Hanseatic League. The saga itself tells us in a prologue that it was put together by *norrœnir menn* 'Norse men' according to accounts of Germans, and also refers to old German poems, and certainly the stories of Sigurðr's killing of the serpent and Gunnarr's death differ in important ways from the Icelandic sources. For example (ch. 166), Sigurðr kills the serpent (here called Reginn) by cutting off its head, and cooks the whole of the serpent in a broth, rather than roasting its heart, though the result is the same, that he can understand the speech of birds.[184] The saga therefore lacks some of the important details of the story discussed above, found in both images and texts, such as the fact that Sigurðr killed the serpent from below, and that he roasted its heart over an open fire. Gunnarr does die in a snake-pit, though there is no mention of his playing the harp (ch. 383).[185] The immediate German sources for the saga cannot be identified, and the saga may have incorporated local Norwegian traditions as well, as shown for example by the way in which the names of several of the major characters are given in their Scandinavian, and not their German, forms.[186]

The rewriting of the Sigurðr cycle did not end with the thirteenth century, as versions can be found in both prose and poetry from late medieval Iceland, and in Danish, Faroese and Norwegian ballads, some recorded as late as the nineteenth century, with the Norwegian ones from the same part of the country as the carvings discussed below.[187] Then there are the surviving German analogues, most prominently the early thirteenth-century *Nibelungenlied*, with yet another version of the story-cycle substantially different from both the Old Icelandic texts and *Þiðreks saga*. There are also other German versions from the fifteenth century or later, and scattered references throughout much other literature, not to mention modern reworkings, from Wagner to Tolkien.[188]

The twelfth- and thirteenth-century literary flourishing of the cycle, in particular, should be seen in the context of a similar flourishing of artistic interpretations. Pre-eminent among these are the carved wooden portals of five stave churches in Norway, also dated to the late twelfth or thirteenth centuries. Three of these are from Aust-Agder (Austad, Hylestad and Vegusdal), one (Mæl) from neighbouring Telemark, and one from the not-too-distant Lardal in Vestfold.[189] The best-known of these is Hylestad, which tells the story in episodic form in a series of roundels, corresponding to the accounts of *Reginsmál* and *Fáfnismál*, with the forging of the sword, the killing of the dragon, the roasting of the heart and the warning speech of the birds, and the horse with the treasure on its back. There is thus no mythological prologue, but there is an allusion to subsequent events, as the final roundel shows Gunnarr in the snake-pit, playing the harp with his toes, a scene also found on the Austad portal. Two of the other portals, Lardal and Mæl, do however allude to the mythological prehistory by showing the otter skin, stretched out over the gold, in an image reminiscent of the Ramsey otter, discussed above, but without the fish. All of these portals show more than one scene from the cycle, but there are also some other carvings from medieval Norway which show individual scenes which can likely be associated with the Sigurðr cycle, from four churches in Telemark and one in Numedal, Buskerud.[190]

The geographical distribution of these depictions is thus relatively restricted (to four Norwegian counties), and far from identical to the overall distribution of stave churches, though these may also have an unrepresentative distribution through their extensive destruction over the centuries, being built entirely of wood. Nevertheless, the Sigurðr carvings do seem to be a phenomenon closely related to that particular time and place in southern Norway.[191] Unlike the early representations from the Isle of Man and Sweden, these carvings are from a time when Christianity was well established, so they cannot be said to derive from a hybrid situation in which the old stories are used to acculturate new Christians. Rather, they reflect a confident, local assertion of pride in the local and national past, expressed in terms derived from common European culture, for example Sigurðr is depicted as a medieval knight, with a kite-shaped shield.[192]

Although the carvings are a specific regional phenomenon, there are interesting parallels with some of the literary texts from Iceland. Hylestad shows Reginn forging the sword in his smithy along with an assistant, also mentioned in *Vǫlsunga saga*, though not elsewhere.[193] Also, the marble capital from Lunde in Telemark shows Sigurðr killing the dragon from below, positioned in one of three pits, the multiple pits being another detail that is only found in *Vǫlsunga saga*, where they are said to result from Óðinn's advice to the hero, so that he does not drown in the serpent's blood.[194] *Vǫlsunga saga* (ch. 23) also depicts Sigurðr as a medieval knight.[195] Although Sigurðr must have meant something different in the literary culture of thirteenth-century Iceland than in the wealthy inland valleys of southern Norway at roughly the same time, both show a parallel concern to meld indigenous traditions with the common cultural currency of their period.

These parallels can be seen in the context of diasporic contact between southern Norway and Iceland. *Háttalykill*, as noted above, was composed in twelfth-century Orkney by the Icelander Hallr Þórarinsson and the Orcadian Earl Rǫgnvaldr, but Rǫgnvaldr, though he had an Orcadian mother, was born in and grew up in Agder, the very region where somewhat later pictorial depictions of the Sigurðr cycle appear.[196] Rǫgnvaldr also spent time in Bergen, where it appears that German versions of the Sigurðr story were assimilated to Norse textual culture in the thirteenth-century *Þiðreks saga*. Although there may not have been many Germans there in his time, the Norse traditions that mingled with the German ones in *Þiðreks saga* a century later could well have been current already then. The exact routes these stories took cannot be reconstructed in detail, nor how the medieval interest in the story-cycle relates to the Viking Age evidence discussed above, though skaldic poetry may be an important link. But it is clear that, in the twelfth and thirteenth centuries, wealthy, educated and mobile individuals from Iceland, Orkney and Norway had a shared interest in the traditional stories of their ancestors, that collected around the central heroic figure of Sigurðr the Serpent-Slayer.

Myths and identities

The Viking Age evidence discussed above shows that the central Sigurðr story of how he killed the serpent, and probably other parts of the cycle, were known in the British Isles and Sweden, and probably Norway, by the tenth and eleventh centuries. By the twelfth and thirteenth centuries, there is further evidence for the story from Iceland and Orkney, and certain evidence from Norway. It is unlikely that this distribution arose from a simple dispersal from the Scandinavian homelands to the British Isles and Iceland at the time of the Viking Age migrations. Rather, it is clear that the vitality of the story was fed by the ongoing contacts between these regions after the initial migrations, contacts that were the result of the Viking diaspora. Furthermore, the evidence of the twelfth and thirteenth centuries shows the ways in which this diasporic consciousness flourished in a context which was opening up to new regions of the world through trade and cultural contacts. Although the Sigurðr story probably had its origins in the Migration period (fourth to sixth centuries) and in the Germanic-speaking areas of the European continent, the German connections of *Þiðreks saga* arise from the Hanseatic trading networks which were pulling Norway away from its ancestral ties to the north and west, and making new, southern links. But in the thirteenth century, the ties to the north and west were still strong, and it was in this fruitful mix of southern and northern that the traditional Sigurðr story came full circle and was assimilated to its distant German analogues.

The Sigurðr cycle was clearly important to the identities of different groups of people in the Viking diaspora. On the Viking Age memorials, it could be used to emphasise the heroic and social status of the newly Christian deceased in the Viking Age, through a hero who harked back to the traditional, and even mythological, past, without offending Christian sensibilities, indeed a hero who could easily be assimilated to Christendom's pantheon of dragon-slaying heroes. The literary versions of the story from medieval Iceland show a strong interest in the fates of the female characters involved in the whole sorry cycle, and reflect a growing interest in literary themes that feature women. Indeed the love triangle of the Sigurðr cycle is replicated in *Laxdœla saga* (whose heroine is called Guðrún), while the conflicts of loyalty that the Guðrún of the Sigurðr cycle experienced are alluded to in *Gísla saga Súrssonar*, both sagas that foreground the feminine experience of tragedy and feud, and were undoubtedly influenced by the versions of the story found in the Eddic poems.[197] The aristocrats of twelfth- and thirteenth-century southern Norway used the Sigurðr cycle to affirm their unique brand of both Christianity and local political power, as expressed in that quintessentially Norwegian form of religious architecture, the stave church. In thirteenth-century Bergen, the exposure of Norwegian story-tellers to an alternative version may have helped in the acculturation of a new group of people, the Hanseatic Germans. The Viking diaspora enabled the use of the Sigurðr cycle in these confident and contemporaneous assertions of both traditional values and new ideologies.

The stories of the Sigurðr cycle appealed to a variety of groups at different times, but these are specific social groups that can fairly easily be identified. Many other aspects of the Viking diaspora helped to establish and maintain the identities of a range of other groups, as will be discussed in the next chapter.

Notes

1 Turville-Petre 1964.
2 Abram 2011, vii–viii.
3 Nordberg 2012, 142.
4 Nordberg 2012, 125–30.
5 *OED*, 'mythos'.
6 For an outline of these and related written sources, see Abram 2011, 10–31.
7 Abram 2011, 53–9.
8 Turville-Petre 1964, 1–34.
9 Holmberg 1991, 154.
10 Andersson 1992, 77.
11 Holmberg 1991; see also Andersson 1992, Sandnes 1992 and Brink 1999. The examples in the following, and discussion of the relevant elements, are taken from these articles, which contain further references to earlier scholarship. The classic study is Olsen 1926, which is now superseded in much of its detail, but is still an important reference point.
12 Andersson 1992, 86; Brink 1999, 32. This site is discussed further, below.
13 Andersson 2006.
14 Sandnes 1992, 16.
15 Vikstrand 2001.
16 The information in the table is taken from Brink 2007, who also provides distribution maps.
17 Nordberg 2012, 130–1.
18 *SnEGylf*, p. 26; *SnESkskm*, p. 19; *SnE*, pp. 26, 76.
19 *SnEGylf*, pp. 25, 28–9; *SnESkskm*, p. 19; *SnE*, pp. 25, 29, 76.
20 Data in the table are based on the interpretations of Peterson 2007. Elements are given in their Old East Norse form reflecting the geographical bias of the evidence. Monothematic names, and hypocoristic forms such as *Dísa*, are not counted. See also Meldgaard 1992, Shaw 2011.
21 For a general survey of Old Norse personal names, see Janzén 1947b.
22 See the frequency tables in Peterson 2007, 271–82.
23 Peterson 2007, 235.
24 Kousgård Sørensen 1989.
25 For recent surveys, see Ratke and Simek 2006, and Ratke 2009. See also http://guldgubber.de/ [last accessed 20 November 2014].

26 *Edda*, pp. 61–8; *PE*, pp. 57–64; *SnEGylf*, pp. 30–1; *SnE*, pp. 31–2.
27 Ratke 2009.
28 See also the 'valkyrie' figurine from Hårby discussed in ch. 4, above.
29 Turville-Petre 1964, 13.
30 Christensen 2009.
31 *ÍF* XXVI, 13, 19; *Hkr*, pp. 8, 11.
32 A range of possible parallels, including the Aska figure, are illustrated and discussed in Christensen 2009. For the Freyja interpretation, see also http://scienceblogs.com/aardvarchaeology/2009/11/13/odin-from-lejre-no-its-freya/ [last accessed 16 June 2014].
33 Price 2006.
34 *AB*, p. 207.
35 Olsen 1966.
36 Olsen 1926, 231–2.
37 Larsson 2006, 2007. The following details are taken from these articles.
38 A few such other sites are briefly summarised in Larsson 2007, 13, 22.
39 Larsson 2007, 22.
40 Lidén *et al*. 1969.
41 Nordeide 2011, 107–13, 279–80.
42 E.g. *ÍF* XXVI, 172, 317, XXVII, 178–80, XXIX, 8, 80; *Hkr*, pp. 111, 207, 365–7; *Ágrip*, pp. 10–11; *Fsk*, p. 60.
43 *ÍF* XXVI, 317; *Hkr*, p. 207; *ÍF* XXV, 279; *SOTOS*, p. 105. See also the discussion of Þórhaddr the Old in *Landnámabók*, below.
44 Nordeide 2011, 107–8.
45 Karlsson 2000, 23–6.
46 Runic inscriptions can be traced by their identifier or location in *SR*; references to editions and discussions are also given below.
47 *DR*, Text, cols 223–8; Moltke 1985, 154–6.
48 *DR*, Text, cols 248–53; Moltke 1985, 224–8.
49 For a survey of interpretations and some cautious suggestions, see Lerche Nielsen 1997.
50 Both are discussed in Brink 2002. Neither has yet been treated in a corpus edition.
51 Brink 2002, 107.
52 *ÍF* I, 102–3, 374; *BoS*, pp. 39, 139.
53 *ÍF* I, 307–8; *BoS*, p. 117.
54 *ÍF* I, 368–9; *BoS*, p. 137.
55 *ÍF* I, 362–5; *BoS*, p. 135.
56 *ÍF* I, 78–9, 125, 268, 310–11, 319, 350–1, 385; *BoS*, pp. 31–2, 45, 102, 119, 121, 131, 144. The *hof* is also imagined as a building in *ÍF* I, 220; *BoS*, p. 84.
57 *ÍF* I, 315.
58 This is a variant form of the term *goði* (pl. *goðar*), though one more likely to be found in East Scandinavia.
59 *ÍF* I, 313.
60 Brink 2002.
61 Olsen 1966, 192.
62 Friðriksson and Lucas 2009, 3–4.
63 The details below are all taken from Lucas 2009b.
64 Nordeide 2011, 104–7, 127–8.
65 Friðriksson and Lucas 2009, 10; Lucas 2009b, 400.
66 *ÍF* XV, 9–10; *BoI*, p. 36. For a slightly different interpretation of the stanza, see *SPSMA* IV, forthcoming.
67 *BoI*, p. 60.

68 For Sigvatr's biography, see *SPSMA* I, 532–3, for the circumstances giving rise to the poem, pp. 578–83, and for the stanzas discussed, pp. 589–92.
69 Peterson 2007, 282.
70 Data extracted from Fellows Jensen 1968.
71 The data have been extracted manually from the index of *ÍF* I, 441–525. Here, the elements are given in their Old West Norse form, and deuterothemes are not extracted because of the difficulty of doing this manually.
72 Again, the data have been extracted manually from the index of *ÍF* I, 441–525.
73 Jesch 2011b, 16–17.
74 Jesch 2011b, 19–20.
75 Jesch 2009c, 52–4, 58–9.
76 *CASSS* II, 108–9; Kopár 2012, 64–8.
77 Kopár 2012, 72.
78 Kopár 2012, 110–21.
79 *CASSS* II, 102; Kopár 2012, 77, 91–2.
80 *CASSS* II, 102; Kopár 2012, 91–2.
81 *CASSS* II, 102; Kopár 2012, 92.
82 *CASSS* I, 143–4, VI, 161; Kopár 2012, 72–5.
83 *CASSS* III, 214–15; Kopár 2012, 110.
84 Buckland 2010, 57; Kopár 2012, 77–8, suggests it is a trial piece.
85 Jesch 2009c, 58; 2011b, 17–19.
86 Kopár 2012, xxiv–xxv, 167–79.
87 Bailey 2000, 20; McKinnell 1987, 335; Abrams 2001, 122.
88 Stocker 2000, 195.
89 Nordberg 2012, 126.
90 Townend 2002, 121–43.
91 Jesch 2001b, 319–20.
92 Abrams 2012.
93 Antonsson 2014, 56.
94 Nordal 1999; see also Jesch 2009c, 57–8.
95 There is a useful survey, with full references, in Antonsson 2014.
96 Brink 2004, 163; for a more general discussion, see Nordberg 2014.
97 Jochens 1999.
98 *ÍF* I, 17; *BoI*, p. 9.
99 Vésteinsson 2000.
100 Svanberg 2003, II, 147–50; Nordeide 2011; Antonsson 2014, 58–9.
101 Søvsø 2010.
102 *DN* I, nos 285, 361, II, no. 280, III, nos 341, 399, 966, 1009, IX, no. 402, X, nos 166-7, XI, no. 601.
103 For a recent summary, see Nordeide 2011, 140–6.
104 Nordeide 2011, 145–6, 151–3.
105 Brink 2004, 170–1.
106 Vretemark and Axelsson 2008, 211.
107 Vretemark and Axelsson 2008, 216.
108 See Abrams 2014 for a summary.
109 Abrams 2014.
110 Abrams 2014, 336–7.
111 Antonsson 2014, 61–2.
112 Eldjárn 2000, 590, 609.
113 Kristjánsdóttir 2011, 425–31.

114 Musin 2014, 313; specific Thor's hammer finds are mentioned in several of the articles in Bauduin and Musin 2014.
115 Musin 2014, 315.
116 *RPC*, pp. 73–7, 89–90.
117 *RPC*, pp. 74, 77, 90.
118 *Edda*, pp. 88–95; *PE*, pp. 74–9; *SnEGylf*, pp. 44–5; *SnESkskm*, pp. 11, 14–17, 50, 65, 86–7, 96; *SnE*, pp. 46–7, 69, 72–4, 106, 116, 135, 142.
119 *SnEGylf*, pp. 48–9; *SnE*, pp. 51–2.
120 McKinnell 2001.
121 Abram 2011, 123–69.
122 Abram 2011, 142.
123 *FGT*, pp. 208–9.
124 Abram 2011, 199.
125 *Saxo* I, 5.
126 See e.g. *Saxo* I, 25–6.
127 *Saxo* I, 69–75; *SnEGylf*, pp. 45–6; *SnE* pp. 48–9.
128 *Saxo* I, 76.
129 *ÍF* XXVI, 11; *Hkr*, p. 7.
130 For a list and brief summary of the mythological poems, see Abram 2011, 17–19.
131 Gunnell 2005, 83.
132 Meulengracht Sørensen 1991.
133 *Saxo* I, 5.
134 Jesch 2005; 2009b.
135 *SnESkskm*, p. 72; *SnE*, pp. 122–3.
136 *SnE1931*, p. 259; *ÍF* XXXIV, 169; *OS*, p. 256.
137 *SnESkskm*, p. 73; *SnE*, p. 123; see also *SPSMA* III, forthcoming.
138 *Saxo* I, 179.
139 *FAS* I, 367–82; *SBFP*, 43–57.
140 *SnESkskm*, p. 52; *SnE*, p. 107.
141 *SnESkskm*, pp. 52–7; *SnE*, pp. 107–9; *ÍF* XXXV, 5–7, 39–40.
142 On Rǫgnvaldr see *SPSMA* II, 575.
143 *ÍF* XXXIV, 185; *OS*, p. 269; *HL*, p. 26; *SPSMA* III, forthcoming.
144 *SBFP*, 217–19.
145 *SPSMA* II, 592–3.
146 Jesch 2009b, 157–8.
147 Johnston 1910, 297.
148 *SPSMA* II, 575–630. For Eddic versions of these myths, see *Edda*, p. 40; *PE*, p. 32; *SnEGylf*, pp. 47–8; *SnESkskm*, pp. 3, 6–7, 11–14, 40–1, 44, 46–7; *SnE*, pp. 50–1, 61, 66, 70–1, 94–5, 99, 101–2.
149 Nordal 2001, 32.
150 *RIMO*, 178–86.
151 These are based on the interpretations or reconstructions of sts 2b, 3a, 4a, 10b, 24a, 26a, 27a, 28b, and 36a in *Hl*. An edition of the poem is forthcoming in *SPSMA*.
152 Nordal 2001, 309–38.
153 See sts 8, 9, 27 and 29 in Frank 2004, 25, 30. An edition of the poem is forthcoming in *SPSMA*.
154 Whaley 1998, 73–6.
155 *SPSMA* II, 231–2, 258–9.
156 Nordal 2001, 48.
157 Nordal 2001, 310–11.

158 *SnESkskm*, p. 5; *SnE*, pp. 64–5.
159 A useful and concise summary of the whole cycle is in *SnESksm*, pp. 45–51; *SnE*, pp. 99–106.
160 Düwel 1986; Guðmundsdóttir 2012a.
161 Margeson 1980, 184.
162 Margeson 1980, 185–95.
163 *CASSS* IX, 181–2.
164 *SöR*, pp. 71–3, 306–11; *UR* IV, pp. 621–31, 659–62. Stern 2009, following some earlier scholars, would add three stones from Gästrikland to the Swedish corpus, but admits that these are 'controversial'.
165 *SnESkskm*, p. 45; *SnE*, p. 99.
166 Margeson 1983, 101; Stern 2009, 898.
167 *SnESkskm*, pp. 48–9; *SnE*, p. 104; Guðmundsdóttir 2012b.
168 Stern 2009, 899.
169 Guðmundsdóttir 2012b, 1039–41.
170 Stern 2009, 902.
171 *SPSMA* II, pp. 282–5.
172 *SPSMA* I, pp. 845–7.
173 *AÍ* I, 13; Magoun 1944, 323–4, 347.
174 *Edda*, p. 241; *PE*, p. 205.
175 *AÍ* I, 16; Magoun 1944, 340, 350.
176 *AÍ* I, 17; Magoun 1944, 345–6, 350.
177 *Hl*; *SPSMA* III, forthcoming.
178 *Edda*, pp. 163–274; *PE*, pp. 138–234.
179 *SnESksm*, pp. 45–51; *SnE*, pp. 99–106.
180 *SnEHt*, p. 18; *SnE*, p. 188.
181 *SnEHt*, p. 161.
182 *VS*, pp. ix–x, xxxvi–xxxviii.
183 *ÞS*, p. 4.
184 *ÞS*, pp. 235–6.
185 *ÞS*, p. 517.
186 Uecker 1996.
187 *VS*, pp. x–xi; Nordanskog 2006, 261.
188 *VS*, pp. xi–xiii.
189 Margeson 1980, 196–203.
190 Margeson 1980, 202–4; see also Nordanskog 2006, 236–57, 373, for more detail, especially about the less certain representations.
191 Nordanskog 2006, 286–7.
192 Nordanskog 2006, esp. pp. 275–310.
193 *VS*, p. 27.
194 *VS*, p. 30.
195 *VS*, pp. 40–1.
196 Jesch 2013a, 154–5.
197 Jesch 1991, 191–8.

6

NETWORKS AND IDENTITIES

Networks

Raiding, trading, settlement

There has been little or nothing in this book so far about warriors and kings, merchants and craftsmen, categories of people most would expect to meet in a book about the Viking Age. There is no doubt that their traditional Viking activities of raiding and trading are not only closely linked to, but probably a prerequisite for overseas settlement and the subsequent phenomenon of diaspora. The raiders and traders who spread east, south and west from Scandinavia sometimes did not return home. If they survived, they often morphed into settlers, sometimes individually, sometimes establishing themselves in certain places in large numbers, together with others of Scandinavian origin. Both raiding and trading could be motivated primarily by financial gain, this wealth was then either returned to the homelands or used to establish the overseas settlements. But both raiding and trading are also intimately associated with power and its exercise, and the multifarious activities of the Viking Age were also an important factor in the concentration of power in the hands of monarchies which, cooperating closely with the Christian Church, consolidated the homelands as the modern nations of Denmark, Norway and Sweden towards the end of the Viking Age. These new political structures provided further opportunities for diasporic connections in a transnational context.

Diaspora is the concept that has been used here to explain how these raids and trading voyages led, not only to migration and settlement, but to a whole interconnected transnational world of Scandinavian origin and using Scandinavian language that outlasted the Viking Age. A 'dynamic factor' in these outcomes was Scandinavian culture, as pointed out by Lesley Abrams:[1]

> raiding, trading, and land-taking stimulated new ways of doing things with Scandinavian culture in new environments, and this sometimes involved stressing, not abandoning, Scandinavian ancestry and exploiting selective elements of Scandinavian culture; arguably, Scandinavian identity could therefore at times have been strengthened by the raiding or immigrant experience.

The dynamics of identities will be explored in the second half of this chapter, after some consideration of another essential, but relatively little-studied, concept highly relevant to the Viking Age, that of networks. If diaspora is the 'uniting [of] scattered communities of common origin in a new global network', then these networks have to be identified.[2] Who was connected with whom? Were there particularly well-travelled routes and frequently visited hubs? What kinds of connection were there beyond the obvious ones that took place in the contexts of warfare, trade (both of which the Vikings were very good at, but by no means unique) and migration? How do linguistic and cultural connections, in particular, map onto the more tangible connections of trade and migration? In a mobile world, communications and connections are key. One way of exploring what has been called this 'pervasive connectivity' of the Viking Age is through complex network theory.[3]

Diasporic networks

Using evidence from both texts and archaeology, network theory can suggest new models of how trade and exchange, in particular, operated. Søren Sindbæk used this approach to analyse a group of early Viking Age sites, and the people and things that travelled between them, and found that 'the results can be interpreted as the imprint of a complex communications network', organised on a large scale.[4] In the *Vita Anskarii*, an account of the travels in Denmark and Sweden of the Carolingian missionary Anskar in the ninth century, Sindbæk found that 55 named individuals or groups of people visited 22 sites. At the centre of this network of connections are four of the great emporia of the Viking Age: Dorestad in Frisia, Hedeby and Ribe in Denmark, and Birka in Sweden. Although many of the places mentioned in the text are in fact on the European continent, these are actually peripheral to the 'small world' of the text which, being an account of the mission to Scandinavia, locates this mission in these Viking Age trading centres, the hubs or nodes of the larger network.

Sindbæk's parallel archaeological analysis is based on 72 excavations at 71 sites, using only artefacts that can be dated to the early Viking Age and which are from sites with documented activity in the early ninth century. The links between these sites are not as straightforward as in the case of the people travelling to them in *Vita Anskarii*, as they are based on shared types of 31 common artefacts. The fact of sharing an artefact type does not necessarily indicate direct contact between sites, in the way that people travelling does, rather this kind of commonality could have resulted from regional patterns of production, or regional patterns of exchange, and could therefore indicate no more than a group within which each site had contact with at least one other member of the group. Nevertheless, the overall pattern again reveals a small number of 'intensively connecting sites' such as Hedeby and Ribe. These are stations of long-distance communication, and contrast markedly with rural sites that had few or no external links. These local clusters connect with each other mainly through the hubs, implying a hierarchical system of connections at different levels.

At the highest level, Sindbæk concludes, 'global connections . . . were held together by a tiny core of travellers, passing between an even smaller number of locations. While this network was sometimes remarkably effective, it was also extremely vulnerable.'[5] Viking Age connections were generally vulnerable in this way, given the relative smallness of the populations concerned, and the restricted nature of the people able to form long-distance contacts, identified by Sindbæk as 'specialised travellers'. Such a model is close to the model of elite diaspora posited by Lesley Abrams (as discussed in ch. 3, above), although hers has a broader timescale. In the elite diaspora model, direct cultural connections are restricted to a certain echelon of society, with perhaps subsequent trickle-down effects.[6] But Sindbæk's model in particular is based on evidence from the early Viking Age. As time passed, it is possible to see that other kinds of network, broader and further-reaching, could develop as a result of these more limited networks of the early Viking Age, and this is an area that would certainly reward further study.

Another recent, and rather different, study using the methods of statistical physics explored the personal networks of Iceland in the Saga Age, the period of Iceland's earliest history (the ninth to eleventh centuries), as seen from the perspective of its literate culture in the thirteenth and fourteenth centuries.[7] The authors compared 18 *Íslendingasögur*, or 'sagas of Icelanders', and related texts in order to gather quantitative information on the interrelationships between characters in those sagas, with the aim of comparing the society implied in those sagas to other social networks. At the level of individual sagas, this analysis was able to show differences between those texts which suggest highly assortative social networks, that is, those in which there are many and complex social and familial interrelationships not dominated by any particular character (e.g. *Laxdœla saga*), and those in which the networks are disassortative, that is, in which the focus is very much on the protagonist, as in an outlaw story such as *Gísla saga Súrssonar*. But the differences between the sagas are not great, and the overall picture from the 18 texts they studied suggests that the networks deducible from the sagas correspond closely to real-life social networks.

The authors, who are applied mathematicians, did not draw any substantial conclusions from their analysis beyond noting that 'the saga societies . . . are realistic'.[8] The implications of this 'realistic' quality of the sagas are significant for an understanding of the effects of the diaspora in Iceland. Since the networks depicted in the sagas ostensibly existed two to three hundred years before the sagas were written, where does this 'realism' come from? If the sagas are fictional, and everything in them was invented by their authors, an extreme version of a view held by some scholars, how did the authors manage to come up with thousands of characters and produce something so similar to real-life social networks? On the other hand, if the thirteenth-century saga authors were not making it all up but had access to information about the social networks of their ancestors two or three centuries earlier, in what form did they access this information and how accurate was it? There are still many unanswered questions and the authors of the study acknowledge that 'more holistic information from other fields' is required to answer them, as well as network analysis.[9]

One interesting aspect emerges from their analysis of both hostile and friendly links in saga society. Unlike other early epics which also feature conflict (the authors had previously analysed the *Iliad*, *Beowulf* and the *Tain*), in the sagas, the hostile links are essentially the same as the friendly links. In other words, the conflicts depicted in the sagas are blood feuds between characters who are already acquainted with each other, in contrast to the *Iliad*, for instance (the early text which they found otherwise to be most like the sagas), in which armies meet on the battlefield. Although this insight is not surprising, highlighting it through the application of network theory suggests the need for a closer look at the intimate links between various sections of Icelandic society, both in the Saga Age and in the thirteenth century, when stories from the Saga Age found their surviving written form. The sagas of Icelanders are well known to be anonymous works, despite the efforts of some editors, especially Icelandic ones, over the years to assign them named authors from among medieval people whose names are known to us. But this focus on authorship may be misguided. Slavica Ranković has in a number of papers argued that 'the remarkable representational complexity and realism of the sagas' is facilitated by what she calls their 'distributed authorship'.[10] They are produced by a 'network of authors (oral story-tellers, writers, scribes)' and have evolved through time, in a context in which their listeners/readers have knowledge that is relevant to, but goes beyond what is in, the text. These are the processes that enable the 'realistic' depiction of social networks, as the sagas are the products of a community, a network, that existed in both space and time.

The implications of this understanding of the sagas is that they are neither entirely of the age in which they are set, nor entirely of the age in which they were written. Rather, they are an inevitable product of the Viking diaspora, of a community with a high degree of awareness of how it came into being and a strong interest in its own origins. The social networks of the sagas are new social networks peculiar to Iceland, not those brought from the homelands, since, as *Landnámabók* makes perfectly clear, the first settlers came from many different parts of the Viking world (as discussed further below). So the sagas do not just construct these social networks, rather they come into being both as a result of and in order to record the networks, as indicated clearly by the elaborate genealogies that are such an obsession of most sagas as well as *Landnámabók*. The sagas of Icelanders, unique in world literature, are cultural innovations brought about by new material conditions, the new material conditions being the coming together of people of various origins in a new land and the consequent necessity of establishing new networks not necessarily related to those of the homeland.[11]

The uses of network theory discussed here have very different emphases and come to rather different conclusions. On one hand, there is a picture of small, elite networks of specialised travellers who connect through a small number of important hubs in the early Viking Age, the picture perhaps slightly widened as the Viking Age goes on, but still dependent on elite contacts in certain arenas which might also then spread out locally, or down the hierarchy. On the other hand, the sagas of Icelanders reveal a close-knit society which has come into being in Iceland as the result of a complex migration process, and it is clear that the sagas are intimately bound up with the creation of this society. The difference is not only one of chronology, but also one of the contrast between the wide-ranging, almost global, connections of the Viking Age in some of its aspects, and the more local nodes which develop their own characteristics as they spring up on the expanding networks.

Diaspora theory has the greatest explanatory power when it takes account not only of communications between homeland and overseas, but also between overseas communities of common origin, and some examples show both local and wide-ranging networks.[12] Mac Carron and Kenna's study revealed, as might be expected by anyone who has read it, that *Egils saga* consists, not of one coherent network, but of several overlapping ones, since so much of the story takes place outside Iceland, both before and after the settlement. This is significant in that the Icelandic networks of the saga overlap not only with the Norwegian networks of its long prehistory (chs 1–27), before the protagonist's family arrive in Iceland, but also with other networks outside Iceland during the protagonist's long and eventful life. These networks are illustrated by the saga's tale of Mousa Broch in Shetland.

Case study – Mousa Broch

The origins and functions of the brochs are still debated, but in essence they are 'prehistoric drystone roundhouses with a range of architectural features such as internal stairs and galleries' found in the north and west of Scotland and dating to between 600 BC and AD 100.[13] Although none of these brochs now survives to its full height, they would have been imposing structures in their own day. When the Scandinavians first encountered them, the broch sites had long been abandoned, but many of them would have still been visible in the landscape and some were re-used by the incomers. The broch of Gurness on the Mainland of Orkney, for instance, had at least seven Viking Age graves dug into its ruins.[14] The broch on the small island of Mousa in Shetland (illustrated on the cover of this book) is both the tallest and the best-preserved of these pre-Viking Age structures.[15] Mousa is located on a main sailing route into the heart of Shetland, itself the first landfall for those travelling west from Norway. Mousa also has a high degree of intervisibility with other monuments and locations in Shetland – it is totally unmissable even today. Its iconic status, resulting from this visual prominence, is captured in two saga anecdotes which encapsulate the diasporic networks that linked Norway, the British Isles and Iceland. These networks relate not only to the Icelanders' cultural memory of their migration, but also to the more recent past of thirteenth-century saga authors.

Egils saga (chs 32–5) tells of Bjǫrn, a young man from Aurland deep in the Sognefjord, in western Norway, who is described as a great traveller, 'sometimes on Viking raids, and sometimes on trading voyages', and a very capable man.[16] At a party somewhere in *Firðafylki* (modern Fjordane, to the north of the Sognefjord), he falls in love with a beautiful girl, Þóra *hlaðhǫnd* 'Lace-Sleeve'. His proposal of marriage is rejected by her brother, a chieftain called Þórir. Bjǫrn's reaction is to abduct Þóra from her home while her brother is away. His father Brynjólfr, who is friends with Þórir, ensures that the young lovers live like brother and sister, but does not insist on sending her back home. He tries to get Bjǫrn out of harm's way by buying him a merchant ship full of goods for a trading voyage to Dublin. In the end, with the connivance of Bjǫrn's mother, Þóra elopes with Bjǫrn on this ship, her mother-in-law-to-be having also made sure she had all her clothes and possessions with her. On their voyage south, the young couple are shipwrecked on Mousa. Bjǫrn and Þóra quickly get married then and there, and spend the winter in the broch. They get to hear that the king of Norway has sent a message to the Earl of Orkney, and also to the Hebrides and all the way to Dublin, that he wants Bjǫrn killed. So they make off to Iceland and end up at Borg, in the west of the country, at the farm of Skalla-Grímr, father of the saga's protagonist, Egill. It turns out that Skalla-Grímr knows both Brynjólfr and Þórir, and happily lets the couple stay. He is less happy when he later discovers that their marriage was without her family's consent but eventually the families are reconciled. Bjǫrn and Þóra return to Norway, leaving behind their daughter Ásgerðr, who comes to marry first Þórólfr Skalla-Grímsson and then, on his death, his brother Egill. Back in Norway, meanwhile, the chieftain Þórir becomes the father of Arinbjǫrn, who becomes important to Egill not only as his best friend and protector, but also as his wife's first cousin.

The elopement of Bjǫrn and Þóra has further ramifications for the plot of the saga, too long to be relayed here in detail, except to note that this particular strand culminates in Egill's ultimate recovery in Norway of his wife Ásgerðr's lawful paternal inheritance which had been appropriated by the husband of Bjǫrn's daughter from a second marriage. Here, as in other episodes in the saga, Egill's success depends heavily on the help he gets from his friend Arinbjǫrn, though the plot is further complicated by the hostile relationship between Egill and the Norwegian king Eiríkr *blóðøx* 'Blood-Axe'. Both the hostility and the friendship extend even to York, in England, where, in a famous episode (chs 59–61), Arinbjǫrn once again rescues Egill from his royal enemies.[17] Even this brief summary has shown how closely the story weaves together the fates of various families and friends in Norway and Iceland, throughout a large portion of the saga. The Icelander Egill's successes in Norway and York depend closely on his family's diasporic networks, symbolised by the marriage in the central location of Mousa.

Strangely enough, the other reference to Mousa in saga-literature also involves an elopement. In Chapter 93 of *Orkneyinga saga* the Orcadian earl Haraldr Maddaðarson sets off from Caithness to Shetland, intending to kill a certain Erlendr *ungi* 'The Young' who had proposed to Haraldr's mother Margrét, but had been refused by her son. Erlendr carries Margrét off to Mousa, where Haraldr attempts to ambush them, but finds it impossible to attack the broch. In the end, the two men are reconciled and become allies (going to Norway together to get support for Haraldr's bid for power in Orkney), and the couple get married. Having played her part in Northern Isles politics, Margrét is then out of the saga.

In both anecdotes, women help to cement alliances between families, thus establishing successful personal networks. The *Egils saga* anecdote is more colourful and wide-ranging, concerning a romantic young couple, that of *Orkneyinga saga* more local and restricted, with a less romantic middle-aged couple. There may be a relationship between the two anecdotes. The *Orkneyinga saga* elopement is set in a time (the mid-twelfth century) not long before the writing of the saga and, like much of the saga, is very likely based on oral traditions from Orkney itself.[18] It has a greater claim to historical authenticity than the *Egils saga* story, set in the tenth century, and it is possible that the latter is modelled on the former.[19] Yet even if the story of Bjǫrn and Þóra's elopement is fictional, the extensive personal networks which it symbolises, and their reach across the North Atlantic from Norway to Iceland, are unlikely to be entirely made up. Moreover, the choice of a Northern Isles setting is significant in its recognition of the centrality of Orkney and Shetland, not only to the Viking diaspora, but also to literary and cultural communication in the late twelfth and thirteenth centuries.[20]

The Mousa anecdotes therefore show not only the personal and geographical links operating during the Viking Age migrations westwards, but also the resulting personal and cultural links between the homeland and the different parts of the diaspora that persisted for several centuries afterwards, and which were particularly strong in the twelfth and thirteenth centuries when the sagas were coming into being. These cultural links are particularly notable in two important forms of evidence: runic inscriptions and skaldic verse.

Runic networks

The significance of having a common language across the diaspora, often called the *dǫnsk tunga* 'Danish tongue', has already been discussed in Chapter 3, above. Even though many people in the Viking Age and the diaspora were, and needed to be, multilingual, there is clear evidence for their recognition of how the common Scandinavian tongue united the homelands and the diaspora. Indeed, the diaspora was an important factor in maintaining this commonality of language long after the end of the Viking Age. Cultural products that are essentially linguistic also help to bind the regions of the diaspora together, maintaining connections and networks, as well as the language itself. Two of these that are found around the diaspora are the practice of writing in runes, and that of composing skaldic poetry.

As outlined in Chapter 1, the habit of writing runes has a wide geographical and chronological spread among peoples speaking the Germanic languages, but it is overwhelmingly a Scandinavian phenomenon, as the largest number of surviving runic inscriptions are from both Scandinavia and the diaspora, and from the Viking Age and the post-Viking medieval period. The latter, in particular, are significant

TABLE 6.1 Runic inscriptions from the Scandinavian homelands

	Older futhark	*Viking Age*	*Medieval*	*Total*
Denmark	165	462	394	**1021**
Norway	66	139	1445	**1650**
Sweden	51	2978	691	**3720**
Total	**282**	**3579**	**2530**	**6391**

for understanding linguistic and cultural contacts in the diaspora. While it can be difficult to get an overall picture of the Scandinavian runic corpus, since its variation is both diatopic and diachronic, it is an excellent source because of the large number of inscriptions (at the time of writing 6,751, though the number rises by a few each year) and their widespread geographical distribution.[21]

The corpus discussed here includes all inscriptions, of all kinds and on all materials, with a find-spot in the Scandinavian homelands, or those written in Scandinavian runes regardless of find-spot. It is conventional to divide Scandinavian runic inscriptions into three broad categories, those in the older futhark (before *c.* 750), those in Viking Age runes (*c.* 750–1100) and those in medieval runes (after *c.* 1100), based on the particular variant of the runic alphabet (or 'futhark') used. Although the numbers can never be exact because of new finds, or the difficulty in some cases of dating or classifying inscriptions, the overall patterns are likely to be representative. The distribution of all runic inscriptions from the Scandinavian homelands is shown in Table 6.1.[22]

These raw numbers can be unpicked in various ways, and it is important to note that they are subject to the vagaries of classification and error, and that the inscriptions themselves are subject to the vagaries of discovery and preservation, but also runic fashions. Danish inscriptions in the older futhark are on small portable objects, often of precious metal (like the gold bracteates) and thus their ultimate provenance can be uncertain, whereas a high proportion of the Norwegian inscriptions before 750 are on stone and therefore have a much more certain provenance. Sweden has by far the highest number of Viking Age rune-stones, though these are overwhelmingly from the late Viking Age, while the relatively high number of Danish inscriptions from this period is inflated in part by runic coins and in part by the fact that certain provinces now in Sweden are classified as Danish on historical grounds. The large number of medieval inscriptions from Norway (and to some extent Sweden) come from extensive excavations of urban sites such as Bergen. But even allowing for such distortions, the distribution is quite uneven, and shows that, although writing in runes is a long-lived cultural phenomenon in Scandinavia that lasted well over a millennium, it is also a fluctuating one, blossoming at certain times, in certain places and in certain contexts. When and where runic writing takes place can therefore be indicative of contacts and connections in the diaspora.

Both Viking Age and medieval inscriptions have been found outside the homelands as shown in Table 6.2.[23]

In many cases, these are inscriptions on portable objects, or travellers' graffiti, and so their find-spots do not necessarily relate directly to diasporic communities;

TABLE 6.2 Viking Age and medieval runic inscriptions found outside the Scandinavian homelands

	Viking Age	*Medieval*	*Total*
France	0	1	**1**
Netherlands	0	3	**3**
Germany	8	4	**12**
Poland	3	0	**3**
Latvia	1	0	**1**
Finland	2	0	**2**
Russia	5	0	**5**
Ukraine	1	1	**2**
Byzantium	3	0	**3**
Italy	0	1	**1**
England	13	6	**19**
Isle of Man	33	2	**35**
Ireland	16	0	**16**
Scotland	7	8	**15**
Orkney	18	37	**55**
Shetland	5	2	**7**
Faroes	2	7	**9**
Iceland	1	46	**47**
Greenland	1	100	**101**
Total	**119**	**218**	**337**

this is particularly true of the small number of inscriptions from the first 10 locations in Table 6.2. But the inscriptions of the British Isles and the North Atlantic are worth further consideration in a diasporic context.

The relatively small number of Viking Age inscriptions in England is particularly surprising in view of the extensive evidence otherwise for Scandinavian raiding, trading and settlement there.[24] Most notably, the 'Viking' town of York, so rich in significant archaeological remains, with such a wide range of trading and cultural links, has not yet turned up a single runic inscription. Inscriptions from the south of England, meanwhile, clearly relate to the time of the Danish monarchy in the eleventh century and immigrants who came with them, rather than those who settled in the Danelaw in the ninth and early tenth centuries. On the other hand, the medieval inscriptions of north-west England show a continued interest in Scandinavian runic writing after the Viking Age, though perhaps of a rather specialised antiquarian nature, such as the font from Bridekirk in Cumbria (E 1), in which a Middle English text is written in good Scandinavian runes (though also with some bookhand characters).[25] But even an antiquarian interest must be fed by something, and it is likely that continued contact with Scandinavia, or Scandinavian parts of Britain, stimulated these late inscriptions.[26]

The Isle of Man has an extraordinary number of Viking Age inscriptions in relation to its small size, most of which have been dated to the tenth or very early eleventh century.[27] Traditionally, these memorial stones have been linked to Norwegian runic practice, in part because of evidence that the Vikings of the Irish Sea region had their ultimate origins predominantly in Norway, and in part because of perceived similarities between the Manx inscriptions and those of south-west Norway. These similarities, however, are not as obvious as has been claimed, and there is in addition a problem of chronology, in that it is not at all clear that the Manx inscriptions are later than the Norwegian ones they have been compared with.[28] It is not only difficult to find Norwegian models for the Manx inscriptions of the right date, there is also surprisingly little evidence for Viking Age inscriptions in the places between Norway and Man that must be passed on the way from one to the other. But if not obviously derived from Norwegian models, the Manx corpus is hardly likely to be *sui generis* either. The language is sometimes a bit wonky (as discussed in ch. 4, above), but both the use of runes and the content of the inscriptions definitely fit in the Scandinavian tradition.

Even if we cannot pin down the exact origins of the Manx corpus, it illustrates the many ways in which diaspora leads to new cultural forms. The settlers who established themselves on the Isle of Man around 900 are generally thought to be Vikings of ultimately Norwegian origin who had nevertheless spent a generation or two in the Irish Sea region.[29] If the runic monuments are due to them or their descendants, then they were consciously harking back to a homeland tradition with which they might not have had direct contact for some time. If, on the other hand, the monuments are due to impulses from an individual or group who had come to the Isle of Man directly from Norway (or just possibly elsewhere in Scandinavia) a bit later in the tenth century, then this shows that the islanders had continuing contacts with the Scandinavian homeland. It would also suggest that the Manx-Norse, in choosing to invoke such homeland traditions a generation or more after their settlement, were doing the typically diasporic thing of both rediscovering and emphasising their ultimate ancestry.

Ireland is numerically not too far behind the Isle of Man, though since most of its inscriptions are on portable objects and do not say anything sensible, it is rather harder to judge their significance.[30] Scotland, which is hard to avoid when travelling from Norway to the Irish Sea region, has very few Viking Age inscriptions, either on the mainland or on the islands.[31] The total given in Table 6.2 for Orkney is almost certainly too generous, as many of these inscriptions are fragmentary and hard to date, and the true figure is probably nearer 10 Viking Age inscriptions. Medieval inscriptions are more numerous but, although the total for Orkney looks impressive at first sight, it has to be remembered that, of the 36 medieval inscriptions, 33 are in fact individual graffiti in the prehistoric chambered cairn of Maeshowe. These do not represent a local tradition, developed from their ancestral practices by Orcadians. Rather, it is as good as certain that they were carved, either on a single occasion or within a short period of time, by the pilgrims who had accompanied Earl Rǫgnvaldr to the Holy Land in the 1150s, who were a mixed bunch of Norwegians, Icelanders and Orcadians.[32] Indeed, the inscriptions show a clear dependence on the contemporary runic practices of Norway. Thus the medieval runic inscriptions in Orkney are not on the whole a throwback to a practice introduced during the Viking Age settlement of the islands, but rather reflect the network of their contacts with both Norway and Iceland that continued long after the Viking Age settlements, and which complicate our understanding of when certain cultural phenomena spread around these networks.

As to the rest of the North Atlantic, this is also clearly not a distribution reflecting the export of a strong runic tradition from Norway westwards along with the settlement period export of people in the Viking Age. However, like Norway, much of the North Atlantic has a larger number of medieval inscriptions, suggesting rather that later Norwegian developments in runic writing influenced similar developments in the settlements. This is in itself evidence, not only for the continued contacts between the regions after the initial migrations, but more importantly for the sense of cultural and linguistic connection between the people of those regions.

In the North Atlantic, the largest number of medieval inscriptions from outside Norway comes from Greenland, and this is most likely to have come about through direct contact with Norway, rather than being mediated through Iceland or other intermediate links. Not only is the Greenland number higher than that of Iceland, the Icelandic total is also misleading. The Icelandic inscriptions are generally later and represent a uniquely Icelandic development of late medieval recumbent gravestones that differs in important respects from neighbouring traditions, both runologically and as a monument type. Despite its 46 inscriptions, therefore, Iceland cannot be considered a link between the runic traditions of Norway and Greenland. The Greenlandic inscriptions, on the other hand, have many similarities with contemporary runic practice in Norway. The runic evidence thus bears out other evidence that Greenland's trading contacts with Norway were often direct rather than mediated through Iceland in the medieval period, as is also shown by the relatively scanty knowledge of Greenland in the Icelandic sagas, and the evidence for mainland Scandinavian influence on Greenlandic architecture.[33] The picture may yet change, if more runic inscriptions are found in the excavations of Viking Age sites in both Iceland and Greenland, but for the moment it remains uncertain how much runic writing, if any, actually took place in Viking Age Iceland or Greenland.

Overall, the evidence suggests that runic writing was only practised in very particular circumstances in the Viking Age North Atlantic, in both Norway and the settlements. It was not an automatic cultural export during the process of migration, nor does the distribution of inscriptions correlate with the overall distribution of migrants and settlers that we can gather from other sources. Clearly, the runic distribution, like most other distributions, is affected by the vagaries of preservation and, in places like Greenland, also reflects extensive excavations. The distributions may therefore not be representative, but are still suggestive. At the very least, the runic corpus as a whole demonstrates very clearly the continuing movements, and consequent cultural contacts, around the North Atlantic world, not just in the period of migration but even more so in the centuries after 1100. In fact, it is fair to say that the use of runic writing in the North Atlantic was largely a product of the diaspora rather than of the initial migrations.

Skaldic networks

There is an interesting overlap between the runic and the skaldic evidence, in the form of the Karlevi stone from the island of Öland, off Sweden's Baltic coast. This bears a runic inscription which incorporates a regular stanza in *dróttkvætt* ('court metre'), in praise of the deceased who lies in the mound beneath it, for all the world like the praise poetry of the tenth and eleventh centuries, using the same forms and the same kind of diction.[34] The monument is complex and many aspects of it hard to pin down, but it is reasonably certain that it is from the late tenth century or around 1000, that it commemorates someone who ruled in Denmark, but who died away from home, and that some aspects of the stanza suggest it was composed by a poet who was schooled in Norway or Iceland. Other than this single monument, however, the bulk of the skaldic poetry that survives today does so in medieval Icelandic manuscripts (as outlined in ch. 1). For this reason it is easy to assume that, after probably originating in Norway, the genre became the exclusive preserve of Icelandic poets, who made their living travelling around the courts of Scandinavia, composing in praise of kings and chieftains. In this model, the genre lived on in Iceland and developed new contents and contexts. But both runic inscriptions, and a closer look at the skaldic corpus itself, suggest that for much of its time it was a pan-diaspora phenomenon.

Karlevi is the only Viking Age runic inscription that is closely comparable to the *dróttkvætt* praise poetry preserved in the Icelandic manuscript tradition, though a considerable number of Swedish rune-stones have more informal inscriptions that can be described as laudatory verse.[35] But the medieval inscriptions of Norway, particularly from Bergen but also found sporadically elsewhere, and mostly ephemeral carvings on organic materials, provide extensive evidence for the practice of skaldic poetry there in the thirteenth and fourteenth centuries.[36] There is even one clearly skaldic (though sadly not yet fully interpreted) stanza on a wooden stick found in excavations at Qorlortup Itinnera in Greenland in 1997.[37] These suggest that the skaldic genre was much more widespread than the Icelandic manuscript tradition reveals. In this, the vast majority of skaldic verse is preserved in prose contexts, either as examples for handbooks like Snorri's *Edda*, or as interspersed evidence or comment or dialogue in a variety of saga-genres. Within this manuscript tradition, it can be seen that certain literary genres favour certain types of poetry. Thus, most skaldic poetry with mythological content is found in Snorri's *Edda* while the kings' sagas naturally favour poems in praise of kings and princes. The sagas of Icelanders mostly cite stanzas that are presented as the spontaneous utterances of characters in the saga and many have doubted their Viking Age authenticity as a result, unlike the poems cited by Snorri or in the kings' sagas. As an oral genre, the survival of skaldic poetry depended on its being chosen for citation in these texts, while the runic inscriptions suggest that there was a lot more of it about which never got formally written down to survive for posterity.

In terms of that which did get recorded in manuscripts, we can see the processes of diaspora in operation. Many of the skalds were much travelled in the course of practising their profession and they ranged across the Scandinavian world, as they composed for kings and princes in many countries. Most, but not all, were Icelanders. The recent publication of the first two volumes of *Skaldic Poetry of the Scandinavian Middle Ages* enables an up-to-date survey of the praise poem genre from the ninth to the thirteenth centuries, as it is recorded in the king's sagas.[38] The bulk of the recorded and surviving poetry in this genre is for Norwegian rulers, so these will be considered first.

The earliest recorded court poets are Norwegian, like Þjóðólfr whose very by-name proclaims his provenance – he was *ór Hvini* 'from Kvinesdal' (in Vest-Agder). Along with several other Norwegian poets, he composed for Haraldr *hárfagri* 'Fine-Haired' in the ninth and early tenth centuries. Haraldr's sons Hákon *inn góði* 'The Good' and Haraldr *gráfeldr* 'Grey-Cloak' were also patrons of poets, including Eyvindr *skáldaspillir* 'Plagiarist', who has been described as 'the last important Norwegian skald'. The next major grouping of skalds was at the court of the earls of *Hlaðir*, a court renowned for its devotion to both paganism and poetry (as discussed in ch. 5, above) in the late tenth century. This is where there is a major influx of Icelandic poets, since most of the poets of these earls are said in the sources to have been Icelandic. Although some are not given a nationality, none are explicitly said to be from anywhere else.

The heyday of court poetry was in the late tenth and eleventh centuries, when every Norwegian king had an entourage of skalds, often quite a few. A feature of the eleventh-century poetry is the importance of the poet as witness to the king or prince's activities. While this was always an aspect of praise poetry, there is increasing emphasis on the poet's presence at significant battles, and those battles are often further-flung than previously. Óláfr Haraldsson's youthful forays around England and the Continent, Magnús Óláfsson's campaigns in the Baltic, Haraldr Sigurðarson's military stint in Byzantium and the Mediterranean, and his attempt to conquer England in 1066, Magnús *berfœttr* 'Bare-Legged' Óláfsson's raids in Britain and Ireland, all of these and more are recorded by poets, often more than one, who went along for the ride, but also to bear witness. Many of these poets returned home to Iceland, where their adventures provided entertainment at the General Assembly. One short tale tells the story of an Icelander who travels to the court of King Haraldr harðráði in Norway and surprises the king by entertaining the court with the real-life story of the king's own adventures.[39] To the king's enquiry as to where he learned this story, the Icelander responds:

> 'Þat var vanði minn, herra, at ek fór hvert sumar til alþingis á váru landi, ok nam ek svá sǫguna, er Halldórr Snorrason sagði.'
>
> 'It was my custom, sir, to go every summer to the General Assembly in our country, and I learned the story just as Halldórr Snorrason told it.'

Though none of his poetry survives, Halldórr Snorrason was remembered as one of several Icelandic poets who accompanied Haraldr on many of his voyages and was an eyewitness to his deeds, news of which he brought back to Iceland.[40] No doubt such poets brought other interesting stories back to Iceland with them, not just those that were then recycled in the kings' sagas. The story quoted above suggests one way in which these stimuli from the diaspora encouraged the growth of saga-literature in Iceland.

Poetry in the old style continued to be composed in the twelfth and thirteenth centuries, though sometimes under different circumstances. Poets still documented their patrons' travels and battles, but adapted the old conventions to new circumstances. Sigurðr *jórsalafari* 'Jerusalem-Traveller' Magnússon's journey to the Holy Land still involved lots of warfare, but the purpose was now at least ostensibly a religious one, the two aspects being given varying prominence by the poets who accompanied him.[41] In the thirteenth century, the highly literate poets of the Sturlung dynasty in Iceland, Snorri Sturluson and his nephews Óláfr *hvítaskáld* 'White Poet' and Sturla Þórðarsynir composed poetry for various rulers at the glittering thirteenth-century Norwegian court, especially Hákon Hákonarson, but these encomia have a different tone from those of previous centuries and probably arose in different ways. Snorri's *Háttatal*, ostensibly in praise of Hákon and his co-regent and future father-in-law Earl Skúli, also serves as a tour-de-force in which the poet displays his versatility in 102 metrical variants. It has been described as 'an example of the modification of the skaldic tradition brought about by the increasing use of the written word for literature in Scandinavia' and it is assumed that Snorri sent it to the king in manuscript form, rather than performing it orally before him.[42] Snorri also used it as the framework for *Háttatal*, the third main section of his *Edda*, in which he explained the metrical basis of skaldic poetry. Similarly, his nephew Sturla composed four poems about Hákon, but only one of these while the king was still alive. All of these are preserved in *Hákonar saga Hákonarsonar*, also written by Sturla, and it is likely that most of the poetry was composed at the same time as the saga was being written, unlike earlier skaldic poetry which was rather a source for the authors of the kings' sagas.[43] These Sturlung poets were composing in a particular tradition of which they were very much aware, now out of date but which they were trying to recreate.

Although the majority of the praise poetry from the ninth to the thirteenth centuries was composed for Norwegian rulers, there are also fragments for various Swedish and Danish rulers, and a substantial corpus of poetry for Knútr Sveinsson (a.k.a. Canute or Cnut), king of England and Norway, as well as Denmark, in the early eleventh century.[44] Other English rulers, not all of Scandinavian origin, are also celebrated in skaldic verse, and the composition as well as recital of skaldic verse in England, for a variety of rulers, is well attested.[45] We may wonder whether rulers such as Æthelstan (recipient of an encomium by no less than Egill Skalla-Grímsson) actually understood what was being said to them, and what they made of this particular genre, but Æthelstan, at least, was quite used to foreign cultural practices at his court, and poetry in a variety of languages.[46] A more unusual example is the *Valþjófsflokkr* of Þorkell Skallason.[47] Valþjófr, or Waltheof, was an Anglo-Saxon earl of Huntingdon and Northumbria, though with Scandinavian ancestry, who was executed by William the Conqueror in 1076 for treachery.[48] This execution, and an earlier battle with some Norman warriors, are the events commemorated in what survives of Þorkell's poem. We know nothing about this Þorkell or his origins, but the two stanzas make clear that he was partisan, and that he was in the paid service of Waltheof whom he calls *minn harri* 'my lord'. His use of the expression *véla í tryggð* 'deceive in a state of truce' is exactly paralleled on a tenth-century runic inscription from Braddan in the Isle of Man (IM MM138). Whether Þorkell was an Icelander or Norwegian in Waltheof's service, or whether he was a home-grown skald (perhaps less likely), it is clear that somewhere in northern England in the late 1070s, there was a patron and, presumably, an audience, imbued with Norse concepts of loyalty and treachery, conversant with the conventions and cultural values of skaldic poetry, and willing to pay for and listen to poetry with these values and in this form.[49]

Apart from England in the tenth and eleventh centuries, the other main centre for Old Norse poetic activity in the British Isles was the Earldom of Orkney, and this will be discussed separately below, since it involves a range of types of poetry from a broader chronological period, not all of it conventional praise poetry. But before leaving the survey of praise poetry, it is worth mentioning that the genre was even practised in Iceland, a place without any kings or princes. Some Icelanders had ambitions to be like their high-ranking colleagues in Norway, and there are fragments of evidence for praise poems in the same genre as those for Scandinavian rulers being composed for Icelandic chieftains in the eleventh century.[50] Orkney however provides an interesting test case of the roles skaldic poetry could play in the diaspora, as there is evidence, not all of it equally robust, for the practice of poetry there from its earliest settlement by Scandinavians through into the thirteenth century.

Case study – poets of Orkney

The first recorded poet associated with Orkney is Einarr Rǫgnvaldsson who ruled over it in the early tenth century and who was called *Torf* 'Turf'-Einarr, apparently for his adoption of peat as a fuel in Orkney. He was the son of a Norwegian earl who was awarded the rule of Orkney by Haraldr *hárfagri* 'Fine-Haired' in compensation for the killing of his son, in the late ninth or early tenth century. Rǫgnvaldr then delegated the rule of Orkney to several members of his family in turn, none of whom made a success of it until Einarr, his illegitimate son, took it on. Various sagas preserve five stanzas in which Einarr exults in the vengeance he has taken for the killing of his father by two of Haraldr's sons.[51] Both the authenticity and the date of these stanzas can be, and have been, challenged, but this is in any case a problem with all early skaldic poetry. The stanzas do imply an island location for Einarr's vengeance killing of Halfdan Haraldsson, using the term *Eyjar* 'Islands', which in Old Norse most commonly refers to the Northern Isles of Orkney and Shetland. If genuine, the poems suggest a complex political context for the beginnings of the Orkney earldom, the earls being the beneficiaries of Haraldr's gift of the isles, but embroiled in subsequent hostilities with his sons. Even if not genuine, the poems are important in providing a founding myth for the earldom, which was to reach a high level of power and influence in the eleventh century, under Earl Þorfinnr Sigurðarson, a ruler responsible for the next phase of skaldic activity in Orkney.

As already outlined in Chapter 1, Þorfinnr's family roots were mainly in Scotland, but his political and cultural affiliations were with his Norse paternal ancestry. These affiliations included the patronage of the Icelandic poet Arnórr Þórðarson, who received his nickname *jarlaskáld* 'Earls' Poet' precisely because of his employment by both Þorfinnr and his nephew and sometime co-ruler Rǫgnvaldr Brúsason.[52] By the time Þorfinnr and Rǫgnvaldr ruled in Orkney in the eleventh century, the practice of court poetry was well-established in Norway, and it is likely that is where they got the idea of employing a poet. Arnórr was well-connected, in both poetry and politics. His father, Þórðr Kolbeinsson, is said to have been a court poet to one Danish and two Norwegian kings, as well as the earl of *Hlaðir*, Eiríkr Hákonarson, though only his poem on the latter survives.[53] Þórðr's son Arnórr may have composed for Knútr Sveinsson, king of Denmark, England and Norway, and certainly composed several outstanding poems for Knútr's great rivals Magnús Óláfsson and Haraldr Sigurðarson, kings of Norway. It seems that Arnórr spent some time in Orkney, and composed one long praise poem for each of the earls, *Rǫgnvaldsdrápa* and *Þorfinnsdrápa*.[54]

Rǫgnvaldsdrápa (st. 2) mentions a marriage alliance, suggesting that Arnórr also had a more personal interest in Orkney, though unfortunately further details are not known. In a free-standing verse, Arnórr expresses his dismay at having to take sides in the conflict between Rǫgnvaldr and Þorfinnr, with the implication that his heart is with the former, presumably because of their kinship.[55] But in the end, he supported the winner, who was Þorfinnr. While only a few stanzas of *Rǫgnvaldsdrápa* survive, *Þorfinnsdrápa* is quite well preserved, and provides a wealth of information about Þorfinnr's career, and warfare, politics and winter feasting courtesy of the earl in eleventh-century Orkney. An abundance of place-names demonstrates both the poet's familiarity with local conditions and the geographical range of Þorfinnr's raiding activities. The poem concludes with the stanza quoted at the beginning of this book, along with another one in which the poet asks for God's mercy for Þorfinnr.

At the end of Arnórr's career, he seems to have returned to Iceland, while keeping up his contacts with Norway, in particular. But he is also credited with the composition of poems in praise of the Icelandic chieftains Hermundr Illugason and Gellir Þorkelsson, both characters well known from the sagas.[56] Although only fragments of these poems survive, they are important evidence for Icelandic attempts to adapt the praise poem genre to the slightly lesser figures of Icelandic chieftains as well as to Scandinavian kings and earls. It is significant that it was Arnórr who composed these, his diasporic experience in Orkney contributing to his sense that it was not only Norwegian earls and kings who could be praised in this way.

Chapter 46 of *Orkneyinga saga* refers to one or more praise poems (the manuscripts disagree on their number) for the earls Hákon Pálsson and Magnús

Erlendsson. In the early twelfth century, these two were cousins whose enmity eventually led to the killing of Magnús by Hákon, and Magnús' subsequent elevation to sainthood. But before they fell out, they had fought together against a distant relative called Dufníall, and against a wealthy Shetlander called Þorbjǫrn, both of whom they killed. These and other deeds were celebrated in one or more poems about the cousins, which do not survive, and neither does the name of any poet responsible for them. Chapter 43 of the saga also refers to a praise poem about Hákon, according to which he accompanied the Norwegian king Magnús *berfœttr* 'Bare-Legged' Óláfsson on a raiding expedition to Götaland in Sweden. Whether or not this was the same poem as the one described above is impossible to tell, as this does not survive either. However, these scraps of information do suggest that, once Arnórr had brought the practice of skaldic verse to Orkney, it did not die out when he left, and that later earls were also interested in this form of cultural ostentation. This fact may be relevant in understanding the case of Earl Rǫgnvaldr, although his is more complex and illustrates the ways in which skaldic poetry was changing later in the twelfth century.

Rǫgnvaldr Kali Kolsson, earl of Orkney, has already been mentioned (ch. 5, above) in connection with the interest in Norse myth in twelfth-century Orkney. As a poet, he is a particularly interesting figure, since he represents a new direction for skaldic verse in several ways. Unlike his predecessors, he did not hire court poets to sing his praises, though he did like to surround himself with poets. Together with the Icelander Hallr Þórarinsson, he composed *Háttalykill*, a 'key to metres', which could only have come out of detailed study of the traditional metres of skaldic verse but also a knowledge of poetry in Latin.[57] The content of the poem is historical, and it too shows that its authors must somehow have studied the kings of Scandinavia, from legendary times through to their own day. As a metrical exercise, *Háttalykill* provided a model for the metrical section of Snorri's *Edda* known as *Háttatal*.[58]

Rǫgnvaldr's own poetry is entirely in the form of *lausavísur* or 'free-standing verses', ostensibly composed on the spot to react to events as they happened.[59] The most dramatic events that he composed about include a shipwreck on Shetland, and, most famously, a crusade-cum-pilgrimage-cum-viking-expedition that he undertook to the Holy Land in 1153–4. On this journey, Rǫgnvaldr and his associates passed through Narbonne, in Provence in the south of France, for a memorable encounter with the Viscountess Ermengarde, about whom they composed poetry that is clearly influenced by the European literary conventions of courtly love and the unattainable beloved. According to *Orkneyinga saga*, Rǫgnvaldr's companions on this voyage were Norwegians and Icelanders as well as men from the Northern Isles, and they included four poets. Two of these, Oddi and Ármóðr, are variously said in different manuscripts of the saga to be either Shetlanders or Icelanders, while a third, Þorbjǫrn, is given no nationality.[60] The fourth poet said to have accompanied Rǫgnvaldr is a certain Sigmundr, nicknamed *ǫngull*, which might mean 'fish-hook', but might also allude to Sigmundr's possible origins on the island of Anglesey in Wales (Old Norse

Ǫngulsey).[61] Sigmundr's father, Andrés, was probably a Manxman, his mother (of uncertain origin but with the Norse name of Ingiríðr) subsequently married Sveinn Ásleifarson, a major character in *Orkneyinga saga*, and Sigmundr was brought up in Orkney. While not all of Rǫgnvaldr's entourage were poets, it is virtually certain that the same group of islanders, Icelanders and Norwegians was responsible for the runic graffiti in the prehistoric chambered cairn of Maeshowe, on the Mainland of Orkney, as noted above.[62]

As well as the four poets who accompanied Rǫgnvaldr on his journey, *Orkneyinga saga* also cites verse by two Icelanders said to be resident in Orkney, one Bótólfr, and Hallr Þórarinsson, who has already been mentioned as co-author of *Háttalykill*.[63] Hallr's stanza is particularly interesting, since it shows awareness of issues of national identity and national stereotypes. According to the saga, Hallr arrived in Orkney and asked his first host, a man called Þorsteinn on the island of North Ronaldsay, to introduce him to Rǫgnvaldr's court, where he was refused:

> Hafa kvezk hodda rýrir,
> hinns mestum veg stýrir,
> — neitti grúpans granna —
> gnótt vígligri manna.

> The diminisher of hoards [GENEROUS MAN = Rǫgnvaldr], who possesses very great honour, said that he had plenty of men more warlike; he refused the neighbour of the sausage [= Icelander].

The stanza plays on an obscure joke that is also recorded elsewhere, in which Icelanders are derogatorily associated with sausages and suet. Hallr was eventually admitted to Rǫgnvaldr's court through the intervention of Þorsteinn's mother, Ragna.[64] The Orcadian chieftain Sveinn Ásleifarson, not to be outdone by his rival Rǫgnvaldr, also had an Icelandic poet, Eiríkr, accompanying him on a raiding voyage around Wales.[65]

Rǫgnvaldr clearly enjoyed surrounding himself with poets, of whatever nationality, and discussing the craft with them. It is an interesting question where he learned his poetry, since there is no evidence that he ever went to Iceland. In fact, Rǫgnvaldr grew up in Agder, in Norway, as the son of a Norwegian nobleman and the Orcadian Gunnhildr Erlendsdóttir, sister of St Magnús.[66] Rǫgnvaldr's grandfather, Kali Sæbjarnarson, was also a poet, from whom only one stanza survives, and it is possible he gave Rǫgnvaldr his first instruction in the skaldic art.[67] Some early poetry by Rǫgnvaldr, composed before he came to Orkney for the first time to take up his inheritance, suggests that he was a fully formed poet before then. In general, both Rǫgnvaldr's poetic and his runic skills are most likely to have been acquired during his youth in Norway, particularly in the towns of Bergen and Tønsberg, where he might also have met some poetical Icelanders.[68] But once in Orkney, if not before, he must also have been aware of the poem in praise of his uncle Magnús, mentioned above. Rǫgnvaldr's poetry and his interest in runic writing exemplify the diasporic process in which inherited cultural traditions from the homeland are reinvigorated and even reinvented in the context of multilateral cultural encounters.[69] He demonstrates both internal diasporic connections, between Norway, the Northern Isles and Iceland, and the external cultural connections deriving from his extensive travels in the south. The fact that his poetry was preserved in Icelandic texts demonstrates the Icelanders' consciousness of their ongoing connectedness to the various regions of the Scandinavian homelands and the Viking diaspora.

Bjarni Kolbeinsson, bishop of Orkney, also had a diasporic background. He was brought up on the island of Wyre, in Orkney, but his father had Norwegian connections, while his mother was of noble Orcadian ancestry.[70] He was well connected in Iceland as well as Norway, and often travelled to, and probably died in, Norway.[71] Bjarni was instrumental in promoting the canonisation of Rǫgnvaldr, but his main connection with the earl seems to be their shared interest in poetry.[72] One long poem is attributed to him in medieval sources, *Jómsvíkingadrápa*, which relates historical and legendary traditions about the late tenth-century battle at Hjǫrungavágr between the earls of *Hlaðir* and the *Jómsvíkingar*, a legendary Danish-Baltic fighting force.[73] The poem shows the same interest in legendary history as *Háttalykill*, and is also innovative in ways that seem to echo Rǫgnvaldr's poetry. In particular, its refrain, in which the poet laments his unrequited love for a married woman, introduces to the story both a theme and a note of ironic humour which are reminiscent of Rǫgnvaldr's poetry. Bjarni may also have been responsible for *Málsháttakvæði*, a poem usually understood as a collection of proverbs, hence its name, 'Proverb-Poem'.[74] In fact, it contains much more, including sententious sayings, aphorisms, lyrics, and allusions to fables and to Norse myths and sagas (as noted in ch. 5, above). As in *Jómsvíkingadrápa*, the speaking persona comments deprecatingly on his own verse-making, and has been unlucky in love. But unlike *Jómsvíkingadrápa*, it is not a narrative, but a kind of commonplace book in verse, drawing on a wide-ranging knowledge of both Norse and international literary traditions. The manuscript association, some of the content and certain linguistic features suggest an Orcadian origin, but the ascription to Bjarni Kolbeinsson is less sure than for *Jómsvíkingadrápa*.

The last known poet to have Orkney connections is a certain Snækollr Gunnason, probably the great-grandson (through his mother and grandmother) of Rǫgnvaldr Kali Kolsson himself. Not much is known about him except that he had to leave Orkney after participating in the killing of an earl.[75] He established himself in Norway, as a district chieftain in Sunnmøre, and seems to have become just as involved in turbulent politics there as back home – his one surviving stanza refers to his capture by King Hákon's men in 1239. If nothing else, Snækollr demonstrates how the Norwegian homeland was still a place of refuge for those in trouble in the diaspora. With this, the evidence for poets and poetry in Norse Orkney dies out completely, though it is possible to find other evidence of Norse language and culture there for some centuries to come. The diasporic connections were maintained, but these were no longer expressed in the form of poetry, or at least not in any that has survived.

Identities

Viking identities

The inevitable question raises itself: how did people understand their own identities within the complexities of the networks outlined above, and in the framework of a diasporic world bound together by a common material culture and a common use of the *dǫnsk tunga*? Before addressing this, we have to ponder the ways in which we attempt to understand past identities. Archaeologists, for instance, use both objects and scientific methods of analysis to interpret or even construct the identities of past people. Thus, the occupant of a late ninth-century grave discovered in Adwick-le-Street, South Yorkshire, England, in 2001, is identified in the publication as a 'Viking woman', or 'Norse', through her brooches and other objects found in the grave, while the burial type identifies her as 'pagan'.[76] Isotope analysis of her teeth establishes her origins in Norway, or possibly north-eastern Scotland. But are we just imposing our modern categories of 'female', 'Norse' (or 'Viking' or 'Scandinavian'), 'pagan' or 'from Norway' on the woman from Adwick, and how would she have identified herself? Did she even think in those categories and what words would she have used for them if she did? We can be pretty sure that she did not call herself a 'Viking' (see discussion of this word in ch. 1). While life experience taught her very early on that she was female rather than male, did her 'pagan' and 'Norse' (or 'Norwegian' or 'Scandinavian') identity only become clear to her during her time spent in Christian England? Did she conceptualise these aspects of her identity at all, or were they more important to the people who chose the objects with which to bury her than to herself? If so, how did they conceptualise them?

The nature of identity, both group and individual, has been a matter of debate among archaeologists and historians of the British Isles in the last few decades.[77] This debate is ongoing, and has been further complicated by the advent of new scientific techniques, such as DNA analysis, or stable isotope analysis. There seems to be, if no longer a consensus, then still a very strong tendency to view identity as shifting, indeed malleable, constructed and situated rather than essential, and to stress the agency of early medieval people in defining, selecting or even constructing their own identities (which are nowadays almost always plural). This post-modern emphasis on diversity and complexity has brought many interesting new insights and taught us to question overly simplistic categories for the past. But it may also be that the urge to classify people in this way is more a product of a modern interest in identities and identity politics than a historical reality. The anthropologist Thomas Hylland Eriksen has argued that '[c]omplex modern societies seem to imply processes of identity and boundary maintenance which are much more acutely felt, and more self-consciously fashioned, than has been the case in other kinds of societies', while what he calls 'reflexive self-identity' is one of the 'aspects of . . . interethnic processes which are less likely to come about in non-modern than in modern contexts'.[78] Yet modern scholars are obsessed with identifying such identities in, for example, the Icelandic population. So they return repeatedly to questions of where the Icelandic settlers came from, whether men and women originated in different places, and the extent to which the earliest settlers were pagan or Christian, free or slave.[79] These are the categories which currently interest us about the past.

It is remarkable how little scholars have explored the ways in which identities were expressed in linguistic forms, rather than in clothing, jewellery or other material culture. Recent discussions of past identities have on the whole proceeded from the analysis of material culture and not addressed how it is expressed in language. Yet words, too, are artefacts of the past, and can in some ways give us a better idea than the study of objects of how people in the past thought of their own identities, and which aspects of identity were especially important to them. In a recent study of *Landnámabók*, for instance, I have attempted to show that its primary concern is with individuals and their identities, in particular their gender, their family relationships and their associations with the land.[80] The text is not especially concerned with establishing group identities and, while people are occasionally identified according to their ethnicity, religion or social status, which suggests that those categories were at least recognised, these were not important enough to be mentioned consistently. This can partly be explained by the nature of *Landnámabók* as a catalogue of people and places, not particularly interested in larger social and cultural structures, so that it shows little inclination to classify people into social groups. To the thirteenth-century Icelanders, thinking about their country's past and their Viking Age ancestors, the questions they asked were primarily what were people called, where did they live, how were they related to each other, and how were they related to us? Judging from *Landnámabók*, place and genealogy were the categories by which they classified people, with gender, family and locality being the real keys to identity, but the same urges can be seen in the sagas of Icelanders, which is why they respond so well to the network analysis discussed above. The basic vision is quite small-scale, even if the bigger picture, both geographical and historical, can be glimpsed behind these catalogues and narratives of individual men, women and their families. This may however reflect the particular situation of Iceland in the settlement period, where the diasporic displacement of people from various parts of the Viking world gave them a new focus on their immediate surroundings and situation, rather than on their origins. That came later, as will be discussed below.

The subject of identities in the broader Viking Age, and not just Iceland, integrating the study of both words and objects, would be worth a book in itself and cannot be discussed as fully here as would be desirable. What can be attempted here is some preliminary discussion in the form of two case studies which demonstrate how the processes of diaspora in the Viking Age created completely new identities, in two different parts of the Viking world.

Case study – Scandinavian identities in northern England

It is a fair assumption that the first Scandinavians who settled in England from the ninth century onwards would have differed from their new neighbours in many or all of the really important matters of life such as language, religion, social and family structure, clothing, jewellery, house structure and ornamentation, food habits, occupational skills, poetry and art. In the course of time, though probably not all at once, people of Scandinavian origin became indistinguishable from other people in such matters. It is hard to tell which of these differences they would have considered essential to their personal and group identity, and therefore hung on to for a long time, and which they abandoned quickly in favour of the culture and practices of their new neighbours. Does religion last longer than language or vice versa? Do people adopt new ways of eating more quickly than new clothing? The question to be considered here is whether the adoption of a Christian identity entailed the abandonment of a Scandinavian identity, or whether the former could take place before the latter. A small body of epigraphic texts will be discussed, as they have a bearing upon the newly Christian people of Scandinavian origin in England. These are of interest because they represent both material and verbal culture, so covering more than one way of expressing identity. Much of this material is well known and thoroughly studied, yet little if any of that scholarly effort has been focused on its implications for the study of identities.

A small number of carved stone sundials, which seem to cluster, as far as they can be dated, in the eleventh century, are found in eastern Yorkshire, all associated with churches, namely those of Aldborough, Great Edstone, Kirkdale and Old Byland.[81] All four of them bear inscriptions, in a language that can best be described as late Old English, but with some elements of Latin. All are written in the roman alphabet, in the Anglo-Saxon capitals commonly used for monumental inscriptions at the time. The content of the four inscriptions has been summed up in this way:[82]

> These texts define the church in which the dial stands, and/or tell who made the dial or ordered its construction, and/or inform the passer-by that this is a time-piece . . . or mention its function in a more allusive way.

Nine of the twelve names mentioned in these inscriptions (if they are all correctly interpreted) are Scandinavian – the only non-Norse names are those of Christ and St Gregory, to whom the church in Kirkdale is dedicated, and the English king Edward the Confessor, to whose reign that inscription is dated. Eight of these nine Scandinavian names are the patrons, dedicatees or craftsmen of the monuments, or members of their families. There is also possible evidence of Scandinavian influence on the language of the inscriptions.[83] The pronoun *hanum* in the Aldbrough inscription appears to be Old Norse, though it is grammatically problematic. In the Kirkdale inscription, the word *solmerca* is usually understood as a Norse loan-word. *Huscarl*, if that is what the Old Byland inscription has, is indeed a Norse loan-word, attested in other Old English texts.[84] In the Kirkdale inscription, the English word *eorl* has its usual late Old English meaning of an aristocrat second in rank to the king, which has been influenced by the meaning of the Old Norse cognate *jarl*. It is also possible that the grammatical confusions and loss of endings in the Aldbrough and Kirkdale inscriptions may be due to the more general influence of Norse on English. Nevertheless, the only accurate description of the language of the inscriptions is that they are all in late Old English.

In spite of this, this small group is clearly in some sense a Scandinavian phenomenon and not only because of the Scandinavian names recorded in them. East and North Yorkshire both have heavy concentrations of place-names of Scandinavian origin, and the region shows continued use of Scandinavian personal names well into the twelfth century and even beyond.[85] Moreover, the few parallels for this kind of monument with a vernacular text are mostly close by. Geographically closest is the St Mary's Castlegate dedication stone from York, which is dated to the same period, and also has an inscription in Anglo-Saxon capitals in a mixture of Old English and Latin.[86] Three patrons of the church are named in the inscription; of these one name is certainly and the other two possibly Norse. It has no other Scandinavian features, though, and lacks a sundial. Similarly, a dedication stone from St Mary-le-Wigford in Lincoln has an Old English dedication inscription (with some Latin elements) on a re-used Romano-British monument, again with no sundial, but with a name of possibly Old Norse origin.[87]

There are at least four other contemporary sundials with inscriptions, two of them quite close to the group already discussed from Yorkshire. The sundial from Skelton-in-Cleveland (once North Yorkshire) will be discussed further below. There is also a fragmentary sundial with an Old English inscription from Stow, a large minster church in north Lincolnshire.[88] Sundials from further away are Bishopstone in Sussex, which has a single Old English personal name, but the inscription may not be contemporary with the sundial and it is in any case not a dedication inscription, and one from Orpington in Kent which has inscriptions in both Latin and Old English, and some mysterious runes which may show Scandinavian influence.[89] Sinnington in North Yorkshire seems also to have had an inscribed sundial but it is lost.[90] The fashion for such sundials continued in Yorkshire after the Conquest, as shown by an example from Weaverthorpe, which has a dedication inscription in Latin.[91]

These inscribed sundials are clearly a type of monument that was fashionable among the Scandinavian-origin inhabitants of Yorkshire in particular. But what does it mean to say that these people were Scandinavian, or should they rather be described as Anglo-Scandinavian? They certainly had names of Old Norse origin, but as we know personal names follow fashion and may not reflect ethnicity. The monuments themselves show that these people were good Christians. The inscriptions are in Old English, and the few runic letters used are no more than those which we find in Old English manuscripts, adopted into the Old English alphabet. One could question whether the identity of the people who commissioned these monuments was in any way, or any longer, Scandinavian.

It may be that the patrons of the Yorkshire sundials and similar monuments considered themselves, and could therefore be considered by us, as Christian Anglo-Saxons, who simply happened to have Norse names, and who spoke a form of English with a slight Norse substratum deriving from the Norse settlement of Yorkshire some two centuries earlier, probably without realising it. This interpretation seems likely on the evidence of the monuments themselves. In this model, the names have no significance – either they just represent the incorporation of originally Scandinavian names into the naming-stock of the area a century or two earlier, or, given the eleventh-century date of the inscriptions, they could be the result of a naming fashion set at the court of the Danish king Knútr which had trickled up to Yorkshire. However, there are some weak assumptions in this model, the most important one being that the language of the inscriptions represents the spoken language of the patrons.

Setting aside this assumption allows a second possible interpretation, that the patrons of the Yorkshire sundials had a strong Scandinavian identity that was expressed in their naming practices, in their daily speech and in their regionally specific choice of monument. The main non-traditional, non-Scandinavian element in their culture was that they were Christian. Although this interpretation appears at first to fly in the face of the inscriptions themselves, a case can be made for it. Matthew Townend has argued that Old Norse flourished as a spoken language in England, while noting that there is little or no evidence of it having been written there.[92] The inscriptions are therefore in Old English with bits of Latin simply because these were the only possible languages for this kind of writing at this period, 'whatever language the patrons of these monuments spoke'. Townend does not go so far as to argue that the patrons of these inscriptions spoke Old Norse, and it may be foolish to do so. Yet I think there is some useful parallel evidence which suggests that this could have been the case.

In the Aldbrough inscription we find the Old English word for 'church' *cirice*. This common word acquired a form *kirk* in northern dialects under the influence of Old Norse *kirkja* and, in this form, is found in a number of place-names.[93] Because the word was established in Middle English dialects, the use of *kirk* in a place-name is not always a sign that the name was coined in the Old Norse language. However, there is one category of name where this is likely to have been the case. There are 15 villages in Yorkshire with the name Kirby or Kirkby (there are of course many such villages in other parts of northern and eastern England, and the name-type is found throughout the Viking world).[94] This category of name is still not fully understood, and deserves further study. For the moment, it is sufficient to note that, in Yorkshire at least, the combination of *kirk* with the Scandinavian generic *-by* strongly suggests that the names were coined by speakers of Old Norse, in the Viking period. The modern pronunciations confirm the Scandinavian origin of the first element, yet the literate tradition of the Aldborough inscription required the word to be spelled in the Old English way.

On this basis, it could be argued that this small corpus of sundials is indirect evidence of a community that was still largely Scandinavian in its language. A community that held onto its language in this way is likely to have held onto many other traditional cultural practices, though that is more difficult to demonstrate. The one thing they clearly have not held onto is their religion. This Scandinavian community in England is Christian and proud of it, and has adopted certain associated practices, such as the use of English for writing, when writing is called for.

Their particular use of writing, for monumental sundials, uses the adopted cultural practices to create something new. The Christian identity of the Yorkshire sundial communities is something particular to themselves, not something they borrowed from their neighbours when they became Christian. This particular expression of Christian identity also seems to be symbolically related to their relatively recent entry into the community of Christianity. The Old Byland sundial is not in its original position, having been put into the east wall of the church upside-down, but the other three are all on the south walls of their churches (though Aldbrough is inside). The south wall is usually where the main entrance was in an Anglo-Saxon parish church. The location of these inscriptions thus symbolises the patrons' entry into the sacred space (both literal and metaphorical) of the Church, while the choice of sundials symbolises their submission to the Church's organisation of time and thus of their lives.[95]

In these monuments celebrating a recently acquired Christian identity, a parallel Scandinavian linguistic identity is revealed in the naming practices of the community who commissioned the sundials, but partially or fully concealed by the habits of literacy of those who made the monuments. However one aspect of Scandinavian culture which is not found on these particular monuments, but which when used proclaims that Scandinavian identity loud and clear, is the use of runes. While the Scandinavian runic inscriptions of England are a small, anomalous and often obscure corpus, their very existence is telling, for they often carry the same message of Christian identity, but with a strong and particularly Scandinavian tinge.

This is most clearly seen in the rune-stone found at St Paul's Cathedral, London's main church. In terms of decoration and inscription, the stone is entirely Scandinavian. The runes are Scandinavian, the language is Scandinavian, the names are Scandinavian, and the Ringerike-style quadruped entangled with a serpent is entirely in the Scandinavian artistic tradition. Yet the stone in which it is carved is local, and the monument was found in St Paul's churchyard.[96] This is thus a monument produced in England, but for a Scandinavian patron, by a craftsman or craftsmen who were entirely and convincingly au fait both with Scandinavian art and with Scandinavian literacy. What makes the monument Christian is its location and, probably, its form. It is most likely to be just one stone from a composite monument, a grave-cover with head- and foot-stone – a form of monument entirely appropriate for a Christian graveyard. As a monument in that location it makes a clear statement of Christian identity. What the words, and the art, add to that statement is an equally clear statement of Scandinavian identity.

There are no real parallels to the St Paul's stone elsewhere in England's small corpus of Scandinavian runic monuments. It is rather different from the northern monuments in that it can almost certainly be related to a context among the followers of Knútr, mostly recent immigrants. However, the use of runes to proclaim a Scandinavian identity can be seen in other contexts which also proclaim a Christian identity in the Scandinavian-settled areas of the north. Not far from the Yorkshire sundials already discussed is Skelton-in-Cleveland, now on Teesside, but historically also in Yorkshire. This church has a fragmentary sundial with an inscription both in Anglo-Saxon capitals and Norse runes (E 8).[97] Unfortunately, the stone is too badly damaged to decipher what the inscription might have said. It is not even clear whether the roman-alphabet inscription is entirely in Old English – some have argued that it may be in Old Norse, or in some kind of hybrid language, or in a heavily Scandinavianised form of English. The runes are distinctively Scandinavian but the only recognisable word is *ok*, presumably the word meaning 'and'. The monument has to be seen as closely related to the Yorkshire group, but with a higher degree of Scandinavianness through the use of runes, perhaps because the region in which it is located, near the River Tees, is on the edge of the Scandinavian-settled area. Was there greater need for a public proclamation of Scandinavian identity in the face of non-Scandinavian neighbours?

Until very recently, the Skelton sundial was unusual in being the only monumental use of Norse runes in the whole of Scandinavian-settled eastern England. Found in 2013 and recognised as a Scandinavian runic inscription in 2014, a fragment from Sockburn, Co. Durham (E 19), is now an important addition to the corpus.[98] The inscription on this fragment is entirely in runes, and the monument itself seems to have been a cross, since the inscription very clearly contains the word *kross*. Although this word is more widely found in place-names, in inscriptions it has so far only been found in the Irish Sea region, especially the Isle of Man, as discussed in Chapter 4, above.[99] Links to the west are further suggested by the fact that the inscription appears to contain the Gaelic name *Maelmuire*, the same name as is found on the Kirk Michael stone from the Isle of Man (IM MM130), also discussed in Chapter 4. The significance of this newest runic find is not yet fully understood, but two points are of interest. Sockburn is an important site, with previous finds of a wide variety of Anglo-Scandinavian sculpture, including nine hogbacks (including one with apparently mythological motifs, as noted in ch. 5, above). The sculpture is in a variety of styles and seems to suggest that Sockburn was a centre to which people from different parts of the Anglo-Scandinavian north of England flocked, for reasons that are still obscure, though perhaps to bury their dead and display their new type of Christian identity.[100] The new find strengthens this impression.

Runic inscriptions from the north-west of England are a fascinating but obscure group, post-Conquest, probably from the twelfth century, and because of their date they have been much discussed in relation to the question of how long the Scandinavian language was used in England.[101] As noted above, inscriptions are problematic as evidence for spoken language, particularly in this period, and this is illustrated by the tympanum from the church of Pennington on the Furness peninsula, once in Lancashire, now in Cumbria (E 9).[102] Although the inscription seems to be preserved more or less in its entirety, it still has obscurities. The language is not regular Old Norse, but Townend sees it as 'perfectly acceptable Old Norse, albeit with weakened inflexions'.[103] He argues that the displacement of Old English or Latin, and the roman alphabet, by Norse literacy in runes indirectly indicates the strength of Norse as a spoken language in the area. The linguistic history of the north-west of England still remains to be written, but the Pennington tympanum can plausibly be seen as yet another manifestation of Scandinavian identity in a Christian context. The inscription mentions one, two or three names, depending on which reading you adopt – one is almost certainly not Norse, the other two are Norse if correctly interpreted. The onomastic habits of the region are thus diverse, yet the issue of Scandinavianness is still important, as indicated by the use of runes. The tympanum is now inside the Victorian church but presumably was originally located above the main south entrance, and has parallels with the sundial group discussed above, in the mention of both a patron and a craftsman, and in recording the building or repair of the church. In relation to the discussion of the sundial inscriptions, it is worth noting that the Pennington inscription contains the word *kirk* – by the twelfth century, at least in the north-west of England, writing in a form of Old Norse that appears to represent local speech, and in runes, was possible in a way it does not seem to have been in the early eleventh century in Yorkshire.

This approach to eleventh- and twelfth-century inscriptions may also shed some light on the non-inscribed Anglo-Scandinavian sculpture of the tenth century, especially but not only that which contains traditional Scandinavian iconography which might be described as 'pagan'. The best known and most remarkable is the collection of sculpture still at Gosforth, in Cumbria, but there is a fair number of others both in the north-west and Yorkshire with 'pagan' Scandinavian iconography. Indeed most of the sculpture from the tenth and early eleventh centuries in northern and eastern England is 'Anglo-Scandinavian' in some sense and it is clear that this great flowering of sculpture in the late Anglo-Saxon period results in some way from the social and cultural upheavals of the Scandinavian settlement. This Anglo-Scandinavian sculpture contrasts in many ways with the Anglo-Saxon sculpture that went before it, which was generally of much higher quality and ambition, was ecclesiastical in impetus, and was clearly an elite art form restricted to monasteries and other important church sites. The Anglo-Scandinavian sculpture is secular, and more broadly distributed, in both the social and the geographical sense, while still retaining a connection with the church.

It is often remarked that the Scandinavians came from a culture which did not have a tradition of carving in stone. This has led to the assumption that the direction of influence was from the Christian Anglo-Saxons towards the new arrivals. The phenomenon is sometimes explained in terms of acculturation or accommodation, as discussed in Chapter 5, above. The dominance of Christianity was certainly assured in the long run of history, though whether it was clear at the time is debatable. The extent to which the monuments have 'pagan' elements has probably been overstated. It may be more fruitful to see these apparently hybrid monuments not purely within the pagan–Christian dichotomy, but in a broader context of the Scandinavians and their concern for their identity, whether linguistic, epigraphic, cultural or religious. A comparison with the inscriptions already discussed suggests that the forging of a new identity was a major motivation behind all of these monuments. They are all public and often quite large, and the display of a particular new-found identity seems an obvious function for them. In the north-west, as in Yorkshire, people of Scandinavian origin remained proud of, and anxious to assert, their Scandinavian identity. At the same time, they had the confidence to take on or develop a new Christian identity, and to appropriate Christian cultural forms to assert that identity. In Yorkshire they used the Old English language and the roman alphabet, in Gosforth and elsewhere it was ecclesiastical sculpture with both figurative images and ornament. They also invented completely new forms such as the hogback, an important monument type not yet fully understood.[104]

The Scandinavians adopted and adapted and invented these forms of cultural expression in ways that had no exact parallels among the Anglo-Saxon inhabitants. As a result, their message may not have been 'we have become Christians in order to integrate with you', but was perhaps rather 'we are still Scandinavians; we have chosen to become Christians, but we are doing it in our own way, which is not quite the same way as you have done it'. It could be seen as a case of Scandinavian culture incorporating new and interesting elements, rather than the usual view of a dominant Anglo-Saxon culture accommodating the Scandinavians. It was a way of doing things that lasted to the end of the eleventh century at least, and is represented in England by what I have previously called the 'cultural paganism' of the poetry composed at the court of Knútr – the ultimate assertion of Scandinavianness, through the use of pagan motifs, despite his being the most Christian of Christian kings.[105] But it is typical that the evidence for Knútr's cultural paganism is almost entirely from medieval Icelandic manuscripts, not from any Anglo-Saxon sources. The Anglo-Saxon dominance of the surviving evidence from England has sometimes made it difficult to see the confident assertion of Scandinavian identity that underlies so much of it, just as the use of Old English and the roman alphabet hides the Scandinavianness of the Yorkshire sundials.

All of this suggests a remarkable confidence and persistence of Scandinavian culture in Anglo-Saxon England, even as it incorporates innovations or those elements of the host culture which it finds useful or interesting, in a way that is entirely typical of diaspora. This process is realised in different ways in different regions, but the underlying tendency of the Viking Age is clearly the confident appropriation by Scandinavians of new lands, new religions, new languages and new cultures, when it suited them, and the resulting creation of new identities for themselves. While in England and elsewhere the Scandinavians created new local identities in response to their neighbours and surroundings, in previously uninhabited Iceland, we can observe the creation of a whole new national identity.

Case study – migration, diaspora and Icelandic identity

Most of Europe has been continuously populated since the last Ice Age, despite the ebb and flow of population movements and migrations. The study of population change on such a large land mass and its closely associated islands is complicated, not least because it has been going on for such a long time. This means that for most nations, or groups of people, it can be hard to pinpoint a particular moment in history when they came into being, and often difficult to decide when the change in population was extreme enough to suggest that a new nation or group of people had come into being. Many of these decisive moments are prehistoric or proto-historic, and have left little or no trace in written or other documentary sources. In the case of the North Atlantic island of Iceland, however, it is possible both to pinpoint the arrival of a particular group of people in a previously uninhabited island, and to get a glimpse of the processes by which they settled that island and by which their nation came into being. Moreover, the nation established in Iceland over a thousand years ago has continued in existence until the present day, with relatively little population change, at least in the form of immigrants, before the twenty-first century. This makes Iceland an ideal case study for the migration of populations, in particular a single founding migration, and how this migration relates to a larger diaspora and the subsequent formation of diasporic identities.

A range of different types of evidence points to the arrival of a Scandinavian-speaking population in Iceland in the last quarter of the ninth century:

- archaeology, which can both suggest a date for their arrival and indicate the culture(s) from which they came;
- various biological indices, especially and most recently DNA, which can indicate the current population's affiliations with neighbouring and possible source cultures;
- language, in the form of place-names and the language currently spoken by the Icelanders, both of which appear to have an unbroken history back to the time of the Scandinavian settlement;
- a number of medieval written sources, mostly in the vernacular, which are explicitly or implicitly about the Scandinavian settlement of Iceland.

The first three of these have already been addressed in previous chapters. Here, the focus will be on a few of the written sources which have much to contribute to an understanding of the migration process that brought Iceland into being. Two sources, or groups of sources, deal explicitly with the Viking Age migration to Iceland in what could be argued to be a documentary or historical way: *Íslendingabók* or 'Book of the Icelanders' and *Landnámabók* or 'Book of Settlements'.[106] Both have been referred to frequently in this work already, but are always worth returning to, as extraordinary documents for their time, and it is this extraordinariness that makes them important sources for this topic. So it is important to understand their nature as texts, and their textual transmission.

Íslendingabók opens with a prologue in which the author declares that he originally wrote it for the two bishops of Iceland, Þorlákr and Ketill, and showed it to Sæmundr the Priest. He then revised it according to their suggestions and according to knowledge that became available to him subsequently, and it is this revised version which he presents. The author's name is not, however, revealed until the very last word of the present text, in which a genealogy which begins with the legendary King of the Turks Yngvi ends with 'and I am called Ari'. From this we discover that he was Ari Þorgilsson (*c.* 1067–1148), an author widely acknowledged and respected in later Icelandic historical works. From these facts and from other chronological pointers in the text, it is possible to date the work with some precision to the 1120s. The Icelanders were converted to Christianity in 999 (as discussed in ch. 5, above), when the practice of writing in the roman alphabet was introduced. Within 130 years of this event Ari was able to produce a vernacular history of remarkable sophistication in terms of its obsession with correct chronology and its careful explanation of the reliability of its oral sources. The author does not refer to any native written sources, unless his reference to a 'saga' of St Edmund (ch. 1) was to an Icelandic text rather than a Latin one, which seems unlikely. Otherwise, his references to popes and foreign rulers, in some cases using Latin chronological markers such as *Kalend. Junii* and *obiit Paschalus secundus* (ch. 10) suggest that he had some annalistic sources in Latin, but he does not mention them specifically. The work also contains an important reference to writing in Iceland in the vernacular, when it says that the decision was taken to write the laws of Iceland down in a book (ch. 10). We can deduce that this happened in 1117, just a few years before the 1120s, and it is thus very hard to find evidence of any vernacular writing in Iceland much earlier than Ari, except possibly that of his mentor Sæmundr, who was later known as a historian, but nothing of his work survives, and it is not certain that it was in the vernacular.

A further important aspect of *Íslendingabók*, in addition to its early date, is the author's frequent and careful reference to the (oral) sources of his information, named individuals whom he knew personally and whom he identifies as 'wise' or 'learned' or 'knowledgeable'. By this means, the chain of tradition extends back to the time of the conversion of Iceland, through Ari's teacher Teitr who had spoken to someone who had been an eyewitness to the events. Almost every major event in the book is ascribed to one or another of these informants, or someone they had spoken to. As a whole, the work is a remarkable example of source criticism applied to an oral tradition. The book covers the history of Iceland, and particularly of its church, up until the time of writing. Clearly, its earliest sections, which describe the discovery and settlement of Iceland, are the furthest removed in time from Ari and his informants, and therefore probably based on less reliable information. Nevertheless, the nature of the work has meant that Ari's information has generally been accepted.

It is worth noting how schematic Ari's account of the discovery and settlement of Iceland (chs 1–3) is, and how much it is geared to his programme of writing a history of his relatively young nation, which he identifies as *Ísland*, the name of both the island and the polity established there. According to Ari, Iceland was settled entirely from Norway, so much so that there was a danger of the depopulation of Norway. The process happens quickly and neatly, within 60 years. Ari names one discoverer and primary settler, a Norwegian called Ingólfr. He then names four prominent settlers in each of the four quarters of the island (these four quarters were the basis of the legal and administrative structures, the establishment of which is also described at some length by Ari): Hrollaugr Rǫgnvaldsson, Ketilbjǫrn Ketilbjǫrnsson, Auðr Ketilsdóttir and Helgi Eyvindarson (ch. 2). All four are described as Norwegian, using the term *norrœnn* for Ketilbjǫrn and Helgi, and Auðr's father Ketill, while Hrollaugr is identified as the son of the earl of Møre in Norway (mentioned above in connection with *Torf*-Einarr in Orkney). Auðr's father Ketill is further identified as a *hersir*, a high-ranking class of chieftains in Norway. All four turn out to be the ancestors of Icelandic bishops. Despite its early date, and the author's attachment to chronology and source criticism, *Íslendingabók*'s account of the migration to and settlement of Iceland is a bit too neat, and not especially informative. A much fuller picture of the migration to Iceland emerges from *Landnámabók*.

This is not in fact one text, but both a work in progress and a group of related texts. Five versions of it survive, three medieval and two modern (i.e. seventeenth century). The two modern versions have text-critical value as they both used lost, earlier manuscripts. There are indications in the text that the process of gathering information about the settlement of Iceland started in the twelfth century, possibly even with Ari himself. The earliest surviving version, *Sturlubók*, can be dated to the late thirteenth century, and it is possible to reconstruct a lost version from earlier in the thirteenth century that was its source.[107] So *Landnámabók* cannot compare with *Íslendingabók* in terms of date, or closeness to and critical use of its sources. The traditional scholarly view has been that the text is a gradual accumulation of oral and written traditions in the form of genealogies and anecdotes about the first settlers of Iceland, by medieval Icelanders who valued knowledge about their ancestry and origins, and that much of it is based on local knowledge. Revisionist views of the text have on the other hand presented it either as an attempt by the landowners of the twelfth century to justify their holdings by tracing them back to, or even inventing, original settlers; or as a product of twelfth-century learning, which did not hesitate to speculate where it had no information, or to make up the names of settlers from place-names.[108] It is also true that the extant texts are widely 'contaminated' by the sagas that were being written in the thirteenth century, at the same time as the surviving versions, though the fact that the two do not always agree in detail demonstrates the complexities of working out the origins and textual histories of both.

Landnámabók is structured geographically, going clockwise around the island, and naming the first settler for some 430 farms (13 of whom are in fact women). Most of the time, a chapter is devoted to each settler, and the basic information is the name of the settler and the name of the farm he/she settled – compare Chapter 38 of the *Sturlubók* version cited in Chapter 2, above.[109] Usually, there is more information, which can include some account of the settler's ancestry and place of origin, further information about the extent of the land-claim, or information about the settler's wife, children and descendants. Many of the chapters have grown into mini-anecdotes about the settlers or sometimes even later generations, and this is where the intertextuality with the sagas comes into play.

There is no doubt that *Landnámabók* is a messier, more complicated source for the discovery of and migration to Iceland than *Íslendingabók*. Certainly the work is deceptive in the level of detail it seems to provide, and it cannot necessarily be used as a source for the history of any one individual, family or farm. But precisely because it has so much information, it is possible to study some of the patterns in *Landnámabók* without necessarily believing every word it says. In particular, there are two aspects of it that are relevant to discussions of migration and diaspora. The thirteenth- and fourteenth-century versions of *Landnámabók* have already evolved from a mere catalogue of settlers into something approaching a historical narrative, as demonstrated both by the way they introduce and re-arrange the text, and by the introductory material appended to the catalogue. This introductory material presents an interesting and complex narrative of the discovery of Iceland, to be discussed below. Futhermore, while most of the chapters have a purely Icelandic perspective, in that they concentrate on the first settler, his land-claim and his descendants, a significant proportion of the chapters give additional information which illuminates their settlement in terms of the migration to Iceland, and its diasporic context.

Completely in contrast to Ari's monolithic idea of Iceland having been discovered and first settled by one man, followed by an orderly migration from Norway, led by four distinguished Norwegians, the narrative that emerges from *Landnámabók* is more complex. This narrative is developed in the two most important medieval versions of the text, the late thirteenth-century *Sturlubók* and the early fourteenth-century *Hauksbók*. Such introductory chapters do not appear in the third medieval version of the text, known as *Melabók*, which appears to have a more archaic structure in that it is a purely geographical catalogue. The two revised versions introduce the catalogue with introductory chapters on Iceland and its location, followed by a series of voyage and discovery narratives, and also re-arrange the geography of the text by starting with Ingólfr's settlement, in the middle of the Southern Quarter, rather than at the quarter boundary as seems to have been the original arrangement, represented in *Melabók*. In this they follow Ari in privileging Ingólfr's settlement, at the same time complicating matters by also telling the stories of several earlier 'discoverers' who however did not make permanent settlements in Iceland. *Sturlubók* (chs 3–5) names these as:

- a *víkingr* called Naddoddr who, with his companions, is driven off course when sailing from Norway to the Faroes;
- a man of Swedish origin called Garðarr Svávarsson;
- and another *víkingr* called Flóki Vilgerðarson from the west of Norway.

Hauksbók (chs 3–5) revises the crucial first discoverer of Iceland, naming Garðarr before Naddoddr, and adds some detail to several of these mini-narratives of discovery. Both versions agree, however, that Iceland was discovered by accident, by voyagers sailing to the north of Britain, who were driven off course, and both versions agree that Iceland was discovered several times, both accidentally and by people intending to find this place that they had heard of, but none of whom stayed there permanently until the significant primary settlement by Ingólfr.

These multiple narratives of discovery may arouse suspicion in the literary-minded, particularly that of Flóki, who finds Iceland by following three ravens in a story which has reminded readers of Noah and his Ark. The story is also suspiciously schematic in that Flóki has three companions who have different opinions about the viability of Iceland as a place for farming, and a Hebridean companion who apparently gives his name to Faxaóss, the big bay which has Reykjavík on its southern shore. The narratives about the 'discoverers' are then followed in both versions (chs 6–10) by a more or less identical and quite lengthy story of Ingólfr and his foster-brother Hjǫrleifr, both from Norway, and their various adventures before settling down in Iceland, and the tribulations of Hjǫrleifr, in particular, after arriving in Iceland. This narrative also contains both a number of literary motifs and some anecdotes that seem to be derived from place-names.

The overall patterns of migration and diaspora which can be deduced from these texts reveal an account of the discovery and settlement of Iceland that is infinitely more realistic than that of *Íslendingabók*. Flóki's ravens have their counterparts in known navigational methods, which included using the migration patterns of birds and whales to establish the proximity of land. The differences of opinion in Flóki's party about whether Iceland was a viable place for Norwegian-style farming also seem eminently realistic and reasonable. Other points to note include that:

- the early voyagers reported back on their experiences;
- the island is given two different names before the name of 'Iceland' sticks;[110]
- this name is already established and the country well known when Ingólfr's primary settlement takes place;
- the explorers have trouble coping with the climatic conditions;
- the early voyagers originate in Sweden, Norway (including several different parts of Norway) and the Hebrides, and have experience of or connections with Denmark, the Faroes, Shetland, the Hebrides and Ireland;
- three of them are described as '(great) vikings' and several of them engage in typically viking activities, primarily in the British Isles;
- several of them have slaves, some of whom are said to be Irish;
- the presence of slaves creates tensions and problems;
- the voyagers are pagan, though at least one of them will not sacrifice, and Christianity is introduced three generations later.

While Ari's picture of the settlement of Iceland was that of an orderly migration from Norway, *Landnámabók* presents a much more diffuse and less linear model. This model fits what we know of the Viking Age, and suggests that the settlement of Iceland is not so much a unique migrational event, but an inevitable consequence of the Viking diaspora and, so, closely linked with Viking activities in the west. The migration to Iceland took place from many different points of origin, by many different types of people, who had different reasons for going there. The migration happened as a result of information trickling back to many parts of the Viking world from a few intrepid explorers who arrived in Iceland, either by accident or because of curiosity. These first explorers did not necessarily have settlement or colonisation in mind, but the idea that one could make a living in this empty land arose out of discussions between those who went there.

This picture deriving from the introductory chapters is borne out by many of the subsequent chapters of *Landnámabók*. Around a quarter of the 399 chapters in *Sturlubók* give information about settlers that fits this diasporic pattern. Thus we get a picture of where the settlers originated and where they departed from on their voyage to Iceland (not always the same thing), the places they stopped off along the way, and whether they were pagan, Christian or undecided. We are also given a sense of the motivations behind their migration to Iceland. Mostly this is expressed in political terms – those who are given a reason for emigration are often presented as the political opponents of the Norwegian king, and it is indeed possible that this is a thirteenth-century view of the migration (as discussed in ch. 3, above). But other motivations are also listed, including several settlers who were supporters of King Haraldr, and therefore the political opponents of the earls of *Hlaðir*.

The settlers whose origins are given can be divided into those who came from Norway (70/91 or 77%) and those who came from somewhere else.[111] Whether they came from Norway, or Britain and Ireland, the geographical origin of the settlers can be stated either in a general way ('Norway', 'the British Isles'), or in more geographical detail, specifying the regions from which the settler came. In the case of Norway, these include most of that country: Oppland, Valdres, Telemark, Agder, Rogaland, Hordaland, Sogn og Fjordane, Møre og Romsdal, Trøndelag, Hålogaland. In the case of Britain the regions mentioned are Orkney, Caithness and the Hebrides, as well as Ireland.

In addition to the strong representation of Norway overall, a point of interest is the emphasis on regional identity within Norway.[112] Very few people (seven references, or 10%) are said just to be 'Norwegian' or to have come from just 'Norway'. The rest are identified with either a wider region in Norway, as noted above, or a specific location, such as a valley, within that region. In fact, a large number of the references (30/70, or 43%) are actually to a specific valley or other place within the region. A second point of interest is that these Norwegian regional identities could be transferred to Iceland, as shown by an interesting concentration of people from the inland Norwegian settlement of Voss in the East Fjords of Iceland.[113] A third point of interest is the strong representation of settlers from the northern districts of Trøndelag and Hålogaland, which complicates the received wisdom that the settlers were predominantly from the south-west of Norway (although Sogn og Fjordane and Hordaland are well represented, Rogaland is not). There could of course be many explanations for this, not least that *Landnámabók* is not representative, or that certain groups maintained their historical traditions better than others (like the Vossings in the East Fjords). Similarly, the relatively small number of references to settlers from places other than Norway is not entirely consonant with the well-aired contemporary genetic patterns which suggest that a substantial proportion of not only female but even male Icelandic settlers actually came from Britain and Ireland.[114] Again, various possible explanations can be found for this mismatch in addition to possible class and gender disparities, but the question is still open to debate.[115]

The key to the differing interpretations of the discovery and settlement of Iceland to be found in *Íslendingabók* in the twelfth century and *Landnámabók* in the thirteenth can be expressed in terms of the differences between 'migration' and 'diaspora'. Ari was writing at a time when the Icelandic nation was only just over two centuries old, and was still in the throes of nation-building: establishing legal and administrative structures, adopting literacy and developing a unifying national religion. Ari's book about Icelanders and their nation locates this infant polity in relation to world history and aims to pinpoint its origins as well as its development. Ari creates an Icelandic identity at the national level by a number of means. He sees the origins of the Icelandic nation very much in terms of a migration from Norway and the re-establishment of Norwegian law, specifically that of western Norway. He does not acknowledge that any of the settlers were Christians, but presents them as pagans who brought their practices with them, until the conversion of 999 established a new kind of Icelandic collective identity. It is significant that the whole nation agrees to adopt Christianity at once, at the General Assembly. Ari's four prominent settlers demonstrate the transplantation of social and family structures that would be expected of a straightforward migration. Each settler is identified by a patronymic and is said to be the ancestor of a particular group of people. Two of them have high-ranking social origins, and all four are said to be Norwegian, ignoring the strong British Isles element in the personal history of both Helgi and Auðr suggested by other sources. By presenting a model of migration from a single country, followed by a linear development of the migrant society, Ari effectively creates the Icelandic nation and an Icelandic identity.

Landnámabók may not show the same tendency to source criticism and strict chronology as *Íslendingabók*, but it may nevertheless reflect a truer picture in its overall patterns, which give a picture of various kinds of diversity. Firstly there is the diversity of the early voyagers. The first four come from a variety of places for a variety of reasons, and react to Iceland in a variety of ways. The process by which sailors are blown off course and 'discover' Iceland, and then report back, encouraging others to set out specifically for the new country, and the difficulties of finding it again, must have been how it really happened. The first reactions of the settlers include their astonishment at the high mountains, the early snow, the sea ice and the great bays in the west of Iceland. Their varying opinions about the suitability of the country for settlement must also represent the considered judgement of experienced farmers, depending however on their previous experience of farming. Even Ingólfr does not settle in Iceland on his first voyage of exploration, but has to make extensive preparations for his second voyage of settlement, preparations that are both financial and spiritual. His settlement is a great undertaking and a great risk. Hjǫrleifr's undertaking comes to grief because he has not made sufficient preparation (expressed in the text as a failure to sacrifice). The diversity of the Icelandic settlement is also reflected in the places the settlers came from, their religious views, and their motivations for going to Iceland. Again, we do not need to believe these in every detail to acknowledge that the origins of a settlement as substantial as that of Iceland must have been geographically diverse, and that such a diverse community must have had a diversity of religious views and motivations for their settlement.

This diversity arises no doubt from the ways in which *Landnámabók* was put together – it is a work of collective scholarship extending over several generations. Different sections of the text tend to have different characteristics, suggesting it was put together on a local or regional basis first, before becoming a grand catalogue of the settlement of the whole of Iceland. Whether or not the local and probably oral traditions on which it is based are 'true' in any objective sense, it is very likely that the overall picture it presents of the settlement of Iceland is true. Once it became known that there was an opportunity to claim virgin land on an island in the North Atlantic, this opportunity drew people from the Viking diaspora as well as their Scandinavian homelands. The Icelanders of the twelfth and thirteenth centuries were well aware of their origins in this diaspora, and their traditions recorded in *Landnámabók* reflect their consciousness of connection both to the people and traditions of their homeland and to others elsewhere in the world who shared the same connection. If Ari knew this more complicated picture of the origins of his homeland, he had his reasons for wanting to simplify it – he wanted to tell a linear history of migration and nation-building, and had no room in his account for the messiness and diversity of the diasporic processes that formed that migration.

This tension between the two different views of Iceland's origins, as a straightforward migration from Norway, or as a product of the Viking diaspora, continues throughout much of medieval Icelandic literary and historiographical production, and indeed into the scholarship of the present day. The thirteenth- and fourteenth-century Icelanders had a complicated relationship with the Norwegian homeland, and the authors of both *Sturlubók* and *Hauksbók* spent significant portions of their careers in Norway. In the late thirteenth century, Iceland became subject to Norway, and the 'mother country' became both oppressor and opportunity. The idea that the Icelanders were originally freedom-loving Norwegians who left home to escape the tyranny of the king must have resonated with medieval Icelanders at the time of the submission to Norway, and was a frequent motif in the sagas (as discussed in ch. 3, above). At the same time, the Icelanders were the official historiographers of the Norwegian kings, and cultivated the skaldic poetry that both celebrated and recorded their deeds.

The diasporic experience always lurks behind the binary relationship between Iceland and Norway. It is no accident that the Sagas of Icelanders are set in the Viking Age, and frequently feature characters originating in the British Isles, or engaged in viking activities both in the British Isles and further afield. Icelanders of the twelfth to fourteenth centuries were still in touch with diasporic communities in the north and west of the British Isles, the Faroes and Greenland, indeed they wrote sagas about all of these places. In Orkney, or Shetland, or Faroe, or Greenland, Icelanders met people who spoke the same language, who used the same onomasticon, who wrote using runes, and who still remembered some of the old myths and legends, even though they had also all become Christians at about the same time as the Icelanders. This North Atlantic community was held together by the rule of the Norwegian king and then gradually fell apart, starting with the cessation of the Hebrides to Scotland in the late thirteenth century and ending with the extinction of the Greenland colony sometime in the fifteenth, with Norway itself having succumbed to Denmark in the meantime, leaving both Iceland and the Faroes isolated, poor and weak, and ruled by a distant Danish administration, until achieving their independence in the twentieth century (an independence that is, in the twenty-first century, still only partial in the case of the Faroes). With this independence, the Icelanders finally shook off their diasporic heritage and achieved the individual identity that Ari envisaged for them, but it took the best part of one thousand years.

Conclusion

Iceland is the most visible and lasting monument to the Viking diaspora, not only in its very existence but also in its rich medieval literary culture, an achievement which is a jewel in its own right, but also an important interpreter of the Viking Age to subsequent generations. The diasporic consciousness of the medieval Icelanders is revealed in this literature and in their culture more generally, as in the legal provisions which recognised the interconnectedness of their world. In addition to maintaining their connections with the Scandinavian homelands, and with the western settlements that preceded them, such as Orkney, Icelanders were also central to the extension of the diaspora westwards, to Greenland and, for a time, as far as North America. This centrality of Icelanders to the diasporic consciousness emerges from their literary achievements, but these should not be seen as a repository of old traditions somehow fossilised in a conservative colonial situation. Rather, the Icelanders' interest in the Viking Age past, its history, mythology and heroic stories, was a result of a dynamic creative process that depended on continuing contact and engagement with both the homelands and the other regions of the diaspora, and this interest can also be documented in many of those other regions.

Skaldic poetry is a good example of a cultural product which had its roots in the Viking Age Scandinavian past but which developed and flourished in the continuing engagement of the poets, many of whom were Icelanders, with their patrons, both in the Scandinavian homelands and in other diasporic lands such as England and Orkney. These skaldic networks thrived particularly in the mobility and fast-changing cultural and political environments of the eleventh and twelfth centuries, showing that one typical diasporic response to social change is to adapt ancient practices and traditions to the latest ideas. Runic inscriptions, on the other hand, reveal continuing connections across the Viking diaspora that flourished after the Viking Age but which did not depend on Icelandic transmission. Icelanders were well aware of runes, and wrote about them in their poetry and sagas, but they did not use runes as a means of communication, either in the Viking Age or the medieval period. Yet even they developed a late and peculiar (to them) tradition of runic gravestones which suggests that they were still dipping into the cultural streams of the post-Viking Age diasporic world in the fourteenth and fifteenth centuries, at the same time as they were still reading and copying the sagas about that Viking Age. In Norway, the British Isles and Greenland, on the other hand, the use of runes flourished even (and especially) after the Viking Age not because of a conservative mindset wedded to ancient practices, nor because of specific local developments, but because of continued contacts between these Scandinavian-speaking, rune-using communities which continually refreshed this practice into the thirteenth and fourteenth centuries. The innovative tenth-century runic inscriptions of the Isle of Man show a very early example of this diasporic process. They were produced, not by settlers straight off the boat from Norway, but by people who had already spent some generations in the Irish Sea region, once again showing how diaspora leads to the combining of traditional practices with new ideas.

Although language is key to the maintenance of the Viking diaspora, these processes can be observed in material culture as well as texts. The oval brooches discussed in Chapter 4 demonstrate how a key cultural signifier develops and adapts in the diaspora. In the early Viking Age, these brooches came in a variety of styles. As they spread geographically, following the Scandinavian women who wore them both east and west, their diasporic significance, which linked these women to a common cultural origin, led to a certain standardisation and internationalised mass production which would make this significance clearer and more consistent. Other forms of material culture, such as houses, clearly had to adapt to local environmental conditions, but they too retained a certain common design across the diaspora. Diasporic networks are also revealed by the spread of certain forms of material culture. Vessels and other objects made of steatite might be unremarkable in places like Norway and Shetland where the mineral occurs naturally, but in the diaspora they spread beyond these places, east to Russia, south to the trading centre of Hedeby, and west across the North Atlantic. Yet other objects, like the Norse bells discussed in Chapter 3, have no obvious connection with the Scandinavian homeland, but arose in the creative encounters between various diasporic communities.

This is not to say that the culture of the Viking diaspora was uniform throughout the Viking world, nor indeed throughout the long, broad Viking Age. But these examples and others show how an awareness of historical connections, and continuing contacts, with both the homelands and other regions, led people to choose certain aspects of both linguistic and material culture to signify a common identity that transcended their own place and time. Diaspora theory, which is most relevant when people migrate to several destinations, and where those settlements endure for some time, is the model that best explains these processes.[116]

The Viking Age saw Scandinavian expansion for the purposes of raiding and trading to many parts of the then-known world. Frequently, this raiding and trading was accompanied by, or led to, migration, in the form of settlement in those same places by Scandinavians who had not necessarily been involved in the raiding and trading but followed in their wake. There was also further migration, to areas which had not been subject to raiding and trading, because they were uninhabited, or sparsely inhabited. As already noted in Chapter 3, diaspora is not possible without migration, but not all migrations necessarily develop into diasporas. The migrations which happened in the Viking Age can be studied using evidence contemporary to that period and a restriction to such evidence will inevitably lead to a focus on the processes of migration, processes which are limited in time. The later diasporic connections that develop from these processes are not migrations as such, but depend on the earlier migrations. In contrast to migration, diaspora is often a lengthy process and can only properly be understood in the context of the 'long and broad Viking Age', as outlined in Chapter 3. To understand the Viking diaspora, we need to look beyond the Viking Age proper and investigate its longer-term effects, whether that be on the environment of pristine landscapes, on the slow emergence of a Scandinavian form of Christianity, or on the language and literature of medieval Iceland. Diaspora is the idea that helps to explain the world created by the migrations of the Viking Age.[117]

Notes

1 Abrams 2012, 38.
2 Kenny 2013, 39.
3 Sindbæk 2007, 59.
4 Sindbæk 2007, 63.
5 Sindbæk 2007, 71.
6 Abrams 2012, 21.
7 Mac Carron and Kenna 2013.
8 Mac Carron and Kenna 2013, 8.
9 Mac Carron and Kenna 2013, 8.
10 Ranković 2006, 42.
11 Kalra *et al.* 2005, 37.
12 Kenny 2013, 13.
13 Armit 2003, 13.
14 Armit 2003, 138.
15 Armit 2003, 59.
16 *ÍF* II, 83–90; *CSI* I, 69–73.
17 *ÍF* II, 175–95; *CSI* I, 114–24.
18 Jesch 2010.
19 *ÍF* II, 249, n. 4.
20 See e.g. Jesch 2009b and ch. 5, above.
21 All data below are taken from *SR* version 3.0 (released in 2014).
22 Country classifications follow those of *SR*, in which places like Skåne (now in Sweden) are counted as Danish, for historical reasons.
23 The geographical classifications are those of *SR*.
24 *SRIB*, pp. 278–337; see also Holman 1996, 14–85.
25 *SRIB*, pp. 278–85.
26 Holman 1996, 81–5.
27 These have not yet received a full scholarly edition, though one by Michael P. Barnes is forthcoming.
28 Barnes 2012b.
29 Wilson 2008, 52–6.
30 *RIVAD*. Cf. discussion of the Killaloe stone at the end of ch. 4.
31 *SRIB*, pp. 117–278.
32 *RIMO*, p. 60; Jesch 2013a, 156–8.
33 Grove 2009, 43–4; Guðmundsson 2009, 73; Høegsberg 2009, 98, 104.
34 Jesch 2001a, 1–6.

35 Jesch 2008a.
36 Barnes 2012a, 109–12; *SPSMA* VI, forthcoming.
37 Stoklund 1998, 10–11.
38 *SPSMA* I and II provide a full account of this genre, along with biographies of all the poets and rulers mentioned below, from which all information about them is taken.
39 *ÍF* XI, 335–6; *CSI* I, 384–5.
40 *ÍF* XXVIII, 79–80, 86, 119–20; *Hkr*, pp. 583–5, 607–8.
41 Jesch 2014a.
42 *SnEHt*, p. ix.
43 Jesch 2001a, 271–5.
44 E.g. *SPSMA* I, 649–63, 767–83, 851–76, 1014–30; II, 311–224, 432–60. Other relevant poems from *SnESkm* will be edited in *SPSMA* III, forthcoming.
45 Jesch 2001b.
46 Jesch 2001b, 320.
47 *SPSMA* II, 382–4; see also Jesch 2001b, 321–3.
48 *SPSMA* II, xcvii.
49 Jesch 2001a, 254–65; Jesch 2001b, 322.
50 *SPSMA* II, 177.
51 *SPSMA* I, 129–38.
52 For biographies of both earls, see *SPSMA* II, xciv–xcv, xcvii–xcviii; for Arnórr, see *SPSMA* II, 177–8.
53 *SPSMA* I, 486.
54 *SPSMA* II, 178–81, 229–60.
55 *SPSMA* II, 280–1.
56 Whaley 1998, 35, 134, 311–13.
57 *Hl*, pp. 118–34I.
58 *SnEHt*; *SnE*, pp. 165–220.
59 *SPSMA* II, 575–609; three further stanzas are forthcoming in *SPSMA* III.
60 *SPSMA* II, 614, 620, 624.
61 *SPSMA* II, 626.
62 *RIMO*, pp. 38–43.
63 *SPSMA* II, 610–11, 629–30.
64 *SPSMA* II, 581–2; Jesch 2013a, 157–8.
65 *SPSMA* II, 612–13.
66 *SPSMA* II, 575.
67 *SPSMA* II, 393–4.
68 Jesch 2013a, 155.
69 Jesch 2014a, 60.
70 See chs 33, 84, 108 of *Orkneyinga saga*; *ÍF* XXXIV, 85, 192–3, 289; *OS*, pp. 191, 275, 342.
71 *SPSMA* I, 954.
72 *ÍF* XXXIV, 282; *OS*, p. 338.
73 *SPSMA* I, 954–97.
74 Frank 2004; Roberta Frank's edition of this poem is forthcoming in *SPSMA* III.
75 *SPSMA* II, 654–5.
76 Speed and Rogers 2004.
77 Jones 1997 has been particularly influential in this debate.
78 Eriksen 2010, 95, 107.
79 E.g. Jesch 1987; Sigurðsson 1988; Sayers 1994; Helgason *et al.* 2000a, 2000b, 2001; Hallgrímsson *et al.* 2004; Jacobsen 2005; Price and Gestsdóttir 2006; Karlsson 2009; Vésteinsson 2010; Vésteinsson *et al.* 2012.

80 Jesch 2014b.
81 *CASSS* III, 123, 133–5, 164–6, 195; *SRIB*, pp. 304–5.
82 *SRIB*, p. 305.
83 Pons-Sanz 2013, 40, 103, 276–7.
84 Jesch 2001a, 238–9.
85 Fellows Jensen 1968, 1972.
86 *CASSS* III, 99–101.
87 *CASSS* V, 214–16.
88 *CASSS* V, 258–9.
89 *CASSS* IV, 124–5, 147–9.
90 *CASSS* III, 229.
91 *CASSS* III, 43, 47, 230.
92 Townend 2002, 189–92.
93 *OED*, 'kirk'.
94 Fellows Jensen 1972, 31–2.
95 Hamilton and Spicer 2006, 7–10.
96 *SRIB*, pp. 285–8; Holman 1998.
97 *CASSS* VI, 195–7; *SRIB*, pp. 301–7.
98 See www.languagesmythsfinds.ac.uk/north-east-england [last accessed 20 August 2014].
99 *EPNE*, 'cros'.
100 Cramp 2010, 30–1.
101 Townend 2002, 189.
102 *SRIB*, pp. 307–12.
103 Townend 2002, 194.
104 Lang 1972–4, 1984.
105 Jesch 2004b.
106 All references below are to chapter numbers in *ÍF* I, which are also those of the translations in *BoI* and *BoS*.
107 The detailed study of *Landnámabók* in *ÍF* I, l–cliv is summarised in English in Benediktsson 1969.
108 Callow 2011, 11–12.
109 *ÍF* I, 76; *BoS*, p. 30.
110 See ch. 2, above, for more detail on this.
111 The figures are based on *Sturlubók* only and provide a simple counting of all instances in which places of origin or departure are named. Names are given in their modern forms, where these are known. The numbers do not equate with actual settlers, since some settlers are given a different place of origin and residence, or a different place of origin and departure for Iceland. The numbers are small, given that less than a quarter of the entries in *Landnámabók* specify a place of origin and/or departure, and so these observations are not numerous enough to have overall statistical validity, but the patterns are still instructive.
112 See also Karlsson 2009, 131–2.
113 *ÍF* I, 302–3, 307, 310–11, 319, 368; *BoS*, pp. 115–17, 119, 122.
114 Helgason *et al.* 2000b, 2001; Goodacre *et al.* 2005.
115 Vésteinsson 2010.
116 Kenny 2013, 14.
117 Kenny 2013, 1.

BIBLIOGRAPHY

Primary sources

AB: Adam of Bremen, *History of the Archbishops of Hamburg-Bremen*, trans. Francis J. Tschan, 2nd ed. with new introduction and bibliography by Timothy Reuter. New York: Columbia University Press, 2002.

Ágrip: *Ágrip af Nóregskonungasǫgum*, ed. and trans. M. J. Driscoll. London: Viking Society for Northern Research, 1995.

AÍ: *Alfræði íslenzk. Islandsk encyclopædisk litteratur I*, ed. Kr. Kålund. Copenhagen: S. L. Møller, 1908.

A&N: *Annálar og nafnaskrá*, ed. Guðni Jónsson. Reykjavík: Íslendingasagnaútgáfan, 1953.

ASC: *The Anglo-Saxon Chronicle*, trans. and ed. Dorothy Whitelock *et al*. London: Eyre and Spottiswoode, 1961.

BoI: *Íslendingabók. Kristni saga. The Book of the Icelanders. The Story of the Conversion*, trans. Siân Grønlie. London: Viking Society for Northern Research, 2006.

BoS: *The Book of Settlements. Landnámabók*, trans. Hermann Pálsson and Paul Edwards. Winnipeg: University of Manitoba Press, 1972.

CASSS: *Corpus of Anglo-Saxon Stone Sculpture*, I–XI. Oxford: Oxford University Press, 1984– [in progress].

CSI: *The Complete Sagas of Icelanders*, I–V, ed. Viðar Hreinsson. Reykjavík: Leifur Eiríksson, 1997.

DN: *Diplomatarium Norvegicum*, I–XXI. Christiania/Oslo: Norsk historisk kjeldeskrift-institutt, 1847–1976.

DR: *Danmarks runeindskrifter*, Atlas, Registre, Text, ed. Lis Jacobsen and Erik Moltke. Copenhagen: E. Munksgaard, 1941–2.

Edda: *Edda. Die Lieder des Codex Regius nebst verwandten Denkmälern*, ed. Gustav Neckel and Hans Kuhn. Heidelberg: Carl Winter, 1983. [5th edition].

ENL: *The Earliest Norwegian Laws, Being the Gulathing Law and the Frostathing Law*, trans. Laurence M. Larson. New York: Columbia University Press, 1935.

FAS: *Fornaldar sögur Norðurlanda*, ed. Guðni Jónsson. Reykjavík: Íslendingasagnaútgáfan, 1954.

FGT: *The First Grammatical Treatise*, ed. Hreinn Benediktsson. Reykjavík: Institute of Nordic Linguistics, 1972.

Flat: *Flateyjarbók. En samling af norske konge-sagaer med inskskudte mindre fortællinger om begivenheder i og udenfor Norge samt Annaler*, I–III, ed. Gudbrand Vigfusson and C. R. Unger. Christiania: Malling, 1860–8.

Fsk: *Fagrskinna. A Catalogue of the Kings of Norway*, trans. Alison Finlay. Leiden: Brill, 2004.

GrágásK: *Grágás. Islændernes Lovbog i Fristatens Tid, udgivet efter det Kongelige Bibliotheks Haandskrift*, I–II, ed. Vilhjálmur Finsen. Kjøbenhavn: Brødrene Berling, 1852.

GrágásSt: *Grágás efter det Arnamagnæanske Haandskrift Nr. 334 fol., Staðarhólsbók*. Kjøbenhavn: Gyldendal, 1879.

GS: *Guta saga. The history of the Gotlanders*, ed. Christine Peel. London: Viking Society for Northern Research, 1999.

Hav.: *Havelok*, ed. G. V. Smithers. Oxford: Clarendon Press, 1987.

Hkr: *Heimskringla. History of the Kings of Norway, by Snorri Sturluson*, trans. Lee M. Hollander. Austin: University of Texas Press, 1964.

Hl: *Háttalykill*, ed. Jón Helgason and Anne Holtsmark. Copenhagen: Einar Munksgaard, 1941.

HN: *Historia Norwegie*, ed. Inger Ekrem and Lars Boje Mortensen, trans. Peter Fisher. Copenhagen: Museum Tusculanum Press, 2003.

IA: *Islandske annaler indtil 1578*, ed. Gustav Storm. Christiania: Grøndahl & Søn, 1888.

ÍF I: *Íslendingabók. Landnámabók*, ed. Jakob Benediktsson. Reykjavík: Hið íslenzka fornritafélag, 1968.

ÍF II: *Egils saga Skalla-Grímssonar*, ed. Sigurður Nordal. Reykjavík: Hið íslenzka fornritafélag, 1933.

ÍF III: *Borgfirðinga sǫgur. Hœnsa-Þóris saga. Gunnlaugs saga ormstungu. Bjarnar saga hítdœlakappa. Heiðarvíga saga. Gísls þáttr Illugasonar*, ed. Sigurður Nordal and Guðni Jónsson. Reykjavík: Hið íslenzka fornritafélag, 1938.

ÍF IV: *Eyrbyggja saga. Brands þáttr ǫrva. Eiríks saga rauða. Grœnlendinga saga. Grœnlendinga þáttr*, ed. Einar Ól. Sveinsson and Matthías Þórðarson. Reykjavík: Hið íslenzka fornritafélag, 1935.

ÍF V: *Laxdœla saga. Halldórs þættir Snorrasonar. Stúfs þáttr*, ed. Einar Ól. Sveinsson. Reykjavík: Hið íslenzka fornritafélag, 1934.

ÍF VI: *Vestfirðinga sǫgur. Gísla saga Súrssonar. Fóstbrœðra saga. Þáttr Þormóðar. Hávarðar saga Ísfirðings. Auðunar þáttr vestfirzka. Þorvarðar þáttr krákunefs*, ed. Björn K. Þórólfsson and Guðni Jónsson. Reykjavík: Hið íslenzka fornritafélag, 1943.

ÍF VII: *Grettis saga Ásmundarsonar. Bandamanna saga. Odds þáttr Ófeigssonar*, ed. Guðni Jónsson. Reykjavík: Hið íslenzka fornritafélag, 1936.

ÍF VIII: *Vatnsdœla saga. Hallfreðar saga. Kormáks saga. Hrómundar þáttr halta. Hrafns þáttr Guðrúnarsonar*, ed. Einar Ól. Sveinsson. Reykjavík: Hið íslenzka fornritafélag, 1939.

ÍF IX: *Eyfirðinga sǫgur*, ed. Jónas Kristjánsson. Reykjavík: Hið íslenzka fornritafélag, 1956.

ÍF X: *Ljósvetninga saga með þáttum. Reykdœla saga ok Víga-Skútu. Hreiðars þáttr*, ed. Björn Sigfússon. Reykjavík: Hið íslenzka fornritafélag, 1940.

ÍF XI: *Austfirðinga sǫgur*, ed. Jón Jóhannesson. Reykjavík: Hið íslenzka fornritafélag, 1950.

ÍF XII: *Brennu-Njáls saga*, ed. Einar Ól. Sveinsson, Reykjavík: Hið íslenzka fornritafélag, 1954.

ÍF XIII: *Harðar saga. Bárðar saga. Þorskfirðinga saga. Flóamanna saga . . .*, ed. Þórhallur Vilmundarson and Bjarni Vilhjálmsson. Reykjavík: Hið íslenzka fornritafélag, 1991.

ÍF XV: *Biskupa sögur I: Kristni saga. Kristni þættir. Jóns saga helga*, ed. Sigurgeir Steingrímsson *et al.* Reykjavík: Hið íslenzka fornritafélag, 1998.

ÍF XVII: *Biskupa sögur III: Árna saga biskups. Lárentius saga biskups. Söguþáttur biskups Jóns Halldórssonar. Biskupa ættir*, ed. Guðrún Ása Grímsdóttir. Reykjavík: Hið íslenzka fornritafélag, 1998.

ÍF XXV: *Færeyinga saga. Óláfs saga Tryggvasonar eptir Odd munk Snorrason*, ed. Ólafur Halldórsson. Reykjavík: Hið íslenzka fornritafélag, 2006.

ÍF XXVI–XXVIII: Snorri Sturluson, *Heimskringla*, ed. Bjarni Aðalbjarnarson. Reykjavík: Hið íslenzka fornritafélag, 1979.

ÍF XXIX: *Ágrip af Nóregskonunga sǫgum. Fagrskinna – Nóregs konunga tal*, ed. Bjarni Einarsson. Reykjavík: Hið íslenzka fornritafélag, 1984.

ÍF XXXIV: *Orkneyinga saga. Legenda de Sancto Magno. Magnúss saga skemmri. Magnúss saga lengri. Helga þáttr ok Úlfs*, ed. Finnbogi Guðmundsson. Reykjavík: Hið íslenzka fornritafélag, 1965.

ÍF XXXV: *Danakonunga sǫgur. Skjǫlunga saga. Knýtlinga saga. Ágrip af sǫgu Danakonunga*, ed. Bjarni Guðnason. Reykjavík: Hið íslenzka fornritafélag, 1982.

Jb: *Jónsbók. The Laws of Later Iceland*, trans. Jana K. Schulman. Saarbrücken: AQ-Verlag, 2010.

KM: *The King's Mirror. (Speculum regale – Konungs skuggsjá)*, trans. Laurence Marcellus Larson. New York: The American-Scandinavian Foundation, 1917.

KnS: *Knytlinga Saga. The History of the Kings of Denmark*, trans. Hermann Pálsson and Paul Edwards. Odense: Odense University Press, 1986.

KS: *Konungs skuggsjá*, ed. Ludvig Holm-Olsen. Oslo: Norsk historisk kjeldeskrift-institutt, 1983.

LEI: *Laws of Early Iceland*, I–II, trans. Andrew Dennis *et al.* Winnipeg: University of Manitoba Press, 1980–2000.

LLBH: *The Life of Laurence Bishop of Hólar in Iceland (Laurentius Saga) by Einar Haflidason*, trans. Oliver Elton. London: Rivingtons, 1890.

Mork: *Morkinskinna. The Earliest Icelandic Chronicle of the Norwegian Kings (1030–1157)*, trans. Theodore M. Andersson and Kari Ellen Gade. Ithaca, NY: Cornell University Press, 2000.

NGL: *Norges gamle love*, I–V, ed. R. Keyser, P.A. Munch, Gustav Storm and Ebbe Hertzberg. Christiania: Gröndahl, 1846–95.

NIYR: *Norges innskrifter med de yngre runer*, I–VI, ed. Magnus Olsen *et al.* Oslo: Norsk historisk kjeldeskrift-institutt, 1941–90.

NMD: *Norske middelalderdokumenter*, ed. and trans. Sverre Bagge *et al.* Bergen: Universitetsforlaget, 1973.

OS: *The Orkneyinga Saga*, trans. Alexander Burt Taylor. Edinburgh: Oliver and Boyd, 1938.

PAS: *Portable Antiquities Scheme*. www.finds.org.uk [last accessed 14 July 2013]

PE: *The Poetic Edda*, trans. Carolyne Larrington. Oxford: Oxford University Press, 2014.

RIMO: *The Runic Inscriptions of Maeshowe, Orkney*, ed. Michael P. Barnes. Uppsala: Institutionen för nordiska språk, Uppsala universitet, 1994.

RIVAD: *The Runic Inscriptions of Viking Age Dublin*, ed. Michael P. Barnes *et al.* Dublin: Royal Irish Academy, 1997.

RPC: *The Russian Primary Chronicle: Laurentian Text*, trans. and ed. Samuel Hazzard Cross and Olgerd Sherbowitz-Wetzor. Cambridge, MA: Medieval Academy of America, 1953.

Saxo: *Saxo Grammaticus. The History of the Danes*, trans. Peter Fisher, ed. Hilda Ellis Davidson. Cambridge: Brewer, 1979.

SBFP: *Stories and Ballads of the Far Past*, trans. N. Kershaw. Cambridge: Cambridge University Press, 1921.

SnE: *Snorri Sturluson. Edda*, trans. Anthony Faulkes. London: Dent, 1987.

SnE1931: *Edda Snorra Sturlusonar*, ed. Finnur Jónsson. Copenhagen: Gyldendal, 1931.

SnEGylf: *Snorri Sturluson. Edda. Prologue and Gylfaginning*, ed. Anthony Faulkes. Oxford: Clarendon, 1982.

SnEHt: *Snorri Sturluson. Edda. Háttatal*, ed. Anthony Faulkes. Oxford: Clarendon, 1991.

SnESkskm: *Snorri Sturluson. Edda. Skaldskaparmál*, ed. Anthony Faulkes. London: Viking Society for Northern Research, 1998.

SöR: *Södermanlands runinskrifter*, ed. Erik Brate and Elias Wessén (Sveriges runinskrifter III). Stockholm: Kungl. Vitterhets historie och antikvitets akademien, 1924–36.

SOTOS: *The Saga of Olaf Tryggvason. Oddr Snorrason*, trans. Theodore M. Andersson. Ithaca, NY: Cornell University Press, 2003.

SPSMA: *Skaldic Poetry of the Scandinavian Middle Ages* I–VII, ed. Margaret Clunies Ross *et al.* Turnhout: Brepols, 2007– [in progress].

SRIB: *The Scandinavian Runic Inscriptions of Britain*, ed. Michael P. Barnes and R. I. Page. Uppsala: Institutionen för nordiska språk, Uppsala universitet, 2006.

ThoG: *Thrand of Gotu. Two Icelandic Sagas*, trans. George Johnston. Erin, Ontario: The Porcupine's Quill, 1994.

Þorsk: *A Translation of Þorskfirðinga (Gull-Þóris) saga*, by Philip Westbury Cardew. Lampeter: Edwin Mellen Press, 2000.

ÞS: *Þiðreks saga af Bern*, ed. Guðni Jónsson. Reykjavík: Íslendingasagnaútgáfan, 1954.

TM: *Theodoricus Monachus. The Ancient History of the Norwegian Kings*, trans. David and Ian McDougall. London: Viking Society for Northern Research, 1998.

UR: *Upplands runinskrifter*, I–IV, ed. Elias Wessén and Sven B. F. Jansson (Sveriges runinskrifter VI–IX). Stockholm: Kungliga Vitterhets historie och antikvitetsakademien, 1940–58.

VS: *Vǫlsunga saga. The Saga of the Volsungs*, ed. and trans. R. G. Finch. London: Nelson, 1965.

Standard reference works

EPNE: *English Place-Name Elements*, I–II, ed. A. H. Smith. Cambridge: Cambridge University Press, 1956.

NID: *Norsk-isländska dopnamn och fingerade namn från medeltiden*, ed. E. H. Lind. Uppsala: Lundequist, 1905–15.

NIDS: *Norsk-isländska dopnamn och fingerade namn från medeltiden. Supplementband*, ed. E. H. Lind. Oslo: Dybwad, 1931.

NIP: *Norsk-isländska personbinamn från medeltiden*, ed. E. H. Lind. Uppsala: Lundequist, 1920–1.

OED: *Oxford English Dictionary*. http://www.oed.com.

ONP: *A Dictionary of Old Norse Prose. Ordbog over det norrøne prosasprog*, ed. Helle Degnbol *et al.*, 1989– [in progress].

SR: *Samnordisk runtextdatabas*, Rundata 3.0, 2014. http://www.nordiska.uu.se/forskn/samnord.htm.

VEPN: *The Vocabulary of English Place-Names*, ed. David N. Parsons *et al.* Nottingham: Centre for English Name-Studies, 1997– [in progress].

Secondary sources

Abram, Christopher. 2011. *Myths of the Pagan North. The Gods of the Norsemen*, London: Continuum.

Abrams, Lesley. 2001. 'The conversion of the Danelaw', in Graham-Campbell *et al.* 2001, pp. 31–44.

—— 2012. 'Diaspora and identity in the Viking Age', *Early Medieval Europe* 20, 17–38.

—— 2013. 'Early Normandy', in Bates 2013, pp. 45–64.

—— 2014. 'The conversion of Scandinavians in Britain and Ireland: an overview', in Bauduin and Musin 2014, pp. 327–37.

Abrams, Lesley, and David N. Parsons. 2004. 'Place-names and the history of Scandinavian settlement in England', in Hines *et al.* 2004, pp. 379–431.

Adams, Catrina T., *et al.* 2012. 'Arable agriculture and gathering: the botanical evidence', in Barrett 2012a, pp. 161–97.

Adams, Jonathan, and Katherine Holman, eds. 2004. *Scandinavia and Europe 800–1350: Contact, Conflict, and Coexistence*. Turnhout: Brepols.

Adger, Neil, *et al.*, eds. 2009. *Adapting to Climate Change: Thresholds, Values, Governance*. Cambridge: Cambridge University Press.

Ambrosiani, Björn, and Helen Clarke, eds. 1994. *Developments around the Baltic and the North Sea in the Viking Age*. Stockholm: Riksantikvarieämbetet and Statens Historiska Museer.

Amundsen, Colin, *et al.* 2005. 'Fishing booths and fishing strategies in medieval Iceland: an archaeofauna from the [*sic*] of Akurvik, North-West Iceland', *Environmental Archaeology* 10, 127–42.

Andersen, Flemming G., *et al.*, eds. 1980. *Medieval Iconography and Narrative: A Symposium*, Odense: Odense Universitetsforlag.

Anderson, Atholl, *et al.*, eds. 2010. *The Global Origins and Development of Seafaring*. Cambridge: McDonald Institute.

Andersson, Gunnar. 2006. 'Among trees, bones, and stones', in Andrén *et al.* 2006, pp. 195–9.

Andersson, Thorsten. 1992. 'Kultplatsbeteckningar i nordiska ortnamn', in Fellows-Jensen and Holmberg 1992, pp. 77–105.

—— 2007. 'Wikinger: sprachlich', *Reallexikon der germanischen Altertumskunde* 35, 687–97.

Andrén, Anders, *et al.*, eds. 2006. *Old Norse Religion in Long-Term Perspectives: Origins, Changes, and Interactions*. Vägar till Midgård, 8. Lund: Nordic Academic Press.

Androschchuk, Fedir. 2003. 'The Hvoshcheva sword: an example of contacts between Britain and Scandinavia in the Late Viking Period', *Fornvännen* 98, 35–43.

Androschchuk, Fjodor [*sic*]. 2008. 'The Vikings in the East', in Brink and Price 2008, pp. 517–42.

Androushchuk [*sic*], Fedir. 2009. 'Vikings and farmers: some remarks on the social interpretation of swords and long-distance contacts in the Viking Age', in Olausson and Olausson 2009, pp. 93–104.

Anlezark, Daniel, ed. 2011. *Myths, Legends, and Heroes: Essays on Old Norse and Old English Literature*. Toronto: University of Toronto Press.

Antonsson, Haki. 2014. 'The conversion and Christianization of Scandinavia: a critical review of recent scholarly writings', in Garipzanov 2014, pp. 49–73.

Arge, Símun V. 2005. 'Cultural landscapes and cultural environmental issues in the Faroes', in Mortensen and Arge 2005, pp. 22–38.

Arge, Símun V., *et al.* 2005. 'Viking and medieval settlement in the Faroes: people, place and environment', *Human Ecology* 33/5, 597–620.

Armit, Ian. 2003. *Towers in the North: The Brochs of Scotland*. Stroud: Tempus.

Arneborg, Jette. 2003. 'Norse Greenland: reflections on settlement and depopulation', in Barrett 2003a, pp. 163–81.

Arneborg, Jette, *et al.*, eds. 2009. *Norse Greenland. Selected Papers from the Hvalsey Conference 2008*. Journal of the North Atlantic Special Volume 2.

—— 2012a. *Greenland Isotope Project: Diet in Norse Greenland* AD *1000 to* AD *1450*. Journal of the North Atlantic Special Volume 3.

—— 2012b. 'Human diet and subsistence patterns in Norse Greenland AD c.980–AD c.1450: archaeological interpretations', in Arneborg *et al.* 2012, pp. 119–33.

Arnold, Bettina, and Nancy L. Wicker, eds. 2001. *Gender and the Archaeology of Death*. Walnut Creek, CA: AltaMira Press.

Bäcklund, Jessica. 2001. 'War or peace? The relations between the Picts and the Norse in Orkney', *Northern Studies* 36, 33–47.

Bagge, Sverre. 2010. *From Viking Stronghold to Christian Kingdom: State Formation in Norway, c. 900–1350*. Copenhagen: Museum Tusculanum Press.

Bailey, Richard. 2000. 'Scandinavian myth on Viking-period stone sculpture in England', in Barnes and Clunies Ross 2000, pp. 15–23.

Bandle, Oskar. 1967. *Studien zur westnordischen Sprachgeographie. Haustierterminologie im norwegischen, isländischen und färöischen*. Copenhagen: Munksgaard.

— 1977. 'Die Ortsnamen der Landnámabók', in Pétursson and Kristjánsson 1977, pp. 47–68.

Barnes, Geraldine, and Margaret Clunies Ross, eds. 2000. *Old Norse Myths, Literature and Society: Preprints of the 11th International Saga Conference*. Sydney: University of Sydney.

Barnes, Michael P. 2012a. *Runes: A Handbook*. Woodbridge: Boydell.

—— 2012b. 'Manx runes and the supposed Jæren connection', *Futhark* 3, 59–80.

Barrett, James H., ed. 2003a. *Contact, Continuity and Collapse: The Norse Colonization of the North Atlantic*. Turnhout: Brepols.

—— 2003b. 'Culture contact in Viking Age Scotland', in Barrett 2003a, pp. 73–111.

—— 2008. 'What caused the Viking Age?' *Antiquity* 82, 671–85.

—— 2010. 'Rounding up the usual suspects: causation and the Viking Age diaspora', in Anderson *et al.* 2010, pp. 289–302.

—— ed. 2012a. *Being an Islander. Production and Identity at Quoygrew, Orkney, AD 900–1600*. Cambridge: McDonald Institute for Archaeological Research.

—— 2012b. 'Viking Age and medieval Orkney', in Barrett 2012a, pp. 11–23.

Barrett, James H. and Michael P. Richards. 2004. 'Identity, gender, religion and economy: new isotope and radiocarbon evidence for marine resource intensification in early historical Orkney, Scotland, UK', *European Journal of Archaeology* 7/3, 249–71.

Barrett, James, *et al.* 2008. 'Detecting the medieval cod trade: a new method and first results', *Journal of Archaeological Science* 35, 850–61.

—— 2012. 'Quoygrew and its landscape context', in Barrett 2012a, pp. 25–46.

Bates, David, ed. 2013. *Anglo-Norman Studies XXXV: Proceedings of the Battle Conference 2012*. Woodbridge.

Batey, Colleen E., *et al.*, eds. 1993. *The Viking Age in Caithness, Orkney and the North Atlantic*. Edinburgh: Edinburgh University Press, 1993.

Batey, Colleen E., *et al.* 2012. 'Local availability and long-range trade: the worked stone assemblage', in Barrett 2012a, pp. 207–27.

Bauduin, Pierre, and Alexander E. Musin, eds. 2014. *Vers l'Orient et vers l'Occident. Regards croisés sur les dynamiques et les transferts culturels des Vikings à la Rous ancienne*. Caen: Presses universitaires de Caen.

Baug, Irene. 2011. 'Soapstone finds', in Skre 2011, pp. 311–37.

Bekker-Nielsen, Hans, and Hans Frede Nielsen, eds. 1997. *Beretning fra sekstende tværfaglige vikingesymposium*. Højbjerg: Hikuin.

Benediktsson, Jakob. 1969. '*Landnámabók:* some remarks on its value as a historical source', *Saga-Book* 17/4, 275–92.

Bertelsen, Reidar. 1992. 'Vågan: Nordnorges første by?', in Øye 1992, pp. 84–101.

Bertelsen, Reidar, and Raymond G. Lamb. 1993. 'Settlement mounds in the North Atlantic', in Batey *et al.* 1993, pp. 544–54.

Blöndal, Sigfús, and Benedikt S. Benedikz. 1978. *The Varangians of Byzantium*. Cambridge: Cambridge University Press.

Böldl, Klaus. 2007. 'Wikinger: definition des W.-Begriffs', *Reallexikon der germanischen Altertumskunde* 35, 697–708.

Bolin, Hans. 2004. 'The absence of gender: Iron Age burials in the Lake Mälaren area', *Current Swedish Archaeology* 12, 169–85.

Bond, J. M., and J. R. Hunter. 1987. 'Flax-growing in Orkney from the Norse period to the 18th century', *Proceedings of the Society of Antiquaries of Scotland* 117, 175–81.

Boulhosa, Patricia. 2005. *Icelanders and the Kings of Norway: Medieval Sagas and Legal Texts*. Leiden: Brill.

Bowden, Georgina R., *et al.* 2008. 'Excavating past population structures by surname-based sampling: the genetic legacy of the Vikings in Northwest England', *Molecular Biology and Evolution* 25/2, 301–9.

Brink, Stefan. 1999. 'Fornskandinavisk religion – förhistorisk samhälle. En bosättningshistorisk studie av centralorter i Norden', in Drobin 1999, pp. 11–55.

—— 2002. 'Law and legal customs in Viking Age Scandinavia', in Jesch 2002, pp. 87–127.

—— 2004. 'New perspectives on the Christianization of Scandinavia', in Adams and Holman 2004, pp. 165–75.

—— 2007. 'How uniform was the Old Norse religion?', in Quinn *et al.* 2007, pp. 105–36.

—— 2008. 'Naming the land', in Brink and Price 2008, 57–66.

Brink, Stefan, with Neil Price, eds. 2008. *The Viking World*. London: Routledge.

Broderick, George. 2006. *A Dictionary of Manx Place-Names*. Nottingham: English Place-Name Society.

Brown, Louise. 2013a. 'The coarse pottery from Hamar', in Turner *et al.* 2013, 144.

—— 2013b. 'Summary of the coarse pottery assemblage from the Upper House, Underhoull', in Turner *et al.* 2013, 169–71.

Buchanan, Meg, ed. 1995. *St Kilda: The Continuing Story of the Islands*. Edinburgh: HMSO.

Buckland, Paul C. 2010. 'Ragnarök and the stones of York', in Sheehan and Ó Corráin 2010, pp. 47–59.

Buckland, Paul C., *et al.* 1993. 'An insect's-eye view of the Norse farm', in Batey *et al.* 1993, pp. 506–27.

Buckland, Paul, and Eva Panagiotakopulu. 2005. 'Archaeology and the palaeoecology of the Norse Atlantic islands: a review', in Mortensen and Arge 2005, pp. 167–81.

Callmer, Johan. 2008. 'Scandinavia and the contintent in the Viking Age', in Brink and Price 2008, pp. 439–52.

Callow, Chris. 2004. 'Narrative, contact, conflict, and coexistence: Norwegians in thirteenth-century Iceland', in Adams and Holman 2004, pp. 323–31.

—— 2011. 'Putting women in their place: gender, landscape and the construction of *Landnámabók*', *Viking and Medieval Scandinavia* 7, 7–28.

Capelle, Torsten. 1968. *Der Metallschmuck von Haithabu*. Die Ausgrabungen in Haithabu 5. Neumünster: Karl Wachholtz.

Cavill, Paul, ed. 2004. *The Christian Tradition in Anglo-Saxon England. Approaches to Current Scholarship and Teaching*. Cambridge: D. S. Brewer.

Christensen, Tom. 2009. 'Odin fra Lejre', *ROMU: Årsskrift fra Roskilde Museum* 2009, 6–25.

Church, Mike J., *et al.* 2013. 'The Vikings were not the first colonizers of the Faroe Islands', *Quaternary Science Reviews* 77, 228–32.

Clarke, Howard B., *et al.*, eds. 1998. *Ireland and Scandinavia in the Early Viking Age*. Dublin: Four Courts Press.

Clelland, Sarah-Jane, *et al.* 2009. 'Scientific analysis of steatite: recent results', in Forster and Turner 2009, pp. 106–17.

Clifford, James. 1994. 'Diasporas', *Cultural Anthropology* 9, 302–38.

Clover, Carol. 1988. 'The politics of scarcity: notes on the sex ratio in early Scandinavia', *Scandinavian Studies* 60, 147–88.

Clunies Ross, Margaret, ed. 2000. *Old Norse-Icelandic Literature and Society*. Cambridge: Cambridge University Press.

—— 2005. *A History of Old Norse Poetry and Poetics*. Cambridge: D. S. Brewer.

Clutton-Brock, T. H., and J. M. Pemberton, eds. 2004. *Soay Sheep. Dynamics and Selection in an Island Population*. Cambridge: Cambridge University Press.

Coates, Richard. 1990. *The Place-Names of St Kilda: Nomina Hirtensia*. Lampeter: Edwin Mellen Press.

Cohen, Robin. 2008. *Global Diasporas: An Introduction*. London: Routledge. [2nd edition].

Coleman, Nancy, and Nanna Løkka, eds. 2014. *Kvinner i vikingtid*. Oslo: Spartacus.

Cramp, Rosemary. 2010. 'Sockburn before the Normans', in Stephens 2010, pp. 3–35.

Crawford, Barbara E. 1987. *Scandinavian Scotland*. Leicester: Leicester University Press, 1987.

—— ed. 1995. *Scandinavian Settlement in Northern Britain*. London: Leicester University Press.

—— 1999. 'Final discussion', in Crawford and Smith 1999, pp. 239–48.

—— 2005. 'Thorfinn, Christianity and Birsay: what the saga tells us and archaeology reveals', in Owen 2005, pp. 89–110.

Crawford, Barbara E., and Beverley Ballin Smith. 1999. *The Biggings, Papa Stour, Shetland. The History and Excavation of a Royal Norwegian Farm*. Edinburgh: Society of Antiquaries of Scotland.

Dekker, Kees, *et al.*, eds. 2009. *The World of Travellers: Exploration and Imagination*. Leuven: Peeters.

Diamond, Jared. 2006. *Collapse: How Societies Choose to Fail or Survive*. London: Penguin.

Dockrill, Stephen J., *et al.* 2010. *Excavations at Old Scatness, Shetland Volume 1: The Pictish Village and Viking Settlement*. Lerwick: Shetland Heritage Publications.

Dodgshon, R. A., and R. A. Butlin, eds. 1978. *An Historical Geography of England and Wales*. London: Academic Press.

Drobin, Ulf, ed. 1999. *Religion och samhälle i det förkristna Norden*. Odense: Odense Universitetsforlag.

Duczko, Wladyslaw. 2004. *Viking Rus: Studies on the Presence of Scandinavians in Eastern Europe*. Leiden: Brill.

Düwel, Klaus. 1986. 'Zur Ikonographie und Ikonologie der Sigurddarstellungen', in Roth 1986, pp. 221–71.

Düwel, Klaus, with Sean Nowak, eds. 1998. *Runeninschriften als Quellen interdisziplinärer Forschung*. Berlin: Walter de Gruyter.

Duffy, Seán, ed. 2010. *Medieval Dublin*, X. Dublin: Four Courts Press.

Dugmore, Andrew J., *et al.* 2005. 'The Norse *landnám* on the North Atlantic islands: an environmental impact assessment', *Polar Record* 41/216, 21–37.

—— 2007a. 'Abandoned farms, volcanic impacts, and woodland management: revisiting Þjórsárdalur, the "Pompeii of Iceland"', *Arctic Anthropology* 44/1, 1–11.

—— 2007b. 'Norse Greenland settlement: reflections on climate change, trade, and the contrasting fates of human settlements in the North Atlantic islands', *Arctic Anthropology* 44/1, 12–36.

—— 2009. 'Norse Greenland settlement and limits to adaptation', in Adger *et al.* 2009, pp. 96–113.

Dumville, David. 2008. 'Vikings in insular chronicling', in Brink and Price 2008, pp. 350–67.

Edgren, Torsten. 2008. 'The Viking Age in Finland', in Brink and Price 2008, pp. 470–84.

Edwards, B. J. N. 1998. *Vikings in North West England: The Artifacts*. Lancaster: University of Lancaster.

Edwards, Kevin J., and Ian B. M. Ralston. 1997. *Scotland: Environment and Archaeology, 8000 BC–AD 1000*. Chichester: Wiley.

Edwards, Kevin J., and Douglas B. Borthwick. 2010. 'Peaceful wars and scientific invaders: Irishmen, Vikings and palynological evidence for the earliest settlement of the Faroe Islands', in Sheehan and Ó Corráin 2010, pp. 66–79.

Edwards, Kevin J., *et al.* 2011. 'Is there a Norse "footprint" in North Atlantic pollen records?', in Sigmundsson 2011, pp. 65–82.

Eldjárn, Kristján. 2000. *Kuml og haugfé úr heiðnum sið á Íslandi.* Reykjavík: Mál og Menning. [2nd edition, ed. Adolf Friðriksson].

Emery, Norman, and Alex Morrison. 1995. 'The archaeology of St Kilda', in Buchanan 1995, pp. 39–59.

Eriksen, Thomas Hylland. 2010. *Ethnicity and Nationalism: Anthropological Perspectives.* London: Pluto. [3rd edition].

Ewing, Thor. 2006. *Viking Clothing.* Stroud: Tempus.

Faulkes, Anthony, and Richard M. Perkins, eds. 1993. *Viking Revaluations.* London: Viking Society for Northern Research.

Fell, Christine E. 1987. 'Modern English *Viking*', *Leeds Studies in English* 18, 111–23.

Fell, Christine, *et al.*, eds. 1983. *The Viking Age in the Isle of Man.* London: Viking Society for Northern Research.

Fellows Jensen, Gillian. 1968. *Scandinavian Personal Names in Lincolnshire and Yorkshire.* Copenhagen: Akademisk forlag.

—— 1972. *Scandinavian Settlement Names in Yorkshire.* Copenhagen: Akademisk forlag.

—— 1978. *Scandinavian Settlement Names in the East Midlands.* Copenhagen: Akademisk forlag.

—— 1985. *Scandinavian Settlement Names in the North-West.* Copenhagen: Reitzel.

Fellows-Jensen, Gillian, and Bente Holmberg, eds. 1992. *Sakrale navne. Rapport fra NORNAs sekstende symposium i Gilleleje 30.11.–2.12.1990.* Uppsala: NORNA-förlaget.

Fenton, Alexander, and Hermann Pálsson, eds. 1984. *The Northern and Western Isles in the Viking World: Survival, Continuity and Change.* Edinburgh: John Donald.

Feveile, Claus. 2010. 'Ribe: continuity or discontinuity from the eighth to the twelfth century', in Sheehan and Ó Corráin 2010, pp. 97–106.

Forster, Amanda. 2009. 'Viking and Norse steatite use in Shetland', in Forster and Turner 2009, pp. 58–69.

Forster, Amanda, and Val E. Turner, eds. 2009. *Kleber: Shetland's Oldest Industry.* Lerwick: Shetland Amenity Trust, 2009.

Frank, Roberta. 2004. *Sex, Lies and Málsháttakvæði.* Nottingham: University of Nottingham.

Franklin, Simon, and Jonathan Shepard. 1996. *The Emergence of Rus 750–1200.* London: Longman.

Fredriksen, Britta Olrik. 2005. *Opuscula* 12. Copenhagen: Reitzel.

Frei, K. M., *et al.* 2009. 'Provenance of ancient textiles – a pilot study evaluating the strontium isotope system in wool', *Archaeometry* 51/2, 252–76.

Friðriksson, Adolf, and Gavin Lucas. 2009. 'Introduction', in Lucas 2009, pp. 1–25.

Fullerton, Brian, and Alan F. Williams. 1972. *Scandinavia.* London: Chatto and Windus.

Gade, Kari Ellen. 2000. 'Poetry and its changing importance in medieval Icelandic culture', in Clunies Ross 2000, pp. 61–95.

Gammeltoft, Peder. 2001. *The Place-Name Element* bólstaðr *in the North Atlantic Area.* Copenhagen: C. A. Reitzel.

—— 2006. 'Scandinavian influence on Hebridean island-names', in Gammeltoft and Jørgensen 2006, pp. 53–84.

Gammeltoft, Peder, and Bent Jørgensen, eds. 2006. *Names through the Looking-Glass. Festschrift in Honour of Gillian Fellows-Jensen July 5th 2006.* Copenhagen: C. A. Reitzel.

Garipzanov, Ildar, ed. 2014. *Conversion and Identity in the Viking Age.* Turnhout: Brepols.

Gillham, Nicholas Wright. 2011. *Genes, Chromosomes, and Disease: From Simple Traits, to Complex Traits, to Personalized Medicine*. London: FTPress.

Goldberg, P. J. P., and Felicity Riddy, eds. 2004. *Youth in the Middle Ages*. York: York Medieval Press.

Goodacre, S., *et al.* 2005. 'Genetic evidence for a family-based Scandinavian settlement of Shetland and Orkney during the Viking periods', *Heredity* 95, 129–35.

Gräslund, Anne-Sofie. 1988–9. '"Gud hjälpe nu väl hennes själ": om runstenskvinnorna, deras roll vid kristnandet och deras plats i familj och samhälle', *Tor: Tidskrift för nordisk fornkunnskap* 22, 223–44.

—— 2001. 'The position of Iron Age Scandinavian women: the evidence of graves and rune stones', in Arnold and Wicker 2001, pp. 81–102.

—— 2009. 'How did the Norsemen in Greenland see themselves? Some reflections on "Viking identity"', in Arneborg *et al.* 2009, pp. 135–41.

Graham-Campbell, James. 2013. *Viking Art*. London: Thames and Hudson.

Graham-Campbell, James, *et al.*, eds. 2001. *Vikings and the Danelaw*. Oxford: Oxbow.

Griffiths, David. 2010. *Vikings of the Irish Sea*. Stroud: The History Press.

Grove, Jonathan. 2009. 'The place of Greenland in medieval Icelandic saga narrative', in Arneborg *et al.* 2009, pp. 34–55.

Guðmundsdóttir, Aðalheiður. 2012a. 'The origin and development of the *fornaldarsögur* as illustrated by *Völsunga Saga*', in Lassen *et al.* 2012, pp. 59–81.

—— 2012b. 'Gunnarr and the snake pit in medieval art and legend', *Speculum* 87, 1015–49.

Guðmundsson, Guðmundur J. 2009. 'Greenland and the wider world', in Arneborg *et al.* 2009, pp. 70–7.

Guðmundsson, Helgi. 1997. *Um haf innan. Vestrænir menn og íslenzk menning á miðöldum*. Reykjavík: Háskólaútgáfan.

Gunnarsson, Þorsteinn, ed. 2004. *Um Auðunarstofu*. Reykjavík: Hólanefnd.

Gunnell, Terry. 2005. 'Eddic poetry', in McTurk 2005, pp. 82–100.

Hadley, D. M. 2006. *The Vikings in England: Settlement, Society and Culture*. Manchester: Manchester University Press.

—— 2008. 'Warriors, heroes and companions: negotiating masculinity in Viking-age England', *Anglo-Saxon Studies in Archaeology and History* 15, 270–84.

Hadley, Dawn M., and Julian D. Richards, eds. 2000. *Cultures in Contact: Scandinavian Settlement in England in the Ninth and Tenth Centuries*. Turnhout: Brepols.

Hallgrímsson, Benedikt, *et al.* 2004. 'Composition of the founding population of Iceland: biological distance and morphological variation in early historic Atlantic Europe', *American Journal of Physical Anthropology* 124, 257–74.

Halsall, Guy, ed. 1998. *Violence and Society in the Early Medieval West*. Woodbridge: Boydell.

Hamilton, Sarah, and Andrew Spicer. 2006. 'Defining the holy: the delineation of sacred space', in Spicer and Hamilton 2006, pp. 1–23.

Hansen, Steffen Stummann. 2010. 'Toftanes and the early Christianity of the Faroe Islands', in Sheehan and Ó Corráin 2010, pp. 465–73.

Hansson, Pär, ed. 1997. *The Rural Viking in Russia and Sweden*. Örebro: Örebro kommuns bildningsförvaltning, 1997.

Harding, Stephen, *et al.* 2010. *Viking DNA: The Wirral and West Lancashire Project*. Birkenhead: Countyvise.

Harland, Jennifer F. 2012. 'Animal husbandry: the mammal bone', in Barrett 2012a, pp. 139–54.

Harland, Jennifer F., and James H. Barrett. 2012. 'The maritime economy: fish bone', in Barrett 2012a, pp. 115–38.

Harrison, Jane. 2013. 'Building mounds. Longhouses, coastal mounds and cultural connections: Norway and the Northern Isles, c. AD 800–1200', *Medieval Archaeology* 57, 35–60.

Harrison, Stephen H. 2010. 'Bride Street revisited – Viking burial in Dublin and beyond', in Duffy 2010, pp. 12–-52.

Hayeur Smith, Michèle. 2004. *Draupnir's Sweat and Mardöll's Tears: An Archaeology of Jewellery, Gender and Identity in Viking Age Iceland*. BAR International Series 1276. Oxford: Archaeopress.

Heide, Eldar. 2005. '*Viking* – rower shifting? An etymological contribution', *Arkiv för nordisk filologi* 120, 41–54.

Helgason, Agnar, *et al.* 2000a. 'mtDNA and the origin of the Icelanders: deciphering signals of recent population history', *American Journal of Human Genetics* 66, 999–1016.

—— 2000b. 'Estimating Scandinavian and Gaelic ancestry in the male settlers of Iceland', *American Journal of Human Genetics* 67, 697–717.

—— 2001. 'mtDNA and the islands of the North Atlantic: estimating the proportions of Norse and Gaelic ancestry', *American Journal of Human Genetics* 68, 723–37.

—— 2003. 'A reassessment of genetic diversity in Icelanders: strong evidence from multiple loci for relative homogeneity caused by genetic drift', *Annals of Human Genetics* 67, 281–97.

—— 2009. 'Sequences from first settlers reveal rapid evolution in Icelandic mtDNA pool', *PLoS Genetics* 5/1, 1–10.

Helle, Knut, ed. 2003. *The Cambridge History of Scandinavia. Volume I: Prehistory to 1520*. Cambridge: Cambridge University Press.

Henriksen, Mogens Bo, and Peter Vang Petersen. 2013. 'Valkyriefund', *Skalk* 2013/2, 3–10.

Hermann, Pernille, *et al.*, eds. 2007. *Reflections on Old Norse Myths*. Turnhout: Brepols.

Hines, John, *et al.*, eds. 2004. *Land, Sea and Home: Proceedings of a Conference on Viking-Period Settlement*. Leeds: Maney.

Hjaltalín, Thor. 2009. 'The historic landscape of the Saga of the People of Vatnsdalur: exploring the saga writer's use of the landscape and archaeological remains to serve political interests', *Medieval Archaeology* 53, 243–70.

Hodder, Ian, and Scott Hutson. 2003. *Reading the Past: Current Approaches to Interpretation in Archaeology*. Cambridge: Cambridge University Press. [3rd edition].

Høegsberg, Mogens Skaaning, 2009. 'Continuity and change: the dwellings of the Greenland Norse', in Arneborg *et al.* 2009, pp. 86–105.

Holman, Katherine. 1996. *Scandinavian Runic Inscriptions in the British Isles: Their Historical Context*. Trondheim: Tapir.

—— 1998. 'Scandinavian runic inscriptions as a source for the history of the British Isles: the St Paul's rune-stone', in Düwel and Nowak 1998, pp. 629–38.

—— 2001. 'Defining the Danelaw', in Graham-Campbell *et al.* 2001, pp. 1–11.

—— 2007.*The Northern Conquest: Vikings in Britain and Ireland*. Oxford: Signal.

Holmberg, Bente. 1991. 'Om sakrale sted- og personnavne', in Steinsland *et al.* 1991, pp. 149–59.

Hough, Carole, and Kathryn A. Lowe, eds. 2002. *'Lastworda betst': Essays in Memory of Christine E. Fell with her Unpublished Writings*. Donington: Shaun Tyas.

Hraundal, Thorir Jonsson. 2013.*The Rus in Arabic Sources: Cultural Contacts and Identity*. Bergen: Centre for Medieval Studies.

Hunter, John, *et al.* 2007. *Investigations in Sanday, Orkney. Vol. 1: Excavations at Pool, Sanday. A Multi-Period Settlement from Neolithic to Late Norse Times*. Kirkwall: The Orcadian.

Imsen, Steinar, ed. 2003. *Ecclesia Nidrosiensis 1153–1537*. Trondheim: Tapir.

Jacobsen, Grethe. 2005. 'The Celtic element in the Icelandic population and the position of women', in Fredriksen 2005, pp. 284–303.

Jakobsen, Jakob. 1936. *The Place-Names of Shetland*. London: David Nutt (A. G. Berry). [reprinted Kirkwall: The Orcadian, 1993].

Jakobsson, Ármann. 2005. 'Royal biography', in McTurk 2005, pp. 388–402.

—— 2013. *Nine Saga Studies: The Critical Interpretation of the Icelandic Sagas*. Reykjavík: University of Iceland Press.

Jakobsson, Sverrir. 2007. 'Strangers in Icelandic society 1100–1400', *Viking and Medieval Scandinavia* 3, 141–57.

Jansson, Ingmar. 1985. *Ovala spännbucklor. En studie av vikingatida standardsmycken med utgångspunkt från Björkö-fynden*. Uppsala: Uppsala University Institute of North European Archaeology.

—— 1997. 'Warfare, trade or colonisation? Some general remarks on the eastern expansion of the Scandinavians in the Viking period', in Hansson 1997, pp. 9–64.

Jansson, Sven B. F. 1987. *Runes in Sweden*. Stockholm: Gidlunds.

Janzén, Assar, ed. 1947a. *Personnavne*. Stockholm: Bonniers.

—— 1947b. 'De fornvästnordiska personnamnen', in Janzén 1947a, pp. 22–186.

Jensen, Kurt Villads. 2001. 'Introduction', in Murray 2001, pp. xvii–xxv.

Jesch, Judith. 1987. 'Early Christians in Icelandic history – a case-study', *Nottingham Medieval Studies* 31, 17–36.

—— 1991. *Women in the Viking Age*. Woodbridge: Boydell.

—— 1994. 'Runic inscriptions and social history: some problems of method', in Knirk 1994, pp. 149–62.

—— 2001a. *Ships and Men in the Late Viking Age: The Vocabulary of Runic Inscriptions and Skaldic Verse*. Woodbridge: Boydell.

—— 2001b. 'Skaldic verse in Scandinavian England', in Graham-Campbell *et al.* 2001, pp. 313–25.

—— 2002a. 'Old Norse *víkingr*: a question of contexts', in Hough and Lowe 2002, pp. 107–21.

—— 2002b. *The Scandinavians from the Vendel Period to the Tenth Century: An ethnographic perspective*. Woodbridge: Boydell.

—— 2004a. '"Youth on the prow": three young kings in the late Viking Age', in Goldberg and Riddy 2004, pp. 123–39.

—— 2004b. 'Scandinavians and "cultural paganism" in late Anglo-Saxon England', in Cavill 2004, pp. 55–68.

—— 2005. 'Literature in medieval Orkney', in Owen 2005, pp. 11–24.

—— 2006. 'Viking "geosophy" and some colonial place-names', in Gammeltoft and Jørgensen 2006, pp. 131–45.

—— 2008a. 'Poetry in the Viking Age', in Brink and Price 2008, pp. 291–8.

—— 2008b. 'Myth and cultural memory in the Viking diaspora', *Viking and Medieval Scandinavia* 4, 221–6.

—— 2009a. 'Namings and narratives: exploration and imagination in the Norse voyages westward', in Dekker *et al.* 2009, pp. 61–9.

—— 2009b. 'The Orcadian links of *Snorra Edda*', in Jørgensen 2009, pp. 145–72.

—— 2009c. 'The Norse gods in Scotland', in Woolf 2009, pp. 49–73.

—— 2010. '*Orkneyinga saga*: a work in progress?', in Quinn and Lethbridge 2010, pp. 153–73.

—— 2011a. 'Runic inscriptions and the vocabulary of land, lordship, and social power in the late Viking Age', in Poulsen and Sindbæk 2011, pp. 31–44.

—— 2011b. 'The Norse gods in England and the Isle of Man', in Anlezark 2011, pp. 11–24.

—— 2013a. 'Earl Rögnvaldr of Orkney, a poet of the Viking diaspora', *Journal of the North Atlantic* Special Volume 4, 154–60.

—— 2013b. 'Some Viking weapons in Sigvatr's verse', in Reynolds and Webster 2013, pp. 341–57.

—— 2014a. 'Christian Vikings: Norsemen in Western Europe in the 12th century', in Bauduin and Musin 2014, pp. 55–60.

—— 2014b. 'Women and identities in Viking Age Iceland', in Coleman and Løkka 2014, pp. 268–86.

Jochens, Jenny. 1999. 'Late and peaceful: the conversion of Iceland through arbitration in 1000', *Speculum* 74, 621–55.

Jørgensen, Jon Gunnar, ed. 2009. *Snorra Edda i europeisk og islandsk kultur*. Reykholt: Snorrastofa.

Johansen, Olav Sverre. 2003. 'Borg: the local setting', in Munch *et al.* 2003, pp. 25–32.

Johnston, Alfred W. 1910. 'Grotta söngr and the Orkney and Shetland quern', *Saga-Book* 6/2, 296–304.

Jones, E. P., *et al.* 2012. 'Fellow travellers: a concordance of colonization patterns between mice and men in the North Atlantic region', *BMC Evolutionary Biology* 12, 35 [doi:10.1186/1471-2148-12-35].

Jones, Michael, and Olwig, Kenneth R. eds. 2008. *Nordic Landscapes: Regions and Belonging on the Northern Edge of Europe*. Minneapolis: University of Minnesota Press.

Jones, Siân. 1997. *The Archaeology of Ethnicity: Constructing Identities in the Past and Present*. London: Routledge.

Jorgensen, Alice, ed. 2010. *Reading the Anglo-Saxon Chronicle: Language, Literature, History*. Turnhout: Brepols.

Jorgensen, Tove H., *et al.* 2004. 'The origin of the isolated population of the Faroe Islands investigated using Y chromosomal markers', *Human Genetics* 115, 19–28.

Joseph, John E. 2004. *Language and Identity: National, Ethnic, Religious*. Basingstoke: Palgrave Macmillan.

Kalra, Virinder S. *et al.* 2005. *Diaspora & Hybridity*. London: Saga.

Karkov, Catherine E. 2012. 'Postcolonial', in Stodnick and Trilling 2012, pp. 149–63.

Karlsson, Gunnar. 1996. 'Plague without rats: the case of fifteenth-century Iceland', *Journal of Medieval History* 22/3, 263–84.

—— 2000. *The History of Iceland*. Minneapolis: University of Minnesota Press.

—— 2009. 'The ethnicity of the Vinelanders', in Arneborg *et al.* 2009, pp. 130–4.

Karnell, Maria Herlin, ed. 2012. *Gotland's Picture Stones: Bearers of an Enigmatic Legacy*. Visby: Gotlands Museum.

Keller, Christian. 2010. 'Furs, fish and ivory: medieval Norsemen at the Arctic fringe', *Journal of the North Atlantic* 3, 1–23.

Kenny, Kevin. 2013. *Diaspora: A Very Short Introduction*. Oxford: Oxford University Press.

Kershaw, Jane. 2013. *Viking Identities: Scandinavian Jewellery in England*. Oxford: Oxford University Press.

Keynes, Simon. 1997. 'The Vikings in England, *c.* 790–1016', in Sawyer 1997, pp. 48–82.

Khvoshchinskaya, Natalya V. 2007. 'Small steatite moulds from the collection from Ryurik Gorodischche and other steatite finds in Rus', in Nosov and Musin 2007, pp. 199–202.

King, Turi E., and Mark A. Jobling. 2009. 'What's in a name? Y chromosomes, surnames and the genetic genealogy revolution', *Trends in Genetics* 25/8, 351–60.

Kisbye, Torben, and Else Roesdahl, eds. 1989. *Beretning fra ottende tværfaglige vikingesymposium*. Aarhus: Hikuin.

Knirk, James E., ed. 1994. *Proceedings of the Third International Symposium on Runes and Runic Inscriptions, Grindaheim, Norway, 8–12 August 1990*. Runrön 9. Uppsala: Uppsala Universitet.

Knudson, Kelly J., *et al.* 2012. 'Migration and Viking Dublin: paleomobility and paleodiet through isotopic analyses', *Journal of Archaeological Science* 39, 308–20.

Kolodny, Annette. 2012. *In Search of First Contact: The Vikings of Vinland, the Peoples of the Dawnland, and the Anglo-American Anxiety of Discovery*. Durham, NC: Duke University Press.

Kopár, Lilla. 2012. *Gods and Settlers: The Iconography of Norse Mythology in Anglo-Scandinavian Sculpture*. Turnhout: Brepols.

Kousgård Sørensen, John. 1989. 'Om personnavne på -vi/-væ og den førkristne præstestand', *Danske studier* 1989, 5–33.

Kramarz-Bein, Susanne, ed. 1996. *Hansische Literaturbeziehungen. Das Beispiel der Þiðreks saga und verwandter Literatur*. Berlin: Walter de Gruyter.

Kristjánsdóttir, Steinunn. 2011. 'The Vikings as a *diaspora*: cultural and religious identities in early medieval Iceland', in Sigmundsson 2011, pp. 422–36.

Krüger, Jana. 2008. *"Wikinger" im Mittelalter. Die Rezeption von* víkingr *m. und* víking *f. in der altnordischen Literatur*. Berlin: Walter de Gruyter.

Lane, Alan M. 2010. 'Viking-Age and Norse pottery in the Hebrides', in Sheehan and Ó Corráin 2010, pp. 204–16.

Lang, James T. 1972–4. 'Hogback monuments in Scotland', *Proceedings of the Society of Antiquaries of Scotland* 105, 206–35.

—— 1984. 'The hogback: a Viking colonial monument', *Anglo-Saxon Studies in Archaeology and History* 3, 86–176.

Larrington, Carolyne. 2008. 'A Viking in shining armour? Vikings and chivalry in the *fornaldarsögur*', *Viking and Medieval Scandinavia* 4, 269–88.

Larsen, Anne-Christine. 2013a. 'Aspects of the Viking and Late Norse economy at Belmont', in Turner *et al.* 2013, pp. 205–8.

—— 2013b. 'The environmental evidence', in Turner *et al.* 2013, pp. 208–13.

—— 2013c. 'Belmont: summary and discussion', in Turner *et al.* 2013, pp. 214–16.

Larsen, Anne-Christine, and Mads Drevs Dyhrfjeld-Johnsen. 2013. 'The artefactual evidence from Belmont: selected finds', in Turner *et al.* 2013, pp. 194–205.

Larsson, Lars. 2006. 'Ritual building and ritual space: aspects of investigations at the Iron Age central site Uppåkra, Scania, Sweden', in Andrén *et al.* 2006, pp. 248–53.

—— 2007. 'The Iron Age ritual building at Uppåkra, southern Sweden', *Antiquity* 81, 11–25.

Lárusson, Ólafur. 1939. 'Island', in Olsen 1939, pp. 60–75.

Lassen, Annette, *et al.*, eds. 2012. *The Legendary Sagas: Origins and Development*. Reykjavík: University of Iceland Press.

Lawson, Ian T. 2009. 'The palaeoenvironment of Mývatnssveit', in Lucas 2009, pp. 26–54.

Lawson, M. K. 2004. *Cnut: England's Viking King*. Stroud: Tempus.

Lerche Nielsen, Michael. 1997. 'Runologien mellem sprogvidenskaben og arkæologien – med et sideblik på de forskellige tolkninger af Glavendrupindskriften', in Bekker-Nielsen and Nielsen 1997, pp. 37–51.

Lidén, Hans-Emil *et al.* 1969. 'From pagan sanctuary to Christian church: the excavation of Mære church in Trøndelag', *Norwegian Archaeological Review* 2, 3–32.

Liestøl, Knut. 1929. *Upphavet til den islendske ættesaga*. Oslo: Aschehoug.

Lind, John H. 2001. 'Consequences of the crusades in target areas: the case of Karelia', in Murray 2001, pp. 133–50.

Lindkvist, Thomas. 2001. 'Crusades and crusading ideology in the political history of Sweden, 1140–1500', in Murray 2001, pp. 119–30.

—— 2003. 'Kings and provinces in Sweden', in Helle 2003, pp. 221–34.

Loe, Louise, *et al.* 2014. *'Given to the Ground': A Viking Age Mass Grave on Ridgeway Hill, Weymouth*. Oxford: Oxford Archaeology.

Lucas, Gavin, ed. 2009a. *Hofstaðir: Excavations of a Viking Age Feasting Hall in North-Eastern Iceland*. Reykjavík: Fornleifastofnun Íslands.

—— 2009b. 'Hofstaðir in the settlement period', in Lucas 2009a, pp. 371–408.

Mac Carron, P., and R. Kenna. 2013. 'Network analysis of the *Íslendinga sögur*: the Sagas of Icelanders', *The European Physical Journal B* 86, 407 [doi: 10.1140/epjb/e2013-40583-3].

Mac Niocaill, Gearóid. 1975. *The Medieval Irish Annals*, Dublin: Dublin Historical Association.

McGovern, Thomas H., *et al.* 2007. 'Landscapes of settlement in northern Iceland: historical ecology of human impact and climate fluctuation on the millennial scale', *American Anthropologist* 109, 27–51.

McKinnell, John. 1987. 'Norse mythology and Northumbria: a response', *Scandinavian Studies* 59, 325–37.

—— 2001. 'Eddic poetry in Anglo-Scandinavian northern England', in Graham-Campbell *et al.* 2001, pp. 327–44.

McLeod, Shane. 2011. 'Warriors and women: the sex ratio of Norse migrants to eastern England up to 900 AD', *Early Medieval Europe* 19, 332–53.

McTurk, Rory, ed. 2005. *A Companion to Old Norse-Icelandic Literature and Culture*. Oxford: Blackwell.

Magoun, Francis P., Jr. 1944. 'The pilgrim-diary of Nikulas of Munkathvera: the road to Rome', *Mediaeval Studies* 6, 314–54.

Margeson, Sue. 1980. 'The Völsung legend in medieval art', in Flemming G. Andersen *et al.* 1980, pp. 183–211.

—— 1983. 'On the iconography of the Manx crosses', in Fell *et al.* 1983, pp. 95–106.

Martens, Irmelin. 1994. 'Norwegian Viking Age weapons: some questions concerning their production and distribution', in Ambrosiani and Clarke 1994, pp. 180–2.

—— 2004. 'Indigenous and imported Viking Age weapons in Norway: a problem with European implications', *Journal of Nordic Archaeological Science* 14, 125–37.

Marwick, Hugh. 1952. *Orkney Farm-Names*. Kirkwall: W. R. Mackintosh.

Melchior, Linea, *et al.* 2008. 'Evidence of authentic DNA from Danish Viking Age skeletons untouched by humans for 1,000 years', *PloS One* 3/5, e2214 [doi: 10.1371/journal.pone.0002214].

Meldgaard, Eva Villarsen. 1992. 'Sakrale personnavne', in Fellows-Jensen and Holmberg 1992, pp. 185–97.

Meulengracht Sørensen, Preben. 1991. 'Om eddadigtenes alder', in Steinsland *et al.* 1991, pp. 217–28.

—— 1993. 'The sea, the flame and the wind: the legendary ancestors of the Earls of Orkney', in Batey *et al.* 1993, pp. 212–21.

Milner, Nicky, and James H. Barrett. 2012. 'The maritime economy: mollusc shell', in Barrett 2012a, pp. 103–13.

Mirdal, Gretty M., and Lea Ryynänen-Karjalainen. 2004. *Migration and Transcultural Identities*. ESF Forward Look Report 2. Strasbourg: European Science Foundation.

Moen, Marianne. 2011. *The Gendered Landscape: A Discussion on Gender, Status and Power in the Norwegian Viking Age Landscape*. Oxford: Archaeopress.

Moltke, Erik. 1985. *Runes and their Origin: Denmark and Elsewhere*. Copenhagen: National Museum.

Monk, Mick. 2013. 'Viking Age agriculture in Ireland and its settlement context', in Reynolds and Webster 2013, pp. 685–718.

Montgomery, J. E. 2008. 'Arabic sources on the Vikings', in Brink and Price 2008, pp. 550–61.

Mortensen, Andras, and Símun V. Arge, eds. 2005. *Viking and Norse in the North Atlantic: Select Papers from the Proceedings of the Fourteenth Viking Congress, Tórshavn, 19–30 July 2001*. Tórshavn: Føroya Fróðskaparfélag.

Mourant, A. E., and I. Morgan Watkin. 1952. 'Blood groups, anthropology and language in Wales and the western countries', *Heredity* 6, 13–36.

Munch, Gerd Stamsø, *et al.*, eds. 2003. *Borg in Lofoten: A Chieftain's Farm in North Norway*. Trondheim: Tapir.

Murray, Alan V., ed. 2001. *Crusade and Conversion on the Baltic Frontier 1150–1500*. Aldershot: Ashgate.

Musin, Alexander E. 2014. 'Les Scandinaves en Rous entre paganisme et christianisme', in Bauduin and Musin 2014, pp. 311–26.

Myhre, Bjørn. 1993. 'The beginning of the Viking Age: some current archaeological problems', in Faulkes and Perkins 1993, pp. 182–204.

—— 1998. 'The archaeology of the early Viking Age in Norway', in Clarke *et al.* 1998, pp. 3–36.

Näsman, Ulf, and Else Roesdahl. 2003. 'Scandinavian and European perspectives: Borg I:1', in Munch *et al.* 2003, pp. 283–99.

Naumann, Elise, *et al.* 2014. 'Changes in dietary practices and social organization during the pivotal Late Iron Age period in Norway (AD 550–1030): isotope analyses of Merovingian and Viking Age human remains', *American Journal of Physical Anthropology* 155/3, 322–31.

Nelson, Janet L. 1997. 'The Frankish Empire', in Sawyer 1997, pp. 19–47.

Ney, Agneta. 2012. 'The welcoming scene on Gotlandic picture stones, in comparison with Viking period and medieval literary sources', in Karnell 2012, pp. 73–82.

Ney, Agneta, *et al.*, eds. 2009. *Á austrvega. Saga and East Scandinavia: Preprint Papers of The 14th International Saga Conference, Uppsala, 9th–15th August 2009*, Gävle: Gävle University Press. [http://urn.kb.se/resolve?urn=urn:nbn:se:hig:diva-4837].

Noonan, Thomas S. 1994. 'The Vikings in the east: coins and commerce', in Ambrosiani and Clarke 1994, pp. 215–36.

Nordal, Guðrún. 1999. 'Odinsdyrkelse på Island. Arkæologi ok kilderne', in Drobin 1999, pp. 139–56.

—— 2001. *Tools of Literacy: The Role of Skaldic Verse in Icelandic Textual Culture of the Twelfth and Thirteenth Centuries*. Toronto: University of Toronto Press.

Nordanskog, Gunnar. 2006. *Föreställd hedendom: tidigmedeltida skandinaviska kyrkportar i forskning och historia*. Lund: Nordic Academic Press.

Nordberg, Andreas. 2012. 'Continuity, change and regional variation in Old Norse religion', in Raudvere and Schjødt 2012, pp. 119–51.

Nordeide, Sæbjørg Walaker. 2011. *The Viking Age as a Period of Religious Transformation: The Christianization of Norway from AD 560–1150/1200*. Turnhout: Brepols.

Nosov, Evgeniy, and Alexander E. Musin, eds. 2007. *The Origins of the Russian State*. St Petersburg: Russian Academy of Sciences.

Ó Corráin, Donnchadh. 2008. 'The Vikings and Ireland', in Brink and Price 2008, pp. 428–33.

O'Brien, M. A., and R. Baumgarten. 1973. 'Old Irish personal names', *Celtica* 10, 211–36.

Olausson, Michael, and Lena Holmquist Olausson, eds. 2009. *The Martial Society: Aspects of Warriors, Fortifications and Social Change in Scandinavia*. Stockholm: Archaeological Research Laboratory, Stockholm University.

Olsen, Magnus. 1926. *Ættegård og helligdom. Norske stedsnavn sosialt og religionshistorisk belyst*. Oslo: Aschehoug. [Also published in English as *Farms and Fanes of Ancient Norway: The Place Names of a Country Discussed in Their Bearings on Social and Religious History*. Oslo: Aschehoug, 1928.]

—— ed. 1939. *Stedsnavn*. Stockholm: Bonniers.

Olsen, Olaf. 1966. *Hørg, hov og kirke*. Copenhagen: H. J. Lynge & Søn.

Owen, Olwyn, ed. 2005. *The World of Orkneyinga Saga*. Kirkwall: The Orcadian.

Owen, Olwyn, and Christopher Lowe. 1999. *Kebister: The Four-Thousand-Year-Old Story of One Shetland Township*. Edinburgh: Society of Antiquaries of Scotland.

Øye, Ingvild, ed. 1992. *Våre første byer*. Bergen: Bryggens Museum.

Parsons, David N. 2002. '*Anna, Dot, Thorir* . . . Counting Domesday personal names', *Nomina* 25, 29–52.

Pedersen, Anne. 2004. 'Anglo-Danish contact across the North Sea in the eleventh century: a survey of the Danish archaeological evidence', in Adams and Holman 2004, 43–67.

Perdikaris, Sophia. 1999. 'From chiefly provisioning to commercial fishery: long-term economic change in Arctic Norway,' *World Archaeology* 30, 388–402.

Perdikaris, Sophia, and Thomas H. McGovern. 2008. 'Codfish and kings, seals and subsistence: Norse marine resource in the North Atlantic', in Rick and Erlandson 2008, pp. 187–214.

Peterson, Lena. 2007. *Nordiskt runnamnslexikon*. Uppsala: Institutet för språk och folkminnen. [5th edition]

Pétursson, Einar G. and Jónas Kristjánsson, eds. 1977. *Sjötíu ritgerðir helgaðar Jakobi Benediktssyni 20. Júli 1977*. Reykjavík: Stofnun Árna Magnússonar.

Pierce, Elizabeth. 2009. 'Walrus hunting and the ivory trade in early Iceland', *Archaeologia Islandica* 7, 55–63.

Pollard, A. M., *et al.* 2012. '"Sprouting like cockle amongst the wheat": the St Brice's day massacre and the isotopic analysis of human bones from St John's College, Oxford', *Oxford Journal of Archaeology* 31, 83–102.

Pons-Sanz, Sara M. 2013. *The Lexical Effects of Anglo-Scandinavian Linguistic Contact on Old English*. Turnhout: Brepols.

Poulsen, Bjørn, and Søren Sindbæk, eds. 2011. *Settlement and Lordship in Viking and Early Medieval Scandinavia*. Turnhout: Brepols.

Price, Neil. 2006. 'What's in a name? An archaeological identity crisis for the Norse gods (and some of their friends)', in Andrén *et al.* 2006, pp. 179–83.

—— 2013. 'Viking Brittany: revisiting the colony that failed', in Reynolds and Webster 2013, pp. 731–42.

Price, T. Douglas, and Hildur Gestsdóttir. 2006. 'The first settlers of Iceland: an isotopic approach to colonisation', *Antiquity* 80, 130–44.

Price, T. Douglas, *et al.* 2011. 'Who was in Harald Bluetooth's army? Strontium isotope investigation of the cemetery at the Viking Age fortress at Trelleborg, Denmark', *Antiquity* 85, 476–89.

Quinn, Judy. 2007. '"Hildr prepares a bed for most helmet-damagers": Snorri's treatment of a traditional poetic motif in his *Edda*', in Hermann *et al.* 2007, pp. 95–118.

Quinn, Judy, *et al.* 2006. 'Interrogating genre in the *fornaldarsögur*: round-table discussion', *Viking and Medieval Scandinavia* 2, 275–96.

Quinn, Judy, *et al.*, eds. 2007. *Learning and Understanding in the Old Norse World: Essays in Honour of Margaret Clunies Ross*. Turnhout: Brepols.

Quinn, Judy, and Emily Lethbridge, eds. 2010. *Creating the Medieval Saga: Versions, Variability and Editorial Interpretations of Old Norse Saga Literature*. Odense: University Press of Southern Denmark.

Ranković, Slavica. 2006. 'Golden ages and fishing grounds: the emergent past in the *Íslendingasögur*', *Saga-Book* 30, 39–64.

Ratke, Sharon. 2009. 'Guldgubber: a glimpse into the Vendel Period', *Lund Archaeological Review* 15, 149–159.

Ratke, Sharon, and Rudolf Simek. 2006. 'Guldgubber. Relics of pre-Christian law rituals?', in Andrén *et al.* 2006, pp. 259–64.

Raudvere, Catharina, and Jens Peter Schjødt, eds. 2012. *More than Mythology. Narratives, Ritual Practices and Regional Distribution in Pre-Christian Scandinavian Religions*. Lund: Nordic Academic Press.

Redknap, Mark. 2000. *Vikings in Wales: An Archaeological Quest*. Cardiff: National Museums and Galleries of Wales.

—— 2004. 'Viking-Age settlement in Wales and the evidence from Llanbedrgoch', in Hines *et al.* 2004, pp. 139–75.

Renaud, Jean. 2008. 'The Duchy of Normandy', in Brink and Price 2008, pp. 453–7.
Reynolds, Andrew, and Leslie Webster, eds. 2013. *Early Medieval Art and Archaeology in the Northern World: Studies in Honour of James Graham-Campbell*. Leiden: Brill.
Rick, Torben C., and Jon M. Erlandson, eds. 2008. *Human Impacts on Ancient Marine Ecosystems: A Global Perspective*. Berkeley: University of California Press.
Ridel, Elisabeth. 2009. *Les Vikings et les mots. L'apport de l'ancien scandinave à la langue française*. Paris: Editions Errance.
Ritchie, P. Roy. 1984. 'Soapstone quarrying in Viking lands', in Fenton and Pálsson 1984, pp. 59–84.
Roberts, B. K. 1978. 'Perspectives on prehistory', in Dodgshon and Butlin 1978, pp. 1–24.
Roesdahl, Else. 1998. *The Vikings*. London: Penguin. [2nd edition].
—— 2005. 'Walrus ivory: demand, supply, workshops, and Greenland', in Mortensen and Arge 2005, pp. 182–91.
Roesdahl, Else, and Preben Meulengracht Sørensen, eds. 1996. *The Waking of Angantyr: The Scandinavian Past in European Culture*. Aarhus: Aarhus University Press.
Roth, Helmut, ed. 1986. *Zum Problem der Deutung frühmittelalterliche Bildinhalte*. Sigmaringen: Jan Thorbecke Verlag.
Rowe, Elizabeth Ashman. 2005. *The Development of Flateyjarbók: Iceland and the Norwegian Dynastic Crisis of 1389*. Odense: University Press of Southern Denmark.
Safran, William. 2005. 'The Jewish diaspora in a comparative and theoretical perspective', *Israel Studies* 10/1, 36–60.
Sand, Shlomo. 2010. *The Invention of the Jewish People*. London: Verso.
Sandnes, Jørn. 1992. 'Norske stedsnavn og hedensk kultus', in Fellows-Jensen and Holmberg 1992, pp. 9–21.
Sawyer, Birgit. 2000. *The Viking-Age Rune-Stones. Custom and Commemoration in Early Medieval Scandinavia*. Oxford: Oxford University Press.
Sawyer, Peter, ed. 1997. *The Oxford Illustrated History of the Vikings*. Oxford: Oxford University Press.
Sayers, William. 1994. 'Management of the Celtic fact in *Landnámabók*', *Scandinavian Studies* 66, 129–53.
Schledermann, P., and K. M. McCullough. 2003. 'Inuit–Norse contact in the Smith Sound region', in Barrett 2003a, pp. 184–205.
Schoenfelder, Meagan, and Julian D. Richards. 2011. 'Norse bells: a Scandinavian colonical artefact', *Anglo-Saxon Studies in Archaeology and History* 17, 151–68.
Schofield, J. Edward, *et al*. 2013. 'Palynology supports "Old Norse" introductions to the flora of Greenland', *Journal of Biogeography* 40/6, 1119–30.
Scully, Marc, *et al*. 2013. 'Remediating Viking origins: genetic code as archival memory of the remote past', *Sociology* 47/5, 921–38.
Searle, Jeremy, *et al*. 2009. 'Of mice and (Viking?) men; phylogeography of British and Irish house mice', *Proceedings of the Royal Society B*. 276, 201–7.
Seppälä, Matti, ed. 2005. *The Physical Geography of Fennoscandia*. Oxford: Oxford University Press.
Shaw, Philip A. 2011. 'The role of gender in some Viking-Age innovations in personal naming', *Viking and Medieval Scandinavia* 7, 151–70.
Sheehan, John. 2008. 'The *longphort* in Viking Age Ireland', *Acta Archaeologica* 79, 282–95.
Sheehan, John, and Donnchadh Ó Corráin, eds. 2010. *The Viking Age: Ireland and the West. Proceedings of the Fifteenth Viking Congress*. Dublin: Four Courts.
Shepard, Jonathan. 2008. 'The Viking Rus and Byzantium', in Brink and Price 2008, pp. 496–516.
Sigmundsson, Svavar. 2009. *Nefningar*. Reykjavík: Stofnun Árna Magnússonar í íslenzkum fræðum.

—— ed. 2011. *Viking Settlements and Viking Society*. Reykjavík: Hið íslenska fornleifafélag and University of Iceland Press.

Sigurðsson, Gísli. 1988. *Gaelic Influence in Iceland. Historical and Literary Contacts*. Reykjavík: Bókaútgáfa Menningarsjóðs.

Sindbæk, Søren. 2007. 'The small world of the Vikings: networks in Early Medieval communication and exchange', *Norwegian Archaeological Review* 40/1, 59–74.

—— 2011. 'Urban crafts and oval brooches: style, innovation and social networks in Viking Age towns', in Sigmundsson 2011, pp. 407–21.

Sjøvold, Thorleif. 1974. *The Iron Age Settlement of Arctic Norway: A Study in the Expansion of European Iron Age Culture within the Arctic Circle. II: Late Iron Age (Merovingian and Viking Periods)*. Tromsö: Norwegian Universities Press.

Skre, Dagfinn, ed. 2011. *Things from the Town: Artefacts and Inhabitants in Viking-age Kaupang*. Aarhus: Aarhus University Press.

Smith, Brian. 2001. 'The Picts and the martyrs or did Vikings kill the native population of Orkney and Shetland?', *Northern Studies* 36, 7–32.

Søvsø, Morten. 2010. 'Tidlig kristne begravelser ved Ribe Domkirke – Ansgars kirkegård?', *Arkæologi i Slesvig / Archäologie in Schleswig* 13, 147–64.

Speed, Greg, and Penelope Walton Rogers. 2004. 'A burial of a Viking woman at Adwick-le-Street, South Yorkshire', *Medieval Archaeology* 48, 51–90.

Spicer, Andrew, and Sarah Hamilton, eds. 2006. *Defining the Holy: Sacred Space in Medieval and Early Modern Europe*. London: Ashgate.

Sporrong, Ulf. 2003. 'The Scandinavian landscape and its resources', in Helle 2003, pp. 15–42.

Stalsberg, Anne. 2001. 'Visible women made invisible: interpreting Varangian women in Old Russia', in Arnold and Wicker 2001, pp. 65–79.

Steinsland, Gro, *et al.*, eds. 1991. *Nordisk Hedendom*. Odense: Odense Universitetsforlag.

Stemshaug, Ola. 1985. *Namn i Noreg*. Oslo: Det Norske Samlaget. [3rd edition].

Stephens, Laura, ed. 2010. *Tapestry of Time. Twelve Centuries at Sockburn*. Middlesbrough: Quoin.

Stern, Marjolein, 'Sigurðr Fáfnisbani as commemorative motif', in Agneta Ney *et al.* 2009, pp. 898–905.

Steuer, Heiko. 1998. 'Datierungsprobleme in der Archäologie', in Düwel and Nowak 1998, pp. 129–49.

Stig Sørensen, Marie Louise. 2009. 'Gender, material culture, and identity in the Viking diaspora', *Viking and Medieval Scandinavia* 5, 253–69.

Stocker, David. 2000. 'Monuments and merchants. Irregularities in the distribution of stone sculpture in Lincolnshire and Yorkshire in the tenth century', in Hadley and Richards 2000, pp. 179–212.

Stodnick, Jacqueline, and Renée R. Trilling, eds. 2010. *A Handbook of Anglo-Saxon Studies*. Chichester: Wiley-Blackwell.

Stoklund, Marie. 1998. 'Arbejdet ved Runologisk Laboratorium, København', *Nytt om runer* 13, 4–11.

Storemyr, Per. 2003. 'Stein til kvader og dekor: Trøndelags middelalderkirker – geologi, europeisk innflytelse og tradisjoner', in Imsen 2003, pp. 445–64.

Streeter, Richard, *et al.* 2012. 'Plague and landscape resilience in premodern Iceland', *Proceedings of the National Academy of Sciences of the United States of America* 109/10, 3664–9.

Svanberg, Fredrik. 2003. *Decolonizing the Viking Age*, I–II. Stockholm: Almqvist & Wiksell.

Svane, Gunnar. 1989. 'Vikingetidens nordiske låneord i russisk', in Kisbye and Roesdahl 1989, pp. 18–32.

Sveinbjarnardóttir, Guðrún. 2011. *Reykholt: Archaeological Investigations at a High Status Farm in Western Iceland.* Reykholt: Snorrastofa.

Sveinsson, Einar Ól. 1958. *Dating the Icelandic Sagas: An Essay in Method.* London: Viking Society for Northern Research.

Thomas, Mark. 2013. 'To claim someone has "Viking ancestors" is no better than astrology', the *Guardian*, 25 February. [http://www.guardian.co.uk/science/blog/2013/feb/25/viking-ancestors-astrology?INTCMP=SRCH; last accessed 5 June 2013].

Thomson, William P. L. 1995. 'Orkney farm-names: a reassessment of their chronology', in Crawford 1995, pp. 42–63.

Toolis, Ronan, *et al.*, 2008. 'Excavation of medieval graves at St Thomas' Kirk, Hall of Rendall, Orkney', *Proceedings of the Society of Antiquaries of Scotland* 138, 239–66.

Townend, Matthew. 2002. *Language and History in Viking Age England: Linguistic Relations Between Speakers of Old Norse and Old English.* Turnhout: Brepols.

Tulinius, Torfi. 2005. 'Sagas of Icelandic prehistory (*fornaldarsögur*)', in McTurk 2005, pp. 447–61.

Turner, Val E., *et al.*, eds. 2013. *Viking Unst.* Lerwick: Shetland Heritage Publications.

Turville-Petre, E. O. G. 1964. *Myth and Religion of the North.* London: Weidenfeld and Nicolson.

Turville-Petre, Thorlac. 2001. 'Representations of the Danelaw in Middle English literature', in Graham-Campbell *et al.* 2001, 345–55.

Uecker, Heiko. 1996. 'Nordisches in der *Þiðreks saga*', in Kramarz-Bein 1996, pp. 175–85.

Valk, Heiki. 2008. 'The Vikings and the Eastern Baltic', in Brink and Price 2008, pp. 485–95.

Vésteinsson, Orri. 2000.*The Christianization of Iceland: Priests, Power, and Social Change, 1000–1300.* Oxford: Oxford University Press.

—— 2010. 'Ethnicity and class in settlement-period Iceland', in Sheehan and Ó Corráin 2010, pp. 494–510.

Vésteinsson, Orri, *et al.* 2002. 'Enduring impacts: Social and environmental aspects of Viking Age settlement in Iceland and Greeland', *Archaeologia Islandica* 2, 98–136.

—— 2012. 'The peopling of Iceland', *Norwegian Archaeological Review* 45/2, 206–35.

Vikstrand, Per. 2001. *Gudarnas platser. Förkristna sakrala ortnamn i Mälarlandskapen.* Uppsala: Kungl. Gustav Adolfs Akademien för svensk folkkultur.

Vretemark, Maria, and Tony Axelsson. 2008. 'The Varnhem archaeological research project: a new insight into the Christianization of Västergötland', *Viking and Medieval Scandinavia* 4, 209–19.

Wallace, Birgitta. 2003. 'L'Anse aux Meadows and Vinland: An abandoned experiment', in Barrett 2003a, pp. 207–38.

Wallace, Patrick. 2008. 'Archaeological evidence for the different expressions of Scandinavian settlement in Ireland', in Brink and Price 2008, pp. 434–8.

Walsh, Aidan. 1998. 'A summary classification of Viking Age swords in Ireland', in Clarke *et al.* 1998, pp. 222–35.

Wamers, Egon. 1998. 'Insular finds in Viking Age Scandinavia and the state formation of Norway', in Clarke *et al.* 1998, pp. 37–72.

Wawn, Andrew. 2000. *The Vikings and the Victorians. Inventing the Old North in 19th-Century Britain.* Woodbridge: Boydell.

Weber, Birthe. 1999. 'Bakestones', in Crawford and Smith 1999, pp. 134–9.

Whaley, Diana. 1998. *The Poetry of Arnórr jarlaskáld. An Edition and Study.* Turnhout: Brepols.

—— 2000. 'A useful past: historical writing in medieval Iceland', in Clunies Ross 2000, pp. 161–202.

—— 2006. *A Dictionary of Lake District Place-Names*. Nottingham: English Place-Name Society.

Wicker, Nancy L. 1998. 'Selective female infanticide as partial explanation for the dearth of women in Viking Age Scandinavia', in Halsall 1998, pp. 205–21.

—— 2012. 'Christianization, female infanticide, and the abundance of female burials at Viking Age Birka in Sweden', *Journal of the History of Sexuality* 21/2, 245–62.

Wilson, David M. 2008. *The Vikings in the Isle of Man*. Aarhus: Aarhus University Press.

Woolf, Alex, ed. 2009. *Scandinavian Scotland – Twenty Years After: Proceedings of a Day Conference held on 19 February 2007*. St Andrews: Committee for Dark Age Studies, University of St Andrews.

INDEX